CU00751578

The Great Fear of 1857

# The Past in the Present

EDITOR IN CHIEF

Francis Robinson, Royal Holloway, University of London


EDITORIAL BOARD

Beth Bailey, Temple University
C.A. Bayly, University of Cambridge
David Bindman, University College London
Peter Burke, University of Cambridge
John Carey, University of Oxford
Justin Champion, Royal Holloway, University of London
Peregrine Horden, University of Oxford and Royal Holloway,
University of London
Jonathan Riley-Smith, University of Cambridge
Jim Samson, Royal Holloway, University of London
Andrew Wallace-Hadrill, University of Cambridge

# The Great Fear of 1857

Rumours, Conspiracies
and the Making of the Indian Uprising

Kim A. Wagner

Peter Lang Oxford

First published in 2010 by

Peter Lang Ltd
International Academic Publishers
Evenlode Court, Main Road, Long Hanborough, Witney
Oxfordshire OX29 8SZ
United Kingdom

www.peterlang.com

Kim A. Wagner has asserted the right under the Copyright, Designs
and Patents Act of 1988 to be identified as the Author of this Work.

© Peter Lang Ltd 2010

All rights reserved.
No part of this book may be reprinted or reproduced or utilised
in any form, by any electronic, mechanical or other means,
now known or hereafter invented, including photocopying and recording,
or in any information storage or retrieval system, without the prior permission,
in writing, of the Publishers.

A catalogue record for this book is available from the British Library

ISBN 978-1-906165-27-7

COVER ILLUSTRATIONS:
Front: watercolour by R. M. Jephson, 1858, reproduced with the kind permission of
Peter Harrington and the Anne S. K. Brown Military Collection, Brown University Library.
Back: a battle during the Uprising (Charles Ball, *The History of the Indian Mutiny*).

Every effort has been made to trace copyright holders and to obtain their permission
for the use of copyright material. The publisher apologises for any errors or omissions
and would be grateful for notification of any corrections that should be incorporated
in future reprints or editions of this book.

Printed in the United Kingdom
by the MPG Books Group

# Contents

# Maps and Plates

## Maps

## Plates

The plates are to be found between pages 128 and 129.

# Abbreviations

| | |
|---|---|
| APAC | Asia, Pacific, and Africa Collections (formerly Oriental and India Office Collections), British Library |
| BLC | Bengal Light Cavalry |
| BNI | Bengal Native Infantry |
| *Depositions taken at Meerut* | *Depositions taken at Meerut by Major G. W. Williams* (Allahabad, 1858) |
| *FSUP* | S. A. A. Rizvi and M. L. Bhargava (eds.), *Freedom Struggle in Uttar Pradesh*, I–V (Lucknow: Publications Bureau, 1957–61) |
| *MAS* | *Modern Asian Studies* |
| NLS | National Library of Scotland |
| *Selections* | George W. Forrest (ed.), *Selections from the Letters, Despatches and Other State Papers Preserved in The Military Department of the Government of India, 1857–58* (Calcutta: Military Dept. Press, 1893) |
| *Trial* | Pramod K. Nayar (ed.), *The Trial of Bahadur Shah* (Hyderabad: Orient Longman, 2007) |
| *Two Native Narratives* | Charles T. Metcalfe (trans.), *Two Native Narratives of the Mutiny in Delhi* (Westminster: A. Constable and Co., 1898) |

# Glossary

| | |
|---|---|
| *atta* | flour |
| *ayah* | Indian nanny |
| *badmash* | ruffian or bad character |
| *bania* | trader or moneylender |
| *barkandaze* | a matchlock man or guard |
| *batta* | extra pay for military service outside British territories |
| *bazaar* | market |
| *bhang* | a cannabis preparation, sometimes containing opium |
| Bhumihar | agricultural Brahmin, often employed as *sepoys* |
| *bibi* | Indian mistress |
| Brahmin | high-caste Hindu, often employed as *sepoys* |
| Chamar | caste of tanners, untouchable |
| *charpoy* | light bed |
| *chauki* | police post |
| *chaukidar* | police officer or watchman |
| *chauprassi* | police officer or messenger |
| *cote* | bell-of-arms, small structure where muskets were kept |
| *dak* | official mail |
| *darogha* | police officer |
| *dhoti* | cloth worn by sepoys instead of trousers when out of uniform |
| *doolie* | litter or palanquin |
| *dureewalla* | weaver |
| *fakir* | Muslim ascetic |
| *gange* | market |
| *gharry* | small horse-drawn carriage |
| *ghat* | landing place |
| Gujar | pastoralist caste |
| *havildar* | sergeant, native army |

| | |
|---|---|
| Jat | agricultural caste |
| *jemadar* | lieutenant, native army |
| *jihad* | Muslim struggle |
| *kaffir* | infidel |
| *kahar* | bearer |
| *khalasi* | low-caste worker |
| *khansama* | house-steward |
| *khatick* | butcher |
| *khitmutgar* | servant |
| *koonjra* | greengrocer |
| *kossid* | private post |
| *kotwal* | head of police in town |
| *kotwali* | police station |
| *lathi* | metal-studded stick |
| *lota* | brass vessel used by high-caste Hindus |
| *maulavi* | Muslim scholar |
| Mehtar | caste of sweepers and scavengers |
| *munshi* | scribe or learned man |
| *naik* | corporal, native army |
| *nautch* | Indian dancing girl and prostitute |
| *nullah* | ravine |
| *pagri* | cloth used for turban |
| *panchayat* | meeting |
| *pandit* | learned Brahmin or Hindu priest |
| *perwanah* | official proclamation |
| *puja* | religious ceremony |
| *purbiya* | literally: easterner, refers to *sepoys* from Oudh and Bihar |
| *purdah* | seclusion for women |
| Rajput | high-status Hindu warrior or cultivator |
| *ryot* | peasant |
| *salaam* | common greeting |
| Sanyasi | Hindu mendicant ascetic |
| *sati* | widow-burning |
| *sepoy* | private, native infantry – sometimes spelt *sipahi* |
| *serai* | shelter for travellers |
| *sowar* | trooper, native cavalry |
| *subadar* | captain, native army |
| *syce* | groom |

| | |
|---|---|
| *tehsil* | headquarters of the *tehsildar* |
| *tehsildar* | revenue collector |
| *thana* | police post |
| *thanadar* | superior police officer |
| Thug | highway robber and ritual strangler (according to the colonial authorities) |
| Thuggee | the phenomenon or practice of the Thugs |
| *tindal* | overseer of *khalasis* |
| *tulwar* | curved Indian sword |
| *yogi* | Hindu ascetic |
| *zamindar* | petty ruler or landholder |

# Note on transliteration

While I recognise the colonial connotations of nineteenth-century spelling, I have retained the original names as found in the primary sources to avoid confusion.

# Prologue:
# The Ghost of Mutiny Past

1907 was the fiftieth anniversary of the Uprising of 1857 and thus of immense symbolic significance to the British in India.[1] Exactly a century before, in 1757, the East India Company had established its first foothold in Bengal as a political power, and from there the British had expanded their influence over the entire subcontinent. Yet all previous historical markers paled in comparison to the iconic momentousness of 1857, the year the strength of the British had been tested to its utmost and India had almost been lost. Amidst rumours of British attempts to subvert the religion of Hindus and Muslims, years of pent-up resentment had erupted into the violent Uprising of 1857. What started as a mutiny in the East India Company's army soon turned into a popular uprising across northern India, and for a few months, British rule in the subcontinent hung in the balance. In the Victorian imagination, the massacres of British civilians, and the alleged violation of women in particular, came to dominate the understanding of what became known as the 'Mutiny', which was often seen as a struggle between civilisation and barbarism. Depraved Indian rulers and Hindu and Muslim leaders were thought to have instigated the uprising, preying on the perceived superstition and ignorance of the *sepoys* and Indian population. In the end, however, the uprising was suppressed, and in 1858 control over the subcontinent passed into the hands of Queen Victoria. India thus assumed its place as the jewel in the imperial crown.

Commemorative services were held both in Britain and in India on 11 May 1907, and in London more than 700 veterans of the 'Mutiny' were invited to a sumptuous banquet hosted by the famous Lord Roberts at the Royal Albert Hall.[2] The sentimental speeches and nostalgic toasts of the event were followed by a poem written especially for the occasion by Rudyard Kipling, the first verse of which was:

> TO-DAY, across our fathers' graves,
> The astonished years reveal
> The remnant of that desperate host
> Which cleansed our East with steel.[3]

The jubilant jingoism of the poem aptly captured the general sentiment surrounding the memory of the 'Mutiny' in 1907. Several theatrical plays dramatised the events of 1857 and frequently opened with a scene in which the villainous rebels plotted to overthrow the British, who were blissfully unaware of the danger that surrounded them.[4] Central to the spectacle was the surrender of the British garrison at Cawnpore, followed by the infamous massacre of civilians by the deceitful and bloodthirsty rebels. In the end, though, the rebels were defeated by the noble relief-force and summarily executed. The audience cried out in anger when the British men and women were killed on stage, and when the play ended, and the mutineers were blown from cannon, the theatre 'shook with applause'.[5] The plays presented the story as a glorious instance of national catharsis; noble martyrdom followed by righteous revenge. To mark the anniversary, *The Times* had the celebrated military hero Field Marshal Sir Evelyn Wood write an account entitled *The Revolt in Hindustan*, which readers could follow in the newspaper as it ran through eighteen issues.[6] The extensive coverage and exposition of the anniversary brought the memory of the Uprising to the fore during 1907. According to one Indian, then living in London, 'We Indians at once felt that we were now in 1857.'[7]

In India, many Britons probably felt the same. Even as they were celebrating the victory and persistence of the colonial spirit of 1857, they were haunted by the spectre of the Uprising. At its very pinnacle in 1907, the Raj was faced with the greatest threat of internal unrest for fifty years, which had even tinged the celebration of the anniversary with a note of caution. In introducing Wood's written account, *The Times* stated: 'These chapters on the Indian Mutiny have not, however, been written simply to celebrate a memorable epoch in the life of *The Times*. But now, when the unrest in India is raising in many minds the foreboding of perhaps another outbreak, it has been felt that nothing could be more opportune than the publication of a work on the great rebellion in Hindustan by one of the actors in that sanguinary drama.'[8] At the time, another, even more sanguinary, drama did indeed seem to be under way.

The Partition of Bengal in 1905 had given increased impetus to the Indian nationalist movement, and sparked off a radicalisation of Indian politics. In Bengal in particular, revolutionary nationalism began to flourish; secret societies known as *samitis* were set up by young students who were inspired by the European revolutions and writings of people like Mazzini.[9] These groups sought to drive the British from India and some had as their avowed aim to instigate an armed insurrection, accompanied by 'a general revolt of the Indian army'.[10] Indian revolutionaries were also active outside of the subcontinent; in Paris, Bengali extremists came into contact with various anarchist groups and received training in bomb manufacturing from the Russian Nicholas Safranski. The manuals and expertise brought back to India in 1907 were employed to deadly effect; 1908 and 1909 saw what amounted to a terrorist campaign with several successful bombings, and the assassination of British officials and civilians in both India and Britain. What the extremists lacked in numbers, they made up for with their radical views and violent methods.

International politics further exacerbated the general concern: the humiliating defeat of the Tsar in the Russo-Japanese War of 1904–6 sent ripples across India, as described by Stephen Bonsal in *The New York Times*:

> If the English rule of India is doomed, as many who should be well informed think, the future historian will have to say: 'It was only when an Asiatic power met Russia in war on equal terms and reduced her to a second-class power that the Hindu raised his long-downcast eyes and said, "The white man is not a god after all. Nor is the Asiatic born to everlasting dependence upon him."'[11]

By 1907, Japan had assumed Russia's position as Britain's rival in the Far East, and a famous astrologer of Benares, Pandit Tarini Prasad, made several predictions to this effect: Japan would rise in power, subjugating both Korea and China, and challenging Britain at sea; the Pacific Ocean would become the scene of a great naval war.[12] Others envisaged the Mongolians invading India from the north, with the Japanese approaching by sea from the south. The Japanese and Mongolians would join forces with the 'fighting races of India'; this Asian Triple Alliance would defeat the European nations.[13]

The events of the year thus played out against a background of general tension and turmoil. In 1907 alone, an estimated 1.3 million people died from the plague, while severe famine laid barren large swathes of the subcontinent.[14] A general rise in the cost of living and a disruptive review of the revenue settlement furthermore added to the hardship and anxiety of the population. In the canal colonies in Punjab, which had been established and were irrigated by the Government, a new bill extended official powers, which caused great resentment amongst the local landowners and farmers.[15] Coinciding with widespread corruption among low-ranking officials, crop failure, and a substantial increase in the water rates, the protests against the Government grew into a mass movement. As the situation reached a breaking point, political agitators seized the opportunity to take the lead in the protests that racked the province of Punjab during the early months of 1907. The resentment against the new legislation soon coalesced into more general anti-British sentiments.

Through mass meetings and the distribution of printed leaflets the agitation in Punjab spread, penetrating even to the Indian army.[16] Pamphlets spoke especially to Sikh soldiers and military pensioners. The Uprising of 1857 had been suppressed only because the Sikhs had remained loyal to the British and turned their weapons against their own countrymen; now they had the chance to redeem themselves.[17] While some meetings were entirely inconspicuous, there were enough reports of more serious cases to alarm the authorities.[18] At one political meeting, the Indian politician G. K. Gokhale was supposed to have been approached by two native soldiers, who stated that their regiment was prepared to rise against the British if he would but call for them.[19] Native military personnel on leave were also overheard talking about the readiness of their regiments to take part in an uprising against the British.[20] One *sepoy* disclosed that among the native soldiers 'it had been freely discussed what they should do in the event of a mutiny and all had agreed to take the side of their countrymen and that one day a committee of all the native officers was held at the house of a Risaldar'.[21] The *sepoy* in question belonged to a regiment stationed at Meerut, the very station where the outbreak had first occurred in 1857, and the reference to secret meetings in the *sepoys'* lines was also starkly reminiscent of the stories of the 'Mutiny'.[22]

Some reports stated that, similarly to 1857, it was *sadhus*, or ascetic mendicants, who were the harbingers of sedition. They had played a 'dangerous part to seduce' the native troops, and 'Steps were taken to prevent the Sadhus from entering regimental lines. Checked in their effort to reach the troops directly, they set to work at Hardwar and Amritsar in order to get into touch with the soldiers on leave.'[23] The reports also indicated that efforts to spread sedition had in some instances been successful. *Sadhus*, and *fakirs*, their Muslim counterparts, were generally regarded with great distrust by the

British: 'With absolute freedom to go where they will, with access to all quarters, with fellow initiates in every town their powers of underground propaganda may be very great, and their power for evil serious.'[24] The involvement of *sadhus* was, however, mysterious. According to one source, those operating at Hardwar 'are not real Sannyasis but literate men in disguise', and their chief was one Hoti Lal who had several hundred followers 'who go about as Sadhus among the Hindu native troops (including Sikhs and Gurkhas) preaching sedition.'[25] Adding another layer of dissimulation to the affair was the fact that Hoti Lal was said to be the agent of a deposed native ruler, Holkar of Indore.[26] The British thus seemed to be faced with an opaque plot of agitators hiding behind numerous disguises and guided by unseen hands.

In the weeks leading up to the anniversary of the outbreak of the Uprising, on 10 May 1907, the seething cauldron of disaffection seemed about to boil over; riots had broken out in Amritsar, Lahore, and Rawalpindi, and the army was called in to quell the disturbances. One Reuters telegram read: 'The political unrest is hourly assuming graver proportions. Bands of stalwart rustics, armed with bludgeons, who have been enlisted by the leaders of the sedition, are crowding into the native city, and troops of all arms and bodies of police, mounted and dismounted are being drafted into the City of Lahore from all parts of the province.'[27] The prospect of a rebellion in Punjab was truly terrifying to the British; the Government traditionally had the support of its population, which also supplied one-third of the recruits for the Indian army. Another threatening aspect was the fact that both Hindus and Muslims took part, standing together against the British.[28] The one thing that troubled the British Government more than communal violence was the thought of a communal alliance turned against them. With eerie echoes of 1857, pamphlets were calling for solidarity amongst Indians in the fight against the Raj:

> Brothers call out Allah ho Akbar
> Muslims and Hindus all
> Join brothers one and all
> In hundreds and hundreds.[29]

Even though the Viceroy of India, Lord Minto, was reproached for failing to take the unrest seriously, he was under no illusion about the severity of the situation: 'one must not disguise from oneself how little it would take to set the whole of India in a blaze'.[30] To his wife, Minto indeed admitted as much: 'The whole place is a powder magazine …'.[31] Similar assessments were made in the native press, as exemplified by one Calcutta newspaper in March 1907, which asked: 'Who knows what little act of the rulers may some day set fire to the mine?'[32]

With a revolt seemingly imminent, the Lieutenant-Governor of the Punjab, Denzil Ibbetson, sounded the alarm. He reported to the Viceroy that a great conspiracy was unfolding in the Punjab with the aim of overthrowing the British government; central to this plot was the enlistment of Indian troops in a revolt. The trouble in the region was not caused by any real grievances, but was, according to Ibbetson, the work of radical extremists operating through secret societies. The riots and tampering of the troops were in fact directed by a 'secret Committee' of the revivalist Hindu organisation Arya Samaj, and the devious mastermind was allegedly the political agitator Lala Lajpat Rai, who 'keeps himself in the background, but the Lieutenant-Governor has been assured by nearly every Native gentleman who has spoken to him on the subject that he is the organizer-in-chief. His most prominent agent in disseminating sedition is Ajit Singh, formerly a schoolmaster, employed last year by the supposed Russian spy Lassef.'[33]

Ajit Singh was furthermore reported to have been in contact with the Amir of Afghanistan, and a more sinister conspiracy with even greater ramifications was conceivable.[34] Although the rivalry between Britain and Russia had been settled (for a time, at least) by the Anglo-Russian Entente, both Russian and German interference in Afghan matters were suspected at the time.[35] The most alarmist intelligence reports actually spoke of an Afghan–Russian–Punjabi alliance in May 1907.[36] Minto could not ignore the signals emanating from Punjab and gave way to Ibbetson's calls for extraordinary measures to be imposed. By the application of the antiquated Regulation III of 1818, both Rai and Singh were arrested and deported to Mandalay without trial.[37]

The deportation of Lajpat Rai and Ajit Singh set a standard for the British response to political unrest, which also involved the prohibition of political meetings and the vigorous suppression of the native press.[38] The journalist Valentine Chirol defended the censorship of the press in India, as it 'seems to have really arrested the poisonous flow of printer's ink and with it the worst forms of crime to which it maddened the feverish blood of Bengal'.[39] Similarly, Lord Kitchener, Commander-in-Chief of the Indian army, described the native press as 'a canker which is slowly but surely eating into the loyalty and good feeling of our native troops', thus utilising an epidemiological terminology that was becoming ever more common in British descriptions of the revolutionary nationalists and sedition in India.[40]

The impact of events in Punjab resonated throughout the subcontinent, and as a general sense of panic gradually spread, it seemed as if history was repeating itself with uncanny precision. All the portents of the 1857 Uprising were present: astrological predictions, secret signs and rumours, foreign agents and religious fanatics preaching sedition and tampering with the native troops. It was generally acknowledged that the loyalty of the Indian police was put under great strain by the resurgent nationalist movement; and the authorities even thought that the revolutionaries would send coded messages by telegraph, thus appropriating one of the technological hallmarks of progress.[41] Amidst wild reports of secret revolutionary activities, Minto noted how things were getting out of hand: 'The information I get from Calcutta points to a nervous hysterical Anglo-Indian feeling there which I can only call very unpalatable, the beginning of much of the same feeling which is not pleasant to read of in Lord Canning's time during the Mutiny.'[42] Thousands of guns were said to have been secretly shipped to India, some onboard German steamers, some in consignments of sewing machines, while bombs were smuggled into the country in cans of condensed milk.[43] Foreign agents were allegedly about the country and there were rumours of an uprising being planned, during which all Europeans would be murdered by their Indian servants.[44] Even the Viceroy seemed doubtful of the situation and suggested that:

> perhaps after all the gossip which reaches one indicates more truly the dangers of the electricity that is in the air than the best information on reliable authority. It means a good deal when one hears of Europeans arming everywhere: of British soldiers sleeping with rifles by their sides, and of the unauthorised issue by Commanding Officers of Army rifles and ammunition to civilians wherewith to defend themselves.[45]

Relaying the same worries to his wife, he added: 'The recollections of the Mutiny have shed a great influence over both Europeans and Natives …'.[46]

If British fears closely mimicked those of 1857, so did those of the Indian population. The old rumour of contamination was rehashed yet again, as imported sugar and salt was alleged to have been mixed with bone-dust of pigs and cows. This provided an obvious reason for both Hindus and Muslims to respond positively to the calls for the boycott of foreign goods emanating from 'Swadeshi' activists.[47] During a period when cholera and plague epidemics were rife, official medical and quarantine measures in particular became cause for suspicion. It was noticed that only Indians fell victim to the plague, and it was widely rumoured that the British themselves were the source of contagion; in some areas, the Government was suspected of having poisoned wells and the locals ceased using them.[48] While visiting villages in Punjab in 1907, one British officer was met with the allegation that he was secretly carrying pills for this purpose: 'He said to his men: "open up your kits, and let them see whether these horrible pills are in them". The men did as they were ordered, but the suspicion was so great that people insisted upon the glasses of the telescopes being unscrewed, in order to be quite sure that there was no pill behind them.'[49] The distribution of rat-traps in a native bazaar, to stop the supposed carrier of plague, likewise caused a panic among the locals: 'A deep design was at once suspected!'[50] Mutual distrust between the British and Indians brought the situation to fever pitch.

In the press, both in India and in Britain, the fifty years separating 1857 and 1907 counted for nothing, as the symbolism of the two dates merged.[51] Under the alarmist heading 'Aroused India Faces Mutiny and Invasion', *The New York Times* painted a bleak picture of the extent of British authority and control in India: 'The Government, both as represented at Calcutta and in the Indian Office, is wide awake to the dangers of the situation, but probably no better informed as to the secret aspirations of the millions it rules than it was at the time of the Indian Mutiny.'[52] In other words, the situation remained the same: the British administration was as ignorant and out of touch with its native subjects as it had been during the early days of the Raj. In 1857, the British had been impervious to the trouble brewing around them, and their naivety and complacency in the face of impending doom was a key lesson to be learned. After the Collector of Nasik was shot down by three revolutionaries, the journalist Valentine Chirol said of the British official that 'like the earliest victims of the Indian Mutiny he entertained to the very last an almost childlike confidence in the loyalty of the whole people'.[53] The British had been taken unawares once, with terrible consequences, and they were not about to let it happen again. Even Kitchener was gripped by the same feeling of suspicion when describing the situation among the native troops: 'My officers tell me it is all right, but they said the same thing in the Mutiny days till they were shot by their own men.'[54] In a paranoid environment, the absence of signs of unrest proved nothing, and was simply interpreted as the calm before the coming storm, which lurked just below the horizon.

Some Indian nationalists consciously played on British fears of a second 'Mutiny', and the inflammatory terminology they employed kept the authorities in a state of tension. To 'sacrifice a white goat for Kali' became a common euphemism for murdering a European, and for some young militants the actual ritual of sacrificing goats therefore assumed a double significance as both a religious and political act.[55] In May 1907, one of the extremist political leaders held a speech in which he encouraged people to hold special *pujas* (ceremonies in the honour of Kali) and sacrifice white goats. This, he claimed, would not only be religiously propitious, but also have an effect on the British: 'They are trying to demoralise us. We too may perplex and demoralise them by the organisation of these *pujas*. They have already become nervous, and are conjuring up visions of all kinds of troubles. They are still thinking of the mysterious *chapatis*.'[56] In 1857, the outbreak of the Uprising was said to have been preceded by the mysterious distribution of breads known as *chapattis*, the symbolic value of which was not lost on the revolutionaries. The commemoration of the Uprising by Indian nationalists in London in May 1908 was the very mirror-image of the British celebration at the Albert Hall the previous year.[57] The assembled nationalists paid tribute to the Indian 'heroes' and 'martyrs' of the Uprising, including Nana Sahib, the arch-fiend of 1857 according to the British, and there were nationalist songs and prayers. One of the final events of the commemoration was the distribution of *chapattis* as a blessing (*prasad*) among those present, 'because in 1857 chapattis were distributed secretly passing on the message of intended uprising against the East India Company'.[58] By re-enacting the distribution of *chapattis*, and thereby recreating the initial stages of the Uprising, it was hoped that a similar revolt could be brought about fifty years on.

The panics that marred the British celebrations in 1907 are testament to the persistence of the trauma of the Uprising of 1857. In his novel *Love Besieged* of 1909, the author Charles Pearce summarised the common perception of the 'Mutiny':

> More than half a century has passed since the Mutiny of 1857 shook the structure of our supremacy in India to its very foundations. The causes of the disaffection, the identity of the actual leaders, the methods of organisation, are as mysterious now as they were then. Time has done little to add to our knowledge of the native in India. He moves slowly and silently, he goes about his avocations apparently contented, he pays his taxes, and probably grumbles less than the average Englishman. So long as all is quiet, his rulers do not trouble; they are satisfied

everything is well if nothing is seen. But the Eastern nature never changes. It is as it has ever been, subtle, secret, patient. No one at the time of the Mutiny was able to penetrate beneath the surface. The episode of the greased cartridges was but the spark which ignited the fuse. The fuse itself was invisible, the hands that laid it unknown.[59]

The traumatic events of 1857 had a profound impact on the colonial psyche, and the spectre of the Indian Uprising haunted the British until the very last days of the Raj. If colonial rule had been complacent before the Uprising, afterwards it verged on paranoia. Vague fears of indigenous conspiracies, seditious mendicants, and sinister signs thus permeated the colonial experience in British India after 1857. Where did this pervasive fear of indigenous conspiracies, real or imagined, come from? For the past 150 years, most aspects of the Uprising have been subjected to intense scrutiny by historians, yet the nature of the outbreak itself remains obscure. What was the extent of the conspiracies and plotting, and how significant was the circulation of seemingly inconspicuous *chapattis* and strange rumours? What was it about the outbreak of 1857 which made it loom so large in the repertoire of colonial nightmares?

# Preface and Acknowledgements

I remember being at a car boot sale on a remote island in the western-most part of Denmark at some point in my early teens. My meagre pocket-money allowed me to buy only one of the two items that had caught my attention: a camouflage neckerchief or an obscure two-volume novel enticingly titled *India's Days of Terror*, by a certain John Retcliffe. I eventually chose the novel, which turned out to be a rare edition of the German journalist Hermann Goedsche's Orientalist fable *Nena Sahib, oder: Die Empörung in Indien* ('Nena Sahib, or: The Uprising in India') written in 1858–9. Goedsche's bizarre account caught my still malleable imagination through its deft combination of my then favourite subjects: the Thugs and the Indian Uprising of 1857. I eventually got the Thugs out of my system by writing a PhD on the subject, although my own work does rather pale in comparison to the suspense of my childhood readings. In 2007 I had the unexpected opportunity to join the 'Mutiny at the Margins' research project led by Crispin Bates at the University of Edinburgh, and eagerly seized the chance to revisit the colonial conspiracy theories of 1857 that so enchanted me as a youth. Yet again I have found myself peeling away the layers of exotic drama of nineteenth-century accounts, but I think I have managed to replace them with something at least as fascinating, if not as fantastic.

Setting out to write a new book on 1857 is a daunting task because of the enormous amount of literature already in existence. What interest me most, though, are not the sieges and battles, but the alleged conspiracies that preceded the outbreak, as well as the initial outbreak itself. With few exceptions, this early part of the Uprising has not been the subject of detailed studies. This book covers the events of the first six months of 1857; for those interested in a more comprehensive account of the Uprising, there are any number of excellent works easily available. The following is, in my opinion, the most plausible interpretation of the events leading up to the outbreak on 10 May 1857, including the outbreak itself. Other historians would write, and indeed have written, different accounts based on roughly the same material, and it is for the reader to determine the merits of the present work. My account is written in a narrative style, and in order to make the text more readable, I have left out most historiographical or methodological discussions. For those interested in the historiography of 1857, however, I explain my approach to the subject in the Introduction.

Modern Indian historiography on 1857 still seems, at least in part, to be responding to the prejudice of colonial accounts. It is certainly understandable that Indians should take pride in their history and wish to counterbalance the gross misrepresentations of colonial historiography. However, when even the best among contemporary Indian historians describes the Uprising as 'a glorious struggle', I am reminded of the terminology of the likes of Kaye and Malleson. One does not have to glorify the past in order to counterbalance historiographical misrepresentations. If assigning moral responsibility is not the job of the historian, and I agree with Rudrangshu Mukherjee that it is not, then accounts of 1857 have to move beyond the historical indignation that has hitherto characterised much of the post-Independence historiography. Simply reversing the colonial hagiographies and exchanging Lawrence with Tantia Tope, or Nicholson with Mangal Pandey, does not advance our understanding of the past.

The Uprising of 1857 cannot with any accuracy be characterised as a black-and-white struggle between Indians and Britons, as we all know that there were substantial numbers of Indians fighting on both sides. Those who sided with the British were, in my view, no more self-serving collaborators than those fought against them were a fanatic rabble. I have no particular sympathies for any of the parties involved in the conflict, and I do not condone any of the violence that occurred. If there is a preponderance of British civilians being killed in the following pages, it is because the period covered by this book was characterised by these acts – not because I seek to privilege British suffering. Similarly, any balanced account of Brigadier-General Neill's advance or the retaking of Delhi would mostly be about British brutality. I see no reason to downplay, or to exaggerate, the atrocities carried out by Indians simply because such events seem to offend our post-colonial sensibilities. There were hundreds of British but many more thousands of Indian civilian victims of 1857. No amount of academic spin or nationalist fervour can negate their suffering. When writing about the celebration of the Uprising in 2007, the noted historian Shahid Amin warned against an oversimplified interpretation of 1857: 'To hang the story of the Ghadar by a single thread would amount to hanging its myriad of rebels twice over.'[1] This is a view I fully endorse.

I would like to extend a heartfelt thanks to the other members of the 'Mutiny at the Margins' team at Edinburgh: Crispin Bates, Andrea Major, Marina Carter, and Markus Daechsel. It has been a great privilege and pleasure to work with such talented and friendly colleagues, while at the same time retaining the freedom to focus on my own research. The 'Mutiny at the Margins' project was generously funded by the UK Arts and Humanities Research Council (AHRC), without the support of which none of this could have happened. The following pages have furthermore benefited from the insights, critique, and comments of numerous people: in no particular order, Avril Powell, Clare Anderson, Sabyasachi Dasgupta, William Dalrymple, Kaushik Roy, Gavin Rand, Margrit Pernau, Tom Lloyd, Gajendra Singh, the anonymous readers, Nick Reynolds, Chris Bessant and the staff at Peter Lang, and everybody else whom I pestered with unsolicited queries about 1857. Ricardo Roque and the imperial and post-colonial studies group at ICS, Lisbon, were extremely helpful in providing critical feedback during the final stages of the manuscript. I owe a special debt of gratitude to John Jarvis, who had the dubious honour of reading and editing the very first draft of the manuscript; if this experience did not put him off history for good, it is no thanks to me. With my sidekick of old, John Pincince, I enjoyed the hospitality and great company of Gautam Chakravarti in Delhi in December 2007, including late-night discussions about 'kala pani' in the true spirit of Mangal Pandey.

This book was written during a tumultuous period of my life and between Cambridge, Copenhagen, and Edinburgh. I owe its successful completion to the unwavering support of Julie Hartley, for whose love and companionship I am forever grateful. This book is all I have to show by way of an excuse for having dragged her to Delhi in the stifling heat of the summer.

Maps

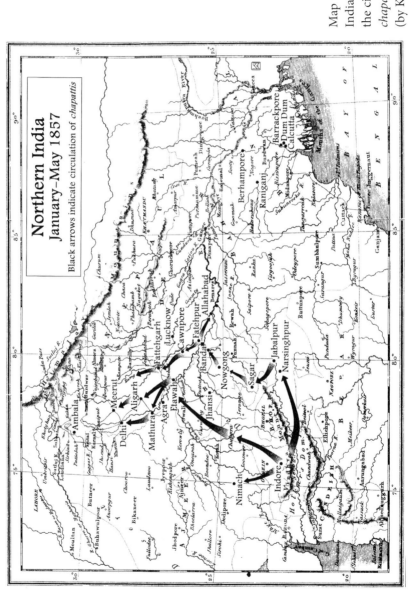

Map 1. Northern India in 1857 and the circulation of *chapattis* (by KAW).

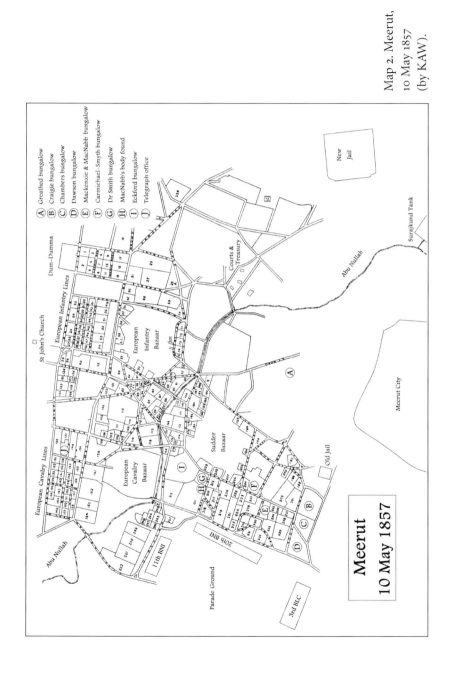

Map 2. Meerut,
10 May 1857
(by KAW).

# Introduction

It appears to be now accepted as a fact that it was the result of a vast Mahomedan conspiracy long organised, and having for its object the re-establishment of its ancient dominion. The Brahminical element in Indian society combined with the Mahomedan for one common purpose, namely, the extermination of the British race.

*Bentley's Miscellany*, 43 (Feb. 1858), 122

The introduction of the new Enfield rifle to the native regiments of the East India Company's army in 1857 was the immediate cause of the Uprising. The cartridge for the new rifle was greased to ease the process of loading, and it was soon rumoured that the lubricant was composed of cow tallow and pig lard. Since the drill required the cartridge to be torn open with the teeth, this would be ritually polluting and highly offensive to both Hindus and Muslims – the cow being sacred to the former, and the pig *haram*, or forbidden, to the latter. The Uprising broke out on 10 May 1857, when the *sepoys* at Meerut murdered their officers and all the British and Christian civilians that they came upon. The mutineers then proceeded to Delhi where the last Mughal Emperor, the enfeebled Bahadur Shah, was proclaimed king and the city became the symbolic centre of the uprising. The unrest spread across northern India, and in many places the military mutiny assumed the character of a popular rebellion. Indian rulers, who had been dispossessed by the British, reclaimed their thrones, most notably at Delhi, Lucknow, and Cawnpore. With the assistance of British regiments diverted to India, and thousands of Indian troops who remained loyal, the Uprising was eventually suppressed, albeit with considerable losses on both sides, both military and civilian. The military campaigns lasted until 1859, when the last rebels were defeated and British authority was re-established.

Thanks to the numerous accounts of the Uprising, including Evelyn Wood's heroic rehash, the reader of 1907 would have been in no doubt that it was the result of a conspiracy and, furthermore, that the ringleader was Nana Sahib, also known as Dandu Pant, the Peshwa of Bithor.[1] Nana Sahib was the adopted son of the late Peshwa Baji Rao, a Mahratta ruler who had been exiled, but who managed to sustain a small kingdom thanks to the generous pension paid by the British. When the Peshwa died, Nana Sahib inherited his title and possessions, but the Government was not prepared to continue paying a pension and the new Peshwa faced the prospect of losing all his privileges. For years Nana Sahib petitioned the Government in order to have the pension resumed, and he even hired a British lawyer to present his case, but all to no avail. Nana Sahib's resentment of British rule was shared by many Indians who had been adversely affected by the expansion of the Company Raj. The kingdom of Oudh had been annexed in 1856 and the British sent the former king to Calcutta so they could keep an eye on him, along with his retinue. Similarly to Nana Sahib, the Rani of Jhansi had failed in getting her son acknowledged as the rightful heir when her husband died, and her state in the Bundelkhand region had 'lapsed' to the British. During the Uprising, Nana Sahib, the Rani, and a number of other dispossessed rulers emerged as important rebel leaders and their activities prior to the outbreak were suddenly regarded in a new light. What had seemed only mildly suspicious during the early months of 1857 now assumed a definitely sinister appearance.

In 1854, Nana Sahib had dispatched a small delegation led by a Muslim retainer, Azimullah Khan, to London in a final attempt to salvage his income and obtain recognition of his official status. Azimullah did not succeed, and the failed mission was said to have deepened his dislike of the British, turning it into a profound hatred. On the way back to India, Azimullah and his companions went by way of Constantinople and the Crimea, where they met *The Times'* famous war correspondent, W. H. Russell, who was covering Britain's war with Russia. Russell later recalled how Azimullah had exhibited a suspicious interest in the recent British setbacks and the depleted state of their troops, and the journalist took an instant dislike to the man. A member of Azimullah's party, Mahommed Ali Khan, subsequently revealed that they had actually met with Russian agents at Constantinople and discussed the possibility of overthrowing British rule in India.[2] Back in India, Azimullah had supposedly lost no time in convincing his master that the only way to regain his former power was to turn against the Company.

In the event, Nana Sahib needed no encouragement and one of his emissaries, Sitaram Bawa, later told the British that his master had been plotting their downfall for years.[3] Nana Sahib had allegedly been sending out letters to all the independent Indian rulers to organise a rebellion, but it was only after the British annexed Oudh that his overtures met with any success. During the early months of 1857, Nana Sahib and Azimullah Khan were said to have toured northern India and visited Lucknow, Kalpi, and Delhi on what they claimed was a pilgrimage.[4] A British officer, who had met Azimullah on the boat back to India, was surprised to see him again at the military station at Ambala and later suggested that he had in fact been on a reconnaissance of all the stations where the Uprising was soon after to occur.[5] Nana Sahib was also supposed to have met with agents of the deposed King of Oudh and the Mughal Emperor Bahadur Shah, who naturally shared his aspirations to rid India of the Company's rule.

Combined with the fact that Nana Sahib later led the uprising against the British at Cawnpore, these accounts seemed to prove that he had indeed taken a leading part in a vast plot. The official historian of 1857, J. W. Kaye, for one, was convinced and stated that 'there is nothing in my mind more clearly substantiated than the complicity of the Náná Sáhib in wide-spread intrigues before the outbreak of the mutiny'.[6] In Kaye's magisterial account, *History of the Sepoy War in India* (1864–76), the existence of a conspiracy was not explicit, and the wording of the main text was rather careful when he discussed the unrest at Barrackpore in February and March of 1857: 'To what extent this idea of overpowering the Government had taken possession of the minds of the soldiery, and how far it was ever shaped into a definite scheme of action by those who were moved against us by religious or political animosities, can only be dimly conjectured.'[7] The circumspection, however, was belied in Kaye's footnotes, where he easily identified the prime movers: 'In my mind there is no doubt of the activity, at this time, of the Oudh people at Garden Reach.'[8] In spite of the obvious uncertainties and inconclusive evidence, Kaye did not hesitate to point out the dispossessed native rulers and their retinue as the ringleaders – in his footnotes.

If Kaye was somewhat cautious in his description of the plots, G. B. Malleson, who completed Kaye's work after the latter's death, showed no such timidity and is perhaps the strongest and most vocal proponent of the existence of a vast prearranged conspiracy.[9] Malleson acknowledged that the identity of all the conspirators might never be known, yet he was quite happy to give a detailed description of the conspiracy and the main plotters.[10] What Malleson described as the 'executive council' consisted of Nana Sahib, the Rani of Jhansi and the so-called Maulavi of Faizabad, a Muslim 'fanatic', who all worked in collaboration with the deposed rulers of Oudh.[11] According to Malleson, the *sepoys* were already discontented and 'ready to be practised upon by any schemer', while the annexations and revenue measures led to more general resentment against British rule amongst the Indian population: 'Conspirators to work upon so promising soil were not wanting to the occasion.'[12]

Malleson claimed to have been told by native informants that the Maulavi of Faizabad had been 'selected by the discontented in Oudh to sow throughout India the seeds which, on a given signal, should spring to active growth'.[13] The evidence was supposedly indisputable, since the Maulavi had, similarly to Azimullah, visited all the locations where mutinies later took place and did indeed lead the rebels at Lucknow:

> That this man was the brain and the hand of the conspiracy there can, I think, be little doubt. During his travels he devised the scheme known as the chapátí scheme. Chapátís are cakes of unleavened bread, the circulation of which from hand to hand is easy, and causes no suspicion. The great hope of the Maulaví was to work upon the minds, already prone to discontent, of the sipáhís. When the means of influencing the armed men in the service of the British Government should have been so matured that, on a given signal, they would be prepared to rise simultaneously, the circulation of chapatis amongst the rural population of the North-west Provinces would notify them that a great rising would take place on the first favourable opportunity.[14]

The introduction of the new Enfield cartridges provided the plotters with a heaven-sent opportunity to turn the *sepoys* against their masters. 'It was so terrible a thing,' according to Kaye, 'that, if the most malignant enemies of the British Government had sat in conclave for years, and brought an excess of devilish ingenuity to bear upon the invention of a scheme framed with the design of alarming the Sipáhi mind from one end of India to the other, they could not have devised a lie better suited to the purpose.'[15] The British had not been adequately alert regarding the components of the grease, and the rumour of its obnoxious components was soon spread. The *sepoys* were thus tricked into thinking that the Government had deliberately tried to pollute them: once they had lost their religion, they could more easily be converted to Christianity. 'The reader may ask how that was possible, considering that the cartridges were similar to those they had used for a century,' Malleson explained. 'The answer is that fanaticism never reasons. The Hindus are fanatics for caste.'[16] The 'executive council' had skilfully manipulated the *sepoys* to rise against the British by exploiting their superstition and caste prejudices. Malleson could reveal that what appeared as contingent events in 1857 were really something much more sinister: 'Indeed I may go as far as to declare that many of the actors in the drama failed to realise to their dying day that the outbreak was not merely a mutiny which they had to combat, but a vast conspiracy, the threads of which were widely spread …'.[17]

## The Great Conspiracy

It is hardly surprising that the Indian Uprising should be perceived as a conspiracy. From the assassination of Caesar to the Gunpowder Plot and the French Revolution, conspiracies have played a significant role in Western history. It was also the classic conspiracies that Russell reverted to when trying to convey a sense of the scope and horrors of 1857: 'Hideous massacres of men, women, and children – compared with which Scylla's proscriptions, the Sicilian Vespers, the great *auto da fé* on Bartholomew's Eve, or the Ulster outbreak of 1641, were legitimate acts of judicial punishment …'.[18] A conspiracy was generally understood as the secret plotting of a group of people to carry out a malevolent and treacherous plan, be it a political intrigue or assassination, a massacre or *coup d'état*, or indeed a mutiny. The existence of actual conspiracies provided more elaborate and imaginary conspiracy theories with a semblance of authenticity. The French Revolution in particular gave rise to a proliferation of conspiracy theories, which became a common form of political analysis in the nineteenth century. Above all, they helped make sense to the human mind of complicated events that were otherwise difficult to fathom.

Whereas the Devil had traditionally been considered to be the malignant force behind events which defied explanation, the Enlightenment placed man at the centre of the universe.[19] Taking the place of a strictly theological world-view, conspiracy theories were, in the words of one historian, 'a rational attempt to explain human phenomena in terms of human intention'.[20] According to this rationale, there was a direct, mechanistic, connection between cause and effect. Events were attributed to deliberate human design – things happened because someone had made them happen, and the cause of events could be inferred from their effect. Hence it followed that wars and revolutions were the result of the malignant intentions of evil men driven by avarice and lust for power. Following the French Revolution, conspiracy theories involved groups like the Jews, Freemasons, Jesuits, and various secret societies, such as the Illuminati, who were attributed with fantastic powers, extensive organisation and diabolic intentions towards the subversion of established society.[21] In the novel *Coningsby* (1844), written before he became British Prime Minister, Benjamin Disraeli thus described the network of influential Jews in powerful positions throughout Europe and explained that 'the world is governed by very different personages from what is imagined by those who are not behind the scenes'.[22] The notion of a conspiracy provided a simple explanation to many different events, subsumed a bewildering number of causes and effects in one single interpretation, and thereby made sense of a chaotic world.

A world-view based on the manipulation of events by hidden forces often led to pervasive panic and what has been described as the 'paranoid style'.[23] Even the most ordinary events assumed a sinister significance, and the absence of suspicious signs was actually seen to confirm the existence of a hidden conspiracy rather than refuting it. The paranoid style, however, was not limited to marginalised and high-strung individuals, and it is hardly an exaggeration to say that most people in nineteenth-century Europe thought that conspiracies of some kind were behind many political events.[24] In the wake of the French Revolution, fear of Jacobinism was endemic in Britain, spurred on in part by the publication in 1797 of Abbé Barruel's sensationalist *Memoirs, Illustrating the History of Jacobinism*, and John Robison's melodramatically entitled *Proofs of a Conspiracy Against all the Religions and Governments of Europe, carried on in the secret meetings of the Freemasons, Illuminati and Reading Societies*.[25] Any kind of secret association was regarded with deep suspicion and the Unlawful Societies Act of 1799 made it illegal for people to meet and take oaths. Oath-taking elicited loyalty to an authority other than the state and thus posed an explicit challenge to the presiding establishment. Following the Chartist movements and the Swing Riots in Britain, the emerging workers' unions were also criminalised as secret societies.[26] There was at the same time also a widespread fascination with secret societies and conspiracies, as exemplified by Thomas De Quincy who wrote a number of works on the subject, including *Secret Societies* of 1847.

Apart from a Western tradition of conspiracy theories, which informed the representation of the Uprising, colonial lore and its ensemble of tropes provided a strong precedent for the more exotic and outlandish claims of writers like Kaye and Malleson. The dramatic events of 1857 were not to be understood simply as the result of a plot or mutiny; they were a conspiracy of 'Orientals' and thus doubly sinister and, to the European mind, mysterious. In the Western imagination, India constituted an unintelligible enigma. G. O. Trevelyan, a civil servant writing in India just after the Uprising, described the huge divide between the British and their Indian subjects:

> We certainly have not yet got to the bottom of the native character. Facts crop up daily which prove incontestably to all … that the depths of that character cannot be fathomed by our ordinary plummet, or marked with certainty on the chart by which we navigate in European waters. Take for instance those extraordinary symptoms which preceded the great mutiny; the marvellous organization of that vast plot; the mysterious but intimate connexion between the mutineers and the independent native powers; the dim prophecies and ghastly rumours which foreshadowed the outbreak; the secrecy; the unanimity; the tokens passed from hand to hand throughout a million villages.[27]

The British in India were in effect faced by a conspiracy of an entire culture of which Nana Sahib's plotting was perhaps only the most radical manifestation. That 'Orientals' were cruel and treacherous was commonly accepted by many British in India and found its expression in descriptions of the ruler Tipoo Sahib, for instance, who had been defeated in 1799.[28] Intermittent rebellions throughout the first half of the nineteenth century, and events like the 1835 assassination of William Fraser, the British Commissioner at Delhi, by an Indian nobleman, only seemed to confirm the stereotype.[29] Above all, however, it was the 'discovery' of the murderous Thugs during the 1830s which provided the most obvious Indian parallel to the conspiracy theories of the West. The Thugs were supposedly a fraternity of ritual stranglers who worshipped the Hindu goddess Kali, and they were first introduced to a European readership in Philip Meadows Taylor's hugely successful novel *Confessions of a Thug* of 1839.[30] In 1854, a British doctor in India noted that: 'Insane patients very generally dislike natives and, when they suspect conspiracies, notions of Thugs, & c. are very common.'[31]

As early as 1812, during the very first British operations against Thugs, a British official had commented that 'It has been said that these people compose a regularly organized and secretly tho' extensively connected society similar to that of the Illuminati or other bodies of that description, the influence of which is widely felt tho' the society itself and its members were concealed by a veil of mystery which none but the initiated can draw aside'.[32] This comparison with secret societies of the West was to become a recurring theme in colonial accounts of Thuggee and other suspicious Indian practices. A key element in the representation of Thuggee was its geographical ramifications, and the elaborate network of gangs supposed to be working in unison; according to a British account of 1833: 'the Thugs have established a regular system of intelligence and communication throughout the countries they have been in the practice of frequenting, and they become acquainted, with astonishing celerity, with proceedings of their comrades in all directions'.[33] At times the Thug informants themselves reinforced this perception and one bragged to the British that 'he could send a message to Calcutta, or any part of the country, and receive an answer in much less time than the dawk [official mail]'.[34] One of the key tropes concerning conspiracies was indeed the alleged ability of the plotters to communicate swiftly and in secret; Barruel, who more than anyone contributed to the notion of a great Jewish conspiracy, gave the following account of the manner in which the 'Grand Master of Freemasons' distributed his orders:

> from neighbour to neighbour and from hand to hand the orders are transmitted with incomparable speed, for these pedestrians are delayed neither by bad weather, nor by the mishaps that normally befall horsemen or carriages; a man on foot can always get along when he knows the country, and that is the case here. They stop neither to eat nor to sleep, for each one covers only two leagues. The mail-coach takes ten hours from Paris to Orleans, stopping for an hour; the distance is thirty leagues. Fifteen pedestrians, replacing one another, can reach Orleans from Paris in nine hours, using short-cuts and above all never stopping.[35]

One significant aspect of Barruel's account is the notion of neighbours and 'local knowledge', which aided the conspirators in communicating with great speed. This is reminiscent of the circulation of *chapattis* in 1857, which were alleged to travel 200 miles in 24 hours, double the speed of mail runners.[36] Kaye himself described the mysteries of indigenous modes of communication:

> We know so little of Native Indian society beyond its merest externals, the colour of the people's skin, the form of their garments, the outer aspects of their houses, that History, whilst it states broad results, can often only surmise causes. But there are some surmises which have little less than the force of gospel. We feel what we cannot see, and have faith in what we cannot prove. It is a fact, that there is a certain description of news, which travels in India, from one station to another, with a rapidity almost electric. Before the days of the 'lightning post,' there was sometimes intelligence in the Bazaars of the Native dealers and the Lines of the Native soldiers, especially if the news imported something disastrous to the British, days before it reached, in any official shape, the high functionaries of Government. We cannot trace the progress of these evil-tidings.[37]

A recurring theme within the colonial sphere was the image of the 'jungle drums' purveying hidden meanings undecipherable to the authorities, or secret societies planning to overthrow the colonial rule. There was a fear of things happening just under the surface, unknown to the colonial administration and kept secret by the indigenous population. This perceived or real threat assumed alarming proportions in times of unrest when the British found themselves unable to get access and gather information from certain social strata of their Indian subjects. In this context, the fears associated with the Thugs were merely a distillate of common fears of the indigenous population more generally. Thuggee was only the most sinister association in what might be described as a continuum of secrecy within Indian society, which was in effect inaccessible to the British. The Thugs and the Uprising of 1857 embodied all that the British feared from their Indian subjects: when combined they constituted the ultimate scenario of colonial paranoia. In a very real sense the accounts of Kaye and Malleson and other British historians emerged from an acute crisis of trust in the Indian population.

Less esoteric and more commonplace perceptions of India also influenced the interpretation of 1857. During the European revolutions of 1789 and 1848, the riotous mobs were usually seen as having been manipulated by the real ringleaders, who nevertheless remained hidden. Such an understanding of popular protest and violent upheavals was easily adapted to an Indian context. Partly in reflection of contemporary British society, but also as a means of distancing the 'Oriental' from the ideal of the free-born Englishman, Indian society was understood as being completely under the sway of a strict social hierarchy imposed by the caste system. Accordingly, it was inconceivable that any Indians could act without the explicit sanction of their betters – in this case the Brahmin priesthood. During the 1830s, similar observations had been made regarding the Thugs who were supposedly guided by the priests in the temples of their goddess: 'It is well known that these priests give information to the thugs of the movements of travellers, and the despatch of treasure. They suggest expeditions, and promise the murderers, in the name of their goddess, immunity and wealth, provided a due share of the guilty spoil be offered up at her shrine.'[38] The more significant implication of the alleged involvement of the priests was that the evil of the Thugs was seen to reflect on all Indians who, due to the caste system, were bound by the commands of the Brahmins: 'How little astonishing is it, then, that we find a class of fellow creatures, like the thugs, so sunk in the depths of infamy, when the people are led by such unprincipled leaders.'[39] Hence it followed that Hindu *sepoys* would never act on their own: indeed, they *could not act* on their own.

If Hindus were bound to follow the biddings of the priestly caste, Indian Muslims were regarded as inherently fanatic, and thus equally susceptible to the bigoted preaching of their *maulavis*. The mutiny of the *sepoys* in 1857 was thus, by inference, guided by the hands of their religious leaders. According to some, it was the different religious groups which manipulated each other; as the *Westminster Review* put it: 'The Hindoo *Sepoys* were made the dupes and instruments of their more crafty Mussulman comrades.'[40] The bottom line was nevertheless the same: the majority of the *sepoys* who mutinied were seen to have no agency of their own. It was, after all, much easier to put faces to a few ringleaders than to the great anonymous 'mob', which was merely the tool of others. Assigning blame to the real masterminds furthermore absolved the British of any responsibility. The Uprising happened because the *sepoys* and Indian population had been misled by 'designing men' and not because they harboured any real grievances against British rule.[41] After British rule had been restored, reconciliation between rulers and subjects would be possible only if a few individuals could be held responsible, and not the entire native population.

The emphasis on the misguided *sepoys* and their religious fears, in regard to the cartridges, meant that any political aspirations they may have held were ultimately discredited. To the British, the Uprising constituted a rejection of modern technology and of the progress offered by British rule, in favour of superstition and idolatry: 'The progress of railways and the mysterious electric wire aroused undefined apprehensions, and it must have appeared that the alien race had, indeed, resolved to establish itself permanently in the land. A conspiracy at such a crisis, among such a people, and for a common object, cannot be considered an unnatural, if it was an unexpected, event.'[42] The Uprising was thus seen to be inherently reactionary and aimed to restore the old order – 'Oriental' despotism and religious fanaticism. Like the Jesuits in Europe, the secret leaders of the Uprising pursued their sinister aims through subterfuge.[43] Hindu and Muslim priests hid base political aims behind feigned religious piety, employing mendicant *yogis* and *fakirs* to spread sedition under the guise of devout asceticism. Similarly, Nana Sahib and other rulers were professing their friendship to the British at the very same time that they were plotting their treason.

During the Uprising, the British were faced not by an ordinary opponent, but by one that embodied in their minds every negative characteristic of the 'Orient': 'From no such hideous picture of vile passion has the veil been ever so suddenly torn away … Faithless to his salt, and true to his vile instincts, the *Sepoy* has all at once become revealed to us as a practised torturer, a cowardly assassin, and a lustful fiend.'[44] There was a sense that the Uprising was not just a political conflict, but a struggle between two races and hence between two basic principles: the British and the treacherous 'Orientals', representing respectively good and evil, progress and barbarism. This dichotomy to some extent mirrored classical conspiracy theories in which the forces of good were threatened by the forces of evil in the shape of the Jesuits, Jews or other malevolent secret societies. One of the key features of conspiracy theories was the pathological terminology; if epidemics were often described in military terms, with disease 'invading' and 'attacking' the body, conspiracies and internal challenges to the state (or the body politic) were often perceived in the distinctly epidemiological language of 'viruses' and 'contagion'.[45] Like an outbreak of the plague, conspiracies and insurgency spread within the healthy body of loyal subjects and had to be cut away for the state to survive. The pathological terminology has perhaps rarely been applied with such consistency as in the context of 1857, and while Kaye described Nana Sahib and his retainers as 'the germs of a cruel conspiracy', Malleson's chapter on the escalation of the Uprising is simply entitled 'The Spread of the Epidemic'.[46] It is also noteworthy that Malleson applied a distinctly Western terminology, commonly associated with secret societies, in his account of 1857. The reference to an 'executive council' implied the existence of a formalised leadership and well-organised secret society, which would make the reader of the day think of revolutionary anarchists or indeed Jesuits and Freemasons.[47]

# V. D. Savarkar and the myth of conspiracy

The account of the conspiracy of 1857 drew upon a well-established repertoire of both Western and Orientalist stereotypes, which provided much of the imagery and terminology.[48] Interestingly, Indian historians of the twentieth century readily appropriated this colonial representation of the Uprising. While the British were celebrating the fiftieth anniversary of 1857, and fearing its second coming, an Indian nationalist in London was reappropriating that same history. Written in 1907–8, V. D. Savarkar's *The Indian War of Independence, 1857* provided a distinctly anti-British account of the Uprising, intended to inspire the ongoing struggle against colonial rule. Savarkar was deeply involved in the nationalist circles based at India House in Highgate and took part in the counter-celebrations during the anniversary years. His book was written in response to the British celebrations in 1907 and simply inverted the account of conspiracies so common to the colonial historiographies that Savarkar consulted in the British Library; Kaye and Malleson's gallery of villains was thus turned into a memorial of national heroes. Curiously, Savarkar adopted the same pathological terminology, only he applied it in reference to the adverse effects of colonial rule. Similar to an epidemiologist, Nana Sahib had supposedly diagnosed the 'chronic symptoms' of the 'terrible disease of slavery' that was afflicting India in the shape of the East India Company, and realised that the sword was the only 'cure'.[49] In describing the resulting upsurge of Indian patriotism, Savarkar nevertheless took recourse to geological metaphors, the first part of the book being 'The Volcano' followed by 'The Eruption'.[50] By describing the Uprising in such terms, the author presented the emergence of Indian nationhood as a natural force – a manifestation of the inherent destiny of the Indian people.

The historical narrative of *The Indian War of Independence* closely followed that of its British sources, with Azimullah Khan first hatching the plan in London, and Nana Sahib subsequently plotting the Uprising with other Indian leaders. In Savarkar's retelling, the conspiracy assumed enormous proportions and involved the tacit support of both Russia and Turkey, while diplomatic relations were allegedly forged with Egypt and Persia.[51] Secret agents and emissaries of the immense 'Revolutionary Organisation' were preaching sedition to the *sepoys* all across the subcontinent, and gypsies told of the imminent downfall of the British to awaken the national feeling among the local population.[52] Not surprisingly, the 'Secret Organisation' of 1857 was said to rely on clandestine meetings and religious oaths, and any traitor to the cause was immediately put to death.[53] The success of the conspiracy was so complete 'that not much inkling of what was going on could reach even such cunning people as the English, until the explosion actually took place'.[54] When the British authorities became suspicious and started opening the letters of the conspirators, 'a sort of code was composed of dots and numbers', which effectively prevented the Government from guessing the dangerous contents.[55] In describing the mysterious circulation of *chapattis*, Savarkar imbued the conspiracy with an overt religious significance and the *chapattis* themselves became a sort of nationalist sacrament:

> Some silly Government officials tried to get hold of these *Charpatees*, cut them to small crumbs, powdered them, and powdered once more, and tried if they could give some message; but, like witches the *Charpatees* had no tongue when they were asked to speak. The *Charpatee* spoke only to those it meant to speak to. It was made from wheat or millet flour. Nothing was written on it; yet it inspired the men who knew it with a strange Revolutionary energy at its very touch. The *Chowkidar* of every village had it. He ate a bit of it first himself and gave the rest, as *Prasâd*, to those who asked. The same number of *Charpatees* were made afresh and sent to the inhabitants of the neighbouring villages. The *Chowkidar* of the latter place would send it to yet another village and so, this fiery red cross of India travelled from village to village, kindling with flames every village it touched.[56]

Accordingly, Savarkar took all the most stereotypical tropes of the colonial representation of 1857 and incorporated them in his nationalist epic by a mere inversion of their moral thrust. In one significant divergence from the standard accounts, however, Savarkar claimed that the British had *deliberately* greased the Enfield cartridges with the blood (*sic*) of cows and pigs.[57] This turned the historical doubt and suspicions into hard facts, and Savarkar thus transformed the outbreak into a justifiable pre-emptive strike against the cunning plans of the British Government. When the *sepoy* Mangal Pandey single-handedly turned on his British officers in March 1857, it was thus an inspiring act of heroic resistance against the calculated subversion of his caste.[58] Similarly, when the *sepoys* eventually broke out at Meerut on 10 May, and murdered British men, women, and children, they were responding to a century of repression and followed a carefully prepared plan.[59] The outbreak was, in other words, a justified thwarting of the attempt by the British to ruin India.

Savarkar's terminology clearly owed more to the likes of Mazzini and other European revolutionaries and anarchists than to the history of nineteenth-century India. Taking his cue from Malleson, Savarkar described the 'secret structure of the Revolutionary Organisation', which involved a 'chief committee' of 'Revolutionary Leaders', as well as 'inner circles' and 'secret societies', thus inventing an anachronistic genealogy for the nationalist revolutionary movement of his own time.[60] The spirit of 1857 was still alive, he proclaimed, and the revolutionaries of the twentieth century were continuing the struggle begun by Nana Sahib and other rebel leaders.

Even before the book was published in English under a pseudonym in 1909 it had been banned due to its seditious contents. The British authorities applied the pathological terminology when referring to the 'virulent poison of the Mutiny Book', and its potential effect on Indian readers was compared to that of drugs.[61] The following year, charges were brought against Savarkar under the Sedition Act, and in 1910 he was sentenced to two terms of transportation for life to the Andaman Islands for his supposed links to an Indian revolutionary who had assassinated a British politician in London. Savarkar later emerged as one of the most important radical Hindu leaders, and was implicated in the assassination of Gandhi in 1948. His work on 1857, however, provided a lasting blueprint for an Indian version of the history of the Uprising – one in which conspiracy assumed a key role. Whether it was viewed as a deceitful plot, or a glorious underground movement, the notion of a grand conspiracy behind the Uprising of 1857 proved to be remarkably persistent.

*

As a true conspiracy theory, the conventional interpretation of the Uprising of 1857 is entirely teleological; because Nana Sahib assumed a leading role in the Uprising, it is assumed that whatever he did prior to the outbreak was related to it. The documentary evidence for the existence of a widespread conspiracy is, however, rather dubious, and in most instances is not supported by any verifiable material. Of the handful of accounts that describe the alleged conspiracy, not a single one precedes the Uprising itself. Although he wrote several letters warning of native discontent in the early months of 1857, it was only seven years later that Lieutenant Martineau remembered his meeting with Azimullah Khan at Ambala and tied it in with the supposed plot:

> Azim-Oollah then, as a skillfull agent, was doubtless feeling his way, was able from his reports to work on the mind of the Nana already incensed by the stoppage of the stipend accorded to the ex Peshwa, to induce him, shortly after his return to visit Lucknow, there doubtless to confer with Alli Nuckee Khan & other servants of the ex king.
>
> Of course I thought little of these things on my meeting Azim-Oollah at the Umballa dak bungalow, tho' rather wondering what exactly could have brought him there.[62]

Similarly, Russell did not write of his encounter with Azimullah Khan at the Crimea until 1860 – long after Nana Sahib had become the evil ringleader of the conspiracy in the British imagination, and the emissary's demeanour could be reinterpreted retrospectively.

The 'confession' of Azimullah's companion, Mahommed Ali Khan, which mentioned the meeting with 'real or pretended' Russian agents at Constantinople, is most likely a literary invention, or a highly embellished tale.[63] The author, Forbes-Mitchell, presented his meeting with Mahommed Ali Khan as a 'strange story' and furthermore provided the preamble that most of the people who were in India at the time had probably forgotten about it. It is actually a moral tale in which the rebel recants on the eve of his execution and acknowledges the fact that the British are more honourable than their opponents. Asked why Nana Sahib had ordered the murder of British women and children, Mahommed Ali Khan explains: 'Asiatics are weak, and their promises are not to be relied on, but that springs more from indifference to obligations than from prearranged treachery. When they make promises, they intend to keep them; but when they find them inconvenient, they choose to forget them. And so it was, I believe, with the Nânâ Sâhib.'[64] This is hardly credible as the confessions of a repentant rebel and the voice is clearly that of the British narrator. Mahommed Ali Khan thus belongs in the same category as Philip Meadows Taylor's famous Thug-informant, Ameer Ali, in the thoroughly fictionalised *Confessions of a Thug*. This form of colonial ventriloquism legitimised British rule by having preconceived notions of Indians and Indian society confirmed by the natives themselves – even if those informants were invented.[65]

The same applies to the famous 'autobiography' of Sita Ram, *From Sepoy to Subedar*, which is often hailed as the only authentic account from the hands of a *sepoy* during 1857.[66] Allegedly told to his British officer, Sita Ram's life and career is a veritable catalogue of colonial lore, covering unlikely attacks by Thugs, amorous adventures, captivity by both Afghans and mutineers, and every single military campaign, from the Nepal War of 1813 to the Uprising of 1857. The narrator, however, is most likely a composite figure based on a British officer's knowledge of the Indian *sepoy* as a generic character.[67] Sita Ram's account of the Uprising thus appears to be culled directly from the pages of Kaye and others, and closely follows the standard version of the conspiracy:

> It is my humble opinion that this seizing of Oudh filled the minds of the *sepoys* with distrust and led them to plot against the Government. Agents of the Nawab of Oudh and also the King of Delhi were sent all over India to discover the temper of the army. They worked upon the feelings of the *sepoys*, telling them how treacherously the foreigners had behaved towards their king. They invented ten thousand lies and promises to persuade the soldiers to mutiny and turn against their masters, the English, with the sole object of restoring the Emperor of Delhi to the throne.[68]

The story has all the hallmarks of the picaresque novel. Like Meadows Taylor's Ameer Ali, who unknowingly strangles his long-lost sister, the loyal Sita Ram is also ordered to execute his own son, who is a mutineer. The 'autobiography' is at best heavily edited and, at worst, a complete fabrication; it certainly does not provide a spontaneous account of 1857 as seen through the eyes of a *sepoy*.

The single most detailed account of Nana Sahib's grand conspiracy was given by one of his emissaries, Sitaram Bawa, who was questioned by the British at Mysore in 1858.[69] As opposed to the accounts of Mahommed Ali Khan and Sita Ram, there is no doubt whatsoever that this highly elaborate description of the conspiracy is authentic – the question is whether the information divulged is credible. According to Sitaram Bawa, Nana Sahib had been involved in several intricate conspiracies, one of which dated back to the 1830s, and was plotting with all the remaining Indian princes and rulers for the overthrow of British rule. At the same time, the main initiative behind the conspiracy is ascribed to Nana Sahib's 125-year-old guru, Dassa Bawa, who was lavishly rewarded for predicting that his master would become as powerful as the former Peshwa.[70] The centegenarian guru is also said to be behind the circulation of *chapattis*:

> The cakes in question were a *jadoo* or charm, which originated with Dassa Bawa, who told Nana Sahib that he would make *jadoo*, and as far as these magic cakes should be carried, so far should the people be on his side. He then took the reed of the lotus, or rumul, called mukhana, and made an idol of it. He then reduced the idol to very small pills, and having made an immense number of cakes, he put a pillet in each, and as far as the cakes were carried, so far would the people determine to throw off the Company's raj.[71]

All Europeans were to be ambushed and killed in one single night, after which Nana Sahib and Bahadur Shah had planned to divide the future rule of India between them. The Russians declined to join in the conspiracy, but they promised that if Nana Sahib captured Delhi, they would help drive the British from Calcutta.[72] 'The military classes were enticed,' Sitaram Bawa further stated, 'by a promise of restoring the old times of license and they all prefer that to a regular form of Government.'[73]

Inconsistent and contradictory, Sitaram Bawa's story appears to be based mainly on rumours and hearsay, and indeed he admitted as much himself: 'Every person, particularly every Brahmin, is well acquainted with all this, and the fact of these letters having been written, why, every Baboo in Calcutta knew of it.'[74] Rather than the solid evidence of a conspiracy from one of the plotters, Sitaram Bawa's testimony thus appears to be no more than an Indian equivalent to the British conspiracy theories: full of intriguing details but short on verifiable substance. It is certainly noticeable that not one of the major Indian rulers whom Sitaram Bawa denounced as co-conspirators actually joined in the Uprising. All the available evidence furthermore speaks against any form of prior communication between Bahadur Shah and Nana Sahib; during the later trial of the Emperor, he was implicated in various and altogether unlikely conspiracies, yet no one suggested a combination with Nana Sahib.[75] Furthermore, not a single letter from Nana Sahib's extensive correspondence in the years preceding 1857, and in which he allegedly plotted the uprising, has ever been found. Sitaram Bawa's grand conspiracy is accordingly not supported by any circumstantial evidence.

Many disaffected rulers *were* involved in intrigues aimed to regain their former status and glory, and inevitably to the detriment of British rule. Often these intrigues amounted to no more than exchanges of letters in which common grievances were listed and hopes for future cooperation expressed.[76] Much of this plotting consisted simply of wishful thinking, and most rulers appear to have been amply supplied with soothsayers, astrologers, and other retainers ready to confirm their masters' aspirations. Similarly to Nana Sahib's guru, a soothsayer interpreted one of Bahadur Shah's dreams to mean that 'the King of Persia with his army would annihilate the British power in the East, would restore the King to his ancient throne and reinstate him in his kingdom, and at the same time the infidels, meaning the British, would be all slaughtered'.[77] Such sycophantic predictions probably served to nourish the dreams of many once-powerful Indian rulers, but rarely led to more concrete actions. It is noteworthy that Sitaram Bawa, who made much of the existence of a conspiracy, nevertheless stated that 'the *sepoys* began to make plans among themselves' and further 'that the plot among the *sepoys* first took place'.[78] This would seem to support the idea that the intrigues at the various Indian courts followed the mutiny of the *sepoys* and did not precede it. The outbreaks at Meerut and Delhi were furthermore said to have been 'mistakes' (i.e. premature), and therefore not under the guidance of Nana Sahib or part of his plot.[79]

It is particularly noteworthy that the three most significant rebel leaders, namely Bahadur Shah, Nana Sahib, and the Rani of Jhansi, all reacted to the initial outbreak of the Uprising by contacting the British. The very day that the Meerut mutineers arrived in Delhi, the Mughal Emperor sent a messenger to Agra, informing the authorities of what had occurred, and 'prayed for assistance, and the restoration of order'.[80] Later the same day he nevertheless did assume the formal command of the Uprising and bestowed his blessings on the mutineers. When Nana Sahib learned of the outbreak on 16 May, he met with his British friends and immediately offered his support against the mutineers.[81] Following an agreement with Colonel Wheeler, the officer in charge, Nana Sahib and his retainers took over control of the treasury five days later, and a native writer even reported that Nana Sahib sent out men 'to apprehend runaway *sepoys* from Delhi and Etawah'.[82] It was not until the beginning of June that Nana Sahib met in secret with the *sepoys* of the station, and even then his support for their cause was not certain.[83] When the *sepoys* broke out in mutiny on 5 June, they gave Nana Sahib an ultimatum: 'a kingdom was prepared for him if he joined them with all his wealth: or death if he sided with the Europeans'.[84] Not surprisingly, Nana Sahib chose the first option. Having plundered the station at Cawnpore, while the British were holed up in Wheeler's entrenchment, the mutineers left for Delhi and

Nana Sahib had to convince them to return and fight the British under his leadership.[85] Nana Sahib had probably been playing it safe all along, waiting to see what the outcome of the disturbances would be, before he finally committed himself to the cause of the mutineers. This, however, is a far cry from his being the mastermind of 'a deep laid plot of conspiracy' that had matured for years and was successfully brought to fruition in May 1857.[86]

Similarly, the *sepoys* at Jhansi broke out on 8 June and massacred the forty-eight British men, women, and children who were then present in the town. Four days later the Rani of Jhansi declared in a letter to the British Commissioner at Jabalpur that she had not been able to prevent the murders, and requested the support of British troops to fight off her local rivals.[87] She later engaged in a lengthy diplomatic exchange with British officials before finally throwing in her lot with the rebels in early 1858.[88] While these alleged members of Malleson's 'executive council' were clearly pragmatic in the policies they pursued, and stood to benefit from the overthrow of British rule, theirs were not the actions of callous conspirators. Whatever role they eventually played in the Uprising, there is nothing to suggest that they planned it and executed it, as is claimed in much of the conventional literature.

## The outbreak reassessed

While a number of noted historians of 1857, such as Majumdar, Sen, and Stokes, have rejected or strongly modified the notion of a widespread conspiracy, it nevertheless remains the standard explanation.[89] The existence of a grand conspiracy is not only one of the most persistent themes in the literature on 1857; it is also one of the most persistently under-researched aspects of the Uprising. Very few authors, popular or academic, dedicate more than a brief opening chapter to the subject of the supposed conspiracies, and the outbreak at Meerut is usually treated as a minor incident which has to be covered in order to get to the really important events of the Uprising. The one exception is J. A. B. Palmer's slim monograph, *The Mutiny Outbreak at Meerut in 1857*, published in 1966.[90] Focusing very narrowly on the events leading up to the outbreak, as I do, Palmer is nevertheless hampered by a thoroughly old-fashioned approach to history. In Palmer's analysis, every single event was the result of a carefully pre-orchestrated plot in which Sunday 10 May was chosen because the heat of the month would work to the disadvantage of the British troops, who would be in church and thus unprepared when the outbreak occurred, exactly an hour and a half before sundown, which would allow the mutineers time to get away in the dark.[91] The panic that initiated the disturbances in the late afternoon of the tenth was deliberately raised in the bazaar, which was on the route that the British troops would have to take, so as to hamper their movements later on. The night before, a British officer was furthermore warned of the uprising, and the telegraph lines between Meerut and Delhi were also cut prior to the outbreak. These were facts, Palmer boldly concludes, 'which make it absolutely certain that the outbreak was indeed premeditated and planned in advance among the Meerut troops'.[92] Within such a mechanistic world-view, there is no room for contingencies or chance, and things happen because someone made them happen. If accounts of the Uprising no longer make use of the crassest stereotypes, which characterised Kaye and Malleson's work, the notion of a conspiracy has changed little since the heyday of colonial historiography.

Written in 2005, Saul David's *The Indian Mutiny* is currently one of the most popular accounts of 1857, and one which reiterates the basic outlines of Malleson's plot as proven fact, including Azimullah Khan's 'nefarious tour'.[93] David claims that the existence of 'secret committees coordinating the uprising is supported by a wealth of documentation', and yet he struggles to reconcile the mounting evidence of *sepoys* plotting with the conventional story of Nana Sahib's master-plan. The resulting account is fraught with tension. If there was a 'civilian' conspiracy, how did it relate to the plotting of the *sepoys*?[94] If Nana Sahib planned the Uprising, why was he forced to join the mutineers under threat of death?[95] With echoes of Palmer's positivism, David also exhibits a rather crude notion of what the *sepoys*' fears were about, stating that, since no greased cartridges were actually distributed, 'the lack of genuine grievance prompts the speculation that some guiding hand – within or without the regiments – was trying to keep the cartridge controversy alive by switching attention from the grease (which was no longer an issue) to the paper'.[96] The implication is that the 'guiding hand' first spread the rumour and subsequently kept it alive by manipulating the *sepoys*. The same teleological take on history is evident in David's description of the Mangal Pandey incident. The 'aborted rising' of the lone *sepoy* failed in part because Mangal Pandey's 'co-conspirators' were not yet ready. And when Mangal Pandey called out that British troops were coming to disarm the *sepoys*, David argues, this 'had clearly been decided upon as the best way to win over waverers'.[97] Time and again, an unnamed agency is invoked, as men and issues are manipulated by agitators and conspirators who, however, remain anonymous. The conspiracy of 1857 is thus cursorily mentioned but never fully explained; it is taken for granted yet not fully proven.

William Dalrymple's hugely successful account, *The Last Mughal* (2006), has set a very high standard for new interpretations of the Uprising, but even he sidesteps the issue of the actual outbreak.[98] In *The Last Mughal*, the Uprising simply arrives in Delhi on 11 May 1857, in the form of the invading mutineers, with only the briefest attempt at explaining the preceding events. While the fall of Delhi obviously changed the nature of what had started as a minor outbreak, Dalrymple's focus on the Mughal capital risks giving the erroneous impression that the Uprising of 1857 began and ended in Delhi. A history of the outbreak at Meerut, on the other hand, can only ever strive to explain the initial stage of the Uprising. That is admittedly a rather less ambitious undertaking, but no less relevant for that. The 150th anniversary of 1857 has seen a spate of new and innovative works on the Uprising, yet none has added significantly to our understanding of the alleged conspiracies and the outbreak itself. The facts surrounding the issue of the greased cartridges are still debated, and often misrepresented, and the interested reader will look in vain for a detailed account of how they affected the *sepoys*. How could rumours of contaminated ammunition spark a mutiny when not a single greased cartridge was ever distributed to the *sepoys*? The character of the outbreak of the Uprising of 1857 is no better understood today than it was at the beginning of the twentieth century. What was this event that set off the bloodiest rebellion against British rule in the nineteenth century and forever changed the history of the Raj?

*

There is today little debate as to why the Uprising of 1857 took place, and only the significance attributed to the individual causes have changed since the days of Sayed Ahmed Khan's *The Causes of the Indian Revolt*, first published in 1858.[99] By the mid-nineteenth century, British rule had radically transformed India: Christian missionaries were increasingly active and the telegraph and railway were slowly but steadily being extended to cover the entire subcontinent. Native rulers and local elites were dispossessed as the East India Company expanded its possessions and introduced new tax and revenue regulations in accordance with Utilitarian ideals. While some Indian classes, such as Hindu moneylenders, were able to benefit from these changes, many others were adversely affected by British policies, and pastoral communities, for instance, were often forced off the land to allow sedentary peasants to settle. The British administration was not only ill-informed of local society and customs, but also arrogant, and it suppressed local resistance with great brutality. At the same time, there was a complete breakdown of communication and trust between the British officers and Indian troops, during a period when new army regulations threatened the status and livelihood of the *sepoys*. The Uprising is therefore often seen as a natural effect of British rule in India.

The apparent inevitability of a rebellion against British rule has neverthe-less overshadowed the interpretation of what happened at Meerut and Delhi on 10 and 11 May 1857, and within the historiography the analysis of the out-break has been overdetermined by a teleological understanding of subsequent events. If a mutiny amongst the native troops of the Bengal Army was inevitable by 1857, and it appears that it was, there was nevertheless nothing inevitable about the time, place, and nature of the outbreak. There was nothing about the situation in northern India in January 1857 that gave forewarning of the violent scenes that were to unfold some five months later. The fact that the wives and children of the native troops who mutinied at Meerut were unprepared and left behind provides a further strong indication that not even the mutineers had anticipated the outbreak when it eventually did occur. Assuming that the oppressive nature of British rule in India is sufficient explanation for the violence of the Uprising also ignores the fact that many Indians sided with the British. The disruption and hugely detrimental effects of the British annexation of Oudh, for example, does not help us understand why individuals acted the way they did on 10 May 1857: why the crowd of the Meerut bazaar so readily joined the mutinous *sepoys*, while one-quarter of the 11th Bengal Native Infantry remained loyal to the British. Or why the butcher Mowla Baksh cut the foetus from Mrs Chambers' womb, while some Indian servants saved their British masters at the cost of their own lives.

The relationship between the long-term causes of the Uprising and the specificities of the outbreak itself is by no means obvious, which is precisely why historians have evoked conspiracy theories as a *deus ex machina* to make the connection between structure and event. In the following, however, I seek to replace the conspiracy theories with an *événementiel* micro-history of the outbreak that foregrounds the contingencies and ambiguities of the event against the backdrop of long-term developments, rather than the other way around.[100] To understand the outbreak, we have to focus on the event itself (to the extent that the sources permit), while keeping in mind the manner in which the wider context and developments of the preceding decades impacted and framed that event. Following the anthropologist Marshall Sahlins' perceptive discussion of the relationship between structure and event, my account seeks to explore the 'basic dynamic of escalation' and how larger issues were expressed through local conflicts and vice versa.[101] Long-term structures created the conditions within which minor issues were endowed with greater significance, and I suggest that a detailed examination of the tipping point – the moment when decades of relatively peaceful coexistence turned into violent animosity – may add to our understanding of the Uprising.

My approach to the subject is further inspired by George Lefebvre's groundbreaking study of rumours and panics among the peasantry during the French Revolution, *The Great Fear of 1789*.[102] I do not pretend to be a historian of equal skill to Lefebvre, though I hope this book might at least go some way towards explaining the outbreak of 1857 in a manner similar to his work on the French Revolution. My ambition is, in the words of George Rudé, 'to chart in precise detail the course of a movement by noting the days, and even the hours, of its appearance: by such means alone can the old bogey of rampaging "mobs" and ubiquitous "conspiracies" be laid to rest, or at least be reduced to proper historical proportion.'[103] That is to say that I make the rumours, panics, and their consequences the object of a study in their own right. The accuracy of rumours is essentially immaterial, and whether or not they were true, they had very real consequences. The fears and grievances of the *sepoys* have to be taken seriously if this event is to be understood; the *sepoys* were not a superstitious rabble, nor were they the passive dupes of scheming conspirators.

Since the middle of the twentieth century, the Uprising has often been interpreted by Indian historians as a peasant rebellion, and Ranajit Guha in particular has analysed 1857 in the context of a model of popular insurgency.[104] This structuralist reading of the Uprising, however, is not quite adequate in explaining events at Meerut and Delhi, where neither the *sepoys* nor the civilians could appropriately be described simply as peasants. When the British wrote of the treacherous betrayal of Indian mobs, who cruelly butchered their masters, Guha reads it simply as noble peasants resisting their oppressors. Yet it is not obvious to me that a mere inversion of colonial accounts constitutes a sufficiently sophisticated approach to the material. I believe that the dynamics of urban riots, which have been eminently described by Stanley Tambiah, Veena Das, Paul Brass, and others, in the context of contemporary South Asia, provide a rather more convincing framework within which to reassess the violence that characterised the events of 1857.[105] If not 'elementary aspects', there are nevertheless certain recurring patterns to be discerned.

In her critique of Rudrangshu Mukherjee and his interpretation of the Cawnpore Massacres, Barbara English suggests that it may be impossible 'to construct a model that could explain the unnecessary and indiscriminate slaughter involved in a massacre'.[106] This is nevertheless what I shall attempt to do with the outbreak at Meerut, and in so doing I will argue that, for those involved, the violence was neither unnecessary nor indiscriminate. The notion that rebel violence 'replicated' that of the British, as Mukherjee has suggested, may perhaps more appropriately be applied to the outbreak at Meerut, albeit with some modification.[107] While British rule was undoubtedly oppressive and brutal, there is no straightforward correlation between colonial and rebel violence in 1857. The desperate ferocity that characterised much of the rebel violence was of an altogether different nature from the sustained everyday brutality of the colonial state.[108] But the violence of the outbreak at places like Meerut and Delhi can be understood as a direct response to the *perceived* threat of British intervention in Indian society more generally. In that sense it was a pre-emptive attack that derived its terms from the intentions ascribed to the British, and this accounts for the retributive character of much of the violence.[109] The violence of the outbreak did not occur in the context of British mass executions or bloody counter-insurgency operations, but as a defensive act against something far more intangible and thus far more threatening: the apparent subversion of the *sepoys'* entire way of life.

Accordingly, the 'Great Fear' of the title refers not only to colonial paranoia following 1857, but also to the fear of Indians, which preceded the outbreak. C. A. Bayly has famously used the notion of 'information panic' to describe the inability of the British to effectively gather and interpret information relating to indigenous practices and movements.[110] This concept can be applied to Indian misreading of the British as well. The Uprising was in fact precipitated by what I think may appropriately be described as an 'information panic' amongst the *sepoys* and part of the Indian population, who saw in British reforms and the introduction of the Enfield rifle a direct attack on their culture and society. Religion represented the social order of Indian society for both Hindus and Muslims, and the *sepoys'* fears of the greased cartridges thus embodied much more general concerns over British intrusion.

*

In the following, I have sought to rely as much as possible on primary sources produced before 10 May 1857, so as to minimise the post-'Mutiny' bias and teleological rationale that characterises much of the later material. The paucity of Indian accounts nevertheless poses a real problem, and historians have access to only a very limited range of sources representing, with greater or lesser accuracy, the voice of a mere handful of either rebel or loyal Indians. Any conclusions based on such a limited amount of material obviously cannot make any claims of being comprehensive in terms of the totality of Indians who took part in these events. It is the best we can do, however, and I have endeavoured to make the most of the native testimonies given during the trial of Bahadur Shah, and the accounts of Mainodin, Shaik Hedayut Ali, and Mohun Lal.[111] The documents collected by George W. Forrest and Major Williams' inquest at Meerut also contain numerous detailed testimonies from Indians, which allow us to approach the subject as more than just an account of what one British officer wrote to another.[112] Accordingly, we have to content ourselves with trying to recover an Indian perspective only when it was recorded by the British. This entails a disproportionate focus on British experience, but I still believe that it provides us with a more complete picture and that it is only by reading the colonial archive against the grain that we might better understand Indian participation in the events of 1857.[113]

In responding to Barbara English's criticism, Rudrangshu Mukherjee defended his use of a specific account of events at Cawnpore in 1857, stating that 'Like all historical sources, Nanak Chand's diary has biases and inconsistencies, but handled with care and with the conventional checks that historians employ when handling any source, it does reveal interesting aspects of the uprising.'[114] The same observations apply to the material upon which this book is based; paraphrasing Mukherjee, I believe I can show that my use of these sources has been careful.[115]

The following pages present my attempt at reconstructing the events of the period between the first murmurs of unrest following the rumour of the cartridges in January 1857, to the final and bloody outbreak at Meerut and Delhi on 10 and 11 May. The argument presented here departs from the conventional histories of the Uprising, which take for granted the presence of a grand conspiracy. While there *were* Indians plotting against the British, the extent of these conspiracies has never been fully assessed and scrutinised in light of the empirical evidence. None of Malleson's 'executive council' plays a significant role in my account of the outbreak and there is in my opinion nothing to suggest that any of the rebel leaders who later emerged took part in events prior to May 1857. Like a number of dispossessed Indian rulers, Nana Sahib probably *was* involved in intrigues against the British all along, but this was a common aspect of Indian politics, and he rose to prominence and assumed a leading role only after events had already been set in motion. Nana Sahib was not a prime mover, nor was Bahadur Shah, the Maulavi of Faizabad or the Rani of Jhansi. Their involvement in the events of 1857 was hesitant and responsive rather than callous and manipulative.

This study instead focuses on the *sepoys* and to a lesser extent the civilians who joined in the outbreak at Meerut and Delhi. It was amongst the *sepoys* that the initial plots were hatched and it was the *sepoys* who first took up arms. This is not to deny the role played by civilians in 1857, but the fact remains that the events of 10 and 11 May constituted a crucial breaking point and created a precedent from which everything else followed. Once the *sepoys* of the 11th and 20th Bengal Native Infantry and the 3rd Bengal Light Cavalry had risen at Meerut, and the Mughal Emperor had been reinstated at Delhi, the Uprising gained a momentum of its own, irrespective of what had previously been planned or plotted. History rarely unfolds according to the plans and aspirations of men, and the history of 1857 is indeed more complicated than implied by the neat assertions of a great conspiracy. The Uprising did not simply erupt or spread like a wildfire; it was smouldering for months and only gradually got under way in the most faltering manner.

# 1

# The Greased Cartridges

In 1853, the East India Company decided to modernise the weapons employed by the *sepoys* of the Bengal Army, and introduce the new Enfield Pattern 1853 Rifled Musket.[1] The musket then in use by the infantry of the Bengal Army was the muzzle-loading smoothbore Brown Bess, which had changed little since the eighteenth century, except for the replacement of its flintlock with a percussion lock in 1842.[2] The ammunition for the Brown Bess consisted of a paper cartridge with a pre-measured amount of powder and one round; in order to load the weapon, the cartridge was torn open with the teeth, the powder was poured into the barrel, and then the cartridge with the bullet was rammed down. A percussion cap was placed on the nipple of the lock and when the trigger was pulled, the hammer would ignite the fulminate and fire the musket. The *sepoys* of rifle companies, who usually functioned as skirmishers, were, however, armed with the 1838 Brunswick two-groove rifle.[3] The rifled barrel allowed for a tighter fit of the bullet and gave it a spin when fired that greatly increased its speed and accuracy. To ease the process of ramming down the bullet and to make a tight fit once loaded, the rifle necessitated the use of a lubricated patch that was wound around the ball, instead of the paper cartridge used in the smoothbore musket. A small number of native troops on the North West Frontier were also armed with the Minié Rifle, which relied on its conically shaped bullet with applied grease for a tight fit.[4] The grease for the patches of the Brunswick two-groove rifle, and for the Minié, was supposed to be composed of linseed oil and beeswax, but it appears that various other types of lubricant were also used, including mutton-fat, wax, and coconut oil.[5] Small numbers of the *sepoys* would accordingly have been familiar with the use of greased ammunition.[6] Native cavalry were armed with either the 1842 Victoria Carbine or the 1842

Lancer Pistol, both of which were smoothbore and loaded similarly to the Brown Bess.[7]

The ammunition for the 1853 Enfield rifle, which was to replace both the Brown Bess and the Brunswick, combined the paper cartridge of the former with the greased patch of the latter. One end of the Enfield paper cartridge was thus lubricated with grease to facilitate loading and to ensure a tight fit.[8] The *sepoy* would have to hold the greased end, where the bullet was, and tear open the other end to pour the powder down the barrel, before ramming the paper cartridge with the bullet down the barrel, greased end first. For firing drills with either the Brown Bess or Enfield, troops used ungreased cartridges without balls, as the aim was simply to practise the process of loading and firing.[9] The paper cartridges for the Brown Bess and the Enfield were not the same and had to be pre-fabricated by trained men.

Prior to the official introduction of the Enfield rifle, the pre-greased cartridges had to be tested to see if they could withstand the climate. *Sepoys* in India and Rangoon accordingly carried the cartridges around for several months in 1853 before it was determined that they were suitable, and during this trial the troops made no objections. At the time a British officer did actually make the Military Board aware of the potential problem posed by the grease, stating that: 'unless it be proven that the grease employed in these cartridges is not of a nature to offend or interfere with the prejudices of caste, it will be expedient not to issue them for test to Native corps, but to European soldiers only to be carried in pouch'.[10] Unfortunately this warning went unheeded.

The only troops to be armed with the Enfield rifle, and hence the greased cartridges, were the British HM 60th Rifles stationed at Meerut, who were initially supplied with pre-greased ammunition from Britain. However, from August 1856 onwards, the grease for the cartridges was made at the arsenal of Fort William in Calcutta.[11] The grease was thus made in India, following instructions from Britain, using beeswax (stearine) and tallow (animal fat), the latter of which was supplied locally by Gangadarh Banerji & Co. Greased cartridges were eventually manufactured at the arsenal of Fort William, Calcutta, and at the stations at Dum Dum and at Meerut, but the grease itself appears to have been made at the former location only. From January 1857, *sepoys* in groups of five from the various regiments of the Bengal Army undertook instruction in the drill and use of the Enfield rifle at the stations of Dum Dum, Ambala, and Sialkot.[12] Although the making of cartridges was part of this drill, no *sepoys* came into contact with the grease or handled greased cartridges at any point during the instruction prior to 10 May.[13] In January 1857, a rumour nevertheless spread at Dum Dum, that the grease on the Enfield cartridges consisted of the fat of pigs and cows.[14]

To come into close contact with fat from these two animals would be extremely offensive to both Hindus and Muslims, and as the loading of the Enfield required that the cartridge was torn with the teeth, it followed that the *sepoys* might even come to ingest some of the odious grease.[15] Having one's ritual purity defiled was no trifling matter for high-caste Hindus; they would be regarded as untouchables and shunned by relatives, friends, and other members of their caste. In order to have their caste restored, they would have to undergo elaborate rites of purification, which included feasting Brahmin priests and making offerings at important pilgrimage sites. Apart from the obvious social and religious stigma, having one's caste restored thus entailed a significant economic burden as well. For the Muslim *sepoys*, the eating of pork was strictly forbidden, but the impurity itself could be allayed through prayers and repentance.

This was by no means the first time this issue was raised. During the First Afghan War, 1839–42, the *sepoys* had had to forgo a number of their observances, such as washing before each meal, and they also had to accept food prepared by Muslims.[16] Their British officers personally supplied them with warm *poshteens* or sheepskin coats against the cold of the mountainous region, but wearing these was offensive to the Hindus. The Muslim *sepoys* also found it hard to reconcile the fact that they were serving an infidel government against other Muslims. The campaign was a catastrophic disaster, but once the *sepoys* who survived the gruelling retreat from Kabul returned, the real implications dawned on them; as one Indian officer described it: 'None of the Hindoos in Hindoostan would eat with their comrades who went to Afghanistan, nor would they even allow them to touch their cooking utensils; they looked upon them all as outcasts, and treated them accordingly.'[17] In practice, the socio-religious doctrines were more flexible than the scriptures allowed, and for both Hindus and Muslims exceptions were often made if the pollution was accidental or through necessity. The rumour of the greased cartridges nevertheless constituted a significant affront to their religious sensibilities.

It certainly caused a very 'unpleasant feeling' among the *sepoys* who were receiving instructions in the use of the Enfield rifle at Dum Dum.[18] The story of how the rumour actually came about was later to be endlessly repeated: allegedly a *khalasi* or labourer of low caste, who worked at the depot, asked a *sepoy* of the 2nd Bengal Native Infantry for some water from the soldier's *lota* or drinking vessel. Brahmins and high-caste Hindus always carried a *lota* so that they could drink water anywhere without having to bring to their mouth anything that might have been polluted by the touch of a person from a lower caste. The *sepoy* indignantly declined the inappropriate request, and the *khalasi* responded: 'You will soon lose your caste, as ere long you will have to bite the cartridges covered with the fat of pigs and cows.'[19] Was this true?

According to the Inspector-General of Ordnance, Colonel A. Abbott, 'No extraordinary precaution appears to have been taken to insure the absence of any objectionable fat.'[20] During a later inquiry into the composition of the lubricant, Lieutenant Currie, Commissary of Ordnance at the arsenal at Fort William, was questioned on the issue:

Question:  You stated in your evidence on Saturday, that before the 27th January, cartridges were issued to the Delhi magazine from the arsenal, already greased; what are the orders you have received on the composition of grease for the use of cartridges?

Answer:    The grease was to be made of six parts of tallow and one part of bees-wax.

Question:  Of what ought that tallow to consist?

Answer:    No inquiry is made as to the fat of what animal is used.

Question:  You do not yourself know what fat is used?

Answer:    No, I don't know.

Question:  Is not the intention of Government that the tallow to be used in the preparation of grease should be mutton or goat's fat?

Answer:    It is *not* the intention of Government that all grease used in any preparation in the magazine is to be made of goat's and sheep's fat only [italics added].[21]

Similarly, Colonel Abbott stated that he 'was told that the composition was that which the regulations prescribed, and that the tallow *might or might not* have contained the fat of cows or other animals [italics added]'.[22] Accordingly, the army did not actually know what the tallow used for the grease was made of and could not exclude the *possibility* that it contained cow tallow and pig lard. Since the presence of obnoxious grease could not be ruled out, and may indeed have been likely, the Governor-General, Charles Canning, later stated that the *sepoys'* worries were 'well founded'.[23] When the story of the *khalasi* was repeated, from one *sepoy* to the next, and from the military lines to the civilian quarters and beyond, the Indian troops certainly did not doubt the tale. A contemporary native account of the affair, by one Nund Singh of Amritsar, provides a good indication of how the story might have been told amongst the *sepoys*:

> Near Calcutta, five coss [about 14 miles] distant from it, there is a place called Achanuk [Barrackpore]. There is a Government cantonment at that place. At that place a Hindostanee[24] was drawing water out of a well. A 'Chumar'[25] came in and asked the Hindostanee to give him water to drink. The Hindostanee told him that he had better go to some other place to drink water.
>
> 'How,' said the Hindostanee, 'can I give you water to drink? You are a Chumar.'
>
> Upon this words were exchanged between them. The Chumar said: 'You do not give me water to drink and affect to be so religious; and the fat of the cow and pig which I prepare with my own hands you will bite off with your teeth.'
>
> These and similar words having been exchanged between them, they came to blows. The other people, who had heard the talk about the 'fat,' rescued the 'Chumar,' and made inquiries from him in a conciliatory manner.
>
> Then two men went along with him to that place [the place where cartridges were said to be made], which was a little removed from the cantonment. There they saw with their own eyes about fifty or sixty Chumars working and putting on the fat of both animals on the cartridges. They returned from thence homewards, and described all to the Soubahdars[26] and other officers.[27]

Though not very accurate, this version did emphasise the key elements of the rumour and furthermore added 'proof' of its veracity. If the British authorities could not ascertain the composition of the tallow, it is nevertheless unlikely that the Indian labourers possessed more concrete knowledge or that a simple visit to the factory could settle the issue. According to another account, a Bengali clerk at Calcutta was given the task of translating into vernacular the manual for the Enfield rifle in early January 1857, and in the process learned that the prescribed grease contained the fat of cows and goats.[28] The British manual, however, simply referred to the use of 'tallow' without any indication of what animal it should come from – hence the confusion. According to *The Delhi Gazette*, the Government's inquiries had revealed that 'the mutton fat ordered, had really been exchanged by the contractor for bullock's fat'.[29] This was also incorrect, but when even Anglo-Indian newspapers reported that the cartridges were greased with cow's fat, it is not to be wondered that the story was widely believed.

The rumour was actually said to have spread all over India, and some of the *sepoys* undergoing instruction at Dum Dum explained to their British officer that when they returned to their respective regiments their friends would refuse to eat with them. The officer, Brevet-Captain Wright, sought to allay the *sepoys'* fears, assuring them that the grease was made up with mutton fat and wax, which were, given the context, both inoffensive substances. The *sepoys* replied: 'It may be so, but our friends will not believe it; let us obtain the ingredients from the bazaar and make it up ourselves; we shall know what is used, and be able to assure our fellow-soldiers and others that there is nothing in it prohibited by our caste.'[30] Thus it seems that the main concern of the *sepoys* was the stigma associated with handling the cartridges, and the actual nature of the grease might have been secondary to the fear of being ostracised.

The day after he spoke with the *sepoys*, Brevet-Captain Wright informed his superior, Brevet-Major Bontein, who commanded the depot at Dum Dum, and suggested that the men be allowed to purchase the materials for greasing the cartridges as they had suggested. Bontein immediately ordered a parade, on 22 January, and called for the *sepoys* to come forward if they had any complaints, which two-thirds of them did. In 'a manner perfectly respectful' they stated that the composition of the grease used on the new cartridges was 'opposed to their religious feeling' and they suggested that a mixture of oil and wax be used instead.[31] Apparently Bontein was already familiar with the rumour, but now felt compelled to report the matter to his superiors, and thus the issue of the greased cartridges became official and began its way through the bureaucracy of the East India Company.

The fact that these concerns were raised before the cartridges had even been distributed is testament to the impact of the pre-emptive rumour and its potentially devastating consequences to the social status of the *sepoys*. Whether they had actually handled the cartridges or not, whether the grease contained pig and cow fat or not, the *sepoys* who went for instruction at the depots were all in risk of being stigmatised – that is, unless they made a public disavowal of the cartridges. But then the *sepoys* of the Bengal Army were no ordinary soldiers.

## The Company and the *sepoy*

A number of the castes, the status of which was taken more or less for granted in 1857, had actually emerged a mere century before.[32] The decline of the Mughal Empire had caused significant political and social turmoil, but it also enabled groups such as the Rajputs and Bhumihars, or agricultural Brahmins, of eastern Uttar Pradesh and Bihar, to establish a high-caste status through military service. This entailed a combination of the warrior ideal with the ritual purity and social privilege of Brahmin priests, who were at the very top of the traditional caste hierarchy. These peasant soldiers were known as *purbiyas* or easterners.

During the second half of the eighteenth century, the East India Company became increasingly entangled in politics and slowly changed from a trading venture into a state in its own right. To protect its trade, honour local alliances, and later expand its territorial possessions, the Company had to rely on Indian soldiers and for that purpose built an army of *sepoys* trained by British officers on European military principles. At the time, however, the British were still an emergent power and as such had to compete on equal terms with political rivals, both Indian and European, in the recruitment of native troops. Much of the Company's legitimacy as a state power was in fact derived through the continuation of pre-colonial practices, which included the establishment of an army of high-caste Hindu *sepoys*. As a result, the Company in Bengal tapped into the military labour market of north India and used the existing networks of patronage and clan-ties by recruiting peasant regiments directly from the *zamindars* or landholders of Bihar, Benares, and Oudh. This resulted in an extremely homogeneous body of *sepoys* in the Bengal Army, composed mainly of Brahmins, Bhumihars, and Rajputs. Accommodating high-caste usages and practices within its regiments was an effective means by which the East India Company could become an attractive and legitimate military employer in eighteenth-century India. Reluctant to interfere too much in local governance, British policy-makers during this early period generally sought to adopt and preserve Indian traditions and institutions as far as possible. The Company thus managed to establish a loyal base of recruitment by employing the rhetoric of high-caste status as well as the promise of regular pay.[33]

At the same time, the indigenous military labour market was becoming increasingly constricted as the British, with the help of the *sepoys*, expanded their sphere of influence. By 1818 the Company had established an effective monopoly of power on the subcontinent, having defeated or pacified Indian rulers and states that would otherwise have provided employment for thousands of Indian troops. By formalising and codifying a social system that they understood but poorly, the British in effect constructed a high-caste army, which maintained its status irrespectively of the changes that were taking place in Indian society at large. Whilst the ideal of the high-status warrior was dying out due to the enforced demobilisation of native armies elsewhere, the Company's army kept alive the spirit of the martial tradition of the past. The Bengal Army, which constituted the military force throughout the newly ceded and conquered territories in north India, provided the perfect frame within which the reinvented high-caste military tradition of the Bhumihars and Rajputs could be formally institutionalised. It presented the *sepoys* with the opportunity to improve and secure their new-found status: service in the Company's army thus became one of the most significant means by which high-caste Hindus asserted their socio-religious status.

In order to bolster the high-status profile of its army, the British allowed the observance of the dietary and ritual requirements of Hindus, and encouraged their religious festivals; at times the regimental colours were incorporated in the religious festivals of the *sepoys* and worshipped as idols. This in effect created a military religious tradition, which reflected the exalted status of the *sepoys*. By endorsing and encouraging the high-caste status of the *sepoys*, the British were also able better to control their native troops and ensure continued support from the local landowners in the regions that supplied the recruits. As the Company was extending its foothold on the Indian subcontinent, the *sepoys* not only became the means by which the stability and authority of the colonial state could be maintained; they also became a vital link between the British rulers and their Indian subjects more generally. More than any other Indian group or community, it was the *sepoys* with whom the British came into close contact, and through whom much of their knowledge of the land was initially derived.

Although the British themselves encouraged high-caste practices amongst the *sepoys*, the Western drill and perception of discipline, as well as practical requirements, often clashed with the special considerations of the native troops. The earliest and most serious rupture occurred at Vellore in the Madras Presidency in 1806. In order to make the appearance of the *sepoys* more uniform and in keeping with a Western military aesthetic, it was ordered in 1805 that they could no longer wear caste-marks or jewellery while on duty, and they had to trim their beards.[34] These regulations interfered directly with most visible markers of identity and status, and were thus greatly resented by the *sepoys*. The following year a new type of headgear was introduced to replace the existing model, which the British considered to be impractical and altogether too similar to a turban. The new hat resembled the stove-pipe shako worn by the musicians of the regimental bands, who were often Christians, as well as by the British troops. Being in the service of the British, who were thought of simply as Christians, put the *sepoys* at constant risk of being polluted by their employers' religion. The deeper implications of the new regulations and headdress, as far as the *sepoys* and local population were concerned, were that the troops were being made to look like the British in order to make them Christians. Matters were not helped by the fact that the Madras army had previously suffered from irregularities in the financing and payment of its troops.

Although the East India Company did not allow missionaries to preach and convert in India until 1813, the British were widely believed to be working towards the conversion of all their subjects. The cultural divide between rulers and ruled meant that many official measures and interventions were seen in this predominantly religious light. By wearing the hats of the Christians, the *sepoys* apparently feared they would become Christians themselves and they would certainly be regarded as such by their relatives and caste members. It was openly stated that no one would marry the *sepoys*, and some were apparently told by their own wives that they would no longer cook or sleep with them if they accepted the new headdress. The fear of being ostracised had an immense effect on the *sepoys*, who would do anything to avoid the odious appellation of 'topi-wallahs' or 'men with hats' – a common term of abuse for the British. The bond between the British and their Indian *sepoys* was in part based on the assumption that the rulers would never impose Christianity on their subjects, whose traditional beliefs they were obliged to uphold. Any new regulation or measure that could be perceived as impinging on religious issues was accordingly perceived as a breach of faith on the part of the British. Under such circumstances, the *sepoys* felt they were relieved of their oath of loyalty.

In the fort at Vellore, the sons of the late Tipoo Sahib were kept in exile by the British, and the presence of these representatives of the old order provided the discontented *sepoys* with a cause around which to rally. The *sepoys* had nightly *panchayats*, or meetings, during which they swore to kill all the European troops when the time came and to keep silent about the plot. Some of Tipoo Sahib's sons, along with their retainers, appear to have encouraged the *sepoys* with the promise of increased pay once they were reinstated as rulers. During the early morning of 10 July 1806, the *sepoys* broke out in mutiny, killed most of their officers and other British troops, and took over the fort. They failed, however, to coordinate the mutiny outside the fort, and when British reinforcements arrived the following morning, the rebellious *sepoys* were quickly defeated and several hundred killed or later executed. The mutiny was largely blamed on the religious sensitivity and superstition of the *sepoys*, as well as the treacherous plotting of the exiled princes. The events nevertheless highlighted the fact that the acceptance of British authority in India was rather precarious, even amongst its closest allies, the *sepoys*. Any interference by the British was perceived as part of a conscious plan to convert their Indian subjects, and in that respect the *sepoys* were particularly vulnerable. The loyalty between the army and its native soldiers was conditional on the maintenance of a fine balance that could easily be overturned. Shortly after the Vellore Mutiny, the British officer in command stated that 'there was an idea among the troops that it was the intention of Government to force them to relinquish everything that distinguishes one caste from another, and by degrees to convert them to Christianity; that they also suspected the Europeans intended to massacre the native troops'.[35] This would not be the last time these worries were voiced by *sepoys*.

In 1824, the high-caste observances of the *sepoys* of the Bengal Army led to another violent clash. It was widely claimed that Hindus would lose their caste if they crossed the 'kala pani' or black water: that is, if they crossed the sea. This belief actually had no scriptural precedent, but seems to have been established on the grounds of more practical issues at the time. High-caste Hindus could not eat any food that had been prepared by or been in physical contact with a person of a lower caste; they certainly could not share pots or drinking vessels, or eat in a communal mess. Onboard a ship it was virtually impossible for *sepoys* to observe their dietary purity, such as cooking their own food and eating by themselves, and provisions were likely to be handled by any number of people.[36] A number of general issues commonly associated with long travels amongst Hindus probably played an additional role in the perceived prohibition against crossing the sea. Most of the *sepoys* of the Bengal Army came from a peasant background and had little or no experience of the sea; they may simply have been averse to risking their lives on the ocean and engaging in service far from their homes. Overseas service could entail years of being absent from their families, to whom the *sepoys* were much attached, and to whom they forwarded a large portion of their pay. When parents died, their children were furthermore supposed to tend to their funeral and perform certain rituals, and this added another disincentive for the *sepoys* to leave the shores of their ancestral home. Water from the sacred Ganges river (or one of its tributaries) was also a prerequisite for various purification rituals among north Indian Hindus, including the absolution of sins at the time of death, and being unable to access Ganges water therefore posed a potential problem. As a result, *sepoys* could only be transported by ship if they volunteered for this, and those who did were paid an extra allowance, known as *batta*, which apparently assisted them in overcoming these fears (and the possible financial consequences of their being deemed 'outcast' by villagers at home).[37] The British were in fact prepared to spend considerable resources and time marching troops across land rather than transporting them by sea. In time, however, this notable exemption of service became a key source of contention between the British command and the *sepoys*.

In 1824 several regiments of the Bengal Army were assembled at Barrackpore, waiting to be marched to Rangoon as part of the British campaign in Burma. It would have been faster to sail across the Bay of Bengal, but to avoid the pollution associated with crossing the sea, the regiments were to be marched on foot to Rangoon via Chittagong. Unfortunately, there were insufficient bullocks to carry the *sepoys*' personal possessions, which weighed 23 lbs per man in addition to their equipment, and they were ordered to carry these themselves or leave them behind. But the *sepoys* flatly refused to march without their *lotas* and personal utensils, carpets and quilts, which would allow them to observe their dietary and ritual purity during the march. As at Vellore, they swore an oath on Ganges water, the holy *tulsi* plant, and the Koran, not to march until the British supplied more carriage cattle or increased their extra allowance. It was furthermore rumoured that once they had reached Chittagong, they would be forced to board ships and sail to Rangoon after all.[38] At one point the *sepoys* armed themselves, and when they refused to lay down their weapons and comply with the orders of their officers, the British opened fire on them with artillery. Several hundred of the mutineers were killed immediately or subsequently hunted down and executed. It later emerged that two Muslim officers had told the *sepoys*, most of whom were Hindus, that if they did not obey orders, they 'would there and then make them eat from the same dish', and further that 'they would make them eat cow's flesh and the Mussalmans that they should eat hog's flesh'.[39] The two officers were generally disliked by the troops, and in the tense situation their goading of the recalcitrant troops had the unfortunate effect of reinforcing the *sepoys'* resentment. Peer pressure and threats had furthermore assured solidarity amongst the Hindu and Muslim *sepoys*. According to a Muslim *sepoy*, 'those *sepoys* who were Hindus objected to go on board ship and told the Mohammedan *sepoys* that if they went to the Colonel they would kill them, consequently we did not go but endeavoured to please them'.[40] Following the brutal suppression of the mutiny at Barrackpore, *sepoys* of the Bengal Army seem to have developed an almost paranoid fear of the British turning their artillery against them. To the British, however, the incident demonstrated the impracticality of having a high-caste army unwilling to compromise ritual practices.

By the 1830s the political climate was changing and, motivated by a civilising zeal and the rise of Evangelicalism, the British could no longer defend their non-intervention policy or the need to perpetuate pre-colonial practices and customs.[41] In 1834, a General Order was passed to allow for the recruitment of a wider range of Hindu and Muslim groups in order to break the high-caste monopoly of the Bengal Army.[42] Gurkha battalions had already been established after the Company's war with Nepal in 1814–16, and following the Sikh Wars of 1845–6 and 1848–9, both Sikhs and Muslims from Punjab entered the Bengal Army in increasing numbers. General enlistment constituted an open challenge to the social exclusivity formerly maintained by the high-caste *sepoys*; if low-status groups could enlist alongside the Rajputs, Bhumihars, and Brahmins, service in the Company's army no longer constituted a guarantee of high status. It directly undermined the identity and ritual purity of the *sepoys*. It furthermore fundamentally challenged their security and livelihood, since a father might no longer be followed by his son (as had been commonplace) in the Company's employment.

At the same time, the presence of missionaries was becoming increasingly conspicuous across the subcontinent, and the fear of conversion apparently permeated Indian society.[43] While the actual number of Indians converted during the first half of the nineteenth century was quite negligible, the underhand methods used by some missionaries, including the conversion of orphans they adopted, led to considerable resentment.[44] Missionary schooling, providing an 'English' education with a strong Christian element to Indian pupils, was also becoming more common, and conversion as a means of upward mobility for lower castes challenged the existing social order.[45]

The British were particularly worried that the activities of missionaries might stir up trouble amongst the *sepoys*; a native soldier who converted to Christianity in 1819 was promptly removed from his regiment, and some

Company officials actually blamed the mutiny at Barrackpore in 1824 on the presence of missionaries.[46] It also caused some embarrassment to the Army, when it emerged in 1857 that the British commander of the 34th Bengal Native Infantry had been preaching to the *sepoys*.[47] When called upon to explain himself, Colonel Wheler stated that for the past twenty years he had 'been in the habit of speaking to the natives of all classes, *sepoys* and other, making no distinction, since there is no respect for persons with God, on the subject of our religion, in the highways, cities, bazaars and villages (not in the lines and regimental bazaars)'.[48] Wheler was subsequently declared unfit to command a regiment.

Yet the prevalent fear of conversion was the result not so much of actual missionary activity as of the gradual intrusion into everyday life by a foreign government thought to be inherently Christian.[49] The abolition of *sati* in 1829, for instance, did not directly affect many Indians – it was an extremely rare practice with fewer than a thousand cases being recorded in Bengal between 1815 and 1829.[50] With the passing of the Widow Remarriage Act in 1856, the British nevertheless appeared to continue the same policy by allowing Hindu women to remarry after the death of their husbands.[51] In a highly patriarchal society, this seemed to suggest that the position of women would be completely changed under British rule, which could only be perceived as a threat to the prevailing social order. For the Indian population it was virtually impossible to discern between the civilising and the proselytising zeal of the British, if indeed such a distinction existed. When Christian missionaries told the *maulavis* and *pandits* that they should not keep their women in *purdah*, and that they should not circumcise their children or practise child-marriage, it was simply assumed that they were speaking for the British Government.[52] At Patna in 1845, the authorities came to realise how prevalent these fears were:

> Reports had been for some time current to the effect that the British Government purposed to destroy the caste of the Hindoos, and to abolish Mahomedanism by forbidding the initial ceremony through which admission is obtained to the number of the Faithful. And to this was added another lie, scarcely less alarming, that the Purdah was also to be prohibited, and that Mahomedan females of all ranks were to be compelled to go about unveiled.[53]

When common messing was introduced in the colonial jails during the 1840s, it provided a further impetus to the fears of some that the Government was seeking to undermine the caste and religion of a part of the Indian population entirely in its power.[54] The practice of obliging prisoners of different castes and creeds to eat together was highly offensive to the high-caste Hindu inmates. At the same time, prisoners were no longer allowed to prepare their own food, but had to receive their meals from the hands of cooks whose social status might be polluting. Another cause of contention was the removal of prisoners' brass vessel, the *lota*, which allowed high-caste inmates to maintain their purity – this was not possible with the earthenware vessels that replaced them. The prisoners' protests over these infringements of their dietary practices were widely supported by the Indian community outside, as the native police officer, Shaik Hedayut Ali observed:

> In course of conversation these people said to me, if any of our brothers commit any offence and by the laws of the land they get punished; that is all very right and proper, and we have nothing to say against it, but that law must be bad which by its infliction ruins our religion, – for instance, when any one is sentenced to imprisonment, immediately on his reaching the prison, his beard and moustache is cut; this to us is a great insult. In jail it is ordered that the prisoners should eat in messes, the Mahomedans by themselves and the Hindoos by themselves; this is no outrage to a Mahomedan, but it is a great one to the feelings and religion of a Hindoo. One Hindoo won't eat from the hand of another unless they happen to be brothers or cousins … When a Hindoo is released from prison he is always tabooed by his family and looked upon as having lost caste: on this account both the prisoner and his relatives become disaffected towards the Government.[55]

*Sepoys* openly voiced their fears that they might be the next to suffer the same fate at the hand of the Government. Like the prisoners, *sepoys* were subject to official rules and had their dietary habits disciplined by army regulations. In a show of solidarity with Brahmin and Rajput inmates who had rioted in the jail at Sahabad, several *sepoys* wrote to them that 'the day on which the English shall attempt to destroy our religion, every regiment will revolt'.[56] The unrest in the jails coincided with the war against the Sikhs and the excitement caused by a tentative British attempt to carry out a census in Patna, 'a movement which was at once declared to be part of the great scheme of the Government for the forcible conversion of the people'.[57] Members of the local Muslim elite in Patna were supposedly distributing money to the *sepoys* in order to make them leave the service of the Company, and it was rumoured that the King of Delhi had promised a month's salary to those troops who joined in the plot. Thanks to the information provided by several loyal Indian officers, the planned rising was prevented by the local authorities, although rumours persisted for some time: 'It was stated that a royal mandate had come from the King of Delhi; that the Rajah of Nepaul was ready to send a great army sweeping down into the plains; and again it was said that the Sikhs were the prime movers of the plot.'[58]

There were certainly those who yearned for the old days and thought that the clock might be turned back by ousting the British. As was the case at Vellore, this appears to have happened when the grievances of dispossessed Indian rulers coincided with those of the *sepoys*. In 1822, several anonymous letters were found in Arcot, which called upon Muslims and Hindus to unite against the British, who were taking over the land. The *sepoys* were furthermore encouraged to mutiny and kill their British officers according to a carefully laid plan, with a promise that they would be well remunerated for their participation. Around the same time an anonymous petition from the local troops complained that civilian administrators received the control of land once it had been conquered by the Company, while the soldiers, who had fought for this, were not rewarded.[59] Nothing further came of these communications, although they did indicate a certain level of dissatisfaction. Ten years later a similar plot was discovered at Bangalore, although this time the preparations were well under way. With the aid of the Company's *sepoys* and demobilised troops of the Raja of Mysore, a group of local leaders planned to take over the fort at Bangalore and kill all the British officers. At the same time, a dead pig was placed at an *eidgah* or outdoor mosque along with a wooden cross, to cause an outrage that would be directed at the British authorities.[60] The conspiracy came to light when a loyal Indian officer informed his superiors and the ringleaders were either executed or imprisoned. In these affairs, the promise of increased pay plays a significant part in the attempt to seduce the *sepoys*. When Sitaram Bawa in 1858 claimed that the 'The military classes were enticed by a promise of restoring the old times of license', he was accordingly drawing on a well-established idea of the mercenary character of Indian soldiers.[61] The Indian *sepoys* were not simply hired hands lusting for plunder, but they do seem to have maintained enough of the traditional mercenary instinct to be dissatisfied with the conditions under which they served the British.

By the 1850s, the relationship between the *sepoys* and the British officers was characterised by increasing distance and growing resentment. Grievances over inadequate pay, the removal of privileges, lack of opportunity for promotion, and a corps of British officers with a poor understanding of Indian culture did nothing to improve the *sepoy*'s loyalty to the Company. It is not that the bond between soldiers and officers had suddenly deteriorated; mutiny was endemic in the East India Company army, and indeed was a part of the traditional terms of employment which the *sepoys*, to some extent, still assumed were in place. The century following 1757 was one of continuous negotiations between the British and their Indian troops, caused in part by the incommensurability of British notions of a standing army and Indian terms of military service. In 1838, before the First Afghan War, extra *batta* was introduced for *sepoys* serving beyond the Indus river, but this was withdrawn after the conquest of Sindh in 1843, when fighting came to an end. The *sepoys* of the Bengal Army who were to be stationed in Sindh on a more or less permanent basis were therefore not accorded extra pay, and this was bitterly resented. Several regiments en route to the frontier refused to follow orders or receive the reduced rate of pay, and they were eventually replaced with regiments from Madras. Six ringleaders of the mutinous 65th Bengal Native Infantry were executed and 32 were given prison sentences, while the entire 34th Bengal Native Infantry was disbanded in disgrace.[62] This situation repeated itself during the Second Sikh War when extra *batta* was reintroduced and then withdrawn once the campaign was over. This time, however, the *sepoys* seemed to have been more organised in their protest, as 'Delegates from several corps went about from station to station, and letters were exchanged between those at a distance.'[63] There was a general fear among the officers that the defeated Sikhs might join forces with the mutineers, and at Delhi, the British found 'unmistakable signs of a confederation of many regiments determined not to serve in the Punjab except on the higher pay'.[64] Five ringleaders of the mutiny in one regiment were sentenced to transportation for life, and the 66th Bengal Native Infantry, which had tried to seize the fort at Govindhgarh in 1850, was disbanded and its name struck from the army list. Time and again, the *sepoys* and the Company clashed over issues such as pay and religious practices, as the native troops sought to negotiate their terms of employment. Some events, however, were beyond their reach.

The annexation of Oudh in 1856 had a significant impact on the *sepoys* of the Bengal Army, since some three-quarters of the troops hailed from that region.[65] The British had dispossessed the King of Oudh on the pretext of his alleged despotic misrule, and the takeover caused immense disruption.[66] As a result of the new revenue settlement, the traditional landowners experienced a severe loss of privileges and possessions, as many were expropriated after forfeiture of their lands. The 50,000-strong local army was demobilised, thus flooding Oudh with armed men harbouring a strong resentment against the Company. 'Oude was the birthplace of the Purbeah race,' according to Mainodin, a native police officer well acquainted with the *sepoys*, 'and these feelings of dissatisfaction affected the whole Purbeah race in the service of the British Government. To the native mind the act of annexation was one of gross injustice, and provoked a universal desire for resistance. The King, and all those connected with him, although bowing to the hand of fate, became henceforward the bitter enemies of the English.'[67]

While the links between the *sepoys* and their homeland should perhaps not be exaggerated, it is obvious that the annexation and political turmoil in Oudh provided another source of discord. The British no longer maintained a respectful relationship with the local elites, who had hitherto facilitated recruitment, and the annexation might thus be perceived as a direct affront to the *purbiya sepoys* and yet another infringement of their status. The state they were serving had taken over their home region, by what *sepoys* perceived as a deceitful and treacherous means.[68] One loyal Indian, referring to the British as 'we', overheard *sepoys* complaining about the annexation, stating that 'they did not like our settlement system introduced in Oude, and one of them being a "Subadar" added that, he was a native of "Gaya" in Bengal, he had some landed property there, the more he laboured to improve his land for increasing the cultivation, the more he was assessed by the settlement officer'.[69] For the majority of the native troops, who did not themselves own land back home, the news received from their villages would nevertheless have informed them of how the world to which they once belonged was being turned upside down.[70] A cavalry trooper from Oudh complained that 'I used to be a great man when I went home; the best in my village rose as I approached; now the lowest puff their pipes in my face.'[71]

The General Service Enlistment Order, passed in 1856, was perhaps the final blow to the confidence of the *sepoys*; the order decreed that new recruits would have to serve wherever they were ordered, including overseas. While this applied only to new recruits, it obviously caused concern amongst the *sepoys*, as it seemed to suggest that they might all in time be deployed regardless of the original terms of their enlistment.[72] As one Indian police officer, Hedayut Ali, described at the time, 'Any new order issued by Government is looked upon with much suspicion by the Native Army, and is much canvassed in every regiment.'[73] The days of special treatment, when the British had to ask for volunteers for their foreign campaigns, were definitively over.

The Hindu *sepoys* of the Bengal Army were not simply high-caste – *being* in that army was to a large extent what *made* them high-caste. The concern over pollution amongst the troops in 1857 was actually a throwback to the social struggles and conflicts of the eighteenth century, during which Rajputs and Bhumihars had established themselves as high-status groups through the appropriation of Brahmin practices concerning ritual purity.[74] Status and identity were not rigid, as the notion of the strictly hierarchical caste system seemed to imply, but flexible and in constant flux. Any perceived infringement on their social status by the army therefore threatened to undermine the identity of the *sepoys*. Whereas the British had originally provided the guarantee of *sepoys'* status, service in the army now became a liability. The exalted social status enjoyed by the high-caste Hindu majority in the regiments furthermore extended to the other *sepoys*, including the Muslims, Sikhs and other Hindus. The British had created a distinct military tradition, which provided a shared sense of identity and united the *sepoys* regardless of background and creed. This was indispensable in maintaining the *sepoys'* fighting power and loyalty to the Company, but it also carried the potential for solidarity among the native soldiers *against* their British commanders. And this certainly seemed to characterise the situation in January 1857, as the rumour of the greased cartridges began to take hold.

# 2

# Barrackpore and Berhampore

The rumour that cartridges greased with the fat of pigs and cows were being used in the Enfield rifle spread swiftly amongst the different regiments in the area around Dum Dum during January 1857; the guards of the 70th Bengal Native Infantry, on duty in Calcutta, for instance, were told of the greased cartridges by a barber who had come down from Barrackpore.[1] The subject was widely discussed in the lines and one *jemadar* later recounted an exchange between himself and a comrade, while they were smoking and chatting in his hut: 'He said: "What do you say on the subject of the cartridges? Will you bite them or not?" I replied: "I will." He replied: "I will not cut them with my teeth; I will cut them with my sword."'[2] According to the *Jemadar*, 'The manner of the men was different from usual. It was the talk of the place. The people left the Sudder Bazar through some fear.'[3] There was an expectation amongst the *sepoys* and traders and camp-followers of the regimental bazaars that something dramatic might happen.[4] A native officer, who was later tried for spreading sedition, told his men that there would be a *pukka ghulbah* or serious disturbance during the religious festival of Holi, which in 1857 fell on 10 March.[5]

While the matter was being thought over in the British military administration, events on the ground had already been set in motion by the rumours. Starting on 23 January, several buildings, including the bungalow of a British sergeant-major, were set on fire on consecutive nights at the railway head of Raniganj, 120 miles east of Calcutta.[6] A few days later, the same occurred at Barrackpore, where the telegraph office and some empty bungalows were burned, and one British non-commissioned officer (NCO) actually pulled a fire-arrow out of the roof of his house. The telegraph office was not chosen at random, it seems, and might have been part of a deliberate plan to slow down British communications.[7] According to an Indian police officer, Mainodin Hasan Khan, it was furthermore 'calculated that the burning of a telegraph office would immediately be communicated along the line from Calcutta to the Punjab'.[8] News of the arson attacks would thus rapidly spread to other *sepoy* regiments stationed across northern India. The British thought they noticed a pattern, in that troops from the 2nd BNI were posted at both Raniganj and Barrackpore. The incendiary arrows found at the latter station were said to be of the kind used by the Santhals, and the 2nd BNI had only the previous year been deployed in the tribal area to suppress the Santhal rebellion.[9] Accordingly, this regiment came under suspicion as the British officers began to speculate that something more serious than idle rumours might be brewing.[10] Strong guards were posted in the officers' lines and there were constant patrols, while the thatched roofs of verandas were removed to avoid the risk of further arson attacks.[11]

Amongst the *sepoys* the situation had already come to a head by the end of January; a small group of native officers and *sepoys* of the 34th BNI decided they would no longer serve the British.[12] In their frustration, they turned to the only alternative to British rule that they knew: the erstwhile rulers of Oudh. The 19th Bengal Native Infantry at Berhampore and the 34th BNI at Barrackpore had both been stationed in Oudh when it was annexed by the British in 1856. According to Mainodin, who later communicated with a number of the *sepoys* from these two regiments, the takeover made a deep impression on them:

> Both these regiments were full of bitterness towards the English Government, and from them letters were written to other Purbeah regiments. The 34th took the lead. These letters reminded every regiment of the ancient dynasties of Hindustan; pointed out that the annexation of Oude had been followed by the disbandment of the Oude army, for the second time since the connection of the English with Oude; and showed that their place was being filled by the enlistment of Punjabis and Sikhs, and the formation of a Punjab army. The very bread had been torn out of the mouths of men who knew no other profession than that of the sword. The letters went on to say that further annexations might be expected, with little or no use for the native army. Thus was it pressed upon the *Sepoys* that they must rebel to reseat the ancient kings on their thrones, and drive the trespassers away. The welfare of the soldier caste required this; the honour of their chiefs was at stake.[13]

The deposed King of Oudh, Wajid Ali Shah, and his followers were then living in exile at Garden Reach in Calcutta, and as *sepoys* of the 34th BNI were routinely deployed on guard duties in the city, there were numerous opportunities for communication. Some of the native officers of the 34th BNI also made contact with Raja Man Singh, one of the most powerful landowners in Oudh, and a desperate plot was hatched to seize the fort at Calcutta and reinstate Wajid Ali Shah.[14] The plan was to take advantage of the presence of three companies of the 34th BNI that would make a stop at Calcutta on their way to Chittagong. With their numbers thus augmented, the various units of the 34th BNI on guard duties in Calcutta were to seize the fort with the assistance of the King of Oudh's men as well as the Calcutta Native Militia.[15] The affair, however, was completely botched when the native officer in charge of the plot was relieved and sent back to Barrackpore on the very day the *coup* was to happen. The ringleaders had furthermore failed to secure the assistance of their comrades in key positions and to inform them of the details of the plan. The attempt went ahead on the night of 26 January, but the running back and forth of *sepoy* guards put the British at Fort William on guard, and the whole thing was eventually aborted.

The bungled attempt to take Fort William had all the hallmarks of an impulsive and ill-judged undertaking, brought about by desperation and with little consideration of strategy or likelihood of success. There was a similar attempt in early March, involving the guards of both the 34th and the 2nd BNI, but the details of this affair are vague.[16] What can be said with certainty is that the *sepoy* guards posted at different locations in Calcutta were to varying degrees involved in mutinous attempts during the early months of 1857. The first plot had entailed the involvement of the other regiments stationed in Calcutta, whose loyalty was to be bought by the promise of a pay-rise of Rs 10 a month once the British had been ousted. It is thus significant that, as early as January, the initial response of the frustrated *sepoys* was to seek to re-establish the old order, when being a soldier entailed a high social status and an ability to negotiate wages and terms of employment. The extent of the ex-King of Oudh's actual involvement in these plots remains obscure, but it seems unlikely that the rumours of the greased cartridges alone should have incited the *sepoys* to mutiny so early. As was the case at Vellore, the retainers of the ex-King might have played a more active role; several months later, three of them were apprehended on suspicion of tampering with the *sepoys*. The British certainly believed that the dethroned Wajid Ali Shah was behind the unrest, and Major-General Hearsey, who commanded the Presidency Division at Barrackpore, was said to be 'confident that they have been tampered with, and thinks that he has traced this to the king of Oude's people at Garden Reach.'[17] On 15 June 1857, the ex-King was confined inside Fort William, but nothing conclusive was ever proven against him.[18]

The tense atmosphere and strange goings-on amongst the *sepoys* at the end of January also affected the frame of mind of the British officers, as Major-General Hearsey reported on the 28th: 'I am sorry to add that I this morning heard that the Officer Commanding Her Majesty's 53rd Regiment in Fort William wrote to the officer in command of the wing of that regiment at Dum-Dum to warn a company to be ready to turn out at any moment, and had distributed to the men of the company ten rounds of balled ammunition, informing that officer that a mutiny had broken out at Barrackpore amongst the *sepoys*!!!'[19] Given the nature of the plots amongst the *sepoys* at the time, as well as the turn of later events, the commanding officer of the 53rd Bengal Native Infantry obviously had more foresight than he was ever given credit for. Others, however, were more composed in their response to the rumours and worries of the *sepoys*, and Brevet-Colonel Kennedy of the 70th BNI invited the native officers into his bungalow to talk through their concerns about the cartridges in late January.[20]

By 27 January, the Government had decided to put a stop to the manufacture of greased cartridges. When the cartridges were to be distributed, they would be ungreased and the *sepoys* could then purchase materials from the bazaar and apply the lubricant themselves.[21] This procedure had, of course, first been suggested by *sepoys* at Dum Dum, but it was endorsed by both Major-General Hearsey and Colonel A. Abbott, the Inspector-General of Ordnance and Magazines.[22] In a matter of days, then, the British responded to the reports of the *sepoys*' objections and immediately sought to remedy the cause for concern. This reflects a certain willingness on the part of the Government to accommodate the sentiments of the native troops in order to avoid any discontent or trouble.

In his first report on the complaints regarding the Enfield cartridges, Major-General Hearsey had simply ascribed the rumour to 'some evil disposed persons', such as the *khalasi* at Dum Dum.[23] In view of the subsequent fires at Raniganj and Barrackpore, however, he soon came to the conclusion that this was more than an idle rumour and that the *sepoys* were being manipulated: 'A report has been spread by some designing persons, most likely Brahmins or agents of the religious Hindu party in Calcutta (I believe it is called the *Dhurma Subha*), that they (the *sepoys*) are to be forced to embrace the Christian faith [italics in original].'[24] According to Hearsey, it was thus orthodox Hindus, opposed to British reforms, who were creating trouble for the Government by making 'a party of the ignorant classes in the ranks of the army believe their religion or religious prejudices are eventually to be abolished by force, and by force they are all to be made Christians, and thus by shaking their faith in Government lose confidence of their officers by inducing the *sepoys* to commit offences (such as incendiarism) so difficult to put a stop to or prove, they will gain their object'.[25]

Without any proof apart from his own stern belief that the *sepoys* were being directed by hidden forces outside the army, Hearsey thus conjured up a conspiracy under the guidance of religious fanatics. While the *sepoys'* objections to the greased cartridges obviously related to their religious beliefs, there were no actual indications that the disturbances had been caused by the involvement of outsiders.[26] This was nevertheless the manner in which the rumours and discontent amongst the *sepoys* were interpreted. It must be remembered that at this early stage there was still some kind of open dialogue between the *sepoys* and their British officers, on the subject of the cartridges, which hardly corresponds with the notion of secret conspiracy.[27] In an attempt to counteract the supposed influence of Hindu fanatics over the *sepoys*, Major-General Hearsey ordered a parade at Barrackpore on 28 January and in front of all the native regiments tried to convince them that they had no reasons for concern. A native officer later recalled the speech, made through a British translator:

> The doubt, which you had in your minds regarding cow's or pig's fat being used in the grease, has been reported to Government, who have no desire whatever that you should lose caste, and they have, therefore, forbidden the application of the grease to the cartridges. The paper and the powder will be supplied by Government, and oil and ghee or other greasy substance, according to their own wish, receiving payment for the same from the Government. Some twenty or thirty men, who will be taught here to make these cartridges, will make them up in conjunction with the *tindal*.[28]

It is worth noticing that in the Indian officer's rendition of the speech, there was no denial of the polluting qualities of the grease, and the speech could therefore be interpreted as an indirect confirmation of the rumours' truth. Little details easily got lost in the transmission of such important statements, thereby increasing the possibilities for misunderstandings and the suspicion among the *sepoys*. According to the commander of the 70th BNI, 'the address appeared to have the desired effect upon the men. The men went to their lines, appearing to be perfectly satisfied with the explanation given by the Major-General.'[29] The men were in fact far from happy, and a *havildar* of the 70th BNI described the situation at Barrackpore on the night of 28 January in very different terms: 'It was a panic. Reports of all kinds were flying about the station; some said there was a regiment coming; some said there would be fighting; some said there was a dacoity; and some said there was a fire. The men were all assembled near their bells-of-arms.'[30] If the *sepoys* seemed to accept the assurances given to them when confronted by British officers, they had no such confidence when amongst themselves.

The British persisted in trying to convince the troops that there was no truth to the rumours, and during parades at Barrackpore on both 3 and 4 February the *sepoys* were shown samples of ungreased cartridges and cartridge paper and told that they could themselves apply grease composed of wax and oil.[31] Following this, several officers went into the lines and amongst their men to let them see and feel the samples in order to convince them that, without the grease, the materials were harmless.[32] This strategy, however, backfired as the *sepoys* responded that 'the paper was not the same as that used for the old cartridges, and that they thought there was something in it.'[33] The paper from which the new cartridges were made was actually different from that which the *sepoys* were used to handling, but according to the chemical analysis that was later carried out, 'The paper has not been treated with any greasy or oily matters during or since its manufacture.'[34] In an attempt to get to the root of the matter, Major-General Hearsey set up an inquiry at Barrackpore on 6 February; during the proceedings one *sepoy* of the 2nd BNI was questioned about the new ungreased cartridges:

| | |
|---|---|
| Question: | Did you make any objections to the materials of which those cartridges were composed? |
| Answer: | I felt some suspicion in regard to the paper, if it might not affect my caste. |
| Question: | What reason have you to suppose that there is anything in the paper which would injure your caste? |
| Answer: | Because it is a new description of paper with which the cartridges are made up, and which I have not seen before. |
| Question: | Have you ever seen or heard from any one that the paper is composed of anything which is objectionable to your caste? |
| Answer: | I heard a report that there was some fat in the paper; it was a bazar report.[35] |

Another *sepoy* stated that, after the parade on 4 February, some of the men had dipped a piece of the cartridge paper in water and set it on fire: 'it smells as if there was grease in it'.[36] Questioned if he had any objections to the ungreased cartridges, a native officer stated that 'A report got about, which I think came from the magazine *khalasis* in Calcutta, that there was some grease in the paper; on this account I have some suspicions about it.' The officer was then asked how that suspicion could be removed from his mind, to which he answered: 'I cannot remove it.'[37] The *khalasi* rumour as first reported to the British referred to the grease applied to the cartridges, but since the *sepoys* had never actually seen these, the finer details of the story were lost. The rumour that the cartridges contained the fat of pigs and cows was sufficient for the *sepoys* to object to them, no matter what concessions were made. In the end, the actual nature of the grease and of the paper was immaterial. When asked if he would bite the cartridges after having been satisfied that it was not greased, one *sepoy* responded that 'I could not do it, as the other men would object to it.'[38] The stigma associated with any handling of the cartridges had accordingly not been alleviated by the fact that they would be distributed without grease. Interestingly, several *sepoys* referred to the rumour of the greased paper as a 'bazar-rumour'. This characterisation of the rumour referred to the nature of its transmission, and at the same time absolved the *sepoys* of having to give up the names of whoever was circulating the story. Such a rumour had no specific source, and one native officer actually excused himself for not informing his superiors, stating that he 'could not report it to the officer, it being merely a bazar report'.[39]

The statements of the *sepoys* also revealed a certain fear of change, caused by a general suspicion as to the motives of the British and any alterations made to existing practices.[40] The British had stopped the manufacture of grease and were prepared to hand out the cartridges for the *sepoys* to apply other lubricants themselves. Samples of the cartridge paper were even distributed in what the British intended as a generous attempt to accommodate the concerns of the *sepoys*. To the *sepoys*, however, these measures appeared simply as more acts of subterfuge designed to persuade them to use the cartridges. Anxieties about the potential infringement of their caste and religious status remained. There was, in short, no real rapport between the British officers and the Indian *sepoys*. Faced by what seemed to them irrational concerns, the British all too readily accepted the protestations of some *sepoys* that they were satisfied that the cartridges were harmless. During the trial of a *jemadar* for inciting to mutiny in April, the prosecutor even stated, 'This explanation, it has been shown in court, satisfied the minds of the men.'[41] That was evidently not the case, and it is significant that the British consistently misread the signs of unrest and the objections voiced by the native troops. The British were entirely oblivious to the possibility that the *sepoys*' objection to the cartridges might also have been related to other issues. The Indian troops were effectively being asked to take on new responsibilities, including the use of new weapons and service overseas, for what amounted to less pay and with no consideration of their aspirations for their sons to follow them in the Company's service. Invoking concern over caste and ritual pollution was one way in which the *sepoys* could express general discontent without being prosecuted for mutiny. At the same time, however, there was a culture of suspicion amongst the *sepoys*, who also misread the intentions of their superiors.

On the evening of 5 February, a large group of *sepoys* from the different regiments met in secret on the parade ground at Barrackpore; they all had handkerchiefs tied around their faces so that they could not be identified. The parades held on the preceding days and the British insistence that they should accept the cartridges had brought them into a state of panic, and they were 'apprehensive of being forced to give up their caste and be made Christians.'[42] As with earlier panics, the *sepoys*' fears were exacerbated by the rumour that European troops and artillery were being brought in, from Dinapore in this case, to force them to accept the cartridges.[43] A native officer, who later informed the British of the meeting, was encouraged to join the assembled men, who stated that they were 'willing to die for their religion, and that if they could make an arrangement that evening, the next night (6th February 1857) they would plunder the station and kill all the Europeans, and then go where they liked'.[44] The plan was almost identical to the failed plot of 26 January: after having burned the bungalows and seized the magazine at Barrackpore, the *sepoys* would take Fort William or the treasury in Calcutta.

Representatives of the four regiments at Barrackpore were also to meet on 6 February to take an oath and make the final preparations.[45] Part of the plan consisted in mobilising *sepoys* outside of Barrackpore, where 'the men of other regiments were to be informed of what is going on here, and that they were to be called upon to cooperate with their comrades, the affair being one which concerned them all'.[46] While the British had been hampered in their ability to communicate by the burning of the telegraph office, the *sepoys* thus sought to extend their organisation to muster external support. The administering of an oath was intended to inspire solidarity and make the *sepoys* commit to the plan, which had dire consequences for everybody involved. The *sepoys* were, however, prepared to take the risks. It appears that, by this stage, they were absolutely convinced that the Government intended to deprive them of their caste and religion by forcing them to bite cartridges – at gunpoint if necessary.

As it happened, no outbreak took place at Barrackpore, and the *sepoys'* plans came to nothing.[47] It was significant, however, that large numbers of *sepoys* from all four regiments at the station took part in the plotting, and that they intended to contact other regiments. This was not the only time that *sepoys* at Barrackpore met at night; there appear to have been several such occasions, during which the men met in the lines after dark, with their faces covered, and discussed the cartridges and what they should do.[48] In spite of the murderous intentions of the *sepoys*, the plots that were hatched during the first months of 1857 were characterised by panic and indecision. Although resentment was growing fast, and discounting the occasional act of arson, the *sepoys* were not yet prepared to act on their frustrations and fears. There were furthermore a number of native officers and *sepoys* who were willing to provide the British with information, sometimes at the risk of their own lives; one *sepoy* said that he feared his comrades would 'use violence towards him' if they found out that he was a spy.[49] Some of these informants were probably motivated by personal resentment and there was accordingly no complete unity among the *sepoys*, who did not constitute a homogeneous social or religious group anyway.[50]

Following the inquiry and news of the secret meeting at Barrackpore, Hearsey was becoming seriously alarmed. Apart from the strengthened guards patrolling the cantonment to prevent any further fires, a reward of Rs 1,000 was offered for information on the arson attacks.[51] All camp-followers were now being registered to keep 'bad characters' out of the cantonment, and Hearsey was convinced 'that the *sepoys* are tampered with by designing villains when on duty in Fort William and Calcutta, it having been frequent noticed by old military residents at this station that after frequent absences on such detached duty, many of them return to their lines with strange ideas and unsettled minds'.[52] To counter this, the Major-General suggested that guard duties in Calcutta should henceforth be assumed by European regiments or the native militia.[53] In reporting on the continuing unrest to the Government, Hearsey did not disguise how serious the situation was, making the by now famous statement that 'We have at Barrackpore been dwelling upon a mine ready for explosion'.[54] The Major-General was exasperated at the 'absurd notions' and 'stupid ideas' of the *sepoys*, who persisted in believing the rumours in spite of all the initiatives that had been taken to allay their concerns regarding the cartridges. Significantly, he also suggested that European troops should be posted at Barrackpore 'in case of a mutiny occurring', and even went so far as to paraphrase Sir Charles Metcalfe, who years earlier stated that 'he expected to awake some fine morning, and find India had been lost to the English Crown'.[55]

These were dire predictions, but even so Hearsey was deceiving himself about the efficacy of his explanations to the *sepoys*. On 9 February he ordered another parade of the entire brigade, and tried to impress upon the *sepoys* that, according to the tenets of Christianity, they could not be forcefully converted, and that, besides, the Government had no such intention.[56] Satisfied of his own success, he stated: 'I have since heard from the officers commanding regiments that their Native officers and men appeared quite "khoosh" (pleased) and seemed to be relieved from a heaviness of mind that had possessed them.'[57] Hearsey even got the commanders of the four regiments at Barrackpore to report formally on the sentiments in their respective regiments and they all confirmed that the parade had 'a most beneficial effect on the minds of the men'.[58] Amongst the British there was a general concern for the unrest amongst the *sepoys*, but at the same time there was also a naive belief, bordering on self-delusion, that their efforts to ease the minds of their troops were successful in spite of every sign to the contrary.

## 'A religious question, from which arose our dread'

Shortly after the secret meeting on 5 February, a native doctor at Barrackpore overheard 'a *sepoy* of the 2nd Bengal Native Infantry, mention at the hospital to some one that a *kossid* had been sent to the [19th Bengal Native Infantry] at Berhampore and to the regiments at Dinapore, informing them that ten or twelve of use have raised a disturbance, and we want you to support us.'[59] This was in full accordance with what had been decided at the secret meeting, and it seemed that the *sepoys* at Barrackpore were now actively communicating with other regiments.[60]

The rumours of the greased cartridges had in fact been known in Berhampore since January, at the very least, but had not caused any great concern amongst the men.[61] Around the same time that the *kossid* was sent, however, a native officer asked Lieutenant-Colonel Mitchell, commanding the 19th BNI at Berhampore, 'What is this story everybody is talking about, the Government intends making the native army use cows' and pigs' fat with the ammunition for their new rifles?'[62] Mitchell did not think this was a serious matter, but nevertheless promised that he would ask his superior, Hearsey, to allow the *pay-havildars* to purchase their own grease for the *sepoys*' use.[63] On 11 February, ammunition supplies for the Brown Bess, then in use with the troops, were received at Berhampore.[64] The consignment, which was escorted by a guard of the 65th BNI, came from the magazine at Calcutta, and this seems to have given new life to the rumour of the cartridges.[65] An officer of Mitchell's regiment told him that, according to the story in circulation, there was pig and cow's fat in the grease 'so that when the *sepoys* bit off the end of the cartridges they would lose caste'.[66]

If the men had not yet been swayed by the rumour, that was about to change, as several detachments of the 34th BNI arrived at Berhampore at the end of February. Explaining how the idea of the greased cartridges reached the *sepoys* of the 19th BNI at Berhampore, a native officer later stated: 'It was first talked about after the arrival of a guard of *sepoys* from Calcutta escorting Government stallions, and afterwards another party of the 34th Regiment, Native Infantry, who came with European invalids, confirmed the doubts in the minds of the men ...'.[67] The second detachment of the 34th BNI actually halted at Berhampore for several weeks and were encamped just next to a tank in the vicinity of the lines of the 19th BNI.[68] The men of the 19th and 34th BNI were well acquainted from their deployment in Oudh the previous year, and they now had the opportunity to exchange news with their old friends. This was when the *sepoys* of the 19th BNI learned in detail what had so far occurred at the other stations and how 'there were doubts about the cartridges at Barrackpore'.[69] In the process of transmission the rumour was further elaborated; one officer of the 19th BNI stated that the cartridges 'were composed of the fat of bullocks, pigs, and *jackasses* [italics added]'.[70] The fat of jackasses never figured in any of the other reports, but it was an obvious addition to the rumour, since asses were considered by Muslims to be polluting.[71] The rumour had thus developed from a logical suspicion concerning the fat of pigs and cows, to include a wholly fictitious component that was added simply by virtue of its being obnoxious to the *sepoys*.[72] Be that as it may, the *sepoys* of the 19th BNI were seized by the same worries as their comrades at Barrackpore and were, in their own words, 'very much afraid on the score of our religion'.[73]

On 26 February, the day after the second guard of the 34th BNI had arrived at Berhampore, Mitchell ordered a parade with firing practice for the 19th BNI for the following morning.[74] It was the practice in the regiment to distribute the copper caps for the Brown Bess in the evening preceding a firing drill, while the blank cartridges were handed out only during the parade itself.[75] When the copper caps for the guns were handed out to the *sepoys* on the evening of 26 February, however, they refused them. Their suspicions regarding the cartridges had been reinforced by the arrival of new stores of ammunition on 11 February, and by refusing the caps, they sought to prevent the cartridges from being distributed the next morning.[76] The *sepoys* approached the *Subadar-Major*, who tried in vain to convince them that the cartridges they were about to receive were of the old type; he even opened a bundle to show them.[77]

The native officers and about fifty *sepoys* of the 19th BNI were thus assembled when, at 7.30 p.m., Mitchell came down to the lines and enquired what the objection to the cartridges was. Speaking on behalf of the *sepoys*, the *Subadar-Major* stated that 'There are two kinds of cartridges, and we have hitherto always made up our own; besides, only a few days ago some stores arrived from Calcutta, and on account of reports going about we have doubts on the subject.'[78] On hearing this, Mitchell lost his composure and retorted that if the *sepoys* would not take the cartridges, he would take them to Burma or China where they would suffer and die.[79] The Lieutenant-Colonel told the native officers to reason with their men and explain that the cartridges were the old ones made by the *sepoy* regiment previously stationed at Berhampore. During the parade to be held the next morning, the officers of the individual companies would hand out the cartridges to the *sepoys* and, Mitchell finished, 'those who refuse to take their cartridges I will severely punish them'.[80] On this note, Mitchell considered the issue to have been resolved and retired for the evening. Troubled by the continuing unrest among the *sepoys*, the Lieutenant-Colonel nevertheless thought it necessary to prepare the 11th Irregular Cavalry and the artillery for the parade the next day.[81]

At roll-call at 8 p.m., Mitchell's orders were explained to the remaining *sepoys* of the 19th BNI. Unfortunately, the rendition of the Lieutenant-Colonel's words was a little too literal and Mitchell's outburst had given rise to new concerns amongst the men: 'He gave this order so angrily that we were convinced that the cartridges were greased, otherwise he would not have spoken so.'[82] The men returned to their huts for the night, but the events of the day left them uneasy. A number of the *sepoys* assembled near a tank, which was just adjacent to the shooting range and where the small detachment of the 34th BNI was encamped. Here they allegedly took an oath, and probably swore not to receive what they thought were the new cartridges.[83] This sequence of events was practically identical to what had occurred at Barrackpore in 1824.

During the early night, news of Mitchell's order for the cavalry and artillery to be present at the parade on the following morning somehow reached the *sepoys*. At about 10.30 p.m. on 26 February, a cry of 'fire' was raised in their lines, and the native officer of the quarter-guard gave the order for the alarm to be sounded by drum.[84] In the tumult of the night, the *sepoys* rushed to the *kotes* or bells-of-arms, broke them open, and seized their guns and ammunition, before returning to their lines, ready to defend themselves. The *sepoys* later told their officers that 'the reason was that the artillery and cavalry was sent for, and they thought that they would be attacked'.[85] According to the *Havildar-Major* of the 19th BNI, 'there was a rumour that the cavalry were about to seize the kotes', and accordingly the *sepoys* armed themselves before they were (supposedly) to be disarmed.[86] Hearing the noise, Lieutenant-Colonel Mitchell immediately ordered the cavalry and artillery to prepare for action, but it was getting towards 1 a.m. before the European officers arrived at the lines, where they found the men 'in undress formed in line and shouting'.[87] Some of the native officers called out that the *sepoys* might shoot if they approached any further, and Mitchell ordered two guns to be loaded with grape and moved into position while some of the cavalry were to dismount. Only then did the Lieutenant-Colonel and his adjutants advance a little, and after the bugle call for assembly had been sounded, a group of native officers along with some of the men came forward.

A later petition written by the *sepoys* themselves reflects the general state of panic that prevailed in the lines:

> The same night, about a quarter to eleven, shouts of various kinds were heard; some said there is a fire, others that they were surrounded by the Europeans; some said that the guns had arrived, others that the cavalry had appeared. In the midst of this row the alarm sounded on a drum, then from fear of our lives the greater number seized their arms from the kotes. Between twelve and one o'clock, the 11th Regiment, Irregular Cavalry, and the guns with torches arrived on the parade with the commanding officer, which still more confirmed our

suspicions of the cartridges being greased, inasmuch as the commanding officer appeared to be about to carry his threats into execution by force. We had been hearing of this sort of thing for the last two months or more, and here appeared to be the realisation of it.[88]

The self-fulfilling power of rumours and panic came into play as the *sepoys'* desperate actions brought about the very things they feared. They now expected the British to force them to bite the cartridges at gunpoint.

The fear of British troops being ordered against them had, of course, been a recurrent feature of the *sepoys'* panic since January. About mid-February it was rumoured at Barrackpore that the 'Native regiments at Meerut have mutinied, and have been attacked by the Europeans.'[89] The rumour had no basis whatsoever, even if it was an uncanny anticipation of things to come, but it reflects how big an impression the events at Barrackpore in 1824 had made on the minds of the *sepoys*.

The native officers pleaded with the Lieutenant-Colonel to retire and not use violence against the *sepoys*, whom they described as 'ignorant and stupid'.[90] Mitchell was furious and allegedly retorted, 'I will blow them away though I die myself.'[91] Several of the European officers tried to reason with the men of their companies, but when the *sepoys* were ordered to lay down their weapons, they refused to do so unless the cavalry and artillery were withdrawn. The situation had turned into a tense stand-off between the British officers and the alarmed *sepoys*. At around 3 a.m., however, Mitchell finally gave in when he was told that the *sepoys* were returning their weapons, and the cavalry and artillery retired along with the European officers.[92] The Lieutenant-Colonel even agreed not to have the cavalry and artillery present during the morning parade, which was by then only a few hours away, 'as the men would only believe that they were intended to act against them'.[93]

During the tumult of the night of 26 February, the *sepoys* targeted one man in particular, namely Sergeant-Major Frawley, the drill officer of the 19th BNI. Frawley was warned to leave his bungalow, which was near the lines, and he eventually sought protection from the cavalry when they arrived later with Lieutenant-Colonel Mitchell.[94] While the Sergeant-Major joined the other British officers, the Drum-Major of the 19th BNI saw to it that Frawley's family was brought to safety. After they had left the bungalow, 'a great mob' came looking for the Sergeant-Major and his family, and when they found the place empty, they let out the cattle kept in the nearby pound.[95] It remains unknown what grievance the *sepoys* had with Frawley, but according to

Lieutenant-Colonel Mitchell, he gave him 'thirty days' leave of absence, so as to keep him out of the way, as there was evidently a bad feeling towards him on the part of the men, and I think it would be as well if he was to be removed to another regiment as sergeant-major'.[96] Given the broader concerns of the *sepoys*, resentment against specific British officers was hardly decisive, but probably did worsen an already tense situation.

The parade on the morning of 27 February took place as planned without any incidents, although the serious nature of the events of the night were brought to light: several of the *sepoys* were missing bullets from their pouches, while others had cartridges with extraction marks, thus indicating that their weapons had been loaded during the night and that they had indeed been prepared to fight.[97] No action was taken against the *sepoys* who had loaded their arms, but Mitchell ordered a court of inquiry to get to the bottom of the disturbances.[98] Although tempers had cooled by sunrise on 27 February, the *sepoys* were still nervous; after the parade they were reluctant to return their weapons and leave the parade ground, and that evening, some of the men also left their huts and slept near the *kotes*, although this was entirely against regulations.[99] The reason given by the *sepoys* was that 'We are afraid that the artillery and cavalry may come down on us again.'[100] The following morning Mitchell ordered another parade during which he, like Hearsey at Barrackpore, tried to convince the *sepoys* that they had nothing to worry about, and he also produced samples of the Enfield cartridges for them to see.[101] As had happened before, the *sepoys* noticed that the paper on some of the cartridges had a glazed appearance, and they suspected that these were the new ones sent from Calcutta.[102] During the night of 1 March, a number of *sepoys* rushed to the *kotes* and seized their weapons, but they returned them immediately when ordered to do so by their officers.[103] The fear that had seized the *sepoys* of the 19th BNI during the night of 26 February was not simply a momentary lapse, but a more or less constant state of panic.

On 29 February, the *sepoys* of the 19th BNI submitted a written petition to Major-General Hearsey, as the commander of the division, which presented their version of the occurrences at Berhampore.[104] The regiment had always been obedient and fulfilled its duties, the petition stated, but due to the rumours of the cartridges the men were 'much afraid on the score of our religion'. No explanation was given of how the disturbances on the night of 26 February had started, but fear of being attacked and being forced to accept the cartridges were listed as the prime reasons for the unrest. The *sepoys* ended their appeal by expressing their continued suspicion of the cartridges, as demonstrated to them by Mitchell on 28 February, but they also professed their unwavering loyalty to the British: 'Therefore, with every respect we now petition that since this is a religious question, from which arose our dread, and as religion is, by the order of God, the first thing, we petition that as we have done formerly we may be now also allowed to make up our own cartridges, and we will obey whatever orders may be given to us; and we will ever pray for you.'[105] This petition was not political in any sense, but clearly indicated the intent on the part of the *sepoys* to continue to serve the British as long as their immediate grievances were addressed. It should be remembered that Mitchell had already promised that the *sepoys* would be allowed to make their own cartridges, but not all of them seem to have been aware of that promise. The Lieutenant-Colonel's assurance had furthermore been made in relation to the new cartridges for the Enfield rifle, which had not yet been introduced at Berhampore. The cartridges that the men of the 19th BNI were to have practised with were of the type they had been using all along with the old Brown Bess. Suspicion, however, now attached itself to any ammunition that the British handed out and which the *sepoys* had not made themselves.

On 27 March, Lord Canning ordered that the 19th BNI be marched to Barrackpore and there disbanded in front of the other native regiments: 'Mutiny so open and defiant cannot be excused by any sensitiveness of religion or caste, by fear of coercion, or by the seduction and deception of others.'[106] The General Order was to be read to all other regiments of the Bengal Army. The station at Barrackpore was chosen as the most suitable location for the disbandment due to the presence of European regiments, which could be relied on in case there was any unrest amongst the native regiments.[107] By this time, however, the rumours and panic had spread far beyond the confines of the *sepoys*' lines and were in fact being noted across northern India.

# 3

## Rumours and *Chapattis*

1857 was not a particularly bad year in India: there was no economic depression, drought or failure of harvest, but there was a vague sense of unrest. In Oudh, the recent takeover by the Company was having profound effects on the landholding elite and on peasants as the new revenue settlement was introduced. For many people, it seemed as if the British were slowly but surely dismantling the last vestiges of independent states and kingdoms across the subcontinent. The ex-King of Oudh was kept in exile at Calcutta, while the Mughal Emperor, Bahadur Shah, was about to be removed from the Red Fort in Delhi to a location convenient to the British Government. The British were at the same time waging war against the Shah of Persia, who had taken the strategic city of Heart in 1856. Persia was regarded as a religious ally by Indian Muslims, and the Shah maintained close diplomatic relations with a number of Indian rulers. News of the progress of the war dominated both British and Indian newspapers right up until the end of hostilities in April 1857. In India it was generally believed that Russia was actively supporting Persia and that once the British had been defeated, the Tsar would lead an immense army south. Rumours of impending invasions or intrigues with foreign powers were deeply unsettling and, in the absence of reliable information, created extreme anxiety amongst ordinary Indians.[1]

The ravages of the cholera epidemic of the preceding year had also been extremely disruptive, and it was still causing deaths in some areas. Outbreaks of cholera were often linked with the movement of the Company's armies, and hence there was a widespread belief that the British were in fact responsible for the disease.[2] The local population affected by the epidemic was particularly susceptible to rumours and panics, and possibly had more than the usual number of reasons for being suspicious of the British authorities. Though the population of northern India was not on the brink of starvation or beset by invaders, the calm that seemed to prevail during the early months of 1857 was highly deceptive.

*

During the early months of 1857, a strange phenomenon occurred throughout the districts of northern India. From village to village, the *chaukidars*, or watchmen, passed from one to the other a strange sign in the form of *chapattis* – the inconspicuous unleavened bread that constituted a basic part of the rural population's diet.[3] The *chaukidars* themselves did not know what the *chapattis* signified or from whence they came; they knew only that it was incumbent upon them to continue the transmission. The Magistrate of Mathura remembered how, in late January:

> one day as I entered the office I found four little cakes laid on the table, dirty little cakes of the coarsest flour, about the size and thickness of a biscuit. A man had come to a village, and given a cake to the watchman, with injunctions to bake four like it, to distribute them to the watchmen of the adjacent villages, and desire them to do the same. The watchmen obeyed, but at the same time informed the police they had now reported the affair, sending in the cakes. The following day came similar reports from other parts of the district, and we next learnt from the newspapers that these cakes were being distributed in the same manner over all Upper India.[4]

As reports of *chapattis* started coming in from places hundreds of miles apart, including Delhi, Shajahanpur, Fatehpur, Sagar, Indore and Nimach, the circulation caught the attention of the authorities. One native police officer who was dispatched to investigate the extent of the circulation reported that 'he had travelled over a large part of the Delhi division, and wherever he had gone he found the chupattee had been received from some place still further east. He was beset with questions, but whence the sign had come no one could tell; neither its origin, nor its intention, were known.'[5] In the absence of any certain knowledge, the British were left to guess at the significance of the *chapattis*, which many thought was related to some native superstition: the circulation, it was suggested, might be a 'spell against disease', an attempt to prevent hail from falling (which would ruin crops) or initiated by native dyers when their dye would not clear properly.[6] In spite of extensive inquiries, the *chapattis* thus remained enigmatic and at Delhi the Joint Magistrate,

Sir Theophilus Metcalfe, concluded that 'There is nothing but conjecture regarding them.'[7]

The British regarded with deep suspicion, bordering on paranoia, any type of communication amongst Indians which they could not understand. The only conceivable reason for the natives to keep things hidden was if they were conspiring and plotting against the British. By the very opacity of their circulation, the *chapattis* set off alarm bells among the colonial administrators. During the rebellions of tribal communities, such as the Kol in 1831–2 and the Santhals in 1855–6, the locals had used twigs or branches as signals to mobilise.[8] The British thus had several recent examples of the circulation of objects which would suggest that the *chapattis* were similar to the 'Fiery Cross' or *Crean Tarigh* which traditionally called the highland clans of Scotland to arms.[9]

The circulation of *chapattis* was, like a rumour, a transient phenomenon that passed swiftly through the districts of northern India, one officer stating that 'the signal spread in all directions with wonderful celerity'.[10] By the time the authorities were informed of its transmission within a district, it had already moved on – an understandably disturbing sign of the efficiency of indigenous modes of communication that lay outside colonial control. The Commissioner at Agra claimed that the *chapattis* travelled 160 or 200 miles a night, but this was clearly an exaggeration, and the example he himself provided (south of Mainpuri to Aligarh) implied a rather more moderate speed of less than 100 miles a night.[11] The circulation was nevertheless seen as a rapid spread of a seditious disease; in early March, *The Friend of India* reported how one *chaukidar* passed *chapattis* on to five others: 'The five obeyed orders also, and distributed their message to 25, and so the affair went on, in geometrical ratio, the cakes sweeping over the district at a speed at which no Indian post yet travels. The wave has not stopped yet.'[12]

The circulation of *chapattis* elicited a variety of responses from the British, and one newspaper wrote that 'In India however though conspiracies are possible, secret societies are not, and speculation is *again at fault. Are all chowkeedars about to strike for wages*? Or is anybody trying a new scheme for a parcel dawk? Is it treason or jest? Is there to be an "explosion of feeling" or only of laughter?'[13] A week later, though, as the circulation continued, the same newspaper speculated that '90,000 lazy policemen', the *chaukidars*, would not have troubled themselves without reason.[14] Puzzlement rather than panic seems to have dominated most of the press coverage of the circulation, with one paper stating: 'Had we been politically shaky, people might have been disposed to detect a fiery cross in these local substitutes for a hot-cross-bun: but it will be curious (to say the least of it) to trace the origin of such a stir, even if it affords only another illustration of the ease with which multitudes are set in motion by a hoaxer …'.[15]

Despite the sceptical and calming admonishments of some newspapers, officials took no chances and responded with swiftness against the inconspicuous yet seemingly menacing *chapattis*. At Delhi, Metcalfe dismissed any suggestions that the circulation might be harmless and related to a native practice to prevent disease; his enquiries suggested that the *chapattis* had been distributed only in the Company's possessions, and to him this implied an anti-British significance to the circulation.[16] Through his intervention the *chapattis* were stopped from continuing further north, although they did in fact reach Meerut, and elsewhere the authorities also sought to prevent their circulation.[17] The British even seemed to suspect that there might be something about the *chapattis* themselves that would provide a clue to their meaning, or that some secret message was hidden in their size and shape. Although *chapattis* were common throughout northern India, several reports described the physical appearance of the ones being circulated in great detail, and some officials even dispatched intercepted breads to their superiors.[18] At Meerut, the Commissioner was, however, dismissive of any attempts to see a 'fiery cross' in the so-called 'Chupatee movement': 'Its real origin was, doubtless, a superstitious attempt to prevent any return of the fearful visitation of epidemic cholera which devastated the North-West Provinces the year before, and still lingered in scattered spots.'[19]

The circulation of *chapattis* does appear to have originated at Indore and to have been related to the outbreak of cholera, which persisted in a number of cities long after the greater epidemic of 1856 had ended.[20] Captain R. H. Keatinge, in charge of the Nimar District, made the first documented sighting of the distribution of *chapattis* at the town of Mandleshwar on 12 January 1857:

> At the time they appeared in Nimar, they were everywhere brought in from the direction of Indore. That city was at the time afflicted with a severe visitation of the cholera, and numbers of inhabitants died daily. It was at that time understood by the people in Nimar, and is still believed, that the cakes of wheat were despatched from Indore after the performance over them of incantations that would ensure the pestilence accompanying them … This habit of passing unholy things on is not unknown in Nimar. When small-pox breaks out in a village, a goat is

procured, a cocoa-nut tied to its neck, and it is taken to the first village on the road to Mundatta; it is not allowed to enter the town, but is taken by a villager to the next hamlet, and so passed on without rest to its destination.[21]

The temple of Mandata was actually a popular pilgrimage site and the thousands of travellers who passed through the district were thought to be one of the main causes for the spread of the disease in this region.[22]

It was common practice in India in these times to seek to remove a disease by transferring it on to an object and then physically removing that object, hoping that it would carry away the disease as a scapegoat. This practice was known as *chalauwa* and could involve objects representing the disease, or food or animals offered to the deity associated with the disease, which would thus symbolically remove it.[23] During an outbreak of cholera in Nimach in 1854, and again in 1857, *chapattis* were distributed between villages and fed to dogs, and in 1857, a pariah dog was sent through villages in Gujarat with a basket of food that was distributed amongst the local dogs.[24] Similarly, when cattle disease broke out in Oudh, *chapattis* were distributed in the belief that, once they reached the holy city of Hardwar, the outbreak would come to an end.[25] In 1857 there were also variants of the *chapatti* circulation; south of Delhi pieces of goat's flesh were being distributed, while in a place called Damoodah it was a pot with *brinjal* or aubergine flowers that was being circulated.[26] These, however, were isolated cases and such instances are not recorded elsewhere.

The geographic circulation of the *chapattis* was not systematic or exponential; the transmission was erratically linear and different 'currents' moved at varying speeds. Some currents simply ran cold, while others moved in parallel or paused before continuing. Thus, long after *chapattis* had reached their northern-most point of Meerut, there was another northwards distribution from Cawnpore to Fattehgarh, which was widely reported in the newspapers. Similarly, the first distribution was recorded at Indore on 12 January and by the end of the month the *chapattis* had reached Mathura, while on 9 February a distribution was recorded at Bajranggarh, halfway between Indore and Mathura.[27] The circulation took place along well-established routes of transmission, which followed the main trade and pilgrimage routes between the bigger cities (see Map 1). There were two main currents of distribution: one went from Indore to Etawah and then split into two northbound trails, via Mathura to Delhi and via Aligarh to Meerut; the second main current went from Indore to Narsinghpur to Jabalpur and Sagar and from there via

Nowgong and Banda to Fatehpur, Farrukhabad and Budaon. These places present a very rough outline of the actual circulation and its sequence, and it should be noted that *chapattis* were also distributed from Indore northwards to Nimach and from Cawnpore to Allahabad in a south-easterly direction.[28] No attempt was made at the time to collect all reports of *chapattis* or establish a wider pattern of the circulation.[29]

Some officials, however, recalled earlier instances of strange transmissions, such as the alleged distribution of *chapattis* that preceded the mutiny at Vellore in 1806, or the sprig of millet and morsel of bread that were passed from village to village at the time of the downfall of the Marathas.[30] Painted buffaloes were used to remove cholera in the Bombay presidency during the first big epidemic in 1818, and even that early the British authorities suspected that it was calculated to cause alarm.[31] That same year, an almost identical circulation to that of the *chapattis* had occurred near Indore, which was described by John Malcolm, the Governor of Bombay:

> The war with the Pindarries was then over, and the country was in a state of tolerable tranquillity, when a sudden agitation was produced among the peaceable inhabitants, by a number of cocoa-nuts being passed from village to village with a mysterious direction to speed them to specific directions (usually the chief local authority) … From beyond Jeypoor North to the Deckan South, and from the frontier of Guzerat to the territories of Bhopal, this signal flew with unheard-of celerity. The Potail [chief] of every village where these cocoa-nuts came, carried it himself with breathless haste to another, to avert a curse which was denounced on all who impeded or stopped them even for a moment. No event followed to throw any light upon this extraordinary occurrence. Every inquiry was instituted, and persons were sent who traced the route of the signal for several hundred miles; but no information was obtained; and a circumstance which produced, for upwards of a month, a very serious sensation over all Central India, remains to this moment a mystery. Various conjectures were made at the moment, as to the cause in which it originated, as well as its meaning and purpose. Some thought it a sign of the complete establishment of the British power. Others believed that it indicated a general rise in favour of the Paishwah Bajerow, who had not then submitted; while persons sent to trace it into the Jeypoor country, returned with an account that the pious gratitude of a holy Brahmin had circulated cocoa-nut through his native district to proclaim his joy at the birth of a son, and that the signal, which spread like wildfire, gained a portentous character as it became remote from the simple cause in which it commenced.[32]

It was accordingly not unknown for commonplace native practices of circulation to extend beyond their local context and create a stir across a wider area. The circulation of *chapattis* in 1857 was most likely the result of such a transmission, which, once started, gained a momentum of its own, independently of its origin. At some point, the *chapattis* passed beyond the limits of their meaningful transmission and simply continued through the country as a 'blank' message. This allowed different meanings and interpretations to be attributed to them, and the *chapattis* became an index of people's thoughts and worries. At Nimach, not far from the point of origin, the local officer was simply told that the *chapattis* were distributed to the dogs to prevent cholera: 'There is no attempt to deny or conceal the fact, and apparently it has excited very little notice or wonder.'[33]

One of the peculiar aspects of the circulation was that many Indians assumed that it was carried out on the orders of the Government.[34] When Metcalfe questioned the *chaukidars* who had brought *chapattis* to Delhi from Bolundshar, they explained that they had merely followed what they believed to be the Government's orders. The circulation of *chapattis* was by no means secretive – in some instances the *chaukidar* who delivered the *chapattis* required a receipt written out by the village *patwari* (accountant) and authenticated by the local police.[35] At Narsinghpur the local head of police contacted the British Commissioner to enquire what he should do with the spare *chapattis* that had been left over from the distribution.[36] The *chaukidars* were, after all, representatives of the authorities at the local level. During the outbreak of cholera the preceding year, *chaukidars* had been officially charged with the distribution of pills in their respective villages, and the circulation of *chapattis* by their hand might thus easily be interpreted in a similar vein. Official contact with the rural population occurred through low-level officials, and surveys and censuses often caused considerable consternation amongst villagers who suspected (sometimes with good reason) that increased taxation or other objectionable Government measures would be likely to result.[37] The association of the *chapattis* with Government orders not only ensured the continuing transmission, but also provided the context for the most sinister local interpretation of their significance.

According to a news-writer in Delhi, the *chapattis* were believed either to signal or to warn against official interference with people's food and thus, by inference, their religion and social status. Food and religion were inseparable, and some Indians believed that the *chapattis*:

were circulated by the Government to signify that the population throughout the country would be compelled to use the same food as the Christians, and thus be deprived of their religion; while others, again, said that the chupatties were circulated to make it known that Government was determined to force Christianity on the country by interfering with their food, and intimation of it was thus given that they might be prepared to resist the attempt.[38]

One British officer also made enquiries regarding the *chapattis* amongst the *sepoys*, who only heard of them at their respective cantonments:

> I asked them what they understood in reference to them, and by whom they supposed that they were circulated; they described them to me as being in size and shape like ship biscuits, and believed them to have been distributed by order of Government through the medium of their servants for the purpose of intimating to the people of Hindoostan that they should all be compelled to eat the same food, and that was considered as a token that they should likewise be compelled to embrace one faith, or, as they termed it, 'One food and one faith.'[39]

Accordingly the *sepoys* thought the *chapattis* were part of the Government's design to undermine their religion – a symbolic counterpart to the cartridges. The notion that sharing food meant the sharing of faith was a common characteristic of Indian fears of conversion at the time. Touching directly upon people's eating habits, it furthermore affected the strict rules that governed social interaction between Hindus and Muslims as well as high castes and low castes. Similar concerns had been behind much of the controversy over common messing in jails as well as the apparent dread expressed by *sepoys* at the prospect of travel overseas.[40] It was in fact reported that the *chapattis*, or part of them, had to be eaten by the recipients, and a British officer at Nowgong noted that 'the cakes are distributed by the hands of the very lowest caste men that can be found; and the natives say that it is intended by Government to force or bribe the headmen to eat them, and thus lose their caste.'[41] In this case the *chapattis* were themselves seen to be the means of pollution, very much like the disease transmitters.

Like propitiatory offerings, the *chapattis* were interpreted by some as having beneficial effects, as the royal physician at Delhi noted: 'People also believed that these chupatties were the invention of some adept in the secret arts, in order to preserve unpolluted the religion of the country, which, it was reported, the Government had proposed to themselves to subvert in two years'[42] Other accounts ascribed the circulation to a guru or holy man, while in the Mughal capital locals believed the transmission was 'supposed to portend some coming disturbance, and was, moreover, understood as implying an invitation to the whole population of the country to unite for some secret object afterwards to be disclosed'[43] The perceived warning of some future upheaval or calamity could very well stem from their origin as disease transmitters, which would also explain the perceived urgency with which the *chaukidars* were informed to pass them on: if a symbolic carrier of disease was not passed on, the disease would rest with the recipient. Although the original specific meaning of the *chapattis* had been lost early in the distribution, the dire consequences of breaking the chain of transmission remained, and thus ensured their successful circulation over an immense area. In the event, the *chapattis* were not 'harbingers of the coming storm'[44] They were what people made them into, and the significance attributed to them was a symptom of the pervasive distrust and general consternation amongst the Indian population during the early months of 1857.

## 'One of many costumes worn by the messenger of evil'

The circulation of *chapattis* was not the only expression of concern amongst the Indian population during the early months of 1857. And while the significance of the *chapattis* was indeterminable and open to a range of interpretations, the rumours that circulated at the time were rather more concrete. In March, an Indian merchant sent several tons of *atta*, or flour, from a mill near Meerut to Cawnpore, where he sold it at well under the standard price.[45] When several more shipments of underpriced *atta* reached the market at Cawnpore, some locals became suspicious, and it was soon reported that the flour had been adulterated with the ground bones of pigs and cows. After that, no one would buy the *atta* and the objections led to a complete suspension of grinding at the specific mill. Although several *sepoys* and a *munshi* went to the mill itself to ascertain that the process of grinding was perfectly normal, the rumour had taken hold.[46]

According to other versions of the story, the authorities had prohibited flour to be ground locally and directed all shopkeepers and merchants to buy directly from the public stores that contained the polluted flour. The

Government was even said to have poured polluted flour into wells, so as to make the pollution of all Indians complete.[47] The wife of a British officer at Simla later described how her *ayah* (Indian nanny) had told her that 'there was a report in the bazaar that all the flour was mixed with the bones, finely ground, of cows and pigs. I laughed at her, and said "Ayah, what nonsense! Who says so?" She replied, "It is quite true, all the bazar people say so." I thought it meant merely that the *banniahs* (merchants) did it to increase the weight of their flour.'[48] A contemporary British official noted: 'Bone-dust attah alarm has taken hold of men's minds at several of our stations, and Sepoys, private servants, Zemindars attending Court, have flung away their roti (bread) on hearing that five camel-loads of bone-dust attah had reached the station.'[49] As late as June 1857, long after events had taken a dramatic turn, loyal *sepoys* still harboured suspicions about the flour they were given – at Sitapur they threw two cartloads of *atta* into the river rather than risk being polluted, as they thought they would be.[50] The following day they mutinied.

Not long after the mutiny at Vellore in 1806, Kaye recorded, the exact same story had been current:

> Among other wild fables, which took firm hold of the popular mind, was one to the effect that the Company's officers had collected all the newly-manufactured salt, had divided it into two great heaps, and over one had sprinkled the blood of hogs, and over the other the blood of cows; that they had then sent it to be sold throughout the country for the pollution and the desecration of the Mahomedans and Hindoos, that all might be brought to one caste and to one religion like the English.[51]

In 1857, however, the rumour resurfaced with even greater impact. In Rajasthan, a consignment of salt, which had been transported in bags used for red ochre, was as a result discoloured, and it was immediately reported that it had been defiled with cow's blood.[52] The rumour of pollution assumed numerous shapes, as summed up by Kaye, affecting all possible substances commonly ingested by Indians:

> It was said that the officers of the British government, under command from the Company and the Queen, had mixed ground bones with flour and the salt sold in the Bazaars; that they had adulterated all the ghi with animal fat; that bones had been burnt with the common sugar of the country; and that not only

bone-dust flour, but the flesh of cows and pigs, had been thrown into the wells to pollute the drinking water of the people. Of this great imaginary scheme of contamination the matter of the greased cartridges was but a part, especially addressed to one part of the community. All classes, it was believed, were to be defiled at the same time; and the story ran that the 'bara sahibs,' or great English lords, had commanded all princes, nobles, landholders, merchants, and cultivators of the land, to feed together upon English bread.[53]

By the spring of 1857, the fears of pollution and conversion that had been around for decades reached their apogee. At Lucknow, the Chief Commissioner Sir Henry Lawrence had a conversation with a native officer, who was fully convinced that for the past ten years the British Government had secretly been seeking to convert all Indians to Christianity: 'His argument was, that as such was the case, and that as we had made our way through India, won Bhurtpore, Lahore, &c., by fraud, so might it be possible that we mixed bone-dust with the grain sold to the Hindoos.'[54] Lawrence tried to convince the man, who had served the British for twenty years, that they had thousands of troops and were not dependent on the *sepoys*. The reply was 'that he knew that we had plenty of men and money, but that Europeans are expensive, and that, therefore, we wished to take Hindoos to sea to conquer the world for us'. In response to this, Lawrence pointed out that the *sepoys* were not strong soldiers at sea, due to their food. 'That is just it,' the officer replied. 'You want us all to eat what you like that we may be stronger, and go everywhere.' Lawrence later mentioned this conversation to several other officials, adding that the native officer 'went over all our anti-Hindoo acts of the last ten years, including Gaol-Messing, the General-Service Oath, &c., and did not conceal not only that he and all others saw no absurdity in the *ground-bones atta* belief, but that he considered we were quite up to such a dodge.'[55] Similar stories were reported in native newspapers, where, for instance, it was said that Lord Gough had promised a curious Queen Victoria to convert three *sepoy* regiments within six months so that they could cross the ocean and be presented before her.[56]

These rumours would not have been in circulation if they had not reflected a shared perception of contemporary events, and thus been considered credible by the local population.[57] They were told by travellers and people meeting in the bazaar or at the well, in the lines of native troops or by *sepoys* passing back and forth between the cantonment and their respective villages on furlough.[58] As such, they percolated through a myriad of meetings and encounters.[59] Kaye described this phenomenon, and although his account is clearly loaded with Orientalist prejudice, it nevertheless captures some of the features of the transmission of rumours:

> The Natives of India have an expressive saying, that 'it is in the air.' It often happened that an uneasy feeling – an impression that something had happened, though they 'could not discern the shape thereof' – pervaded men's minds, in obscure anticipation of the news that was travelling towards them in all tangible proportions. All along the line of road, from town to town, from village to village, were thousands to whom the feet of those who brought the glad tidings were beautiful and welcome. The British Magistrate, returning from his evening ride, was perhaps met on the road near the Bazaar by a venerable Native on an ambling pony – a Native respectable of aspect, with a white beard and whiter garments, who salaamed to the English gentleman as he passed, and went on his way freighted with intelligence refreshing to the souls of those to whom it was to be communicated, to be used with judgment and sent on with despatch. This was but one of many costumes worn by the messenger of evil. In whatsoever shape he passed, there was nothing outwardly to distinguish him. Next morning there was a sensation in the Bazaar, and a vague excitement in the Sipáhis' Lines. But when rumours of disaster reached the houses of the chief English officers, they were commonly discredited. Their own letters were silent on the subject. It was not likely to be true, they said, as they had heard nothing about it. But it was true; and the news had travelled another hundred miles whilst the white gentlemen, with bland scepticism, were shaking their heads over the lies of the Bazaar.[60]

Rumours are by definition an authorless and transient phenomenon, and like the *chapattis*, the authorities found it impossible to trace their origins. According to a British officer stationed at Nasirabad in Rajputana, the rumours 'fled about like will-o'-the-wisps – it was impossible to trace their origin or lay hold of them in any shape, or ever to get them accurately detailed. A man would say he heard such and such a report; of course he disbelieved it; but when asked to give up the name of the person from whom he heard it, he would immediately reply, Oh, it was in everyone's mouth, how could he fix upon any one in particular.'[61]

Absurd as they may appear, however, these rumours were not just hearsay or idle chatter.[62] They presented a significant medium through which Indians attempted to comprehend the actions of the British and make sense of an unfamiliar situation. Ordinary Indians depended on oral transmission for the dissemination of news, and rumours constituted an important form of popular communication and collective interpretation.[63] Anxieties and tension were expressed through rumours, which allowed people who were effectively excluded from the political arena to voice their opinion publicly.[64] Central to the concerns of the rumours was an identification of the Government with Christianity and its actions and policies with conversion.[65] Religion in fact provided the exclusive frame through which the British were perceived by many Indians.[66] The *sepoys*' fear of British troops and artillery being turned against them, and forcing them to accept the greased cartridges, may in fact be seen as encapsulating the history of the Raj up until 1857. The specific fear reflected the wider concern caused by the expansion of British rule and the subsequent changes forced upon Indian society. Rather than being distinct rumours, the suspicion of the Enfield cartridges, the meaning ascribed to the *chapattis* and the bone-dust rumour all represented different strands of the same fear: the Christian conspiracy against all Hindu and Muslim Indians.

Unable to understand the motives behind British administrative reforms and interventions in Indian society, parts of the local population simply assumed that the foreign rulers were deliberately trying to undermine their faith, beliefs, and practices. Given the evangelical zeal that influenced a great number of the colonial state's policies after the 1830s, this fear was perhaps not so misplaced, though it was clearly misdirected. Rumours were, in the words of one historian, 'the utterances of a people sharing common preoccupations about a colonial system which thrust them into ambiguous situations where their life and livelihood seemed under attack'.[67] A perceived threat to both Hindus and Muslims, as embodied in the rumours of pollution, mobilised resentment against the British and further increased the sense of solidarity between Indians of different faiths and backgrounds.[68] It was, indeed, an attempt to make sense, in the common parlance of the times, of the unparalleled impact of British colonialism during this period.

The *sepoys*' objections to the cartridges were thus symptomatic of a much wider suspicion of the British, and probably gave credence to the bone-dust rumour. It is worth remembering that the British controlled the provisions that were sold in the regimental bazaars and bought by the *sepoys* through a regimental system of credit. Like the inmates of the prisons, the *sepoys* as well as camp-followers were entirely at the mercy of the authorities in respect to the food they were given. The extent to which the rumours contained a kernel of truth was really immaterial in relation to their impact. Events and non-events were equally important when communicated from mouth to mouth, and baseless rumours affected people as much as genuine news.[69] While the stories of pollution were entirely untrue, the consequences of their circulation and the reactions they elicited were real enough. The rumours were self-enforcing, and panic caused by a rumour would lead to further rumours, thus perpetuating the circulation of panic-inducing rumours.[70] In an atmosphere of heightened tension and increasing panic, even the most trivial events assumed an ulterior and occult significance. At Lucknow, a British doctor of the 48th Bengal Native Infantry inadvertently drank some medicine directly from the bottle in a regimental hospital, which effectively rendered that bottle ritually impure and polluting to high-caste Hindus. The incident seemed to confirm the existent rumours and caused an outcry among the *sepoys*; it was even reported in the native newspapers.[71] When rumours were repeated in the press, their circulation was given a second lease, as the written word gave rise to new verbal rumours. Textual reproduction of rumours often strengthened their impact and authority.[72]

In this charged atmosphere and general climate of apprehension, there were also rumours and stories that reflected the hopes and aspirations of the *sepoys* and local population. If some rumours told of pollution and forced conversion, others responded by invoking divine retribution or foreign aid that would crush the British. One of the most persistent prophecies was that the reign of the East India Company, established after the Battle of Plassey in 1757, would only last one hundred years and British rule would accordingly come to an end in 1857.[73] A Muslim officer in the Company's service was thus recorded as saying that 'it was written in his books that a change would take place, and that the British rule would soon be overthrown'.[74] As previously mentioned, both Nana Sahib and Bahadur Shah were told by their astrologers that they would soon regain their former power and that the British would be defeated.[75]

News of the greased cartridges and the *sepoys*' protests at Barrackpore and Berhampore spread across northern India and was reported in both British and Indian newspapers.[76] At Delhi, the native police officer Mainodin remembered how:

> No extraordinary incident occurred until it was rumoured that on February 26 the 19th Regiment of Foot at Berhampur had refused to take cartridges served out to them, and that the 34th Regiment had behaved in a similar manner,

and that seven companies of that regiment had been dismissed. When I heard this I suspected it was the beginning of a time of trouble. Information of the behaviour of the different regiments was widely circulated by the Press, in a native newspaper published at Umballa.[77]

Since British power and authority was largely maintained by the *sepoys*, this was no insignificant matter. Any serious trouble amongst the *sepoys* was likely to affect the entire subcontinent, and the unrest caused by the greased cartridges was certainly picked up by many Indian rulers. Bahadur Shah's physician later explained how the news was received in the Red Fort at Delhi:

> I do not remember exactly the month in which intelligence was received of the regiment near Calcutta having refused to receive the new cartridges. I only know that the information was obtained from a Calcutta newspaper; and when it was known that the discussion about the cartridges was spreading, it was remarked that, inasmuch as the matter touched the religion of the people, the excitement would spread extensively over the entire length and breath of the country, and the native army would desert the British Government, whose rule would then be at an end. The King remarked that he would, in that case, be placed in better circumstances, inasmuch as a new dominant power would treat him with greater respect and consideration.[78]

According to the Indian writer Mohun Lal, international news likewise had a significant impact on sentiments in India:

> The late war in Europe, the Santhal Insurrection, close to the Government seat, in Bengal, and exaggerated reports of the power and advance of Persia, at the instigation of Russia, upon Heerat, and the disbelief of their having been defeated & now being in a place with the British Government, as well as the unbecoming expressions of the sentiments of the Editors of the native papers have continued to kindle the sparks of dissatisfaction throughout the Indian Empire.[79]

In the native press, which reported extensively on the British war with Persia, the British were usually said to have been defeated and these stories were generally believed.[80] Mirroring British fears of Russian intervention in India, the native papers were awash with news of the Tsar's imminent invasion. One Delhi newspaper wrote:

As for the Russians, however, they make no secret of the readiness with which they are assisting, and will continue to assist the Persians, whether it be with funds or with forces. It may be said that virtually the Russians are the cause of this war, and that using the Persians as a cloak, they intend to consummate their own designs, regarding the conquest of Hindustan. It is to be believed that the Russians will very soon take the field in great force.[81]

At Delhi it was widely believed that the Russians would soon come to rid India of the British.[82] There was also news of a worldwide call for *jihad* that would mobilise all Muslims and result in the eventual defeat of the infidel British rulers.[83] In March 1857, a proclamation was actually pasted on the Jama Mashid mosque in Delhi, allegedly from the Shah of Persia, which urged all Muslims to unite against the infidels in preparation for the Shah's invasion of India.[84] The 'small dirty paper' was immediately removed by the British authorities, who rightly suspected that it might stir up trouble. It was similar to a number of proclamations that were from time to time circulated in towns all over India, and which were as often directed at rival Muslim sectarian groups as at Christian infidels.[85] None of the news-reports accurately described the political situation of 1857; they rather seem to have been an expression of wishful thinking. Faced with the apparent onslaught of the British against the very foundations of Indian society, people sought succour in the 'news' of the *sepoys*' refusals, Persian victories, and Russian support.

In early 1857, various peculiar proverbs were also common amongst Indians. One British officer was told by a local raja in Bundhelkhand that 'a saying passed from village to village that the sister should protect the brother – meaning that the weak should have power over the strong i.e. the natives over the English …'.[86] Another similar aphorism was said to be: 'Pearls (that is, white-faces) are quoted as low in the market; Red Wheat (that is coloured-faces) is looking up.'[87] In Bengal, another saying was noted: 'Sub lal hogea hai' ('everything is to become red'). Some thought it referred to British rule being extended over the entire subcontinent, red being the colour usually denominating British rule as well as the colour of the *sepoys*' uniforms. Others read in the words a more sinister implication and 'hinted that there was something thicker than water, and of a deeper crimson than a British uniform'.[88] As with the *chapattis*, such anecdotes were reported in the Anglo-Indian press and a Calcutta journal published a satirical poem, the final verse being as follows:

Beneath my feet I saw 'twas nought but blood,
And shrieking wretches borne upon the stream
Struggled and splashed amidst a sea of gore.
I heard a giant voice again proclaim,
'Mid shouts of murder, mutiny, and blood,
'SUB LAL HOGEA HAI,' and I awoke.[89]

British responses to the rumours and tension were accordingly varied: while some seemed prone to panic, others dismissed any suggestions of impending danger with ridicule. For the *sepoys* and for the Indian population more generally, on the other hand, such proverbs and sayings seemed to promise a resolution to their problems. Prophecies of the fall of the British reflected common aspirations and served to prepare and mobilise opposition against the Company's rule.[90] Certain kinds of rumour can in fact bring about what they convey.[91] At Delhi, the police officer Mainodin noted that after the circulation of *chapattis*, 'there arose a hue and cry that the English were plotting to destroy the "caste" of the native *Sepoys*, by causing them to use a cartridge dipped in the fat of cows and pigs. The officers of the Government seemed to attach no importance to the matter, and paid no heed to what we regarded as significant warnings of a serious spirit of disaffection, which was spreading far and wide over the country.'[92]

# 4

# Mangal Pandey

At Barrackpore, the *sepoys'* concerns over the cartridges were undiminished. At the beginning of March, a *jemadar* of the 70th BNI allegedly encouraged another officer not to bite the cartridges and told the *sepoys* that a disturbance would soon take place.[1] Numbers of *sepoys* were furthermore assembled in the *Jemadar's* hut on the evening of 8 March, although it is uncertain whether there was anything suspicious about the meeting. It was, however, against regulations and the officer was tried by a court martial and promptly dismissed.[2] Two *sepoys* of the 2nd Grenadiers, who were accused of trying to instigate a mutiny in Calcutta in March, were not let off so easily – both were sentenced to fourteen years of hard labour.[3] The case was reported in *The Friend of India*, which also referred to the widespread tension amongst the native troops:

> There has been a rumour for some days past of an intended mutiny at Fort William. It appeared to have arisen from the sulkiness and insolence of several *sepoys* who have been placed in arrest. The *Hurkaru* [newspaper] states that the *sepoys* put forth as the excuse for their discontent, the idea that the Governor General has promised the *Home Government to convert them all in three years*. The garrison at Fort William has manifested considerable sympathy with the 19th and the 34th Regiments of native infantry, and there is a slight suspicion that if these regiments be punished severely, the sympathy may not only be that of feeling but of action [italics in original].[4]

The rumoured mutiny at Calcutta was supposed to have taken place on 10 March when the Maharaja Scindia, who was visiting the capital of the presidency, had invited all the leading British officials and their wives to a ball at the Botanical Gardens.[5] While the British were thus distracted, the plan was supposedly for the *sepoys* to rise and take control of Fort William with the aid of the agents of the King of Oudh. As it happened, the fête was cancelled on account of a heavy downpour and the plot came to nothing – if indeed it had ever existed.[6]

The extent of the *sepoys'* fears and discontent, however, cannot be overstated. An anonymous petition of March 1857, addressed to Major Matthews of the 43rd Bengal Native Infantry, but intended for Major-General Hearsey, provides a unique insight into the mindset of the native troops at Barrackpore and their interpretation of events:

> The representation of the whole station is this, that we will not give up our religion. We serve for honour and religion; if we lose our religion, the Hindoo and Mahomedan religions will be destroyed. If we live, what shall we do? You are the masters of the country. The Lord Sahib has given orders, which he has received from the Company, to all commanding officers to destroy the religion of the country. We know this, as all things are being brought up by Government. The officers of the Salt Department mix up bones with the salt. The officer in charge of the ghee mixes up fat with it; this is well known. These are two matters. The third is this: that the Sahib in charge of the sugar burns up bones and mixes them in syrup the sugar is made of; this is well known – all knows it. The fourth is this: that in the country the Burra Sahibs have ordered the Rajahs, Thakurs, Zemindars, Mahajans and Ryots, all to eat together, and English bread has been sent to them; this is well known. And this is another affair, that throughout the country the wives of respectable men, in fact, all classes of Hindoos, on becoming widows, are to be married again; this is known. Therefore we consider ourselves as killed. You all obey the orders of the Company, which we all know. But a king, or any other one who acts unjustly, does not remain.[7]

The authors of the petition further stated that it was evident that a British council had decided to distribute greased cartridges to the *sepoys* in order to destroy their caste. As a result they could not use them and requested that, if the cartridges were not withdrawn, Major-General Hearsey should simply discharge the *sepoys*; they would then leave. The petition was evidently written by NCOs and privates, as it clearly stated that all except two of the Indian officers at the station were on good terms with the men. Of the two officers mentioned, one was a Christian, and therefore seen to have abandoned his religion, and the other was a *jemadar* of the 43rd BNI who had apparently refused to submit the petition to the British officers and who was therefore regarded as an outcaste.[8] As a result of the *Jemadar's* refusal, the petition was simply left for someone to find, but the exhortation to deliver it to Major Matthews reflected in very tangible terms the *sepoys'* concern over religious transgression: 'Whoever gets this letter must read it to the Major as it is written. If he is a Hindoo and does not, his crime will be equal to the slaughter of a lakh of cows; and if a Mussulman, as though he had eaten pig; and if a European, must read it to the Native officers, and if he does not, his going to church will be of no use, and be a crime.'[9] In this petition all the different rumours that had troubled the *sepoys* for months came together and gave form and substance to the idea of a fully fledged British conspiracy to ruin the religion of all Indians. The bone-dust and greased cartridges, the *chapattis* and the remarriage of widows were all part of the Company's elaborate plan. The *sepoys* had supposedly exposed this attempt to undermine their religion and now made their British superiors aware of their knowledge, suggesting that they should as a result simply be discharged. The authors of the petition were never identified, but they were likely to belong to the 43rd BNI, which nevertheless remained loyal to the British throughout the tumultuous events of the following months.

On 18 March, Hearsey paraded the entire brigade at Barrackpore, and warned them 'of such characters, who endeavour to take the bread from the mouths of good *sepoys* by making them the instruments of their bad designs'.[10] In an elaboration of the by now well-established ritual of displaying samples of the cartridges, the Major-General sought to allay the *sepoys'* worries as far as the paper was concerned. Hearsey thus demonstrated how ordinary writing paper, commonly employed by natives, had a glossy appearance similar to the cartridges, although it was obviously quite inoffensive. The *sepoys* were even encouraged to visit the paper mill at Serampore and see for themselves how the paper was manufactured. Hearsey further harangued the troops for continuing to suspect the cartridges when he had, on several occasions, proved that they had no legitimate grounds for concern. The 19th BNI at Berhampore had unfortunately been 'misled by designing men' and had as a result mutinied. Now they were to be marched to Barrackpore and would be disbanded in front of all the regiments – including European ones. Mindful of the fears of the *sepoys*, Hearsey added, 'I inform you of this beforehand, because your enemies are trying to make you believe that European troops with cavalry and artillery will be sent here suddenly to attack you; these and such lies are fabricated and rumoured amongst you to cause trouble. That no European or other troops would come to Barrackpore until ordered to do so by me and that I would give [you] timely intelligence of their coming here.'[11] Contrary to his intent, Hearsey may actually have aggravated the situation by confirming the various rumours that had already reached the *sepoys*. Among the *sepoys* lined up for parade, one in particular seems to have been alarmed by the Major-General's speech; this was Mangal Pandey, a Brahmin *sepoy* of the 34th BNI.[12]

The *sepoys'* fear of European troops was evidently no trifling matter, and even the men of the 19th BNI on their way to Barrackpore were concerned by the reports that 'two batteries of guns and Europeans were to be brought out against them'.[13] During the afternoon of 29 March, two days before the 19th BNI was to arrive, fifty British soldiers of HM 53rd Foot came by steamer from Calcutta and disembarked at the Flag-staff Ghat just outside the station at Barrackpore.[14] Mangal Pandey was in his hut in the lines, cleaning his musket, when he heard of the European troops a little after 4 p.m. Affected by the general nervousness among the *sepoys*, he was also inebriated from taking *bhang*, and when the news reached him he was seized by panic.[15] Wearing his uniform jacket, cap, and *dhoti*, Mangal Pandey grabbed his musket and sword, and ran to the parade ground near the quarter-guard building. Clearly agitated, he called out to his comrades as he was loading his rifle, 'Come out, you *bhainchutetes*, the Europeans are here. From biting these cartridges, we shall become infidels. Get ready, turn out all of you.'[16]

Mangal Pandey tried to force a drummer to sound the alarm, threatening him with his musket, but the drummer was too scared to act. *Sepoys* in their civilian clothes were slowly drawn to the parade ground by the shouting, and Mangal aimed his musket at one, saying: 'Why are you not getting ready? It is for your religion.'[17] Inside the quarter-guard, the officer in command, *Jemadar* Isuree Pandey of the 34th BNI, immediately sent two men off to inform the sergeant-major and field officer of the regiment. The *Jemadar* was clearly frightened by the prospect of having to face the agitated *sepoy*. In a state of panic, Isuree Pandey took cover behind a tree next to the building and ordered his men to close the doors of the nearby *kotes*, yelling to the drummer 'not to sound the assembly or he would be blown away from a gun'.[18] Informed by the *Naik*, Sergeant-Major Hewson armed only with a sword arrived at the scene and Mangal Pandey immediately fired a shot at him but missed.[19] The guards were all taking cover behind the quarter-guard, and Hewson asked the *Jemadar* why he had not seized the *sepoy*. Isuree Pandey answered, 'What can I do; my naick is gone to the adjutant; the havildar is gone to the field officer; am I to take him myself?'[20] The *Havildar* now returned, having informed Captain Drury of what was going on, and the Captain had ordered for Mangal Pandey to be arrested. Hewson turned to the *Jemadar*, saying, 'Do you hear?'[21] It was said that Mangal Pandey had taken *bhang* and the frightened Isuree Pandey did not answer the Sergeant-Major but kept repeating 'the man is mad, don't go near him'.[22]

Hewson ordered the guards to load and fall in, which a few of them did, but some of the *sepoys* grumbled and did not react, and all the while the *Jemadar* remained indecisive. From time to time, Hewson looked out from behind the cover of the quarter-guard, and Mangal Pandey, who trained his musket at him several times, yelled: 'Get out of the way or I will shoot you.'[23] By this time, the parade ground was crowded with unarmed *sepoys* who were passively watching the spectacle. Mangal Pandey was still walking back and forth in front of the quarter-guard in a state of extreme excitement, haranguing his comrades: 'Come out, men; come out and join me – You sent me out here, why don't you follow me.'[24] A *jemadar*, Gunness Lalla, tried to reason with the *sepoy*, telling him to lay down his arms: 'Haven't you heard that you are not to bite the cartridges? Don't make a disturbance.'[25]

Summoned by the *Naik*, Adjutant Baugh now rode up to the quarter-guard, calling out: 'Where is he? Where is he?' Hewson tried to warn him. 'Sir, ride to the right for your life, the *sepoy* will fire at you.'[26] The warning, however, came too late, and Mangal Pandey fired and wounded the horse in the leg, bringing down both horse and rider. Once Baugh had disentangled himself, he got up and, seeing that Mangal Pandey was reloading his musket, the officer charged forward with a sword and one of his pistols in his hands. Hewson followed suit and, ordering the guard to follow him, he too advanced on the lone *sepoy*. As Baugh got closer to Mangal Pandey, he fired his pistol but missed and threw the now-useless one-shot weapon at the *sepoy*, who ducked the missile. The two officers both closed in on Mangal Pandey at the same time. Hewson made a cut at the *sepoy*, who parried the blow with his rifle, and the Sergeant-Major's sword broke at the hilt. Mangal Pandey seized his musket in his left hand and unsheathed his *tulwar*, first feigning a lunge at Hewson but then striking Baugh and completely disabling his left hand. The *sepoy* then lashed out at Hewson, who received a wound to the head. As the three men were engaged in the desperate struggle, an unarmed Muslim *sepoy* named Shaik Pultoo came to the officers' assistance and grabbed Mangal Pandey around the waist. Mangal Pandey was still fighting, and Hewson was fending off lunges even as Shaik Pultoo tried to restrain the *sepoy*. At this point, some of the guards came up and stepped in on the side of Mangal Pandey. As Hewson was facing Mangal Pandey, he was struck at the back of his head with a rifle butt by one of the guards, and the officer fell to the ground. Getting up again, Hewson seized Mangal Pandey by the collar and struck him several times with the hilt of his broken sword. Mangal Pandey wounded the officer a second time on the head and Hewson was again knocked down from behind. Once on the ground, Hewson received several blows from the *sepoys*' rifle butts and he lost consciousness. Meanwhile, Baugh had been wounded a second time by Mangal Pandey, this time in the throat, and he, too, was struck from behind by the guards. Shaik Pultoo managed to pull Mangal Pandey away from Baugh, who then made his retreat. When Hewson came to, he 'saw the adjutant walking away, covered with blood',[27] and both officers, heavily wounded, scrambled to safety.[28] Some of the many unarmed *sepoys* who had been passively looking on now interfered. As Shaik Pultoo later recalled, he 'had got Mungul Pandy down; a great number of the *sepoys*, in undress, were assembled around us, they abused me, saying "why don't you let him go," and struck me on the back and on the head with stones and shoes. I then let him go: the adjutant had got out of the way in the meantime.'[29] The Muslim *sepoy* received a light wound from Mangal Pandey as he let go of him.

While the struggle was going on, *Jemadar* Isuree Pandey was frantically trying to retain control of the *sepoys* inside the quarter-guard. There had been at least one shot fired from the quarter-guard, aimed at Baugh and Hewson, and a number of the guards had run out and assisted Mangal Pandey as he was fighting the two British officers, striking them with their rifle butts. Shaik Pultoo even said that someone from the quarter-guard had threatened to shoot him if did not release his hold on Mangal Pandey. The *Jemadar* did not know whom amongst the guard he could rely on, and when one of the guards sought to help the officers, Isuree Pandey asked, 'why are you going towards the sergeant-major?'[30] In the confusion and excitement, the *Jemadar* lost his head and actually prevented four of his men from assisting Baugh and Hewson, saying: 'Don't go unless I give you orders. Am I not in command of the guard?'[31] One of the *sepoys* who had left the quarter-guard and struck Baugh and Hewson returned with blood on his pantaloons, and the *Jemadar* sent him away to change his clothes.[32] Without a commanding officer to take charge, the *Jemadar* feared the consequences, and as the four guards wanted to assist Shaik Pultoo in seizing Mangal Pandey, Isuree Pandey again held them back: 'If you kill that *sepoy* you will be hung; and if he kills you, what shall I do?'[33]

When Hewson walked away from the fight, wounded and covered in blood, Isuree left the quarter-guard and ran after him, asking who had struck him, 'Mungul or another *sepoy*?' Hewson cried out, 'You have acted shamefully, and I will place you under arrest.'[34] The officer reached out for the *Jemadar*'s sword, but the latter retreated back to the quarter-guard. Here he vented his frustration on the *sepoys*, who were assembled inside the house, saying: 'You could have prevented this, if you had liked; you have connived at it?'[35] Realising that the blame for the guards' attack on Hewson and Baugh would ultimately fall on him, *Jemadar* Isuree ran off and reported the situation to the officer of the day at his nearby bungalow. The officer, however, ordered the *Jemadar* to return immediately to the quarter-guard, which was his responsibility. On his return, Isuree ordered the guard to load and got four of the *sepoys* ready.

After Shaik Pultoo had released Mangal Pandey, the latter picked up his musket and was loading it, warning that 'If any one comes near me I will shoot him.'[36] Isuree Pandey later described how he ventured out in front of the quarter-guard, when Mangal Pandey 'loaded his musket and aimed at me. I then retreated, as I thought my sword was of the same kind as the sergeant-major's, which had broken.'[37] Mangal Pandey had come out of the struggle unscathed, but no less agitated. He continued his tirade, calling out to the assembled *sepoys*, now numbering several hundred: 'The magazine has come with the Europeans, and the Europeans are here to make us bite the new cartridges, and destroy our religion.'[38]

When the commander of the 34th BNI, Colonel Wheler, finally arrived at the scene along with Captain Drury, he immediately ordered the guard to load their arms, which a few of them did 'rather sluggishly'.[39] Wheler repeated the order and told Isuree Pandey to get the guards to seize Mangal Pandey. The *Jemadar*, who had not regained his composure, hesitated and said to Captain Drury that 'It's no use, the men won't go; even if you go they won't follow you; they would take the man's part.'[40] The Colonel insisted, and after he repeated the order several times, some of the guards advanced slowly with Isuree Pandey in front. As soon as they realised that neither of the officers was with them, they stopped. 'What! Are not the colonel and Captain Drury coming?'[41] The *Jemadar*, who was none too happy about leading the men against Mangal Pandey, ran back to Wheler to inform him that the men would not follow orders, and they were called back. One of the *sepoys* told Wheler that Mangal Pandey was a Brahmin 'and that no one would hurt him',[42] and the Colonel realised that further attempts were useless. Drury too was not certain of how the guard would act 'from their sulky and reluctant manner, also from their natural disinclination to kill a man of his caste, and also from the fear of opinion of their comrades in the lines, as it is possible to say, there being a very large proportion of Brahmins in the regiment, who were approving or otherwise of what the man was doing'.[43] The Captain eventually went to get a rifle to shoot Mangal Pandey himself.

It was now 5.10 p.m. and as the situation at the quarter-guard had reached a deadlock, the entire station was in a stir: 'all the *sepoys* of the brigade were turning out on their parade, and men were running in that direction from all quarters of the cantonment'.[44] Major-General Hearsey half-expected the native regiments to rise in mutiny, and he made preparations for the British troops and officers to assemble at the Governor-General's house and put up some form of defence. Hearsey, accompanied by his two officer sons, then galloped down to the parade ground of the 34th BNI. There they met with a scene of complete confusion: 'the whole of the front of the bells-of-arms crowded with *sepoys* in their undress and unarmed, the native officers of the 43rd Regiment, Native Infantry, with them, and endeavouring to keep them in order. The men of the 34th Regiment, Native Infantry, had also turned out unarmed to the right and rear of their quarter-guard'.[45]

Ignoring the warnings that Mangal Pandey's musket was loaded, Hearsey ordered Isuree Pandey to follow him with the guard. The hesitant *Jemadar* simply responded, 'What does it matter – *kyapurwa* – he will only shoot some of us'.[46] The Major-General had drawn his pistol and was waving it at Isuree Pandey as he repeated his order, and the *Jemadar* eventually commanded the ten *sepoys* of the guard to load their muskets. Still on horseback, Hearsey advanced on Mangal Pandey, followed by the guard and a group of British officers on foot. As they closed in on the *sepoy*, one of Hearsey's sons called out, 'Father, he is taking aim at you, look out sharp'.[47] The Major-General replied, 'If I fall John, rush upon him, and put him to death'.[48] Mangal Pandey fired a shot, which missed its mark but stopped the advance of the guard for a moment. Mangal Pandey quickly loaded his musket, but realised that there was no way out and that he was about to be overpowered. The *sepoy* sat down and turned the muzzle against his own chest, pulling the trigger with his toe. The shot, however, did not kill Mangal Pandey, but 'made a deep graze, ripping up the muscles of the chest, shoulder and neck, and he fell prostrate'. As he lay on the ground, 'shivering and convulsed', Mangal Pandey's uniform jacket caught on fire from the muzzle-flash, but it was extinguished by Isuree Pandey and a *sepoy* of the guard who rushed up.[49] They also removed the bloody *tulwar* that Mangal Pandey had wielded with such deadly effect. The heavily wounded *sepoy* was then conveyed to the hospital of the 34th BNI. Thus ended the first bloody incident of 1857.

Mangal Pandey survived his wounds and was treated in the regimental hospital. Later he was moved to a tent where the guards kept a close watch on him, as reported in the newspapers:

> The man is in chains and it is needless to say will be hanged. He is however a very high caste Brahmin, and has numbers of friends and relatives in the corps, who will regard his having met such an ignominious fate as almost equivalent to loss of caste in their own cases. They have therefore, it is said, resolved to storm the guard tent and either rescue or kill the prisoner … As to the prisoner himself, he is as dogged and stubborn as can well be conceived. He has resolutely refused food in the hope of starving himself to death, and there was a talk of the stomach pump being, *a la Palmer*, brought into requisition in his case. He also kept tampering with his wound in the hope that it may prove fatal.[50]

During his subsequent trial, Mangal Pandey claimed that he had acted entirely on his own and had been under the influence of *bhang*: 'I was not aware at the time of what I was doing.'[51] The proceedings failed to bring any further information to light. On 8 April, he was hanged in front of all the Indian and European troops at Barrackpore.[52] An eyewitness account of the execution was later published in the papers:

> At about a quarter to 6 a.m. Mungul Pundy was brought on the ground in a cart with the mehters[53] who had been procured to execute the sentence, escorted by a party of the Body Guard and HM 53rd Regiment. The cart was at once drawn up under the gallows, and the rope adjusted round the criminal's neck, when the cart was drawn away and the man left hanging. He appeared to suffer a good deal judging from the apparently convulsive throes. The General then addressed the Native Regiments, when they were marched up to the front of the gallows to see the man hanging and afterwards returned to their lines.
>
> The man, it seems, had previously refused to make any disclosures, which it was expected might have been elicited, so there remained no alternative but to carry out the sentence.
>
> We are told that the spectacle had a most disheartening effect upon the *sepoy* regiments upon the ground. The 34th were completely cowed …[54]

As the only soldier of the 34th Bengal Native Infantry, *Jemadar* Isuree Pandey was also tried for his part in the events of 29 March. According to Isuree himself, he had done everything in his power on that afternoon and he simply stated: 'Some of the *sepoys* on the guard were young, and there were no non-commissioned officers at the moment with me.'[55] While *Jemadar* Isuree was clearly not up to the task of commanding the quarter-guard that day, he did not collude with Mangal Pandey, apart perhaps from a more abstract sense of caste affinity. His first action had been to inform the British officers of what was going on, and he did the same after the guards knocked down Hewson and Baugh. *Jemadar* Isuree Pandey had no control over the situation. When he kept the *sepoys* of the guard from assisting the two officers, it was an ill-judged attempt to retain some sort of order. After all, it was *sepoys* of the guard who had turned against Hewson and Baugh, and Isuree Pandey had no idea how the men under his command would act once they left the quarter-guard. Moreover, the *Jemadar* was not the type of officer to lead by example, and in a tumultuous situation this had disastrous consequences. On 13 April 1857, Isuree Pandey was sentenced to death for failing to take adequate measures to seize Mangal Pandey, for having prevented *sepoys* from assisting Hewson and Baugh, and lastly for not having followed the orders to advance.[56] After some bureaucratic delays, the *Jemadar* was hanged on 21 April.[57] Rather than the defiant speech of a patriotic martyr, the final words of Isuree Pandey were a perfect example of scaffold contrition:

> Sepoys! Listen to me. I have been a traitor to a good Government. I am about to be punished for my great sins. I am about to be hanged, and I deserve my punishment. Sepoys! Obey your officers, for they are your rightful and just rulers, or else you will like me be brought to the gallows. Sepoys! Obey your officers. Listen to them and not to evil advisers; I listened to evil advisers, and you see what I am come to. I call upon God to bless the Governor General, all the great gentlemen, the General and all the *sahib logue* [British] here present – Seeta Ram! Seeta Ram! Seeta Ram![58]

Such a speech was allowed, if not prompted, by the authorities, as it acknowledged the justness of the execution. It also served as an example to the *sepoys* who witnessed this demonstration of the power of the Government. There is little in his actions on 29 March which indicates that Isuree Pandey had actually 'listened to evil advisers', but this was the message that officers like Major-General Hearsey were keen to impress on the *sepoys*.

Mangal Pandey's one-man mutiny was not the result of a carefully planned plot. Like earlier panics, it reflected the general anxiety and sense of despair amongst the *sepoys*. The troops of the 34th BNI had explicitly been told that European soldiers would be coming to Barrackpore to disband the 19th BNI, but this did not put their fears to rest. Mangal Pandey was recorded as having called out, 'You have incited me to do this, and now you *bhainchutes*, you will not join me', and this has been seen by some as proof that he was set up, that he was merely a pawn in a much wider conspiracy.[59] Another, and perhaps more obvious, interpretation of Mangal Pandey's statements would be that he was referring to the general talk and rumours that had been circulating amongst the *sepoys*. It is known that there had been talks in the 34th BNI of rising against their officers and offering resistance before European troops forced the *sepoys* to bite the greased cartridges. When he heard that European troops had arrived at Barrackpore, Mangal Pandey had, in his drug-induced state of mind, simply acted on that impulse. Once he had taken the initiative and done what everybody had been talking about doing, he berated his comrades for not joining him. But that afternoon, Mangal Pandey's fear was not shared by the hundreds of *sepoys* who stood by as he tried to raise the alarm. In contrast with the men of the 19th BNI a month before, none of Mangal Pandey's comrades panicked or tried to arm themselves. The majority of the *sepoys* seem to have regarded his actions as those of a madman, some saying simply that 'He is mad, he has taken *bhang* to excess',[60] while a native officer of the 34th BNI told a friend, 'I don't know what has come over Mungul Pandy'.[61]

The actions of the *sepoys* of the guard clearly indicate that there was some sympathy with Mangal Pandey, but it seems to have been related to different issues. When a British officer of the 34th BNI reproached the men who stood idly by as their officer was being attacked, 'they all seemed to regard the charge as a frivolous one and some of them even laughed at it'.[62] Adjutant Baugh was in fact extremely unpopular with the *sepoys* of his regiment, as he had refused to prevent European troops from bathing in a tank used by the *sepoys*, which polluted the tank.[63] Baugh had furthermore been the cause of the removal of the late *Havildar-Major*, and this resentment seems to have held back the *sepoys* on 29 February when they were called upon to seize Mangal Pandey.[64] As had been the case at Barrackpore in 1824 and Berhampore on 26 February, personal issues between the *sepoys* and their officers thus played an unexpected role. In that connection it is notable that Mangal Pandey, a Brahmin *sepoy*, was being attacked by two British officers, with the aid of a Muslim *sepoy*. The *sepoy* of the guard who struck Baugh and Hewson was a Brahmin, while two Sikh members of the guard sought to come to the officers' assistance, but were held back by the Brahmin Isuree Pandey. What determined the actions of each individual *sepoy* at Barrackpore on 29 March could thus very well have been determined by factors entirely unrelated to Mangal Pandey's fears of the approach of European troops and the polluted cartridges.

## 'Those wicked men who have misled and ruined us'

With order restored, Major-General Hearsey could prepare for the arrival of the 19th BNI, which was to be disbanded at Barrackpore on 31 March. Aside from Mangal Pandey's attack on his officers, and the *sepoys'* general passivity, the British had good reason to be worried, and the arrival of the mutinous regiment was awaited with great trepidation. Just a few days before, on 27 March, Colonel Abbott at the nearby depot of Ishapore had received a stark warning:

> An intelligent native came today to warn me that we must stand upon our guard on the arrival of the 19th Regt at Barrackpore. For that the Sipahis of Barrackpore are determined that if the Govt attempts to disarm the 19th Regt they will oppose it looking first to their officers (I supposed him to mean by this that they would settle them) & then to their own defence.
>
> That not only all the regiments of Barrackpore are engaged in this determination but that they have corresponded with the whole native army & that all the 70 Regiments (as he calls them) are agreed to stand by one another. That they will not suffer the 19th to be disarmed. That they will march in our service whenever ordered, but will on no account enter any vessel lest the Govt make away with them.
>
> That there is much going on which they will on no account reveal to him or to any person not in the plot.[65]

When Abbott had asked why the *sepoys* were prepared to risk everything by turning against the Government, his informant replied 'that all the wealthy natives of Calcutta have promised to support any who lose service in this cause. That they, the sipahis, have told him in the hope that he may be able to furnish them with gunpowder from the agency. That the Bungalows were burnt lately to keep up the spirits of the men.'[66] The Colonel placed great trust in the information, and wrote a hastily composed letter to the army staff at Calcutta, warning them of what might happen when the 19th BNI arrived at Barrackpore. To Abbott it seemed as if the *sepoys* were planning to use the disbandment as an occasion to test the strength of the British, and if possible to provoke a response that might result in the mutiny of native regiments all over India. The Colonel, however, was also aware that he might be considered an alarmist:

> I am aware that it is very difficult for persons dwelling in Calcutta to believe in the existence of such plots. I myself whenever I enter that city are [*sic*] tempted to regard them as a dream. But I have from the first understood this mutiny to be only part of an extensive design. I have from the first understood that the appropriation of Oude would band together against us every native prince in India. The Oude King was the submissive of all the dependent princes. The crime for which he forfeited his sovereignty was that of which every native prince is conscious: he misgoverned his dominion. I have also always foreseen that so soon as the freedom of the press began to be understood by the natives it would be impossible to rule India with a native army. I presume that no argument can be necessary to prove anything so self-evident and I have been sure that the instant war was declared with Russia, her secret agents would be sent to stir up the native princes and to corrupt the army. For it is thus and not by the bayonet that Russia makes war. The native press since the seizure of Oude has understood its own power and no doubt native papers stirring up the people and army are in circulation throughout India unless we suppose the King of Oude to be asleep … For all these reasons I would earnestly recommend that the Govt should be prepared for something much more dangerous than a military mutiny.[67]

Abbott was particularly worried by the fact that no *sepoys* had so far come forward to provide information to the British, which suggested that they were dealing with no ordinary mutiny: 'The ultimate design of the conspirators are [*sic*] probably known to a very limited number. The bulk of the army are acting upon the terror so systematically inspired into their minds by the agents of the conspirators.' Worst of all, he argued, the British had themselves contributed to this situation by prohibiting various indigenous practices such as polygamy, which united all Indians against the Government.[68] Faced with mutinous troops, the British could not afford to take any chances when the time came:

> At the disbanding of the 19th we should be so strong as to render resistance quite hopeless even if the whole native force combines. If [we are] powerful and determined, I doubt whether any but a few of the more desperate will stir. I would guard against treating a whole corps as mutineers because one or two may fire their pieces. I think it certain that those who live with ropes round their necks will go all lengths in order to incite others.
>
> I think that the danger of alarming the force into open mutiny by precautions should give way in this peculiar case to the greater peril of inviting resistance by an insufficient array of force. For I hold it certain that in the latter case we shall have to shed blood freely.[69]

Abbott ended his letter on a sombre note of warning:

> There is a possibility undoubtedly that the information just now communicated to me may have been communicated with a view to deter the Government from disbanding the 19th Regiment. This I do not think to be the case however. The 19th mutinied at the instigation of the mutineers at Barrackpore. According to Hindoo prejudice and their code of honour they are bound to support the 19th and nothing but the certainty of instant destruction as the consequence will prevent them. I have always understood this.[70]

The letter must have confirmed Major-General Hearsey's worst expectations. Barrackpore had, after all, been chosen as the most suitable place to disband the 19th BNI for exactly this reason, but now it seemed as if the British were themselves holding the spark to the powder-barrel. As a last-minute precaution, Hearsey appears to have sent for the Governor-General's bodyguard in order to augment the two British regiments that had already been ordered to attend the disbandment. On the morning of 31 March, Major-General Hearsey personally rode out to meet the 19th BNI as they finally arrived at Barrackpore. It was later reported that there had in fact been an attempt to coordinate a mutiny and that 'in the evening before the 19th regiment marched into Barrackpore, they received a requisition from certain men of the 34th to murder their officers, and to march into the station two hours before the time ordered, when the 34th would at once join them. To this the 19th *sepoys* replied that they had no complaint against their officers, and that they would do nothing of the kind.'[71]

The 19th BNI marched into Barrackpore in perfect order, and was immediately drawn up on the parade ground, where the regiment was officially to be disbanded. Apart from the four Indian regiments of the station, there were of course the British troops at the ready. One newspaper described how: 'The bayonets of two Royal Regiments, and the sabres of the Body Guard on the parades of Barrackpore were calculated to awaken vivid reminiscences of Paget [the famous British surgeon].'[72] The men of the 19th BNI were given their last pay and informed that transportation had been arranged for their baggage for the journeys back to their respective villages. According to Hearsey, the *sepoys* of the 19th BNI 'loudly bewailed their fate, many men saying the regiment had been misled ... by the 34th Regiment, Native Infantry, on which corps they vowed vengeance'.[73] A *sepoy* of the 19th BNI supposedly asked his officer: 'Give us back our arms for ten minutes before we go; and leave us alone with the 34th to settle our account with them.'[74] This seems to confirm that the rumours regarding the cartridges had first been communicated to the 19th BNI by the detachments of the 34th BNI, which were at Berhampore prior to the outbreak there. The men of the 19th BNI may have felt a sense of betrayal; they had refused to accept what they believed to be the polluting cartridges. Now they were suffering the consequences, while the 34th BNI stood idly by on the parade ground, witnesses to their disgrace. Before the proceedings were over, Hearsey addressed the entire brigade, including the 2nd, 34th, 43rd and 70th BNI, and assured them that the Government had no interest in interfering with their religion, and that their lenience towards the 19th BNI was proof of this.[75] In the event, nothing further happened, and the troops quietly dispersed once the ceremony was over. Whether the warnings had been exaggerated or the presence of British troops really did avert a mutiny will never be known.

On the same day as the regiment was disbanded, a section of the men of the 19th BNI submitted yet another petition to Hearsey, in which they stated that if they were pardoned, they would go wherever they were ordered. The petition referred very briefly to the 'advice of some wicked men', which had been the cause of the outbreak of 26 February.[76] Hearsey immediately replied that if the petitioners would provide information on those who were behind the mutiny, he might be able to intercede on their behalf.[77] The petitioners responded with the following account:

We received your honor's answer to our petition, dated 31ˢᵗ March, yesterday evening, regarding our giving up the names and rank of those wicked men who have misled and ruined us, and thoroughly understand the good advice you have written on our behalf. Alas, if we had known the names and rank of those who have misled us, we should have handed them up immediately before this misfortune overwhelmed us.

*Firstly* – The men who are acquainted with the names and ranks of those instigators are at enmity with us and friendly with them, because, being young, they are independent of the Hon'ble Company's service, and they began with this mutiny with a view to our ruin only, and this is the reason they do not tell us.

*Secondly* – On the night that this conspiracy took place, we left them and went to our colonel. By so doing we placed ourselves in opposition to them, neither did they consult us nor tell us their plot; even now they do not trust us. When this is the case, they will never assist us in our miserable state by giving up their names and rank. In our opinion the guard of the 34ᵗʰ was the cause of the mutiny. But we cannot recognise any of the guards who kindled it, that we may prove it against them. We have given you a true statement. You can use it as you like, with a view to our long service and old age, to keep us from starving. Hoping for a speedy answer. We shall ever pray.[78]

The petitioners evidently consisted of the native officers and veterans among the *sepoys* who maintained the desire to serve under the British. The petition thus reflects a significant point relating to the general sentiments of the *sepoys* in the aggrieved regiments during the early months of 1857: a considerable number of them, especially amongst the officers, were not actively involved in the disturbances, but instead provided information to their superiors or acted as mediators between the panicking *sepoys* and the British. This account of the so-called instigators implied that they were younger men who had not been long in the employment of the Company, and therefore did not feel the same sense of duty towards their regiment. Older *sepoys* and native officers, on the other hand, were entirely dependent on their position in the army and the pension provided for them when they retired. Accordingly there seems to be an issue of market forces and opportunities of employment – older *sepoys* had invested their entire careers in service with the Company, while the younger *sepoys* had not. The division between the *sepoys* was between those who still had faith in the paternalistic Company, and those who did not, and this seemed to be a generational issue. It is also noteworthy that the older *sepoys* of the 19th BNI emphasised the role of the 34th as the main agitators in their petition.[79]

Hearsey's curt reply to the second petition was that, as he had previously stated, he could not help them unless they provided information about the 'wicked instigators'.[80] The disbanded *sepoys* of the 19th BNI eventually returned to their respective villages in the districts to the north-west of Barrackpore. Although these men were thought to be 'orderly, respectful and submissive', the authorities were still worried what further trouble they might cause once they left the supervision of British officers.[81] It was thus suggested that the local authorities and police be warned 'to obviate the possible evil effect of so many discharged men being for a time at large in the neighbourhood of the presidency'.[82] Lord Canning personally ordered Mr Ward of the Thagi and Dakaiti Department to have native spies follow the disbanded *sepoys*, but the attempt to gather further information was unsuccessful.[83] The British were clearly not satisfied that the mutiny of the 19th BNI had been spontaneous and they wanted to establish whether the Hindu or Muslim *sepoys* were most disaffected.

In the event, the official concerns were not unfounded. At Cawnpore, disbanded men of the 19th BNI were later heard telling locals that 'we shall quarrel with Government presently; for new cartridges prepared with cows' and pigs' fat are going to be served out, and the *sepoys* refuse to receive them'.[84] According to another native account, the men of the 19th BNI stated, 'We have lost our bread, but have held fast to our religion. The Government wanted us to bite the cartridges, and thus lose our caste, but we would not do it'.[85] Whether the *sepoys* were actively trying to sow discontent or were merely voicing their anger is unclear; what is, however, certain is the fact that the disbandment of *sepoys* in the spring of 1857 led to a further dissemination of fears and resentment against the British Government.

The events of the preceding months had also brought the loyalty of the *sepoys* at Barrackpore into question, especially the 34th BNI. After the trials of Mangal Pandey and Isuree Pandey, a court of inquiry was accordingly set up to determine the state of the regiment. Most of the British officers of the 34th BNI had actually noticed a lack of respect and sullen attitude on the part of the *sepoys*, and the Sergeant-Major remarked that 'he did not know what had come over the regiment'.[86] Adjutant Baugh thought the change in the *sepoys* could be traced back to December and January, when the order arrived for the formation of new rifle depots and the introduction of the new cartridges.[87] During the inquiry, the failed attempt to seize Fort

William in January and more details of the nightly meetings in the lines also came to light, and Colonel Wheler spoke of a 'smothered feeling in the regiment unknown to myself and the European officers'.[88] The most damning finding of the inquiry was the officers' complete lack of faith in the Hindu *sepoys* of the regiment, as opposed to the trust extended to the Sikhs and Muslims, who were considered not to have been affected by the rumours of the cartridges.[89] Asked whether his lack of trust applied to all castes, one captain replied: 'No; it extends to the Brahmins only. I think the men of other castes are inclined to be good and true, but nearly all the native influence in the regiment is in the hands of the Brahmins, who have also a numerical superiority'.[90] What eventually determined the fate of the 34th BNI, however, was the fact that several hundred of its *sepoys* had watched as two of their officers had been wounded by Mangal Pandey. On 6 May 1857, just over a month after the 19th BNI had been disbanded at Barrackpore, seven companies of the 34th BNI were also disbanded, with the exception of Shaik Pultoo and three companies that had not been present at the station on 29 March.[91] The disbandment proceeded without any trouble, but had severe repercussions for the commanding officers of the two regiments; both Lieutenant-Colonel Mitchell and Colonel Wheler were declared unfit to command new regiments in place of the 19th and 34th BNI.[92] Part of the blame for the mutiny at Berhampore and the Mangal Pandey incident was thus placed on the respective officers.

At the time of their dismissal, further evidence of the seditious activities of the 34th BNI also came to light. A *sepoy* of the 37th BNI, who was on leave at Benares, took a letter, supposedly from a native officer of the 34th BNI, to the Raja of Rewa 'offering the support of 2,000 men if the Raja would rise against the English'.[93] The Raja, however, seized the *sepoy* and sent him to the army station at Nagode where the hapless conspirator pretended to be mad. The officer of the 34th BNI was promptly arrested at Barrackpore, and it was reported in the newspapers that the Government 'has made a discovery of some papers belonging to the Subedar-Major of the 34th NI. They consist of a correspondence with, it is said, all or nearly all the native regiments in Bengal, and the contents disclose a general conspiracy to rise at an appointed time, and murder all the Europeans. The *chuppatee* and other mysteries of the same kind are now said to be cleared up'.[94] This illicit correspondence served to spread discontent further amongst the *sepoys* at distant stations as well as mobilising solidarity and establishing networks of resistance. 'By degrees it became known in native society which regiments were disaffected,' according to Mainodin, 'and it began to be inculcated as a creed that every Purbeah must withdraw his friendship from the foreigner; must ignore his authority, and overthrow his rule. Although these sentiments had become national, the methods to be employed in carrying them into action were but indistinctly known ...'.[95] Initially limited to the *sepoys* stationed in the vicinity of Calcutta, the disaffection had now spread far and wide, and from Bengal to Punjab, trouble was stirring amongst the native troops.[96]

As a reward for his assistance to the officers during the struggle, Shaik Pultoo had been promoted to *havildar*, a rank equal to sergeant, and Major-General Hearsey personally recommended him for the Order of Merit.[97] The distinction was conferred upon Shaik Pultoo the day after Mangal Pandey was executed, but the good fortune of the new *Havildar* was not to last. Shaik Pultoo's promotion and distinction were a direct taunt to the disbanded *sepoys* of the 34th BNI, who were not prepared to be so dismissed while a loyal *sepoy* reaped the benefits of siding with the British. Days before the 34th BNI was disbanded, Shaik Pultoo was lured to an isolated spot in the cantonment at Barrackpore and murdered by his former comrades.[98]

# 5

## Arson at Ambala

During the hot season, the headquarters of the Bengal Army was located at Ambala, in the foothills of the Himalaya, some 120 miles from Delhi. The cantonment was home to the 4th Bengal Light Cavalry, with two troops of horse artillery, and the 5th and 60th Bengal Native Infantry, as well as the European regiment HM 9th Lancers. At the depot at Ambala, *sepoys* from no fewer than forty-four different regiments, in groups of five, received instructions in the use of the Enfield rifle between January and May 1857.[1] As at Dum Dum, the instruction at Ambala had not yet reached the stage where the men were actually handling the cartridges, and accordingly no greased cartridges had been distributed at the depot. Captain Edward Martineau, of the 10th Bengal Native Infantry at Fatehgarh, was one of the officers attached to the Ambala depot as Instructor of Musketry, and he was in a unique position to observe the state of mind of the *sepoys* who went through the training.[2] Rumours of the *sepoys'* complaints over the cartridges had reached Ambala from Bengal, but it was not until the mutiny of the 19th BNI at Berhampore, at the end of February, that it dawned on Martineau that the objections portended serious disaffection. In March, one of the *sepoys* came to Martineau with a letter from his brother, who was stationed at Cawnpore, and asked the officer to explain it to him. The letter consisted of the usual greetings and news of family matters, but ended on a curious note of caution: 'But oh brother! Have you eaten any of that flour? Some of it has arrived here, & I have not cooked in consequence for two days, look out for it at Umballa.'[3] Martineau was as puzzled as the *sepoy* and asked him to go back to the lines and make enquiries among his comrades about the peculiar warning. A few days later, the *sepoy* returned to Martineau and told him of the rumour common amongst the native troops at the depot: ground bones were said to have been mixed in flour and 'all the flour from the Government depots for the supply of troops on the march was so adulterated'.[4]

Martineau was, in his own words, 'excessively startled, and saw at once that some brain of more than ordinary cunning had succeeded in combining for the time being [the] parties of both Hindus and Mahomedans [against] us'.[5] Martineau had established a rapport with the *sepoys*, and now he encouraged them to inform him if any one was circulating the injurious rumours. While Martineau was talking to a group of *sepoys*, a native officer from one of the detachments undergoing training asked to make a statement on behalf of all the men, and said: 'The men at this depot object to use any of the new cartridges at all until they have first ascertained that their doing so is not unacceptable to their comrades in the respectable corps, as on their return to the regiments they are apprehensive of being tainted with loss of caste by so doing'.[6] Before Martineau could respond, though, another native officer present, *Subadar* Harbans Sing of the 36th Bengal Native Infantry, intervened and indignantly challenged the speaker: 'By what right or authority do you presume to make such a statement when you know perfectly well that many of the detachments here entertain no such feelings, speak for yourself'.[7] Not all the *sepoys* undergoing training shared the fear of the cartridges, and the *Subadar* was furious that the first officer was bringing 'disrepute on the native army as a body'. He proclaimed that he had full confidence in the Government, that he would fire when ordered to, and that anybody who refused the cartridges on grounds of religion was 'guilty of mutinous and insubordinate conduct'.[8] This bold proclamation apparently caused the applause of many of the *sepoys*; and the first officer later claimed that he had merely passed on what he thought was the general sentiment among the troops – he personally did not believe the rumour to be true. Martineau was nevertheless sufficiently concerned to write a report to his superior, and the following day he continued his endeavours to allay the worries of the *sepoys* by discussing the matter further with the native officers.

With the arrival of the Commander-in-Chief, Major-General Anson, a few days later, however, Martineau's good intentions came to nothing. Anson's escort was made up of a detachment of the 36th BNI, and two native officers from the same regiment, who were at Ambala for instructions at the depot, went down to the camp to greet their comrades on 19 March.[9] What should have been a friendly reunion did not turn out as expected; as a British officer described it:

What was their amazement at finding themselves taunted with having become Christians, and that by a subahdar, a native commissioned officer of their corps! They had looked for the wonted greeting, 'Ram! Ram!' after a separation of some weeks, but instead of this were branded as out-*castes*; the *lotah* and *hookah*, the water-vessel and the pipe, those love-tokens of Hindoo brother-hood, were withheld from them; they had touched the greased cartridge, and become impure.[10]

Thus rebuffed by men of their own regiment, the two NCOs went to Martineau and despairingly told him what had just happened. According to Martineau, one of the two 'blubbered like a child in my room for an hour because his brethren in the corps had refused to eat with him'.[11]

Word of the incident soon spread to the other *sepoys* receiving instructions at Ambala. Many felt the affront as a collective insult, and appealed to Martineau: 'If a subadar in the Commander in Chief's camp, and on duty as his personal escort, can taunt us with loss of caste, what kind of a reception shall we meet on our return to our own corps? No reward that Government can offer us is any equivalent to being regarded as outcastes by our comrades.'[12] That the *sepoys* had been taunted by others for following orders indicated just how divisive and contentious the cartridge issue had become. But Major-General Anson took a different view of the incident. When enquiries were made, the *Subadar* of the Commander-in-Chief's escort claimed that the taunts and refusal to eat and smoke with the men from the depot had been nothing but a jest.[13] Although his conduct was deemed to have been 'unbecoming and unsoldierlike', no further action was taken against him.[14] The two NCOs who had complained to Martineau, however, were severely reprimanded for having caused trouble over such a trifling issue, and one of them had his planned promotion withdrawn 'for having brought discredit on his own regiment!'[15] As there was no real cause for concern among the *sepoys*, so the reasoning went, it was the scare-mongering that was dangerous and that had to be suppressed at any cost. Such actions on the part of the British staff obviously did nothing to improve the already strained relationship between the *sepoys* and their superiors.

During his subsequent enquiries, Martineau made a number of extremely worrying discoveries about the state of the native army. According to Martineau, the *sepoys* at Ambala generally believed that the cartridges for the Enfield had been smeared with cow's and pig's fat to destroy their religion, and that 'in fact, the weapon itself is nothing more or less than a Government missionary [*sic*] to convert the whole army to Christianity'.[16] Martineau was also told that there were *panchayats* or councils in all the native regiments across the subcontinent, which were communicating on the matter of the cartridges. Furthermore, 'the army at large has come to the determination to regard as outcasts, and to expel from all communication any men who at any of the depots use the cartridges at all'.[17] While this information was somewhat conjectural, the recent events at Ambala convinced Martineau of its truth. The *sepoys* with whom he talked certainly believed that all native regiments 'from Calcutta to Peshawar' were colluding, and Martineau noticed that they were no longer in contact with their respective regiments; when they wrote letters, they received no reply. Reporting on these matters to Major-General Anson, Martineau also ventured an explanation for the *sepoys*' grievances:

> It strikes me that we have here been driving the machine of state rather too fast of late to suit their taste, recruiting for general service, absorption of native states (Oude), the recent passing of certain acts by the Legislative Council; these, any, or some of them, may be unacceptable, and tend to make them peculiarly apprehensive of some new, and more explicit move on the part of Government towards what they regard as the final object, their forcible conversation to Christianity.[18]

Anson responded to these reports by speaking directly to the men of the depot following an inspection parade on 23 March. With Martineau as translator, Anson gave a speech virtually identical to the ones previously given by Hearsey at Barrackpore: the Government had no interest in defiling the *sepoys*, who accordingly had nothing to fear from the new cartridges, and the troops were reminded of their duty to follow orders and to stay true to their oath of allegiance.[19] Afterwards Martineau conferred with several native officers to determine whether the speech had been well received and he concluded that 'They know that the rumour is false; but they equally know, that for one man in Hindostan who disbelieves it, ten thousand believe it, and that it is universally credited, not only in their regiments, but in their villages and their homes.'[20]

Using Martineau as a mediator, the *sepoys* undergoing training at the Ambala depot subsequently petitioned Major-General Anson to consider the 'social consequences of military obedience for themselves'.[21] In Martineau's own opinion these men were all loyal but 'prone to fits of religious panic' that no rational explanation or measures could allay. He had been unable to discover what was behind the present unrest, 'but I am disposed to regard the greased cartridges … more as a medium than the original cause of this widespread feeling of distrust that is spreading dissatisfaction to our rule, and tending to alienate the fidelity of our native army'.[22] Martineau further requested that a court of inquiry be set up to examine the rumours, and to obtain some kind of redress for the men attending instructions at the depot who were shunned by their comrades. Major-General Anson, however, did not consider it prudent to conduct a formal investigation into the discontent at Ambala, which might only give rise to further trouble. 'Redress and inquiry were both inconvenient,' Martineau noted with bitterness, 'so the headquarters' camp marched to Simla.' Left at Ambala, with no real authority and unrest increasing amongst the *sepoys* by the day, Martineau felt helpless. Had he been granted an inquiry, he argued, he would have proven to the staff the real state of the native army; 'that is if anything will open their eyes'.[23] During the night of 26 March, an attempt was made to set fire to the hut of the *Subadar* who had publicly stated his willingness to use the cartridges. The fire, however, was treated simply as an accident.[24]

As the Commander-in-Chief, Anson had nevertheless realised that the cartridge issue had reached an impasse and that no amount of reasoning would remove the suspicion of the *sepoys*. At first he considered disbanding the depot at Ambala and sending the men back to their regiments, but this would just postpone the introduction of the Enfield rifle and not actually resolve the matter. Instead he ordered an analysis of the cartridge paper, to exclude the possibility that it contained grease; in the meantime, instruction at the depots was suspended.[25] By 23 March, the unrest amongst the *sepoys* had accordingly forced the Commander-in-Chief to stop further instruction in the use of the Enfield rifle until all objections had been put to rest.

Meanwhile, it had been suggested that the loading drill for the Enfield might be modified so that the *sepoys* could be allowed to tear the cartridges with their hands instead of biting them.[26] Brevet-Major Bontein at Dum Dum had experienced no real objections from the men who were instructed in 'cartridge-making' at the depot there, but one *sepoy* did say that his comrades in his regiment would consider him to have forfeited his caste if he were to bite the cartridge.[27] Although the drill for the Brown Bess musket required the troops to use their teeth to tear the (ungreased) cartridges, the actual practice had for some time been to do so with their fingers. Accordingly, the suggested modification would not constitute a major change, and, more importantly, it was expected to have the favourable effect of finally putting the fears of the native troops to rest. Bontein's suggestion was readily adopted, and according to the new drill, the *sepoys* were no longer required to bite the cartridges for the Enfield rifle or indeed any of the firearms in use at the time.[28] Since any objections to the cartridges were now effectively removed, the authorities reasoned that firing practice at the depots could be resumed.[29]

On 13 April the order was thus passed for firing practice at Ambala to commence; that very night there was a fire in the lines at the depot. Two nights later there was another fire in the lines of the 60th BNI.[30] On 16 April, cartridges were distributed for shooting practice the following day – the ammunition was ungreased, and the *sepoys* themselves applied a lubricant composed of ghee and bee's wax or coconut oil.[31] Firing practice with the new Enfield rifle and self-greased cartridges thus took place for the very first time on 17 April.[32] In spite of the extraordinary precautions taken, however, there were arson attacks for the following ten consecutive nights at either the depot or the cantonment at Ambala. The preventive measures did not only encompass the military personal and all 'fukeers, travellers and idle persons' were expelled from the station.[33] Initially, suspicion fell on the Indian labourers who thatched the roofs and who obviously benefited from the sudden increase in demand for their skills, but it soon became clear that the *sepoys* of either the cantonment or the depot were the most likely perpetrators. According to a British officer: 'There is a general belief in the bazaar and among all classes of natives that these fires are the acts of *sepoys*, and the reason alleged is a dislike to use the cartridges served out to them.'[34]

On several occasions, small earthen pots with combustible material were recovered outside the bungalows of European officers: 'The combustible here used was powder and brimstone, wrapped in "*fine*" *dhotee*; some burnt *cartridge paper* of a bluish grayish colour was also picked up.'[35] The use of cartridge paper obviously implied the involvement of *sepoys*, yet nothing could be discovered at the time. Even a reward of Rs 1,000, or the equivalent of almost twelve years' salary for a *sepoy*, which was proclaimed in the bazaar, failed to produce any results.[36] There was, however, a clear pattern to the arson attacks – the *sepoys* were not just displaying their discontent with the British for making them use the cartridges. On 19 and 20 April, attempts were made to burn the huts of native officers of the 5th BNI, and in the second case, powder and brimstone were found under an officer's bed. Similar to the first instance of arson in March, these were personal attacks aimed at native officers from the cantonment at Ambala who were involved in the instruction at the depot. The reaction followed swiftly; on 21 April six or seven huts belonging to *sepoys* of the 60th BNI were burned to the ground, immediately followed by two more retaliatory arsons in the lines of the 5th BNI. The internal dispute amongst the *sepoys* stationed at Ambala, which had previously expressed itself through taunts and declarations for or against the use of the cartridges, was being pursued through the nightly fires. The men of the 60th BNI looked down on those of the 5th BNI, some of whom had accepted the cartridges, and they expressed their contempt by means of these attacks. The ability of the *sepoys* to reject the cartridges *en masse* was dependent on the solidarity of all, and those who followed orders set a bad precedent for those who wanted to refuse the cartridges.

During this period Ambala was brimming with tension; a British private from HM 9th Lancers claimed that when he came across a meeting of *sepoys* in a garden one night, he was spat at and maltreated.[37] This was perhaps just a coincidence, but it was observed by other Europeans that the bearing of the *sepoys* had become 'more disrespectful and insubordinate'.[38] It was furthermore not just native officers who were personally targeted in the arson attacks. One morning Martineau went for an early ride by himself and was returning when, just outside the cantonment, a native caused him to stop.[39] The man asked if Martineau lived in the house behind the lines of the 60th BNI, and when the officer replied in the affirmative, the man warned him, as Martineau later recalled:

> 'I wish to warn you that your house will be set fire to this evening at 9 o'clock.'
>
> 'If you know this you can also tell me who will do it,' I replied.
>
> The man laughed and said, 'Look round you, there is not a human being in sight, & if you could recognize me again, & get me summoned to give evidence before any court, I would, as a Brahmin take the most solemn oath that I never saw you in my life, or spoke a word to you, and my word would be held as good as yours, be wise, take my advice, get out of that house, & seek to enquire no further concerning me, who, for reasons you know not of, am a well wisher to you, I would not willingly see you come to harm.'
>
> 'Thank you, my friend,' said I, 'I may now tell you that my things are this moment leaving the house you mean, & going to the hotel, where I have taken rooms from today.'[40]

Martineau returned to the cantonment and warned the two officers who were taking over his house. Their response to his warning, however, was decidedly dismissive: 'They, Caulfield & Craigie, laughed, and wouldn't heed, but that evening, the stables and outhouses were in flames, and their horses galloping lose thro' cantonment.'[41] As the instructor at the depot, Martineau's house was perhaps an obvious target, but at least some of the *sepoys* held him in esteem. This, however, was not the case amongst his superiors; Martineau and those of his colleagues who insisted that the fires were evidence of the excited state of the native army were generally dismissed as 'croakers' and 'alarmists'.[42] According to the Deputy Commissioner, Forsyth, 'there was an evident disinclination to believe the fires to be the work of *sepoys*'.[43] While nightly arson attacks ravaged the station at Ambala, the pace of events was picking up at Meerut, 152 miles (244 kilometres) to the south.

# 6

# Meerut

The military cantonment town of Meerut was one of the most popular assignments in northern India. The nineteen-year-old John Campbell MacNabb, newly arrived in India, had unexpectedly been offered the position of Lieutenant in the 3rd Bengal Light Cavalry at Meerut. While waiting for the official paperwork to come through, he wrote to his mother back in Scotland, excited at the prospect of rapid advancement: 'it seemed put in my way and I thought it right to take it, as it was quite different to my having applied for it. I feel sure it will turn out well. The 3rd is a very "crack," and favoured regiment, and they are at Meerut – the best station in India. I think myself very lucky, as a year hence I shall be higher up in my regiment than any body who came out for the last 16 months, and higher than many who came before that.'[1] Meerut was unusual, as Barrackpore was, in that it had a high concentration of European troops in proportion to *sepoys*, which were almost matched in numbers; in early 1857 there were a total of 136,000 Indian troops and just 24,000 European troops in the entire Bengal Presidency.[2]

Meerut, which was the headquarters of the Bengal artillery, was garrisoned by two native infantry regiments and one light cavalry, in addition to HM 60th Rifles and HM 6th Dragoon Guards (Carabineers).[3] As Lieutenant Gough of the 3rd Bengal Light Cavalry recalled:

> It was one of the pleasantest and most favourite stations in the Bengal Presidency. There was a great deal of sport and gaiety, which all subalterns like, and I confess I took my full share of both. The regiments in the garrison were singularly sociable; and in the midst of fun and gaiety, which was to most of us the apparent object of life, there was little thought or apprehension of anything so serious as war breaking out. The Punjab had been completely pacified, our frontiers appeared

unusually quiet, and, seeing all things the same around us, our martial spirit distinctly lay low.[4]

The layout of Meerut reflected the fact that it was a garrison. It was dissected diagonally on a north-west to south-easterly line by a water-course known as Abu Nullah, which could be traversed only by a few bridges. The station church and European lines were located in the northern part of Meerut, on the eastern side of the Abu Nullah, and it was here that most of the British population lived. Further south, on the eastern side of the Abu Nullah, the huge sprawled-out residences of the senior British officials dominated the open landscape, and it was also here that the court-buildings and new prison were located. The centre of Meerut, south-west of the Abu Nullah, was made up of the native city, enclosed by an old wall, and the Sudder Bazaar, which catered to the native troops. This tightly populated and urban part of the city was squeezed in between the Delhi Road and the Grand Trunk Road, which converged just south of the Abu Nullah. To the west of the native city and Sudder Bazaar were the lines and barracks of the Indian troops, located on the three sides of the native parade ground, with the western-most side left open. The British officers and their families lived in bungalows between the native lines and the Sudder Bazaar (see Map 2). In 1857, the cantonment bazaars alone had a local population of some 40,000, while another 35,000 lived in the Indian city. By comparison, there were little more than 600 European women and children living in the station, the families and relatives of the British troops and officials.[5]

The intangible signs of disquiet had also been noticed by the British officials at Meerut during the early months of 1857, although the significance of the *chapattis* remained as obscure here as anywhere else.[6] Reports of the disbandment of the regiments in Bengal, of Mangal Pandey's attack on his officers, and especially of the incessant fires at nearby Ambala reached the station during March and April. Notably, it was the Commissioner of Meerut, Hervey H. Greathed, who paid most attention to the unrest. By 1857, Greathed was an experienced official, having worked for more than twenty years in India, and with several major postings to his credit. In early April, he wrote to a friend in Britain, stating his opinion that:

> The gulf between the European and the Asiatic has naturally grown wider, the latter being a stationary character, and among mortal men superiority must be met by more or less hate; but, as our power of combination increases and theirs

decreases, as long as we feel ourselves in the right, we have nothing to fear. The native army is becoming contemptible; their martial spirit has waned, as might be expected, from our treading all warlike propensities out of the people; and they have no longer the virtues of militiamen, and are neither formidable to foes, nor useful as watchmen. If we wish to have a serviceable native army in this Presidency, we must cease to recruit from the Hindoos of Oudh and Behar, and draw more largely on the warlike tribes across the Sutledge; it is at present a useless expense, and our only source of uneasiness. The disbandment of the 19th was well done. I hope no attention will be paid to the spirit of repentance that has been generated by the loss of pay and of the prospects of pension. It is a comfort to be quartered with as many true men as we have here.[7]

Such acumen was indeed the rarest of things among British officials during 1857, even if it was tinged with racist views. But Greathed was a civil servant and in an entirely different position with the Indian population compared to the military establishment. Having no obligation to maintain pretence, the Commissioner could express his unreserved opinion on the state of the native army. The drawback to the outsider position was that the views of men like Greathed could comfortably be ignored by the British military command. Many British officers relished the notion that the *sepoys* were their children, and they were supremely confident in the loyalty of the men with whom they had fought side by side through many campaigns. Greathed, however, had a more pragmatic view, and not a very high opinion, of the protestations of loyalty from the native officers and veterans of the disbanded regiments.

The letters that circulated amongst *sepoys*, following the disbandment of the 19th and 34th BNI, had also reached the native troops at Meerut. According to a native account:

All the Sepoys in this country, at Kurnaul, Meerut, &c., were some way or other related (to those of the disbanded regiments). (The men of the latter) wrote to the former, telling them what had occurred and stated 'that we have on this account quitted the service, and have seen all with our own eyes. We have written this to you for your information. If you should receive these cartridges, intermarriage, and eating and drinking in common, shall cease between yourselves and us.'[8]

The troops at the depot at Ambala had already experienced the consequences of receiving, not the cartridges, but drill in the use of the Enfield rifle, and this general warning would be hard for *sepoys* anywhere to ignore.

The general sense of disaffection was current also amongst the locals, who were openly debating the disbandment of the 19th and 34th BNI. This was attributed to the fact that the 'kafirs' or British had deliberately mixed pig and cow fat in the cartridges in order to take away the caste of Muslims and Hindus. During a casual meeting on the veranda of the Collector's office at Bijnour, one Indian stated that 'these infidels should not be allowed to remain in India, or there would be no difference between Mahomedans and Hindoos, and whatever they said, we should have to do'. When a Christian native interjected that the British had hitherto left the native population alone, the man retorted: 'What ease have we, they are always inventing new laws to trouble us, and to overturn religion, teach out of their religious books, which are also distributed; is there now any security for Islam, as it used to be?'[9] Such sentiments probably reflected what many Indians were thinking: the British were deliberately working towards the conversion of all natives; every new act or regulation seemed one step closer towards the complete subversion of their religions.

In early April, a *fakir* on an elephant had appeared at Meerut and set up camp at the holy Surajkund tank with a small entourage of followers and horses. The *fakir* was supposedly from Ayodhya and on several occasions he went begging for money from people in Meerut.[10] During his stay, the mendicant was often visited by the *sepoys* of the 20th BNI, and he in turn went to their lines. This traffic attracted the attention of the Magistrate, A. Johnston, who ordered the *fakir* to leave the city, but the mendicant stayed in the lines of the 20th BNI for some days before leaving Meerut in late April.[11] The enquiries later made suggested that, prior to his stay at Meerut, the *fakir* had stayed at Ambala for several months. *The Delhi Gazette* reported that the man, 'painted yellow', had come from Phillaur or Pattiala, and it expected that 'the authorities will have their eyes on him'.[12] The conclusion of the Superintendent of the Cantonment Police, Major Williams, was nevertheless that nothing of a seditious nature could be proven against him.[13] The *fakir* probably brought news from other stations and may have discussed the worries of the *sepoys*; beyond that, however, his role is unlikely to have been suspicious.

Despite the ominous portents, few amongst the British at Meerut suspected that there was anything seriously wrong. The local postmaster did hear 'a good deal of seditious language used by the orderlies of the different native regiments, who used to meet at the post-office two or three times a day when they came to fetch their officers' and regimental letters'.[14] But when he warned the British officers, they made light of it. One artillery officer at the station remembered how 'We heard stories certainly of the *sepoys* at more than one station having set fire to barracks and Bungalows, but as no one around us seemed to take any serious notice of this, or to treat it otherwise than as a [trifle], we could only follow their example.'[15] And so life continued as usual and the British occupied themselves with balls, plays and sandwich clubs. If the *sepoys* occasionally seemed less respectful than usual, no one paid any attention.[16]

The commander of the 3rd BLC, Lieutenant-Colonel G. Carmichael-Smyth, had been away to purchase remounts for the regiment, and before returning to Meerut in late April he took a brief leave at Mussorie.[17] While at the hill station, he heard of some *sepoys* who had been talking about the unrest at Berhampore, and one of them had said: 'I have been 36 years in the service and am a Havildar, but still I would join in a Mutiny and what is more I can tell you the whole army will Mutiny.'[18] This story made a deep impression on the Lieutenant-Colonel, and when he arrived back at Meerut on 23 April, he immediately reported to the Commander-in-Chief how he had heard that '*the whole Army were going to Mutiny*'.[19] On his arrival at Meerut, Smyth found the instructions for the new drill waiting for him and in them he saw the solution to the present problems. Given that the state of the *sepoys* was apparently very serious, he wasted no time in introducing the simple measure that he assumed would defuse the situation with – quite literally – a flick of the hand. Accordingly, the Lieutenant-Colonel ordered a parade for the following morning to demonstrate the new method of loading the carbines of the skirmishers of the 3rd BLC.[20] The new drill applied to all weapons in use, not just the new Enfield, which had yet to be introduced in any Indian regiments. The firing parade of the 3rd BLC thus entailed the use of ungreased cartridges for their old carbines, which the men were perfectly familiar with.[21] Except for the change in the drill, Smyth was forcing nothing new on the troopers.[22]

In preparation for the parade the following day, Smyth had the orderly of the *Havildar-Major* go through the new drill and fire a few shots. This was an important occasion, which the Lieutenant-Colonel believed would finally put to rest the fears of the native troops, and he did not want anything to go wrong.[23] Unfortunately, it did, and much sooner and much more severely than anyone could have anticipated. Having performed the new drill before Smyth, the orderly, Brijmohun Sing, immediately went and told his comrades of the 3rd BLC about it. As an orderly, Brijmohun Sing was somewhat apart from the troopers, who were concerned about the rumours, and he taunted them with the prospect of the parade: the Lieutenant-Colonel and Adjutant would both be present, and then they would finally see if anyone dared refuse the orders. As the orderly's statement was communicated through the lines, from one high-strung trooper to the next, it underwent an unfortunate but perhaps predictable transformation. The troopers told each other that Brijmohun Sing claimed to have fired two of the new greased cartridges, and that they were the ones to be used on the parade the next day. It is easy to imagine how news of a new drill involving cartridges might turn into a drill with the new cartridges. Combined with the general suspicion among the men, the orderly's attitude meant that Smyth's initiative to resolve the cartridge issue had quite the opposite effect.

By 23 April, the *sepoys* at Meerut would have been aware that shooting practice with the Enfield rifle had begun at Ambala and that there were nightly arson attacks at that station. By setting fires at Ambala, the *sepoys* there had taken the first step in protest against the use of the Enfield cartridges, although these were now ungreased. The attacks were partly directed at the British officers and authorities, but they also probably constituted a message to *sepoys* at other stations, to the effect that the troops at Ambala were not placidly accepting the cartridges. According to Mainodin, the very first cases of arson at Barrackpore and Raniganj in January were 'a concerted signal; it was calculated that the burning of a telegraph office would immediately be communicated along the line from Calcutta to the Punjab, and that those in the secret would understand on hearing of it that they too must fire houses. Information of these incendiaries was widely circulated in all directions, and it is said that letters were sent from regiment to regiment inciting them to commit similar acts.'[24] The setting of fires was a powerful symbol of resistance that would be understood by other Indians, which cleared the *sepoys* of the suspicion of acquiescence to the Government. It was now up to the 3rd BLC to make an even stronger protestation. It is, however, worth recalling that at the depot at Ambala the *sepoys* undergoing instructions were using ungreased cartridges for the new Enfield rifle, which they themselves then lubricated. The skirmishers at Meerut, on the other hand, were simply to be taught the new drill with their old carbines and ungreased cartridges. Unfortunately, such details had long ceased to be of consequence to the native troops.

According to a *havildar* of the 3rd BLC, the troops were greatly alarmed: 'a number of us said to each other: If we use the greased cartridges we shall lose our caste, and shall never again be able to return to our homes.'[25] Two *naiks* of the 3rd BLC, Shaik Peer Ally and Ameer Koodrut Ally, now reiterated the story of the *khalasi* at Dum Dum, adding that while Muslims could remove the pollution of having touched pig's fat, the Hindus would irrevocably lose their caste.[26] As the officers who would be approached first on the parade ground, the two *naiks* pledged not to receive the cartridges and made the other troopers swear on the Koran and Ganges water that they would not use the cartridges until all the other regiments had done so.[27] This course of action had very obvious precedents in the oaths taken by *sepoys* at Barrackpore in 1824 and a few months earlier. By making the other troopers swear along with them, the two men on whom the initial refusal of the cartridges would fall, effectively distributed the responsibility for their disobedience of orders. The two *naiks* could also more easily refuse the cartridges if they knew that the remainder of the skirmishers would support them in their actions by joining the refusal.

During the evening of 23 April, men of all six troops of the 3rd BLC decided that they would not receive the cartridges on the following day.[28] The men of the 4th Troop approached their officer, Captain H. C. Craigie, as a group and requested that the parade for the following day be cancelled. Their reason for doing so, they explained, was the commotion amongst all the native troops. If they received any cartridges, they would become *budnam* – stigmatised. Craigie told his men that there were none of the new cartridges at Meerut, but they replied that 'if they fire any kind of cartridge at present they lay themselves open to the imputation from their comrades and from other regiments of having fired the objectionable ones'.[29] Smyth was immediately informed by Craigie, who stated that 'This is a most serious matter, and we may have the whole regiment in mutiny in half an hour if this be not attended to.'[30] The *sowars* of several of the other troops entreated their officers not to proceed with the parade.[31] The Lieutenant-Colonel was nevertheless convinced that the sooner the native troops were shown the new drill, the sooner the issue would be resolved. On the advice of his adjutant, Captain Clarke, he decided to go ahead with the parade.[32] In a repetition of the pattern from Ambala, Smyth's tent and Brijmohun Sing's hut were burned down that very night, as was an old horse hospital near the magazine.[33] Brijmohun Sing was described as a 'mean fellow' by his fellow officers and he now paid the price for having, as they mistakenly believed, received the disputed cartridges.[34] The orderly's actions endangered the reputation of the entire regiment, and the oaths initiated by the two *naiks* were necessary to maintain the unity of the remainder of the troopers.

On the morning of 24 April, the ninety skirmishers of the 3rd BLC were lined up on the parade ground of the garrison at Meerut. By the time Lieutenant-Colonel Smyth arrived, none of the men had taken the cartridges, and Smyth ordered the *Havildar-Major* of the regiment to demonstrate the proceedings. The *Havildar-Major*, Shaik Bucksh Ally, loaded and fired his carbine according to the new drill, which entailed the cartridge being torn by hand rather than the teeth. The echoes of the single shot reverberated across the parade ground as the order was given for the blank cartridges to be served out to the ninety skirmishers. The cartridges were then taken out by the *kot-dafadars* or NCOs, who handed them, three at a time, to each trooper in turn.[35] The first man was Naik Shaik Peer Ally, who remained true to his oath of the previous night and refused the cartridges, stating simply that he would 'get a bad name' if he did so. Lieutenant-Colonel Smyth then personally addressed the reluctant trooper, as he later recalled:

> 'You see the havildar-major has taken and fired one;' he replied: 'Oh, the havildar-major!' in a manner to signify that his position obliged him to do it, adding – 'If all the men will take the cartridges, I will.' He assigned no reason for not taking it, but still refused to do as I ordered him. I then ordered one to be given to Ameer Koodrut, naick, who stood in the rear of Shaik Peer Ally, but he also refused, saying – 'If all the regiment will take cartridges, I will.'[36]

This scene repeated itself throughout the assembled troops, and of the ninety troopers, only five received the cartridges. These were three Muslims and two Hindus, and all of them were NCOs.[37] The remaining eighty-five men simply refused to take the cartridges, but, significantly, none of them cited religious objections, and instead they professed themselves to be ready to accept the cartridges if everybody else did. Yet the five officers who did so obviously did not sway the rest by their example. Smyth tried in vain to persuade the eighty-five men, but they persisted in their refusal, and the only response he got was a murmur to the effect that if all the regiments were ordered to take the cartridges, they would do so as well.[38] The Lieutenant-Colonel pointed out that the cartridges were not greased, but this had no effect whatsoever. Given the number of troopers who had disobeyed orders, Smyth saw no alternative to dismissing the parade and letting the men return to their quarters, after which he reported the matter to the Commander of the Division.[39]

From the perspective of the skirmishers lined up and facing Lieutenant-Colonel Smyth, the events of the parade had assumed a rather different significance. One of the eighty-five troopers, Mattadin *Havildar*, later described how they experienced the parade, following the unrest of the previous evening:

> Early in the morning, as we were ordered to turn out for parade, we all went there without knowing what had been done or said the night before by captains of the troops. The adjutant came down to parade shortly afterwards, and then the colonel stood in front of the skirmishers and said: 'I have invented something; listen to what I am about to say. If you will fire these cartridges, the Commander-in-Chief will be much pleased, and you will have a great name, and I shall likewise get great praise, and I will have the whole affair published in the papers.' The colonel called the havildar-major to the front, and said to him: 'Take a carbine, load and fire it off in the way I showed you yesterday,' and then he said to us that we should have to load and fire in the same manner. The havildar-major brought his carbine to his side, and having handled his cartridges, was about to bite off the end, when the colonel stopped him, saying: 'Tear it with your hands.' He loaded and fired … The colonel went to the right and said: 'Will you take those cartridges?' All said 'No, we won't take them.' We would not take them as we had great doubts about them; so the colonel had to induce us to take them, a thing he had never done before. When the colonel had put us 'threes about' to dismiss us from the parade, we begged to make a statement to him. He fronted us and we said 'If the other regiments will fire one cartridge, we will fire ten.' The colonel said 'There are no cartridges for other men.' We said 'There are pistols.' The colonel then again put us 'threes about' and dismissed us.[40]

If we are to believe the *Havildar*, the skirmishers had no idea what to expect on the parade and were full of trepidation. Lieutenant-Colonel Smyth's explanation of the new drill, which was supposed to remove all causes for concern, was heard simply as 'I have invented something.' Mattadin's description of how the *Havildar-Major* was *about* to bite off the cartridge clearly indicates that the troopers did not understand the point of the parade and the significance of the drill. Nobody wanted to be the first to accept the cartridges, and risk being ostracised by their comrades and relatives. The remark about pistols suggests that the skirmishers were afraid of the response of the rest of the troopers of the 3rd BLC, who were armed with pistols and not carbines, and tacitly sought to include the entire regiment in the new drill. Informing the reluctant troopers, who were concerned for their reputation, that their acceptance of the cartridges would be widely publicised was certainly not the most tactful thing to do. In his very attempt to allay the fears, Smyth was compounding the issue, and the firing-parade thus became yet another crucial failure in communication between the British officers and the Indian troops. At the time, none of the British officers knew of the two *naiks*' exertions at creating solidarity among the men and the oaths that had been taken the night before.

When Smyth informed the Commander of the Division, Major-General Hewitt, of what had passed, the old General responded, 'Oh, why did you have this parade? My division has kept quiet all this time, and in a few weeks this cartridge affair would have blown over!'[41] Hewitt was by no means the only British officer who was critical of Smyth's decision, which MacNabb described as injudicious:

> because there was no necessity to have the parade at all or to make any fuss of the sort just now, no other Colonel of Cavalry thought of doing such a thing, as they knew at this unsettled time their men would refuse to be the first to touch these cartridges, but that by not asking they would not give their men the chance of refusing, and that next parade season when the row had blown over they would begin to fire as a matter of course, and think nothing of it.[42]

According to MacNabb, 'the real case is that they hate Smyth, and, if almost any other officer had gone down they would have fired them off'.[43] But the damage had already been done, and an inquiry was set up to investigate the refusal of the eighty-five troopers, who were kept under guard in an old hospital.[44]

## 'I could not forsake my religion'

During the first week of May, Greathed wrote to a friend in Britain describing the recent development at Meerut:

> There has been an outbreak among the 3rd Cavalry quartered here, which, though pitiably senseless, must lead to serious consequences. I believe the truth to be, that one of the periodical alarms about compulsory conversion to Christianism has seized the army; and it must be remembered, that conversion with Hindoos

and Mohammedans is not a matter of conviction, but the passing through certain forms, or unconscious performance of some act incompatible with their own religion. They are, therefore, more on their guard than we generally imagine against being led to do anything that would sever their ties with their own creed; and the rumour that the Enfield cartridges were greased with hog's lard for Mohammedans, and bullock's fat for Hindoos, spread like wildfire through the army; and in the wildness of their apprehensions, as there was nothing outwardly visible in the cartridges, the resolution not to use any has been adopted, as the safeguard against contamination.[45]

In his bleak assessment, Greathed was much closer to the truth than he realised. According to Lieutenant Gough of the 3rd BLC, 'there were unheeded tokens of an ill feeling among the natives in the bazaars, &c.; but as there was no overt act of insubordination, and no attempt whatever to rescue the prisoners, the authorities never dreamt of any resistance to the orders of Government, whatever they might be'.[46]

Major-General Hewitt subsequently ordered a court of inquiry, to be judged by native officers. The inquiry confirmed that the cartridges distributed on 24 April were the ones the regiment had been using for years, and that they had actually been made under the supervision of *Havildar* Pursaud Sing, one of the five NCOs who had received them on the parade.[47] During the inquiry, several troopers stated that there was 'a general rumour' against the cartridges, although they acknowledged that they were the same ones that they had always used: 'These cartridges are apparently all right, but the army won't use them, as there is some suspicion attaching to them; I do not know of what nature.'[48] One trooper expressed this ambiguity very clearly: 'I know of no objection to them, but yet I have a doubt in my heart.'[49]

It is significant that, with echoes of the old rumours from Barrackpore and Berhampore, only a single trooper of the 3rd BLC actually suggested the presence of polluting grease: 'I have doubts about the cartridges; they apparently look like old ones, but they may, for aught I know, have pig's fat rubbed over them.'[50] And even then, one cannot help but think that this objection was not quite earnest – the cartridges were entirely inconspicuous, and the troopers even admitted as much. No *sepoy* or *sowar* had at any stage been ordered to bite greased cartridges for the new Enfield rifle, but by now anything distributed by the British was, by virtue of this very fact, subject to suspicion. The fear of being ostracised, of being marked by the stigma of accepting the cartridges (greased or not), was the main motivation behind the troopers' refusal on the parade ground at Meerut on 24 April 1857. The British officers clearly had a very poor appreciation of what group pressure and ostracism meant to the *sepoys*, and the Judge Advocate-General of the army stated: 'There is absolutely no apparent reason whatever why the men of the 3rd Regiment, Light Cavalry, should have declined to use the cartridges served out to them, except the fear of being taunted by their comrades or the *sepoys* of other regiments, and it might be supposed that a sufficient answer to any taunt would have been that the cartridges were the same as had always been used.'[51] But the taunting of comrades was the very reason that the men refused the cartridges, be it at Berhampore, Ambala or Meerut, irrespective of the fact that greased cartridges were never distributed. At Meerut, a trooper of the 3rd BLC said of the cartridges, 'We have doubts about them, as none of the *sepoys* in the station will touch them.'[52] Once the men had sworn on the Koran and the Ganges water, and the two *naiks* had set the precedent of refusal, there was no going back.

As for the five NCOs who accepted the cartridges during the parade, we can only surmise what their motives might have been. They might have been somewhat marginalised from the rest of the skirmishers to begin with, and they had probably not taken the oath. As native officers, they may have been less susceptible to the threat of ostracism from the private troopers and probably had greater faith in the benefits of loyalty to the British. Perhaps ambition and the hopes of promotion led them to side with their superiors rather than their comrades. Surprisingly, there appears to have been no retaliation against the five who broke rank.

On 1 May a new native regiment, the 11th BNI, arrived at Meerut to replace the 15th BNI, which had been relocated to Nasirabad a month before. News of the firing-parade and the refusal of skirmishers had already reached the officers and men of the 11th BNI *en route* to Meerut, and when they arrived at the station the outcome of the inquiry was still pending. The arrival of the 11th BNI resulted in a dramatic distortion of the ratio between British and Indian troops at the beginning of May. There were a total of 2,028 European troops at the station, divided between HM 6th Dragoon Guards (Carabineers): 652, HM 60th Rifles: 901, and 475 men attached to the artillery. In real terms, however, the effective force of British troops was several hundred short of 2,000 and thus more than matched by the 2,258 Indian troops present: the 3rd BLC: 405, the 20th BNI: 950, the newly arrived 11th BNI: 780, and finally 123 natives attached to the artillery.[53]

The finding of the initial inquiry was, as expected, that the eighty-five troopers had no reasonable cause for refusing the cartridges, which did not interfere with the religious sentiments of either Hindus or Muslims, 'and if any pretence contrary to this is urged, that it must be false'.[54] In consequence, a court martial was promptly ordered; like the inquiry, it comprised exclusively of Indian officers, some of whom came up from Delhi.[55] The six Muslim and nine Hindu officers heard the evidence for three days in the large mess-hall of the Carabineers, which functioned as courtroom. A British officer described the scene: 'After their first arraignment, all pleading "not guilty," they were allowed to sit on the ground. It was curious to watch their faces – some, especially the older soldiers, men who had seen and done good service, and wore several medals, looking worn and anxious; others sullen and apparently unconcerned, and, native-like, trusting to fate'.[56] But fate was not with the eighty-five men, and by fourteen votes to one they were sentenced to ten years' hard labour on 8 May. The judges requested that Major-General Hewitt, as the supreme authority, should take into consideration the good character of the men and the fact that they had been misled. But the Major-General dismissed this recommendation outright, as 'There has been no acknowledgement of error, no expression of regret, no pleading for mercy'.[57] The sentences of eleven of the men were, however, reduced to five years on account of their youth. The skirmishers were then marched back to the old hospital where they were held under a guard of HM 60th Rifles.[58]

As the inquiries were going on, the unrest kept simmering among the troops at Meerut. When a group of artillery recruits refused to accept cartridges, they were merely dismissed from the army, as they had not yet passed the drill and were thus not fully subject to army regulations. With the troopers of the 3rd BLC in jail for refusing cartridges, new recruits at the station had no choice but to follow suit if they wanted to be accepted amongst the native troops. The British officer in charge recognised this, and noted that 'their conduct was the result of no thoughtless or sudden resolution, but had been well considered and determined on'.[59] There were a few further murmurs among the remaining recruits following this incident, but apart from a few fires in the lines of the 3rd BLC, nothing further happened.[60] Major-General Hewitt, however, did not think that the disaffection had spread beyond the ranks of 3rd BLC and reported as much to the headquarters at Simla on 7 May.[61] Even amongst the locals, no trouble was expected, and according to the native Deputy Collector, 'up to the 8th of May, when some *sowars* were imprisoned for disobedience, no danger was anticipated'.[62]

## 'The threat was treated by us all with an indignant disbelief'

In the very early morning of Saturday 9 May 1857, the entire garrison of
Meerut was paraded to hear the sentences of the eighty-five men read out. The
troops were lined up on the parade ground, forming three sides of a square
with the prisoners in the middle.[63] No chances were taken and the artillery
and British regiments, HM 60th Rifles and HM 6th Dragoon Guards, stood
facing each other with the native regiments squeezed in between them. The
British troops had furthermore been provided with live ammunition, as
opposed to the native regiments: the 11th and 20th BNI, and the remainder
of the 3rd BLC, which was dismounted.[64] Both Major-General Hewitt and
Brigadier-General Wilson were present along with their staff.

MacNabb later described the despondent scene at which he was present:
'We reached the parade at 5, and there *stood* for 2 hours and more, while
the sentence was being read, and the irons put on. Didn't my long back ache
neither! It was luckily a cloudy morning or we would have been grilled.'[65]
Once the sentences had been read out the eighty-five men were stripped of
their uniforms and boots to have leg-irons fitted on them, one by one. During
the painfully slow procedure, the 'troops stood motionless, their nerves at
the highest tension, while the felon shackles were being methodically and of
necessity slowly hammered on the ankles of the wretched criminals, each in
turn loudly calling on his comrades for help, and abusing, in fierce language,
now their colonel, now the officers who composed the court-martial, now
the Government'.[66] There was no response from the rest of the native troops,
who stood 'in sullen silence' while their comrades were shackled, though a
few whose relatives were among the condemned wept audibly.[67] Some of the
prisoners threw their boots at Lieutenant-Colonel Smyth in frustration as they
were finally marched away, while others blessed their troop commanders.[68]
One of the convicted men proudly proclaimed: 'I have been a good *sepoy*,
and would have gone anywhere for the service, but I could not forsake my
religion.'[69] Following the parade, the self-deluding Hewitt reported to the
army headquarters that 'The remainder of the Native troops are behaving
steady and soldierlike.'[70]

Later in the afternoon of 9 March, some of the officers of the 3rd BLC
went to the new jail to give the men their final pay and say goodbye to the
troopers who had served under them. The visit made a big impression on
the young Lieutenant Gough, commanding the second troop:

We found our men imprisoned in one large ward: at first they seemed sullen or impassive, until it entered their comprehensions that it was all a sad reality, that they were now being paid up and discharged from an honourable service, into which as it were they had been born … Once they began to realise all they were losing, and the terrible future before them, they broke down completely. Old soldiers, with many medals gained in desperately fought battles for their English masters, wept bitterly, lamenting their sad fate, and imploring their officers to save them from their future; young soldiers, too, joined in, and I have seldom, if ever, in all my life, experienced a more touching scene.[71]

If many of the native troops had lost faith in the British Government, they were still attached to their regiments and those of the junior officers who maintained close relations with the men. The notion of a regimental brotherhood at times included British officers, and Gough's depiction of the imprisoned men being paid up reflects the extent of mutual friendship and sense of loyalty that prevailed at some levels within the army. A number of the officers of the 3rd BLC felt genuinely sorry for the fate of their 'poor 3rd' and MacNabb commented on the harshness of the sentence: 'They could not have hit upon a more severe punishment as it is much worse to them than death. It is in fact 10 years of living death. They will never see their wives and families, they are degraded, and one poor old man who has been 40 years in the regiment, and would have got his pension, is now thrown back the *whole* of his service.'[72]

And so the affair seemed to have been settled and the clouds of unrest passed. Following the parade, Brigadier-General Wilson, commanding the artillery, wrote to his wife with relief: 'So ends this business. I expected 4 or 5 of them would have been hanged, but I am not very sorry that it was otherwise, as I would have had a very unpleasant and disagreeable duty to superintend. I hope we shall have no more of this feeling here.'[73] A large part of the Brigadier-General's conjugal correspondence, however, concerned the demise of their flower-garden, the health and behaviour of his horses, and how a bearer might have absconded with two towels.[74] The entire cartridge issue was undoubtedly regarded as a cause of annoyance but hardly of any real concern.

Amongst the local population, it was a different matter. In an eerie echo of Berhampore, it was rumoured on 9 May that the European troops would seize control of the magazines of the *sepoy* regiments. Many locals 'fully expected a serious disturbance on this occasion, and that the Goojurs of the neighbouring villages, and bad characters generally, were ready in thousands to take advantage of it, and *plunder the city*. But all went off quietly, and the crisis was evidently considered to be past [italics in original].'[75] One Indian clerk was warned by a relative that the *sepoys* would mutiny and he later stated that 'I believed this, until finding that nothing occurred, I concluded the report was groundless.'[76]

Hervey Greathed, for one, was only waiting for something to happen. He had been away on an official matter and was to have returned on 10 May. When he learned that the sentences of the court martial would be passed, however, he cut his trip short and made sure to be back with his wife in Meerut on 9 May.[77] That evening, the Greatheds nevertheless attended dinner at Colonel Custance's along with the newly arrived Colonel Finnis of the 11th BNI, Lieutenant Eckford of the Engineers, and others. Seated around the dinner table and in the comfortable knowledge that European troops were nearby, the assembled guests could more easily pretend that everything was alright. When Elisa Greathed mentioned that placards had been seen in the city 'calling upon all true Mussulmans to rise and slaughter the English', it was simply dismissed as immaterial. As she later recalled, 'the threat was treated by us all with an indignant disbelief'.[78] Yet under the assumed façade of peaceful normality, her husband must have been tense.

While the Greatheds were dining with the infantry officers, Lieutenant Gough of the 3rd BLC had retired for the day and was resting in his bungalow in the cavalry lines. A native officer from Gough's troop suddenly turned up asking to talk to him on the pretext of making up the accounts. The actual purpose of this late visit soon appeared: the officer warned Gough that 'the men had determined to rescue their comrades, and that the Native guard over the gaol had promised to help them'.[79] Gough immediately informed Lieutenant-Colonel Smyth and Brigadier-General Wilson, but they were incredulous and reproved the young Lieutenant for paying attention to such idle rumours.[80]

The commanders would have done well to pay heed to the warning. During the afternoon of 9 May, several native troops from Meerut travelled down to Delhi by the *dak gharry* (mail-coach) and went straight to the lines of the 38th Bengal Native Infantry; this struck their officer as peculiar, as the native troops rarely travelled by *dak*.[81] These men probably left Meerut shortly after the parade in the morning; now they were the first to spread the news of the sentences of the eighty-five skirmishers. The native news-writer Jat Mal later stated: 'Letters came in from Meerut on Sunday

[10 May], bringing intelligence that 82 soldiers had been imprisoned, and that a serious disturbance was to take place in consequence. Owing to this the guards at the gate of the palace [belonging to the 38th BNI] made no secret of their intentions, but spoke openly of what they expected to occur, which was that some of the troops after mutinying at Meerut would come over to Delhi.'[82]

The garrisons at Delhi, Meerut and Ambala did maintain close links of communication due to their geographic proximity, and at Delhi, the police officer Mainodin stated that 'Information of the behaviour of the different regiments was widely circulated by the press, in a native newspaper published at Umballa.'[83] In the Mughal capital, the *sepoys* were thus well acquainted with the events at the nearby stations. According to Ahsan Ullah Khan, the royal physician, 'the *Sepoys* used to talk among themselves about the burning of the houses at Ambala, coupling the circumstances with the greased cartridges and avowing their determination not to use them.'[84] Later it emerged that 'some one in the magazine at Delhi had been sending circulars to all the Native regiments [at Meerut], to the effect that the cartridges prepared in the Magazine had been smeared with a composition of fat and that they were not to believe their European Officers, if they said anything in contradiction of it'.[85] With all ammunition used at Ambala and Meerut first passing through the magazine at Delhi, a person stationed there would be in a unique position to pass on reports of polluted cartridges. Apart from the letters circulating between the various *sepoy* regiments spread out across the subcontinent, there were accordingly also more tight-knit regional networks of communication.

The pre-existing plan amongst the native troops at Delhi and Meerut extended only so far as a mutual understanding, as Ahsan Ullah Khan later explained: 'I heard a few days before the outbreak from some of the *Sepoys* of the Gate of the Palace [belonging to the 38th BNI], that it had been arranged in case greased cartridges were pressed upon them, that the Meerut Troops were to come here, where they would be joined by the Delhi Troops …'.[86] Following the parade on 9 May, some of the troopers of the 3rd BLC at Meerut evidently contemplated freeing their comrades and fleeing to Delhi, where there would be no British troops, but rather *sepoys* whose sympathy they could rely on.[87] Whether this course of action involved more than a handful of *sowars* must remain unknown; the expectation that there would be an attempt to free the prisoners was at any rate reported both in Meerut and at Delhi after the parade on 9 May.

# 7

## Alarm at Ambala

At Ambala, Major-General Sir Henry Barnard appears to have taken the trouble there rather more seriously than had Major-General Anson. At the end of April, during the height of the incendiary attacks, the Deputy Commissioner at Ambala, Mr Forsyth, was entrusted with the task of making special enquiries into the fires and dissatisfaction among the *sepoys*. As Forsyth described it, 'It was [Barnard's] particular desire that the inquiry should form the subject of no public report, and the information received from time to time was forwarded by him privately to the Commander-in-Chief.'[1] The only way to do so was to acquire native informants and the *kotwal* or chief police officer, acting on Forsyth's orders, managed to convince a Sikh *sepoy* of the 5th BNI to gather intelligence. For the civil authorities to utilise a *sepoy* as an informant was quite extraordinary, and it was with great circumspection that Forsyth reported to Barnard that 'I do not like at present to go further into the cause of these fires as I am conducting a secret, and I must say very difficult and delicate inquiry, which I trust will lead to very satisfactory results … I can only at present state that the investigation is being conducted with all the energy and secrecy which I can bring to bear.'[2]

The initial information provided by the informant corroborated what Martineau had already discovered: that there were cliques among the *sepoys* who held meetings that were kept secret from the majority of the men, and that the Muslim and Hindu *sepoys* were united in their opposition to the cartridges, which they considered as 'tampering with their religion'.[3] The native troops were furthermore said to have resolved that when the order was given for them to use the cartridges, 'every bungalow in the station should be in flames!'[4] A week into May, the intelligence assumed a very specific and more menacing character; by way of the *sepoy*, Forsyth was informed that 'a general rising of the *sepoys*' was planned.[5] As part of this conspiracy, the two native infantry regiments would seize the magazines, the cavalry would take the guns and the *syces* or grooms of HM 9th Lancers would hamstring the horses, thus effectively sabotaging the European cavalry.[6] The Kotwal also reported to Forsyth that a *pandit* in the local bazaar had told him that, according to astrological calculations, 'blood would be shed' within a week, at Delhi, Meerut or Ambala.[7] These warnings were immediately passed on to Anson via Barnard, but as the British officers of the regiments at Ambala remained confident of the loyalty of their *sepoys*, the intelligence was dismissed.[8]

The incendiaries finally seemed to have come to an end, and at the very beginning of May, Major-General Barnard was highly optimistic in his assessment of the situation at the Ambala depot: 'I have no reason to accuse the Sipahi of causing these fires – no overt act has been elicited, and no instance of insubordination has occurred. The musket practice has been resumed with apparent good will and zeal. I have frequently attended it myself, and I will answer for it that no ill feeling exists in these detachments.'[9] The level of self-delusion in certain quarters of the British command was truly staggering. Many of the signs of unrest were either ignored or played down in order to present a more appealing impression of the state of affairs, and to avoid casting aspersions on those in charge. Others, however, saw things only too clearly. On 5 May 1857, Martineau wrote to Becher concerning the continued refusal to grant him a court of inquiry, which could have proved that the real state of the army was 'as bad as can be'.[10] The letter is one of the most remarkable documents that preceded 10 May:

> We make a grand mistake in supposing that because we dress, arm and drill Hindustani soldiers as Europeans, they become one bit European in their feelings and ideas. I see them on parade for say two hours daily, but what do I know of them for the other 22?
>
> What do they talk about in their lines, what do they plot? For all I can tell I might as well be in Siberia.
>
> I know that at the present moment an unusual agitation is pervading the ranks of the entire native army, but what it will result in, I am afraid to say. I can detect the near approach of the storm, I can hear the moaning hurricane, but I can't say how, when, or where it will break forth. Let us look our position calmly in the face[;] we are a small body dotted over the face of the land, entirely unsuspicious and unprepared. Sir Charles Metcalfe once wrote that he never

went to bed feeling quite certain that he might not have his throat cut before morning.

If he could write so 25 years ago I am justified in feeling so now. Why, whence the danger, you say. Everywhere far and near, the army under some maddening impulse, are looking out with strained expectation for something, some unseen invisible agency has caused one common electric thrill to run thro' all.

I don't think they know themselves what they will do, or that they have any plan of action except of resistance to invasion of their religion and their faith.

But, good God! Here are all the elements of combustion at hand, 100,000 men, sullen, distrustful, fierce, with all their deepest and inmost sympathies, as well as worst passions, roused, and we thinking to cajole them into good humour by patting them on the back, saying what a fool you are for making such a fuss about nothing. They no longer believe us, they have passed out of restraint and will be off at a gallop before long.

If a flare up from any cause takes place at one station, it will spread, and become universal, then what means have we for putting it down?

You can view the position more coolly in the Himalayas doubtless than I in the plains in May, and you would like a false prophet to cry to you 'peace, peace,' when I declare there is no peace.

As for myself, as soon as I can get away I start for Futtehgurg, my duty is with my regiment to try to keep it in order. I have some influence with the men, perhaps more than any other officer, and I hope I may succeed, but, if I fail, what then?

No passions stir in the human mind so strongly as religious animosity, and this may yet become a war of races.

Mahomedanism & Paganism (strange union) combine against Christianity, that is, barbarism, retrogression against progress, civilisation, and humanity. Who can doubt the result, but at what sacrifices may not the end be attained, who will survive to witness it?

Well, call me an alarmist, call me a coward if you choose, I calmly await the opening scene of the drama and prophecy, and if it will not be melodramatic enough to make all the world stare, I am vastly mistaken. Any way, I am ever yours sincerely

E. M. Martineau

Martineau could not then have known how painfully accurate his assessment of the situation was, nor how soon the 'flare-up' would happen. He was fortunate enough not to make it back to his regiment at Fategarh before he, and everybody else, was overtaken by the sudden turn of events. 'At Simla … men in high office declared me a troublesome alarmist and joked about the coming mutiny,' Martineau later recalled, 'whilst at Umballa, amidst the open dissatisfaction of the 5th and 60th Bengal Native Infantry we continued our rifle practice [until] the close of the prescribed course, and in the first week of May we all separated to return to our prospective corps, most of us alas! never to meet again.'[11]

Early in the morning of 10 May, the *sepoys* of the 5th and 60th BNI rushed out of their lines at Ambala, broke into the bells-of-arms and seized their weapons, and at the same time the guard of the treasury, composed of men of the 60th BNI, took up arms.[12] As soon as Major-General Barnard was informed of this, he ordered HM 9th Lancers and the horse artillery to prepare, and he then proceeded to the parade ground along with his staff. The *sepoys* were all in a state of excitement, and some of them 'had loaded, and were actually pointing their muskets at their officers'.[13] They threatened to shoot their officers if the European cavalry and artillery approached. HM 9th Lancers were all ready to move and an officer later recalled that 'If our men had had the chance to go in at them, they would have made short work of them, they are so enraged at having so much night-work lately, in consequence of the fires, which are all attributed to the *sepoys*.'[14] Barnard and the British officers, however, managed to defuse the situation, and after an hour-long stand-off, the *sepoys* started to lodge their arms and gradually returned to their lines. The *Subadar* of the 60th BNI was thought to be the main instigator of the affair, and according to Forsyth, 'It was too plain that he had acted on a concerted plan, which, if carried out, would have caused the loss of our treasury.'[15]

The British chaplain at Ambala believed that much more than just the treasury could have been lost that day. According to Cave-Browne, it had long been rumoured that the *sepoys* had plotted an attack on the Europeans at Ambala while they were attending church service.[16] The old church, however, was situated between the barracks of HM 9th Lancers and the artillery, and was therefore not well suited to such a surprise attack. As it happened, a new church was then being built, which was located in the vicinity of the lines of the 5th and 60th BNI and therefore presented a much more susceptible target. The service for 10 May was planned to have taken place in the new church, but was relocated to the old one at the very last moment, thus ruining the rumoured plot. When, later in the day, a *sepoy* of the 60th BNI was confined by his officer for inciting to mutiny, his comrades threatened to rescue him

1 Native recruits are turned into *sepoys* (*Illustrated London News*, 1857).

2 *Sepoys* practising with the new Enfield rifle (G. F. Atkinson).

3 The secret distribution of *chapattis* (*Narrative of the Indian Revolt*, 1858).

4 The *sepoys* refuse to move against Mangal Pandey
(H. Gilbert, *The Story of the Indian Mutiny*, 1916).

5 The execution of a *sepoy* in early 1857
(Thomas Frost, *Complete Narrative of the Mutiny in India*, 1858).

6 A fanciful depiction of the disarmament of the 19th Bengal Native Infantry at
Barrackpore (Charles Ball, *The History of the Indian Mutiny*).

7  A typical British station in India (G. F. Atkinson, *Curry and Rice*, 1859).

8  The Sudder Bazaar in Meerut, early twentieth century
(from collection of KAW).

9  The death of Colonel Finnis (*Narrative of the Indian Revolt*, 1858).

10  A bungalow is attacked by the *sepoys* at Meerut
(*Narrative of the Indian Revolt*, 1858).

11  The massacre at Meerut (Frost).

12  Europeans in hiding from the rebels (Ball).

13 A view of Delhi in 1857 (Ball).

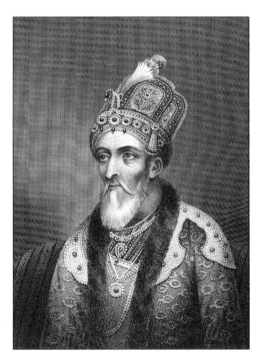

14 The Mughal Emperor
Bahadur Shah (Ball).

15 The massacre of Europeans by Indian rebels. The uniforms and architecture suggest that this image is actually based on a scene from a European conflict (Ball).

16 The capture of Bahadur Shah by Captain Hodson (Ball).

and an outbreak seemed imminent. But the *sepoys* 'had been already baffled and disconcerted that morning; they lost heart, and gave in. The plot had thus been unconsciously counteracted, the *emeute* [outbreak] proved abortive, and Umballa was for the present safe.'[17]

It is possible that news of the sentencing of the eighty-five skirmishers at Meerut had reached Ambala by 10 May and that the *sepoys* expected the same fate to befall them. Ever since the first signs of disaffection at Barrackpore in February, there had been loose talk amongst the *sepoys* of mutinying and killing their officers. Such notions might thus have been acted upon in the spur of the moment following the alarming report of the severe punishment meted out to *sepoys* who stood by their faith and rejected the cartridges. The precedent set by the skirmishers of the 3rd BLC implicitly forced all other native troops to act accordingly, lest they be accused of cowardice and collaboration with the British.

The authorities took a surprisingly lenient view of the affair, but then news of the occurrences elsewhere on 10 and 11 May had not yet reached Ambala. Major-General Barnard simply informed the men of the 5th and 60th BNI that he was satisfied by the fact that they had (eventually) returned to their lines, and stated that their misconduct would be disregarded.[18] The incident was never fully investigated but the extant accounts, however brief, do suggest that it bore more than a passing resemblance to the earlier panic at Berhampore when the 19th BNI took up arms in late February. Colonel Mitchell of the 19th BNI had been severely criticised for taking a soft line with the *sepoys* then, and his military career suffered on account of this. It is not unreasonable to suppose that Barnard and the other British authorities at Ambala afterwards downplayed the nature of the event as it reflected poorly on their ability to control their Indian troops. The details of the bloodless mutiny of the 5th and 60th BNI at Ambala on 10 May will probably never be fully known, but it seems certain that the situation could very easily have escalated. Had this been the case, the course of events might have been very different.

# 8

## The Outbreak

'Sunday, the 10th of May,' Mrs Greathed later recalled, 'dawned in peace and happiness.'[1] Whatever unrest had troubled them the previous night was largely forgotten as the British community of Meerut gathered for the morning service at St John's Church in the European lines. Gough and MacNabb drove to church together, and Gough chided his newly arrived friend for wearing an alpaca frock-coat with the wrong type of lace, which was certain to be noticed by their colonel.[2] The Greatheds sat close to the two young officers, and after the service they chatted for a while before they all went their own ways. Most returned to the shade and coolness of their respective bungalows.[3] While MacNabb went to spend the day with some friends in the artillery lines, Gough later recalled how:

> The day for me was passed as many a careless youngster even now spends the long hot-weather Sunday (for in the middle of May the days are both long and hot). I had many ponies to look after, both my own and my chum Sanford's; and I had several tame pets, amongst them two bears and a leopard: one bear, however, had lately become too savage to be much of a playfellow, and I had been obliged to shoot him, so I amused myself with the other.[4]

If everything seemed quiet in the numbing heat of the afternoon of 10 May, the atmosphere in Meerut outside the confines of the European bungalows was tense. The parade on the previous day had apparently deeply affected the native troops at the station. When the Major of the 20th BNI asked a *havildar* why the *sepoys* of his regiment looked so upset and were weeping, the answer was simply: 'these troopers were comrades'.[5] The sense of humiliation suffered by the eighty-five men during the hour-long parade on 9 May is likely to have had a profound impact on the remaining native troops. The eighty-five had stood fast and maintained their refusal of the cartridges, while their comrades had looked on in despondent apathy. After months of speculation about the greased cartridges, the moment had come and gone, leaving the *sepoys* and *sowars* in despair. The eighty-five were brave men who had steadfastly opposed their British commanders, while the rest had become the stooges of the Christian *sahibs*. Punishing the eighty-five did not have the intended effect of silencing the few recalcitrant voices amongst the troops – quite the opposite. All the British command at Meerut had achieved was to instil a mortal fear in the native regiments. Now, they had tangible proof of what would happen to them if they refused the cartridges.

The old story of ground bone-dust mixed in the flour had resurfaced during the inquiry. Now rumours circulated that batches of polluted *atta* had reached the European bazaar.[6] While the *sepoys* continued to use flour, the story obviously added to the general suspicion of the British. When the British signallers at Meerut telegraphed their colleagues at Delhi, they mentioned the excitement caused by the sentences and stated that the eighty-five skirmishers were to be blown from guns.[7] When such exaggerated stories were being related even by British signallers, it is hardly surprising that wilder rumours were being circulated amongst the *sepoys* and the local population. Only a few days before, the men had been officially informed of the execution of Isuree Pandey – yet another apparent example of the manner in which the British treated their own *sepoys*.[8]

There was a tangible sense of despair; there had been a general understanding amongst the *sepoys* that if any cartridges were forced upon them, the entire regiment should refuse them. This is what had happened on 23 April. Now the crucial sense of solidarity was shattered as the eighty-five men who had stayed true to the agreement were imprisoned. Although emotions were running high, there was no consensus on what they should do. On Sunday afternoon, a number of the troopers of the 3rd BLC stated their intention to present a petition to Lieutenant-Colonel Smyth the next morning, asking for the release of their comrades, and 'if the Government would employ them again, or let them go to their homes free, they would be willing to obey any orders whatever might be given them'.[9] As far as these troopers were concerned, there was still the possibility that things might come to a peaceful resolution.

But others amongst the 3rd BLC had already passed beyond the stage of negotiation. Some time during the afternoon of 10 May, the telegraph line between Meerut and Delhi was cut, in the vicinity of the former station. The telegraph lines ran southward out of Meerut, just a few hundred yards from the barracks of the 3rd BLC and some *sowars* were later reported as having claimed that they had 'broken the telegraph'.[10] The cutting of telegraph lines was an obvious act of sabotage directed against the authorities. In this sense, it was similar in character to the numerous cases of arson that ravaged many of the military stations during the preceding months, including Meerut. The cutting of the telegraph lines was not systematic, and the lines running by a different route to Agra remained intact until much later in the evening of 10 May.[11] The warning given to Gough the previous evening nevertheless reflected just how desperate the native troops were – they were openly talking of taking up arms and freeing their imprisoned comrades.

Most of the local inhabitants of Meerut expected that something would happen on 10 May, and the British noticed that a number of native servants were absent on Sunday morning.[12] The old Indian servant of the postmaster had begged his mistress not to let the children out of the house before they went to church in the morning – his 'earnest entreaties' were ignored.[13] Similarly, a Kashmiri girl who resided with the surgeon Dr Smith, probably as his *bibi* or mistress, was told by another prostitute that 'the troops would mutiny and massacre the Europeans'.[14] She related this to Smith, who dismissed the warning, saying that the girl 'always brought him bazaar reports void of foundation'.[15] Such reports were, of course, no more specific than the warning Gough had received the night before, but they were nevertheless suggestive of the general atmosphere.

In the Sudder Bazaar, the *sowars* of the 3rd BLC furthermore had to suffer the taunts of both the infantry and the local prostitutes for their apathy in allowing their comrades to be imprisoned. The prostitutes were said to have been jeering at the troopers: 'Your brethren have been ornamented with these anklets [shackles] and incarcerated; and for what? Because they would not swerve from their creed; and you, cowards as you are, sit still indifferent to their fate. If you had an atom of manhood in you, go and release them.'[16]

## 'Fly, sahib, fly at once, the Regiments are in open mutiny'

As the authorities later noted, a number of rumours had been circulating at the station following the parade on 9 May: 'A note was received by the Clerk of the Judge's Court, about 6 ½ P.M., from his brother in Cantonments, saying he had better come home, as there was a disturbance going on in the Cantonments; the Rifles having come to take the native Magazines. There was no foundation for this; all was quiet, but the rumour gained strength, evidently with another, that 2,000 fetters were being forged for the native soldiers.'[17] On the afternoon of 10 May, in the tense atmosphere of the Sudder Bazaar, this new and more alarming rumour was causing a stir: the iron shackles would be ready in two nights and one day.[18] The report had no foundation whatsoever, but seemed to confirm what every Indian soldier at Meerut feared: what had happened to the skirmishers would happen to them. Either they would be forced to accept the cartridges, with perhaps disastrous consequences for their social status, or they would be imprisoned by the British at the point of the bayonet. From the exalted status of a proud soldier of the Company Raj, the *sepoy* now seemed to have become its lowly slave, called upon to risk his caste and religion, or be jailed like a common criminal.

In an eerie repetition of the sequence of events at Berhampore, the report of the 2,000 shackles was further embellished by the alarming news that HM 60th Rifles and artillery were coming down to take control of the magazine of the 20th BNI and thereby leave the *sepoys* defenceless. The simmering unrest immediately rose to a fever pitch. The *sepoys* were seized by panic and started making their way back to the lines to warn their comrades. An unperturbed *havildar* of the 20th BNI, who was whiling away time at a peddler's shop, suddenly realised that *sepoys* of both infantry regiments were running pell-mell out of the bazaar. He was then informed by a drummer of his regiment that 'he had just heard from a cook boy of the rifles [HM 60th], that the artillery and rifles were coming to take away the arms and ammunition of the native regiments'.[19]

The soldiers were calling out that the 'Europeans' were coming, and the cry was picked up by the motley crowd of civilians who followed closely behind them. The crowd consisted mainly of the local traders and labourers who were lounging about in the bazaar. The traders and inhabitants of the Sudder Bazaar at Meerut catered to the specific needs of the *sepoys* and were thus finely attuned to the issues of dietary requirements and equally sensitive to any perceived infringements of the status of the troops – and possibly themselves.[20] The British had full control of the provisions made available for the *sepoys* in the cantonment bazaars and even supplied the troops with prostitutes of Brahmin, Rajput or equally 'respectable' background.[21] The army had thus created an entire social community of camp followers, peddlers, and merchants whose livelihood, and social standing, had become closely interwoven with the fate of the *sepoys*. The panic in the bazaar thus affected *sepoys* and civilians alike. Believing they were about to be attacked, this highly volatile crowd oscillated between fear and anger. Some of the locals actually came down to the infantry lines armed with swords and sticks; pushed too hard, they were ready to strike back.[22]

The *sepoys* had taken service with the East India Company on the condition that their employer would safeguard their ritual status and not interfere in any religious practices. The introduction of the greased cartridges, whether real or not, apparently constituted a direct breach of contract as far as the *sepoys* were concerned, and many no longer felt obligated to serve the British. Still worse, entire companies were being imprisoned or dismissed from service, with little sympathy or concern for their fate, probably confirming the *sepoys*' worst fears arising from the proposed reorganisation of the army following the General Enlistment Act. With rumours of an impending attack by British troops, the frustration and alienation felt by many *sepoys* seems to have turned to outright hatred, and they responded as they had been trained to do.

The report that the European troops were coming immediately spread in the native lines as the agitated *sepoys* gathered outside their huts and on the parade ground.[23] Captain Taylor and a handful of British officers of the 20th BNI, along with a few native orderlies, soon arrived at the lines. Since they did not expect any serious disturbance, they went unarmed.[24] The situation was still relatively calm at this stage, and the officers simply talked with the agitated men as they walked through the lines, reassuring them that no one would take over the magazine.[25] The bazaar crowd, however, was completely blocking the road leading to the magazine and was swarming around the building. Taylor ordered the grenadiers of the regiment to drive off the crowd, but the soldiers remained passive and instead the drummers and musicians of the 20th BNI managed to push the crowd back with sticks. A few *sepoys* of the guards, who were the only troops present carrying arms, began to steal away, but the British officers stopped them. Captain Taylor and the others promised the men that, as long as they remained quiet, the magazine would remain under their control. Through their combined efforts, the officers managed to convince the *sepoys* of the 20th BNI to return to their lines.[26]

At this moment a *sowar* galloped on to the parade ground and with raised hand called out that the British troops were coming, and that if they *sepoys* intended to do something, they had to do it at once. Again the cry of alarm was picked up by the crowds from the bazaar, who remained lingering on the outskirts of the parade ground, exacerbating the general confusion caused by the dramatic rallying call of the *sowar*. This was the final straw for the *sepoys* of the 20th BNI, who had at that very moment been on the verge of complying with their officers. Finally giving in to their fears, they rushed to the bells-of-arms and the magazine, breaking them open, and armed themselves. The British officers tried to hold back their men, physically wrenching the weapons from some and punching others, but they could not hold back the hundreds of panicking *sepoys*. As the lines of the 20th BNI descended into chaos, the armed *sepoys* fired their guns into the air and started setting fire to the bungalows, while the shocked officers slowly withdrew.

In the lines of the 11th BNI, the *sepoys* had also gathered on the parade ground and were as agitated as their friends of the 20th BNI just a few hundred yards away. Colonel Finnis and several of the regiment's officers quickly arrived from their bungalows just behind the lines, and though the men were 'violently excited', they managed to keep the situation under control. Finnis tried to reason with the *sepoys* and dispel their fears, but he also ordered the officers to search the lines and make sure none of the men were hiding their arms.[27] By that time, however, the 20th BNI had armed themselves. When they realised that the 11th BNI were not joining them, they moved forwards and opened fire across the parade ground. The *sepoys* of the 11th BNI were in a desperate situation: they were unarmed and, according to one of the officers present, the men 'entreated Colonel Finnis to let them have their arms, saying they would stand by us and drive off the 20th'.[28]

Uncertain of the loyalty of his men, Finnis instead made the bold decision to ride over to the 20th BNI to make them lay down their arms. Ignoring the protestations of his officers, the Colonel rode up and challenged the excited crowd of armed *sepoys*. Brandishing their guns, they told him to leave, and as he seemed to hesitate, someone let off a shot, wounding Finnis' horse. The Colonel belatedly realised the severity of the situation and hastily made his way back to the 11th BNI, closely followed by the disaffected men of the 20th BNI. A *sepoy* of the 20th BNI then ran up and shot Colonel Finnis in the back at close range, and as the officer tumbled to the ground, the *sepoys* charged forward and fired a volley into his prostrate body.[29] This decided the matter. The 11th BNI immediately broke into their bells-of-arms and joined those of the 20th BNI who had only minutes earlier been shooting at them. The 11th BNI had equivocated until Finnis was killed, but as one of their Indian officers later stated, 'Our *sepoys* (fearing from the colonel having been murdered, they would all be hung on the morrow) raised a disturbance.'[30] The 11th BNI was thus forced to mutiny – not because of the greased cartridges, but due to the breakdown of army discipline following the earlier summary trials and dismissals. In the subsequent tumult on the parade ground, the *sepoy* who had fired the first shot at Finnis, and thus sealed the fate of all the troops, was killed by his comrades.[31]

The British officers of the 11th BNI were now forced to beat a hasty retreat. Ensign Phillipps, who had been just next to Finnis when he was shot, later recalled: 'As I mounted my horse, my servant, who was holding him, was knocked over, bullets falling thick as peas. Had not the brutes been such infernally bad shots we would all have perished.'[32] The medical officer of the 11th BNI was at that moment leaving his bungalow just behind the regimental lines:

> I had scarcely got to the gate, when I heard the popping sound of firearms, which I knew at once were loaded with ball-cartridge, and a European non-commissioned officer came running with others towards me from the 11th lines, saying, 'for God's sake, Sir, leave, come to your bungalow, change that dress, and fly.' I walked into my bungalow, and was doffing my uniform; the bullets by this time flying out of the 11th lines into my compound, when the *Havildar-Major* of the 11th rushed into the room, terrified and breathless, and exclaimed, 'fly, sahib, fly at once, the Regiments are in open mutiny, and firing on their officers, and Colonel Finnis has just been shot in my arms.'[33]

With the exception of Colonel Finnis, all the British officers of the 11th BNI miraculously made it to the safety of the European lines. Those of the 20th BNI, however, did not fare so well. Once Finnis had been shot, it seemed as if a magic threshold had been breached and along with the crowd the excited *sepoys* of the 20th BNI now turned against their officers. They knew that none of them could expect any mercy from the authorities: their only hope of survival was to stay together and defeat the British. By killing all their officers, they would leave no one behind to hold them to account, and defeating the invincible Europeans furthermore shored up the solidarity of the *sepoys*. Captain Macdonald and a civilian, Tregear, were shot and killed in the throng of *sepoys* near the magazine, and Captain Taylor had to fight his way through the crowd, at one point knocking down a butcher wielding a sword.[34] The remaining officers of the 20th BNI had retreated into the street leading away from the lines, still desperately trying to hold back their men. But soon the situation became untenable: 'The bullets were flying thickly around them, information was brought of the above murders, and several *sepoys* urged them to leave.'[35] With smoke billowing from the nearby buildings and shots going off everywhere, the confusion was complete; several *sepoys* and Indian officers nevertheless remained loyal and helped their superiors to escape.[36]

Lieutenant Humphrey of the 20th BNI had his horse shot under him as he endeavoured to flee, and lying on the ground he was shot at several times at close range. None of the bullets hit their target, however, and the officer saved his life by hiding in an outhouse nearby.[37] An ensign of the same regiment, who had been shot in the neck, ran through several gardens closely pursued by *sepoys*, until he reached Sudder Street and was picked up by a passing carriage.[38] Captain Taylor and five other officers, unarmed and on foot, escaped together from the lines of the 20th BNI: 'Wherever they moved they were encountered by immense mobs; every street, lane, by-path, and compound was one vast mass of animated villainy, yelling death and destruction to the Feringhees.'[39] They made it to the outhouses of Lieutenant-Colonel Smyth's compound on the other side of Sudder Street but were soon discovered, and as the crowd set fire to their hiding place, they split up. Captain Taylor and two others were caught as they escaped the flames and were cut down, while the remaining three 'took refuge in the temple of Cloacina' (the toilet) and survived.[40]

Lieutenant Gough had been enjoying the calm of the afternoon when the native officer who had warned him of the outbreak the previous night, along with two *sowars*, came to warn him again. Hearing that the infantry were murdering their officers and that the *sowars* of their own regiment were arming themselves, Gough rode down to the infantry lines with his special escort of three loyal troopers:

> These lines, usually a scene of perfect discipline and neatness, with rows of mud barracks neatly thatched, with the quarter-guard ready to turn out, and with groups of well-dressed and happy contented *sepoys* lounging about, were now the scene of the most wild and awful confusion: the huts on fire, the *sepoys* (in each regiment over a thousand strong) having seized their arms and ammunition, dancing and leaping frantically about, calling and yelling to each other, and blazing away into the air and in all directions – absolutely a maddened crowd of fiends and devils, all thirsting for the blood of their officers, and of Europeans generally. I confess I was appalled at the sight, and saw at once it was no place for me: their madness had got the mastery over them, and I was in the extremest peril. The *sepoys* had seen me approaching with my escort, and as I pulled up

in wonder and horror, they shouted to my men to leave me, and began to rush forward, firing as they came. The native officer implored me to turn back; and indeed it was high time, for as I turned to leave, and galloped away, a volley was fired – but fortunately without effect.[41]

Over-dramatic as Gough's account may be, it does suggest the complete chaos that reigned amongst the native troops after they had shot and chased away their officers. The bonds that tied them to the Company had been irrevocably broken.

Even before the shooting broke out in the infantry lines, the rumours had spread to the cavalry lines of the 3rd BLC at the southern end of the parade ground. While the panicking infantry was wavering and confused, the response of some of the *sowars* was more deliberate: rather than turning on their officers, some forty troopers immediately set out to release their comrades locked up in the new jail.[42] According to an Indian eyewitness, they were 'bare headed, with drawn swords', and as they passed through the city, they caused great alarm amongst the local inhabitants.[43] Their departure left the cavalry lines in a state of confusion as the remainder of the *sowars* were caught by the same panic and indecision that had affected the infantry with such a deadly outcome. Across the entire lines of all the native troops, fires broke out at about the same time.

Keeping in mind that no greased cartridges were ever distributed to the native troops at Meerut, it is nevertheless noteworthy that the sepoys readily used their old weapons, and the ungreased cartridges that went with them, against the British once they broke out in mutiny. It should be remembered that on the parade of 24 April it was blank ungreased cartridges for their old smoothbore carbines that the eighty-five skirmishers of the 3rd BLC refused. It thus appears as a glaring inconsistency that their comrades should feel no compulsion against using the very same weapons with live ungreased cartridges during the subsequent outbreak. The point is, however, that the sepoys' rejection of cartridges was largely situational and determined by context. The actual cartridges, old or new, greased or ungreased, were not as important as the circumstances under which the troops were handling them. The same cartridge might thus appear suspicious when handed out by the British, but uncontentious when needed to fight them.

# 9

# Meerut Ablaze

After the *sepoys* and *sowars* had run to their respective lines, the Sudder Bazaar was teeming with unrest. At the time there were a number of British soldiers walking quietly around in the Sudder Bazaar, buying a few knick-knacks at the shops. The quietude of the afternoon was broken by the sudden panic amongst the native troops as people started running around. The British were confused and, seeing a crowd running towards the infantry lines, calling 'ayah, ayah', they first thought that a fire had broken out somewhere.[1] The true nature of the unrest was soon revealed as a trooper of the 3rd BLC rode through the bazaar and somewhat surprisingly warned the British soldiers to leave immediately.[2]

While focused on the *sepoys*, the rumours of the preceding months nevertheless concerned all Indians and had created a deep sense of insecurity. The *sepoys* were the physical manifestation of British rule and the single most important means by which colonial authority was maintained. The moment the link between the British and the *sepoys* was seen to be severed, the entire social order was thrown into chaos. As the native troops turned against their officers, the East India Company's authority evaporated. This sudden implosion of colonial rule and total breakdown of order allowed the locals to act on their disaffection and grievances. This assumed an extremely violent form as fear turned to rage, and the crowd in the bazaar vented their anger on the British troops thought to be the instruments of the disarmament, humiliation, and mistreatment of the *sepoys*.

Realising the danger of the situation, the British soldiers ran towards the *kotwali* in the heart of the bazaar, where there was a guard of *sepoys*. Expecting to find protection behind the red uniforms of the *sepoys*, the British were horrified when the guards turned their weapons and shot at them. Soon the British soldiers found themselves running a deadly gauntlet through the narrow lanes of the bazaar, beaten by sticks and pelted with stones by furious crowds at every turn. One artillerist saved himself by fighting off the crowd armed with just a brick, while his companion was about to be cut down by a policeman when an old Indian intervened and held the attacker back, thus allowing him to escape.[3]

Gunner Hugh McCartney later described his escape from the Sudder Bazaar, where he and two of his friends had been spending the afternoon:

> We then ran, my two companions, who were behind, were knocked down, I got to an open spot clear of the streets, when two parties of natives tried to stop me, one party on my right, headed by two policemen, attacked me. The policemen with drawn swords, and a man with a stick came forward. I had a stick in my hand, I put it up to save my head, but it was cut through by a blow from a sword, and my cap also cut, I received two wounds on the head, I then struck a man a blow, and tried to wrest a stick out of his hand, when I was struck senseless, and left for dead; on coming to my senses, I got over a wall into a compound, and there found a dragoon, who had been wounded, and also three artillery men, I received four wounds on my head, and was severely beaten about the body.[4]

McCartney later made it back to the safety of the British lines, but his two companions were not so lucky – they were cut to pieces by the crowd in the Sudder Bazaar along with several other Europeans.[5]

\*

The tumultuous situation of the bazaar soon spread to other parts of the station and the *tehsildar* saw 'multitudes coming from the sudder into the city, and heard firing', while another local described 'people flying to their houses for protection'.[6] In the confusion and chaos following the initial outbreak, the air was thick with rumours – an Indian clerk later recalled how 'it was noised abroad in the city, that the *sepoys* of the 20th NI, had risen to oppose the Rifles, who had come to deprive them of the charge of the bells of arms, as they feared they would now be dealt with in the same manner that the *sowars* had been, and had murdered Europeans, burnt bungalows, and destroyed property'.[7] As darkness was falling, no one could tell exactly what was really happening; many locals probably believed that the *sepoys* and *sowars* really had defended themselves against the onslaught of the British.

In spite of the complete confusion of the night of 10 May, there were, however, clear patterns in the violence and destruction that swept through Meerut. One notable aspect of the riots that accompanied the outbreak was their distinctively Muslim tenor: 10 May was the fifteenth day of Ramadan, a particularly holy festival for Muslims, during which any perceived infringement or attack on their religion would almost certainly result in an intensely violent response. More importantly, it was supposed to be a time of reverent reflection and peace, which the British had contrived to disrupt. Effectively excluded from any participation in government or access to political power, the urban space provided one of the few outlets through which local Hindu and Muslim communities could publicly express themselves and assert their status in colonial India.[8] This was primarily done through processions during religious festivals, which often led to violent clashes between different communities, and it was apparently such a pattern of ritualised collective behaviour that the largely Muslim crowds resorted to in Meerut on 10 May 1857.

A number of witnesses described the rallying cries of the crowd, including '*Yah! Ali! Ali! Ek nara Haidari*' ('Yeah! Ali! Ali! One shout Haidar')[9] and '*Ali, Ali, aj marlia haie kafron ko*' ('Ali, Ali, today we have taken it upon ourselves to strike the infidels').[10] One of the eighty-five skirmishers of the 3rd BLC later told a comrade that there had been two main groups traversing the city and causing havoc that night: one led by Mahomed Ali Khan and another led by a *maulavi*. Both crowds had been chanting, 'Ali, Ali, our religion has revived' and had assaulted native Christians, particularly those employed by the British.[11] These rallying cries were clearly Shia in character and would normally have accompanied the traditional processions at festivals such as the Muharram or during sectarian clashes.[12] Religious festivals and celebrations were particularly sensitive times, and there was a fine line between religious processions and riots, which sometimes spilled over into one another.[13] The outbreak at Meerut thus constituted a powerful rejection of colonial rule, but because the British were seen simply as Christians, it assumed the form of a sectarian riot. The Government by its actions was believed to be subverting both Hindu and Muslim faiths: anti-British sentiments were thus expressed through the use of religious idioms.

The crowds, which merged with the mutineers and were active in the widespread destruction and violence, were invariably described by the authorities as the 'bazaar rabble', the marginal anti-social elements that even the locals referred to as 'budmashes' or bad characters.[14] While some of them might have matched this description, the majority were in fact

Muslim tradesmen and artisans, semi-skilled workers, and labourers from
the lower rungs of society, amongst whom the presence of butchers (*khaticks*),
weavers (*dureewallas*), and porters was especially notable. Eyewitnesses also
mentioned tanners (Chamars), cooks, and house-stewards (*khansamas*),
servants (*khitmutgars*), grooms (*syces*), watchmen (*chaukidars*), bearers
(*kahars*), grass-cutters, greengrocers (*koonjras*), fishermen, milk-men,
cobblers, and betel-leaf sellers as well as more vaguely designated groups such
as villagers and labourers.[15] A specific urban dynamic informed the spread
of the turmoil. Many in the crowd belonged to specific trades and occupied
specific neighbourhoods and markets in the station and city of Meerut. These
links enabled them to be mobilised quickly. An Indian moneylender looking
out from his rooftop in the native city witnessed the swelling crowds: 'a mob
of bad characters, comprising of mahommedans, pulladars from the gunge
[market], and another of butchers with stones from the goozree [meat stalls],
shouting, Yah Ali, Ali! part of whom went through the Kumboh gate towards
the sudder bazaar, and part to the tehseel [revenue office], great noise and
tumult now arose on all sides, and fires appeared in all directions'.[16]

Due to their profession, Muslim butchers were usually at the forefront of
Hindu–Muslim riots caused by the contentious issue of cow-slaughter, and
they often assumed an aggressive role in the assertion of Muslim community
identity.[17] Muslim weavers were similarly prominent, though for a different
reason: their trade was in drastic decline due to the increasing import of
European textiles and the establishment of mills and factories.[18] It was also
amongst those classes that the reformist Muslim movements, such as that of
Saiyid Ahmad Barelvi, which had emerged during the preceding decades, had
taken strongest root.[19] Saiyid Ahmad's followers were distinctly anti-British
in their views, and this perception of British rule may have affected larger
sections of the lower Muslim classes.

The popular participation in the outbreak at Meerut thus assumed many
of the characteristics of the sectarian riots and violence that broke out in cities
across northern India during the eighteenth and nineteenth centuries. Violent
clashes between local communities, however, were never just about religion.
They were inevitably tied to broader issues concerning access to resources,
or commercial and economic competition, or were brought about by the
intervention of the colonial state. Hindus also participated in the violence
at Meerut, but they did so side by side with Muslims, and one of the *sowars*
of the 3rd BLC was heard calling out: 'Brothers, Hindoos and Mussulmans,
haste and join us, we are going to a religious war. Be assured, we will not harm

those who join us, but fight only against the Government.'[20] The perceived attack on religion created a sense of community in opposition to the British, and made the disorderly crowds of agitated *sepoys*, camp-followers, bazaar traders and artisans coalesce into a coherent group with the common aim of defending their faith and, by implication, their status and social order.

The outbreak was accordingly a pre-emptive attack on the British which derived its legitimacy from the rumour of the impending disarmament of the *sepoys*. The extreme violence that accompanied the riots at Meerut was in part an expression of the moral outrage felt by the *sepoys* and the crowd, and thus assumed a vindictive aspect.[21] As one historian has noted, 'religious violence is intense because it connects intimately with the fundamental values and self-definition of a community'.[22] British rule in India was predicated on the colonial state's complete monopoly on violence, and maintained through the use of force, while everyday interaction was characterised by almost total social segregation between the British and their Indian subjects. The collapse of authority and almost complete inversion of power thus had an immense impact on the *sepoys* and the crowd, who now had complete control over their former rulers. Suddenly empowered, the crowd's fear and awe of the invincible British was no more. The Indian subalterns and servants seized the opportunity to exact bloody revenge on their British masters. All European individuals were seen to represent colonial rule and constituted potential threats. Men, women, and children were attributed with the evil intent of the British Government, as it was perceived, and accordingly the crowd targeted them indiscriminately. Instead of assaulting the British infantry lines and troops, who were allegedly going to disarm the *sepoys*, the crowd turned on the isolated and vulnerable groups of European soldiers and civilians who were within their reach and whom they could attack with impunity. The King's physician at Delhi later claimed that 'Before their defection the native troops had settled it among them to kill all Europeans, including women and children, in every cantonment.'[23] Once the mutiny had begun, the *sepoys* and the crowd would have to eradicate the British completely to leave no witnesses and prevent reprisals. By committing brutal acts of murder, in which all were forced to join in, the crowd could be united through a shared guilt and responsibility. Seemingly mindless killings thus served the purpose of bolstering solidarity and firmly committed everyone to persist in the attack on the British.

The wrath and violence unleashed against the British at Meerut was not simply random and aimless, but in part derived from a well-established repertoire of urban riots.[24] The crowd deliberately targeted official buildings and institutions that symbolised colonial authority, and they thus sought physically to remove the presence of British rule.[25] The attack on the authorities and plunder for personal enrichment became indistinguishable as the crowds pillaged and burned court buildings and revenue offices, and any structures associated with the British and their most important Indian collaborators.[26] There was accordingly an element of redistributive social protest in the widespread pillaging and looting that occurred during the night of 10 May. In several instances *sepoys*, accompanied by the crowd, demanded money from local shop-owners, some of whom managed to buy off the rioters and save their property.[27] Local butchers were stealing bullocks, and one native official ordered his servants to steal grass for his cattle.[28] The poor Muslim crowd not only shared a religious identity, but probably harboured a similar resentment against the rich, and thus turned on the wealthier Hindu merchants and moneylenders, plundering and burning their shops and stores.[29]

Just before sunset, several hundred *sepoys* gathered around the old jail just north of the native city. The head guard of the jail managed to lock them out of the gate into the large compound, but the *sepoys* set fire to the gate by piling up bundles of straw, and soon burst in, freeing all 720 inmates.[30] By releasing the hundreds of local prisoners, the *sepoys* not only added considerably to the general turmoil, but also unleashed an angry and impoverished crowd, intent on plunder and with a strong motivation to turn on the authorities. A native officer of the jail guard of the old prison was later seen leading a large group of freed convicts, and he told them that 'their fetters were cut by the brave *fouj* (army), it were better to do something before going to their prospective homes'.[31] They then proceeded to plunder and burn the nearby bungalow of a British family. According to a native eyewitness, a trooper of the 3rd BLC pointed out the house of Major Williams and 'said that the thuggie officer lives there, let us let lose the prisoners from there also'.[32] After they were freed, these prisoners also joined the crowd. Facing a common enemy, local police, jailers, and inmates all joined in the rioting, and the jail guards, for instance, were seen extorting money from the official treasurer.[33]

The role played by the local *chauprassis* or policemen in the attacks on the British is particularly conspicuous. The institution of the *kotwal* or head of police predated colonial rule, and the *kotwal* and his officers, referred to as either *chauprassis* or *chaukidars*, were deeply involved in the local society from which they themselves were recruited.[34] After the *sepoys* and the crowd merged, many of the local police simply joined in the attack on the British and lent their authority to the outbreak. Some of them thus assumed the leadership of the different crowds; perhaps they felt the need to demonstrate their loyalty by taking the lead in the physical attacks on the former rulers. The *tehsildar*, or native revenue official, on the other hand, answered directly to the British magistrate and was therefore targeted as a collaborator once the disturbances broke out. When a large crowd headed by *sowars* attacked the *tehsil*, the *tehsildar* shot two of them before he had to run for his life, and he spent the rest of the night in hiding.[35]

The Indian Deputy Collector later described the scene as the entire city south of Abu Nullah was engulfed in the riots:

> It was now dark, and fires could be seen raging on all sides. I observed three sowars with drawn swords in their hands coming out of the compound of the Custom House, after setting fire to it, and followed by a crowd of low people shouting 'Yah! Ali! Ali! ek nara Haidari;' amongst them I heard the clanking of iron chains. I heard the sowars saying they had burnt the Cantonments, murdered the Europeans, broken the Electric Telegraph, and overturned the British Rule, and boasting that they had committed these atrocities for the cause of religion.[36]

Such reports not only bolstered support for the mutineers, but also stoked the flames. 'That night,' according to another native official, 'the sowars set it about that no Europeans remained; hearing which the evil disposed having no fear committed great havoc and destruction.'[37] In the confusion of the dark, the horizon lit by distant fires and panicking people running to and fro amidst straying horses and cattle, it seemed as if the world had turned upside down. One Indian clerk remembered how 'it was now rumoured that the bad characters of the city had determined to create as much disturbance and confusion as they might revenge themselves on their enemies, and plunder the rich.'[38] Many of the local elite and wealthier inhabitants of Meerut did not share the general enthusiasm of the crowds, and when the *sowars* galloped through the native city, it 'much alarmed the inhabitants, the respectable portion of whom, fearing the loss of life or wealth, and honour, closed the doors of their houses.'[39] In some cases, the collapse of authority provided the occasion for people to settle personal scores and the so-called 'tuzmabazies' or petty swindlers, who had been released from jail, went looking for the *munshi* of the Dacoity Department who had originally convicted them.[40]

Months of built-up tension, years of increasing resentment, had finally reached a stage when it could no longer be contained and thus came to a violent head on 10 May 1857 as the entire station and city of Meerut rapidly descended into chaos.

## 'The poor old man went nearly mad'

As soon as news of the disturbances in the infantry lines reached Smyth at his bungalow, he ordered the Adjutant, Captain Clarke, to proceed to the lines of the 3rd BLC and take charge there. Smyth himself went in the opposite direction, away from the lines and towards Major-General Hewitt's quarters.[41] Accompanied by his faithful orderlies, including Brijmohan, Smyth had to ride for his life pursued by a crowd of armed natives. Smyth stopped at Greathed's compound on the way, but a servant shut the gate in front of the Lieutenant-Colonel and informed him that his master was out; Smyth eventually reached the safety of the artillery lines, where he joined Wilson and the rest of the command.[42] They had already received warning from an officer of the 11th BNI who had left the infantry lines just before Colonel Finnis was shot. Orders were now given for the artillery, the Carabineers and HM 60th Rifles to assemble and prepare to move out. HM 60th Rifles had been preparing for the church parade when news of the disturbances in the *sepoy* lines reached them, and a company was immediately dispatched to the treasury.[43] Here they took over from the *sepoy* guards, who gave up their arms without a murmur, and the rest of the night the presence of British soldiers meant that the treasury was secure while the surroundings were abandoned to plunder and mayhem.

As the British troops were slowly assembling on the parade ground of the rifles, many of the British civilians were getting ready for church service at 7 p.m. – completely oblivious to the events that were unfolding around them. When the postmaster and his family were leaving for church, for the second time, on the evening of 10 May, their old servant begged them not to go. When they persisted, 'the poor old man went nearly mad, and threw himself on the road before our horses to try to prevent us from leaving the house'.[44] In the end, the old man had to be forcefully removed so that the family could leave. Similar scenes took place in several of the British households as the native servants sought to warn their employers against the disturbances which were by then already well under way.[45]

Elizabeth Muter, the wife of a captain in HM 60th Rifles, was taking in the scenery of the quiet evening, waiting for her husband to bring up the British troops for the church parade:

> The sun was sinking in a blaze of fiery heat that rose hazy and glowing from the baked plain. I drove to church and waited outside the door, expecting every moment to hear the gay march which so strangely heralds the approach of a body of soldiers to divine worship; but – I listened in vain. A dull sound, very different from that I expected, came over the stillness of nature around; but I little heeded the holiday-making in the bazaars, holiday-making, as I then thought it.[46]

She soon found out, however, that what she could hear was not the sound of the natives celebrating Ramadan, and she eventually drove home when she realised that the church service had been cancelled.[47]

While some of the civilians were still disinclined to believe the gravity of the reports, panic soon spread amongst the returning church-goers in the European lines. The postmaster and his family were pulled out of their disbelief by the sight of 'a poor soldier of the European cavalry, whose lines were just across the road from the post-office, run by our back gate with his back cut open, having been mobbed and wounded by the "budmashes" in the Bazaar.'[48] As Elizabeth Muter returned to her house in the buggy, she passed a native crowd pursuing two artillerymen, pelting them with stones, but they paid no attention to her as she turned down the road and reached her own bungalow safely. She was later escorted to the European infantry lines by a sergeant of her husband's regiment.[49]

The *dak*-van going down to Agra left the post office at 6 p.m. but was attacked near the native city. While the driver managed to escape, the mail-bags were plundered and the three British soldiers who were travelling as passengers were dragged out and murdered.[50] Hearing of this, the postmaster's sister, Kate Moore, sent a telegram to her father at Agra around 8 p.m., as they were expecting their aunt to come up with the *dak*-van. The first intimation to the outside world of what was happening was very brief: 'The 20th have mutinied, killed several of their officers, and are setting fire to the Station around us. Don't let aunt start till you hear from me again.'[51] When the telegraph master tried to send another message shortly after, he found that the lines had been cut.[52] With the roads out of Meerut closed off, Moore and her family were soon joined by various travellers stranded at the station. Among those caught up in the situation were the native officers from Delhi who had sat at the court martial of the eighty-five skirmishers and were seeking shelter in the post office. These officers had good reason to fear the wrath of the *sepoys* since they – and not the British – had just sentenced the eighty-five men to ten years' labour. The day he left for Meerut, the officer who presided over the court had actually told his superior in Delhi that 'if I find these men guilty, I will give them the severest punishment in my power'.[53] Now they were scurrying for cover, hiding amongst the *memsahibs* in the safety of the European lines. 'From this time the din grew louder and louder,' Kate Moore recalled, 'and what with the shouting and yelling of the human fiends and the barking and howling of dogs, it seemed as if hell itself were loose on earth. As, too, the evening drew to a close, the firing of houses commenced, and we could see house after house blazing up, till we seemed to be enveloped on three sides by flames.'[54]

The disturbances that enveloped the entire city of Meerut spilt over and encroached upon the perceived safety of the European lines north of the Abu Nullah. While the *sepoys* standing guard at the artillery depot duly saluted the scared Europeans rushing past them, as if nothing had happened, those posted at the Brigadier-General's let off several shots at passing officers before they ran off and joined their comrades to the south. At the School of Instruction, the officers Light and Stubbs with some British troops ordered the two dozen *sepoys* of the guard to surrender; as Stubbs later recalled: 'They brought their muskets to the charge, and one of the bayonets, which were fixed, caught Light in the collar, whereupon the front rank fired and five *sepoys* fell, the rest dropped their arms and bolted.'[55] The two surgeons of the 3rd BLC had been to dinner at Lieutenant-Colonel Smyth's and were returning in a buggy when they were set upon by some *sowars* of their regiment in the eastern parts of the European lines. One was shot and killed while the other survived a deep cut to the face, which left him severely disfigured.[56] The troopers presumably left to join their comrades, but smaller groups of native troops and crowds were seen from time to time in the European lines south of the Mall.[57]

# 10

# The World Turned Upside Down

Around 6 p.m. on 10 May, the wife of Captain Craigie and the sister of Lieutenant Mackenzie, both officers in the 3rd BLC, left the bungalow of the former in a small carriage and drove north along Sudder Street to go to the church.[1] As they passed the compound of the mess of the 3rd BLC, they noticed that all the servants were leaning over the walls, looking down the road to the lines of the 20th BNI. When Mrs Craigie asked what was going on, she was warned to turn back as the infantry had mutinied and there was a fight in the bazaar. The two women now noticed an armed crowd coming towards them and they hastily turned around and drove back to Craigie's bungalow. As they bolted along, they passed a British trooper running for his life, closely pursued by natives trying to hit him with *lathis* and swords. Mrs Craigie stopped the carriage and pulled in the man, and then 'drove off at full speed, followed for some distance by the blood-thirsty wretches, who, being on foot, were soon left behind, not, however, till they had slashed with their *tulwars* in several places the hood of the carriage, in vain efforts to reach the inmates'.[2] They then proceeded on their way and reached Craigie's bungalow safely. Mrs Craigie was the first to inform her husband what had happened. Captain Craigie rushed out, without waiting for his horse, to get to the lines of his regiment a few hundred yards away.

Just up the road, Mackenzie was in his bungalow, which he shared with MacNabb, reading a book 'at the hour when better folk were on their way to church'.[3] His servant came rushing into the room and excitedly told him that a 'hulla-goolla' or riot had broken out and that the *sepoys* were murdering the *sahibs*. Mackenzie did not believe the man, but the sound of shots in the distance was unmistakeable: 'The thought that flashed through my mind was that our men of the cavalry were attacking the native infantry in revenge for the sneers with which we all knew these others had freely, since the punishment parade, lashed their submissive apathy in witnessing, without an attempt at rescue, the degradation of their comrades.'[4] Armed only with a sword, Mackenzie prepared to ride down to the lines, but just outside his bungalow the Quartermaster of the 3rd BLC came running, desperately screaming, 'Oh God, sir! The troopers are coming to cut us up!'[5] Mackenzie suggested that they stay together, but at the rapid approach of a group of native troopers, heralded by a cloud of dust, the Quartermaster ran on right through the Lieutenant's garden. As he was scaling the wall into the neighbouring bungalow, the Quartermaster was attacked by a mob, among which Mackenzie recognised his own *chaukidar*. The Quartermaster was cut in the face by a spear, but, firing off one of the barrels of his gun, he managed to make his escape.[6]

A *sepoy* wielding a sword charged at Mackenzie, but the officer, who had not yet drawn his sword, rode his horse right into the man. Mackenzie continued out of his compound on to Sudder Street, where he found three *sowars* of his own regiment bearing down on him. Not realising the true state of the situation, he called out to the men to stop, which they did; but instead of presenting themselves to their officer, they attacked him. It was all that Mackenzie could do to fend off the sudden onslaught. At this moment Lieutenant Craigie emerged from his bungalow just down the street, and he immediately ran to the aid of Mackenzie. Equally incredulous, Craigie called out to the *sowars*, 'What are you doing? That's my friend,' and the three troopers rode off.[7] The two officers then went down to the cavalry lines.

By the time they reached the lines, the situation was completely out of hand: 'Most of the men were already mounted, and were careering wildly about, shouting and brandishing their swords, firing carbines and pistols into the air, or forming themselves into excited groups.'[8] Many of the officers of the 3rd BLC had come down to the lines and were desperately trying to calm their men and restore some kind of order. Although the troopers were not openly hostile, some of them did warn their superiors to leave, while calling out that 'the Company's Raj was over for ever!'[9] Amidst the confusion, the officers were told that their commander, Lieutenant-Colonel Smyth, 'was flying for his life and had given no orders'.[10] At the same time, they learned that a large group of *sowars* had left to release the eighty-five skirmishers from prison. Relying on his rapport with his men, Craigie managed to gather about 40 *sowars* of his troop, who swore to their loyalty.[11] Although he was not the senior officer present, Craigie simply assumed command and ordered the loyal *sowars* to follow him, Mackenzie and Clarke to the jail.[12] The party then proceeded on their self-appointed mission. This took them across the entire breadth of Meerut, which was by now engulfed in the turmoil. As Mackenzie later described:

> The roads were full of excited natives, who actually roared approbation as we rode through them, for they evidently did not distinguish in the dusk the British officers, and took the whole party for a band of mutineers. We three officers led, and as we neared the jail our pace increased, till from a smart trot we broke into a gallop. Already the *sepoys* and the mob had begun their destructive work. Clouds of smoke on all sides marked where houses had been set on fire.[13]

If the declining light allowed Craigie and the others to pass unnoticed, it also allowed two thirds of the *sowars* in their troop to disappear quietly, thus leaving the three officers with a much depleted force as they reached the jail.[14]

But they were too late, and the eighty-five *sowars* had already been freed. The prisoners had been lodged in the new jail under the supervision of the British jailer, James Doorit, who had been given a guard of just twenty *sepoys* of the 20th BNI in support of his own guards.[15] When Doorit noticed the approaching *sowars* and the smoke appearing from across the city, he ordered his guards to oppose the party. The men of the 20th BNI were in command of the gate, however, and they simply allowed the troopers to enter the gate and free their comrades without offering any resistance. Doorit himself ran off to the Magistrate to report what had happened. Amongst the hundreds of inmates in the new jail, the *sowars* of the 3rd BLC only released their eighty-five comrades, and having brought their uniforms and equipment, many of them left directly for Delhi.[16]

Mackenzie later described the scene that met them at the jail: 'The prisoners were already swarming out of it; their shackles were being knocked off by blacksmiths before our eyes; and the jail guard of native infantry, on our riding up to it, answered our questions by firing at us, fortunately without hitting any of us.'[17] When some of the fleeing *sowars* recognised Craigie, however, their response was very different and one of them ran up to his former officer, crying, 'I am free, my lord. My captain, let me press you to my bosom before I fly.'[18] There was nevertheless nothing more for Craigie, Mackenzie, and Clarke to do at this point, and they decided to turn around and attempt to save the regimental colours in the cavalry lines. Retracing their steps, Mackenzie and the other realised the severity of the situation:

'No sooner had we turned our horses' heads than the full horror of what was taking place burst upon us. The whole cantonment seemed one mass of flames.'[19] As they were riding back in the descending darkness, Mackenzie did not notice a telegraph wire that had been cut and was trailing across the road. The wire caught him in the chest, throwing him off his horse and into the dusty road, right into the path of his companions; as he later recalled:

> Over my prostrate body poured the whole column of our followers, and I well remember my feelings as I looked up at the shining hoofs. Fortunately I was not hurt, and regaining my horse I remounted, and soon nearly overtook Craigie and Clarke, when I was horror-struck to see a palanquin-gharry – a sort of box-shaped Venetian-sided carriage – being dragged slowly onwards by its driverless horse, while beside it rode a trooper of the 3rd Cavalry, plunging his sword repeatedly through the open window into the body of its already dead occupant, an unfortunate European woman.[20]

The officers ahead of their party immediately attacked the *sowar* and 'In a moment Craigie had dealt him a swinging cut across the back of the neck, and Clarke had run him through the body.'[21] Seeing one of their comrades cut down right in front of them, however, angered the remaining *sowars* of Craigie's party, and their loyalty, already greatly strained, wavered as several of them called out '*Maro! Maro!*' ('Kill! Kill!').[22] A shot was soon after fired at Craigie by one of the *sowars*, but the three British officers dared not return fire lest they provoke the remaining troopers. The shooter was a *sowar* whom Craigie had previously removed from his position in the regiment and who was now pursuing a personal vendetta, his face covered by a scarf. As they continued their desperate ride, the man again shot at Craigie, who called upon those of his men whom he knew to be loyal, and they eventually forced back the shooter but did not kill or disarm him.[23] In this perilous manner the motley party finally reached the officers' bungalows and the cavalry lines.

While Craigie with a handful of men went to save the regimental colours, Mackenzie and four *sowars* went to Craigie's bungalow, where Mrs Craigie and Mackenzie's sister had remained. The women had been anxiously waiting in the house as the situation around them gradually worsened. Mrs Craigie first hid the uniform of the wounded trooper whom they had earlier saved, as she thought 'that he alone might be the object of possible attack, as the native troops have been incensed by a guard of carabineers having been over our skirmisher prisoners'.[24] In other words, Mrs Craigie expected the

British troops who had stood guard over the eighty-five skirmishers to be the exclusive targets of the uproar. Crowds of native troops, some in uniform, some without, were hurrying past the house, and the air was rent by shouts and gunshots. The regard with which Lieutenant Craigie was held by his troops nevertheless seems to have saved his house and its occupants. The surrounding bungalows were fired; his alone was left by the crowds.

In the bungalow next door, the pregnant 23-year-old Mrs Chambers had been left by her husband, a Captain of the 3rd BLC, who had gone to deal with the disturbance in the infantry lines. Mrs Chambers, however, had not been entirely forgotten: one of the officers of her husband's regiment, Lieutenant Möller, was riding across the parade ground near the lines of the 3rd BLC on his own, at a time when the rest of the British troops were still miles away. Möller stated that 'I had almost reached the house of Mrs. Chambers, then in her verandah, and looking at me, when five or six Native troopers spread out to cut me off, and forced me back.'[25] Mrs Craigie later recalled how she and Mackenzie's sister were observing Mrs Chambers from the first floor of their house:

> Bungalows began to blaze round us, nearer and nearer, till the frenzied mob reached that next to our own! We saw a poor lady on the verandah, a Mrs. Chambers (lately arrived). We bade the servants bring her over the low wall to us, but they were too confused to attend to me at first. The stables of that house were first burnt. We heard the shrieks of the horses. Then came the mob to the house itself, with awful shouts and curses. We heard the doors broken in, and many, many shots, and at that moment my servants said they had been to bring away Mrs. Chambers, but had found her dead on the ground, cut horribly, and she on the eve of her confinement! Oh! night of horrors! Still I heard shouts of my husband's name, and assurances that our house should be spared, but crowds kept threatening. I almost believed we should escape.[26]

Natives were by now entering the compound, but Craigie's servants drove them out and proclaimed that the master of the house 'was the people's friend, and that no one should burn his house'.[27]

At this stage Mackenzie and the four *sowars* arrived, to the great relief of the women. In their desperation they had gotten out Lieutenant Craigie's guns, but knew not how to load them. The Carabineer had been unable to offer any assistance, as he was in a state of 'nervous collapse'.[28] The situation was, however, far from secure, and Mackenzie was none too sure about the loyalty of the *sowars*. Resolutely, he presented the two women to the four troopers and 'commended their lives to their charge'. The response of the *sowars* was as unexpected as it was reassuring: 'Like madmen they threw themselves off their horses and prostrated themselves before the ladies, seizing their feet and placing them on their heads, as they vowed with tears and sobs to protect their lives with their own.'[29] The Captain had appealed to the very honour of the troopers, and his demonstration of his trust in them, feigned though it may have been, paid off. Mackenzie and the *sowars* were soon busy keeping the ever more aggressive crowd out of the compound. The Lieutenant later described the night in his high-sounding style:

> Through the windows flashed brilliant light from the flaming houses on all sides. The hiss and crackle of the burning timbers – the yells of the mob – the frequent sharp reports of fire-arms, all formed a confused roar of sound … As I stepped out on to the upper verandah I was seen by some of the mob who were wrecking the opposite house. 'There is a feringhi!' they cried; 'let us burn this big *kothi*!' (house). And several of them ran forward with lighted brands to the boundary wall; but on seeing my gun levelled at them they thought better of it and recoiled.[30]

It was nevertheless clear that their position in the house was becoming untenable.

Meanwhile Craigie had managed to save the colours of the 3rd BLC with the help of some of the *sowars* who remained with him. Once he had delivered them to the safety of the Dragoon lines, he returned to his house, passing up and down the length of Sudder Street and the worst trouble on his way.[31] He nevertheless reached his bungalow safely, and once reunited with his wife, he and Mackenzie agreed that it would be safer to leave the building, which they feared would be surrounded at any minute. In the back of the extensive garden, partly hidden by the trees, was an old *chattri* with three of its four sides bricked up, and they decided to hide there.[32] They gathered up their weapons and, with the two women wrapped in blankets, they rushed to their new hiding place where they remained the rest of the night. The next morning the party made it to the safety of the European lines.

The survival of Mrs Craigie and Mackenzie's sister was nothing short of miraculous. Most of the bungalows to the east and south of the native cavalry lines were pillaged and burnt, and several of their inhabitants killed. In the bungalow next to Mrs Chambers and closest to the lines, Dr Dawson and his wife were sick with smallpox and accordingly unable to escape the crowd; as Mackenzie later described: 'they came in their night clothes into the verandah, he carrying a gun loaded with shot, which he discharged at the crowd, only further enraging it. He was instantly shot dead. His wife met with a worse fate. The cowardly demons, afraid to touch her because of the danger of infection, threw lighted brands at her. Her dress caught fire; and she perished thus miserably.'[33] Not far away, Mrs Macdonald was fleeing with her three children, dressed in Indian clothes and accompanied by an *ayah* and some native servants. Unfortunately, they encountered a crowd of armed men who stopped and questioned them. One of the servants explained that the woman was his sister-in-law, but when she did not respond to the questions put to her, a man pulled Mrs Macdonald's shawl aside and promptly cut her down. The children were whisked away by the servants and survived.[34] At least one other European, Mr Hughes, was killed as he tried to escape in disguise while his family was hidden by their Muslim landlord.[35] In one of the bungalows behind the lines of the 3rd BLC, Riding-Master Langdale's seven-year-old daughter Sophia was killed by a single sabre-cut as she lay sleeping on a *charpoy* outside.[36]

## 'We will now kill the kafirs'

As dusk was settling over Meerut, the raging crowds attacked and plundered the bungalows situated between the Sudder Bazaar and the Abu Nullah to the north. A wounded artilleryman had escaped the butchery of the bazaar and made his way to the house of a pensioner, Markoe, and his wife, Emma, who hid the wounded man inside. A crowd of more than 100 broke into their compound and began searching the house for the fugitive. When they found his bloody clothes, they threatened Emma Markoe, demanding she show them where the 'kafirs' and 'feringhees' were. One of the crowd was actually the neighbour's watchman, and grabbing Mrs Markoe's arm he said: 'I only get four rupees as a chuprassie, is that enough to feed and clothe me[?], but we will now kill the kafirs …'.[37] The woman screamed as she was knocked down, and her husband came bursting in through the door with a stick in his hand, which made the crowd take off. Armed with sticks, the couple managed to lock the gate but were both severely wounded by sword-cuts in the process, and they retired to their house stunned and bleeding to take cover in the bedroom. The mob soon returned and broke down the gate, and Mrs Markoe persuaded her husband and the artillerist to escape through the window. The crowd now burst into the room and Mrs Markoe was attacked and beaten with sticks until she lost consciousness. She later described how she came to: 'I opened my eyes, and saw the mob plundering my house, on their leaving the bed room, I took the opportunity of getting out of the window, I could hardly walk, but went in search of my poor husband, and in a garden … I found his body, he had one leg hanging over the wall, as if he had tried to get over, when he was killed by a severe sword cut, nearly dividing the neck, I returned to the garden and hid there till next morning.'[38]

Elisabeth Cahill, a widow who lived in the Markoes' compound, tried to escape when the crowd broke down the gate, but she was seized by a *chauprassi* who dragged her back and threatened to kill her with a knife if she tried to run. As the crowd proceeded to plunder her house, she later recalled:

> another chuprassie, who was with the mob, asked me, if I would become a mahomedan; to save my life, I said I would, he tried to drag me into an empty room, but on my struggling against him, he ran me through the thigh with his sword, he then made a rush at Mrs. Markoe, and I ran out to try and get over the wall of the compound. A sikelgur [knife-grinder] made a cut at me, and wounded my shoulder. A blacksmith who lived close to me, took hold of my hand, and helped me over the wall with Mrs. Millar, and hid us both in his house …[39]

Not far away, Dr Smith was in his garden when he heard the sound of musketry from the nearby infantry lines and saw people running by. His *bibi* or mistress, Golaub Jaun, begged him to flee with her but, unsure of the cause of the disturbance, he refused. A *doolie* (litter) sent by Golaub Jaun's mother now arrived, and parting with Smith she was carried out of the garden just as the crowd surrounded the house. Several of the men wanted to kill her, but she was eventually allowed to pass through the armed crowd. Smith was cut down where he stood, and the next morning his body was found 'naked and frightfully mutilated by sword cuts.'[40]

Just next door, and located almost directly across from the Sudder Bazaar, Lieutenant Eckford's house was surrounded by extensive gardens with several outbuildings. The Lieutenant was consequently informed quite early by his servants that the *sepoys* were killing their officers. From the compound wall of Eckford's house, a British employee, the pensioner Joseph Chapman,

watched as several privates of HM 60th Rifles were chased up Sudder Street
by native policemen and the crowd. They were all bloodied and wounded,
and the pensioner observed how one of them had received a severe cut to the
head, which had almost scalped him, 'the back hair of his head laying on his
shoulders'.[41] One of the soldiers, a rifleman named Fitzpatrick, managed to
get away from his pursuers and into Eckford's compound, where he collapsed,
'the sleeves of his white jacket all saturated with blood'.[42]

Eckford's servants and native guards begged him to send away the
British soldier, as the 'mob particularly sought their lives' and would revenge
themselves on the Lieutenant, but he simply dismissed this warning and sent
Chapman and Fitzgerald into the house.[43] The Lieutenant now learned that
his neighbour, Dr Smith, had been killed and his house set on fire, and that
the crowd was fast approaching. Armed with a double-barrelled gun, Eckford
stepped out on the veranda to face a large crowd of armed natives who were
swarming into the garden, some of them carrying torches. The Lieutenant
fired off both barrels, killing the leader of the crowd, which immediately
dispersed. As no assistance seemed forthcoming and the crowd was bound
to return, Eckford sent his wife, her sister, and their child to hide in a small
hut at the back of the garden. Handing a rifle to Fitzpatrick and a spear to
Chapman, Eckford prepared to defend the building and locked all the doors
before retreating to the portico, where a disheartening sight met him: 'I saw
an immense number of men, *sepoys*, troopers, and bazaar people (in all at
least 4 or 5 hundred) moving quickly towards the house. Whenever they
saw me they aimed at me with their muskets but not a shot struck me.'[44]
Suddenly Eckford and the others heard a loud noise downstairs and realised
that another crowd had entered from the back and broken into the house.
The Lieutenant rushed downstairs, and when he entered the dining room,
he suddenly came face to face with fifteen armed natives:

> I had a double barrelled pistol in each hand. I gave a shout and dashed at them.
> The room was rather badly lighted I knew and went at them, fired my right pistol
> (one barrel after another) at the men on the right (each ball must have told in
> some way on them). They all, with one exception, turned and scrambled out.
> The man who remained – a trooper of the 3rd Cavalry by his dress – came at me.
> About 4 or 5 paces distant I let him have one of the left pistol barrels (he must
> have been very hard hit) – the other would not go off (The body of this man
> was afterwards dragged out by his friends from the burning house – this the
> servants told me). He almost simultaneously gave me a severe gash across the

head with his sabre. I attempted to close with him and we struggled for a few
seconds – in which time I smashed my pistol on his head – a heavy blow for it
broke the trigger guard and swivel ramrod of the pistol which was found next
day. He in return gave me sundry wounds and sabre cuts.[45]

At the very last moment, Eckford was saved when Fitzgerald appeared and
the wounded *sowar* staggered out of the room. Bleeding and stunned, the
Lieutenant decided to make his stand on the flat roof of the portico upstairs,
and the rifleman helped him up and propped him against the parapet.
Chapman had already fled and was hiding in the garden; Fitzgerald was
anxious that they would soon be surrounded. Accordingly, Eckford told
him to make his escape while there was still time – he was himself unable
to move. The Lieutenant gave Fitzgerald his double-barrelled gun and the
rifleman rushed down, promising that he would get help. From his spot on
the roof, Eckford heard several shots from the house downstairs and a lot of
shouting – then all became quiet. 'I lay breathlessly expecting the mutineers
to come and assail me,' he later recalled.[46] Eventually, and very cautiously, the
attackers made their way up the stairs and emerged on the veranda, just next
to the portico where he was lying. As it happened, Eckford was covered by
the deep shade of a nearby tree, and in the bright moonlight the men did not
see him. Finding the other floors empty, they assumed that he was hiding on
the roof and, rather than risking their lives in a fight, they simply set fire to
the furniture and the house, and posted guards around it. Eckford was still
bleeding profusely and slipped in and out of consciousness for several hours
as he lay powerless, the entire building slowly catching on fire.

The European lines were just across the Abu Nullah, a few hundred yards
away, and throughout the evening Eckford expected the British troops to come
to his relief, but this never happened. At one point he overheard the natives
just below him talking about his wife and child, but he was unable to make
out the exact words. Desperate to help his family, the Lieutenant considered
throwing himself from the portico on to the ground, but he realised that he
was too weak even to defend himself. As the fire got closer and closer to his
hiding place, the heat became intolerable and Eckford either had to get away
or risk being burned alive. Mobilising his last strength, he dragged himself
down on to the veranda, where the wooden doors and Venetian blinds were
all on fire. He kept moving along but the effort weakened him and he fainted
– only to be brought back to consciousness as his body was scorched by the
blazing flames. Eckford finally reached the ground, where he collapsed and

was soon after found by a servant who came to his assistance. The crowd had left, and Eckford was taken to the gardener's hut, where he found his wife and child alive and well. A make-shift litter was prepared for him by his servants, and soon after they all crossed the Abu Nullah and reached the safety of the Carabineers' lines. As Eckford and his wife were united, he later described, 'we most sincerely and fervently returned thanks to God for our wonderful escape.'[47] The Eckfords had indeed been lucky, although the Lieutenant was subsequently laid up for six weeks on account of the six wounds he had received, one of which had cut into the skull and left a large scar on his forehead. While the pensioner Chapman also survived and made it back to his wife, Rifleman Fitzpatrick was not so fortunate. His body was found next morning lying naked on the road just behind Eckford's house; the rifle he had carried was found just inside the compound wall.[48]

## 'My love did not know how to plunder'

The eastern part of the station was only little affected by the unrest, although it was the scene of one of the more gruesome attacks during that night. Around 10 p.m., Sergeant Law and his wife had finished praying and were about to turn in – entirely oblivious to the outbreak and conflagration barely a mile away, which had by then been in progress for hours.[49] All of a sudden, a large armed crowd burst into the house, and as they surrounded Sergeant Law, his wife managed to get away with their infant child in her arms. Having left behind both her husband and three other children, Mrs Law was, however, far from safe: 'As I was escaping, two men, both chuprassies in Government employ, one the son of the man who supplied us with milk and butter, and the other, chowkeedar of the school, debated about killing me, the first man said, they had got quite enough in the house and was for allowing me to escape, but the other, who had on a red turban, was for killing me.'[50] Eventually the two men let her go, but Mrs Law and the infant were then set upon by another crowd and severely beaten – she received three wounds on the head and a cut to the arm. Mrs Law finally escaped and was found by a Sergeant Foster, who got her and the baby to safety.

With the help of a few native recruits, Sergeant Foster later fought back a large crowd which had fired a bungalow and was advancing on the artillery barracks. The crowd was led by two men, one in white cloth and another in the uniform of the *chauprassis*, with whom the Sergeant fought desperately: 'The man in white spat at me, and abused me, calling me a feringhee soor [white pig], he cut at me with his sword, and the tall man in police uniform cut at me three or four times, but I being armed with a fursee, a long kind of battle axe, taken in the Santhal war, he could not get at me.'[51] Heavily outnumbered, Foster and the recruits nevertheless scared off the crowd by pretending that reinforcements were approaching, and no further disturbance occurred in that part of the station.

During the late evening, the general turmoil was further exacerbated by the arrival of villagers from the surrounding region who had come into Meerut, attracted by the prospect of plunder.[52] The Gujars made their first appearance here, although they were later to play a significant role in the uprising across the countryside. Gujars were traditionally a powerful semi-nomadic pastoralist caste who controlled land and traded in cattle in the areas surrounding Meerut and the adjoining territories.[53] As a result of the imposition of British rule, however, much of the common land they relied upon for grazing was auctioned off to other groups, such as the Jats, and by 1857 they had in many places been reduced to lowly cultivators. To survive, some engaged in cattle-theft, and they had a bad reputation as thieves, amongst both locals and the British administrators, who described them in the following terms: 'They are cattle-stealers by profession, and, like most of the predatory tribes, take employment (whenever they find officials foolish enough to trust them with it) as watchmen, or village police.'[54] It was certainly not accidental that some of the rumours that flourished after the parade on 9 May referred to 'Goojurs of the neighbouring villages, and bad characters generally' who were preparing to plunder Meerut by the thousands.[55] As late as the early twentieth century, Gujar women would still sing of the pillaging of the city:

> People got shawls, large and small; my love got a handkerchief.
>     There is a great Bazaar at Meerut; my love did not know how to plunder.
> People got dishes and cups: my love got a glass.
>     There is a great Bazaar at Meerut; my love did not know how to plunder.
> People got coconuts and dates; my love got an almond.
>     There is a great Bazaar at Meerut; my love did not know how to plunder.
> People got coins of gold; my love got a half-penny.
>     There is a great Bazaar at Meerut; my love did not know how to plunder.[56]

The outbreak at Meerut on 10 May 1857 was accordingly remembered in local folk-songs mainly for its association with plunder.

The *kotwal* of Meerut, Dhunna Sing, was himself a Gujar and played a dubious role during the outbreak. Many of his officers ran away during the evening, either to join the conflagration or simply to get out of harm's way.[57] The *kotwal* was thus left with a heavily depleted force in a city where large crowds ran riot and plunder and murder occurred all around. When some of his *chaukidars* brought in two Gujars who had been taken with stolen horses and other loot, Dhunna Sing exclaimed: 'why are you making arrests, what will you have me strung up[?]'[58] Towards midnight, the servant of a Bengali merchant came to fetch the *kotwal*, as his master's house was being attacked. Dhunna Sing assembled his few remaining men and went to the Bengali's house, where they encountered a huge group of Gujars armed with swords, axes and *lathis*. The *chaukidars* wounded two of the Gujars, but Dhunna Sing restrained his men and explicitly ordered them not use their swords against his people.[59] The Gujars, for their part, called out to Dhunna Sing: 'thou hast called us, and now turn us out, very well, release our man now in confinement, and we will go away'.[60] It thus appeared that the *kotwal* had informed his fellow Gujars of the outbreak, perhaps even encouraging them to plunder, and now his loyalties were divided.[61] In the midst of the general outbreak against the British, various minor conflicts and alliances thus emerged. In the end, the *kotwal* agreed to release the two prisoners held at the *kotwali* along with their loot, and the Gujars took off to pursue their depredations elsewhere. Dhunna Sing and several of the other policemen later deserted, and the remaining officers dared not tell the British of what had occurred during the night – these details only transpired after months of investigation by Major Williams.[62] Even if some *chaukidars* remained with their officers and did not actively join the rioting crowds, the local police were largely ineffective.

Some time after midnight, the remaining 839 prisoners in the new jail were released by a crowd, which then proceeded systematically to demolish the buildings with remarkable thoroughness. 'On going down to the jail next day,' the jailer Doorit recalled:

> I found the house built for me much destroyed and burnt, the whole of my property cleared out and taken away, the jail godowns plundered of all the bar, flat, and sheet iron, carpenter's, blacksmith's, mason's and other working tools, nails, screws, bolts, and hinges, brass and iron cooking utensils, millstones,

with a large stock of saul timber taken away, and most of the door frames in the barracks inside the jail with iron bars in them pulled out, what they could not move, they burnt and destroyed …[63]

For some, this may not simply have been an opportunity for looting, but through the dismantling of the prison, an attack on one of the most potent symbols of colonial rule.[64]

## 'Whether for life or death they must return to the regiment'

Earlier that evening, when Lieutenant Gough reached the lines of the 3rd BLC, along with his three *sowars*, there were no other British officers present; the magazine was being plundered by the remaining troopers while all the bungalows were in flames. Initially, no one paid any notice to the presence of the single British officer. 'After a time, however,' Gough recalled, 'the disregard of my authority changed to open mutiny; there were loud shouts of "Maro, Maro!" ("Kill him, kill him!") and a few men, chiefly recruits, fired pistol-shots at me, mostly at random, although one shot so far took effect as to pierce the cantle of my saddle.'[65] Joined by another British officer who was fleeing for his life, Gough and his escort were eventually forced to leave the parade ground as the situation became untenable. Once they left the lines, Gough's first thought was to go to the aid of the Greatheds, as the location of their house placed them in the middle of the turmoil and very much in harm's way. 'Though no longer pursued by our men,' Gough remembered, he and his companions 'had to force our way through the only road open to us, and this was the native bazaar, which – such was the singularly unanimous outbreak of fanatical and race feeling – was up in arms; the roads were crowded with foes, and we had literally to cut our way, pelted with stones, through hundreds of men armed with tulwars and *lathies* (iron-bound-cudgels). But our speed saved us, and we got through safely, though bruised and beaten.'[66]

By the time they reached the house of the Greatheds, a large crowd of people were already approaching. At the gateway, however, Gough was informed by the servants that Mr and Mrs Greathed had already left for the safety of the European lines, and so the Lieutenant and his party continued northwards. The truth was that Hervey and Eliza Greathed were then hiding on the roof of their house, and had also been there when Lieutenant-Colonel Smyth had passed by earlier that evening. Like everyone else, the Greatheds had been preparing to go to church when they realised what was going on. Encouraged by their faithful servant Golab Khan, they had taken refuge on the terrace of their house. 'The increasing tumult, thickening smoke, and fires all around,' Eliza Greathed recalled, 'convinced us of the necessity of making our position as safe as we could; our guard were drawn up below. After dark, a party of insurgents rushed into the grounds, drove off the guard, and broke into the house, and set it on fire. On all sides we could hear them smashing and plundering, and calling loudly for us; it seemed once or twice as though footsteps were on the staircase, but no one came up.'[67] Just as the flames and smoke began to make their situation on the roof untenable, Golab Khan convinced the crowd that his masters were hiding in a haystack some way off, and thus lured them away from the house. Once the crowd was out of sight, the servant fetched the couple and they hurried down and hid under the trees in the garden. 'In a very few minutes after our descent,' Eliza later remembered, 'the house fell in with a crash, and we thanked God for His merciful preservation of us.'[68] Clutching a revolver, Hervey stood watch along with Golab Khan throughout the rest of the night, while Eliza rested on a *charpoy* in the shadows – 'The remaining hours till dawn were not without anxiety.'[69] The Greatheds made it to the safety of the European lines the following morning.

Before Gough and his escort reached the artillery lines, the native officer and two *sowars* stopped and bade the Lieutenant farewell, the former stating that 'his duty was with his regimental comrades, and whether for life or death they must return to the regiment'.[70] Gough was genuinely sorry to see the men leave but was unable to persuade them to remain. As his subsequent sentimental account put it:

> And so we parted, after several hours of the most anxious and trying dangers; and for ever – for notwithstanding all my efforts, I never heard again of my friend the native officer. I knew his name, of course; but though I found out his house, in the Oude District, no trace of him was ever again found, and I can only conclude that he met his death at Delhi in the mutineers' camp. A braver or more loyal man I have never met, and, whatever his faults may have subsequently been, in his mutiny against his salt and his military allegiance, all will allow his loyalty to me was beyond praise, and I can never forget him, of how he risked his life again and again to save mine.[71]

And so it was that Gough arrived at the European lines alone, to be greeted by the chaos and noise of the British troops being assembled to respond to the disturbances. In the absence of any reliable information about the extent of the disturbances, the British Command veered on the side of extreme caution and strictly maintained all formalities.[72] After the Carabineers had mounted their horses, armed and ready, a roll-call was taken before they could be dispatched; further delays accrued as they had to wait for a staff officer. Thirty troopers had by that point left on their own account to try and save some of the European civilians, but as soon as this was noticed they were called back.[73] HM 60th Rifles also took a long time getting ready, before they moved down along with the artillery. The officers sought to avoid leading their troops into the narrow streets and lanes of the bazaar, where it would be impossible to manoeuvre, and instead took a huge detour at a slow pace.[74] The Carabineers had at first been ordered to proceed to the new jail, and they had covered half the distance when they were suddenly ordered to turn around and join the other troops.[75] When all the British forces finally assembled on the native parade ground, in front of the now empty lines of the 11th BNI, it was well past 8 p.m.[76] Captain Muter with HM 60th Rifles later described the eerie scene before them: 'The sun had set and the moon had not yet lit up the scene. The illumination … rising out of the thick blackness around was one of awful grandeur. For more than a mile three rows of thatched bungalows were on fire …'.[77] Several volleys of both musketry and grapeshot were fired across the parade ground at the distant shadows that some thought they could discern through the smoke. This effected little more than the dispersal of the last few *sowars* who had not yet left Meerut.[78]

The troops eventually moved eastwards, and then turned back up towards the European lines via Sudder Street, picking up a number of bodies along the way. Lieutenant Gough had joined the force and was moving through the burnt-out remnants of the buildings between the infantry lines and the Sudder Bazaar: 'It was here my sad experience to discover and identify the remains of my brother-officer young Macnabb, from whom I parted that Sunday morning at the church door, now lying on the road dead. Had it not been for his great height and the peculiar braid on his frock-coat, on which I had commented in the morning, I should not have been able to identify him. Happily I had reason to believe his death must have been instantaneous.'[79] Captain Taylor, who had escaped from the first outbreak on the parade ground of the 20th BNI, was found on the road in front of a native shop a few hundred yards away; 'he had apparently been killed by an iron bound lathi, the back of the head was smashed'.[80] Some of the British officers who had been hiding from the *sepoys* were also found alive and brought back with the troops. On the northern side of the Abu Nullah, the entire force set up camp, placing guns and pickets at the various bridges that connected the southern and northern parts of the city. The participation of the substantial British force at Meerut on 10 May was thus limited to a much belated and entirely ineffective excursion into the area of disturbance, followed by a strategically passive defence of the European lines.

During the early hours of the outbreak, several officers offered to ride to Delhi and warn the British authorities there, but their initiative was not followed up.[81] Lieutenant Möller repeatedly begged Major-General Hewitt to let him deliver such a warning, but Hewitt refused to do so unless Möller got Wilson's permission, and it proved impossible to find the Brigadier-General.[82] At the time, there was much frustration over the dithering of the senior officers at Meerut. Hewitt and Wilson, in particular, were singled out; it was said they could have prevented much of the bloodshed, both at Meerut and at Delhi, if they had acted swiftly.[83] This critique was not only made with the benefit of hindsight. On 15 May, Ensign Phillipps, who had been on the parade ground when the *sepoys* first broke out, wrote to his family: 'The *sepoys* were shooting every European they could meet and setting fires to the bungalows – the General and Brigadier General seemed quite paralysed, and for three mortal hours kept marching the Carabineers, Rifles and Artillery backwards and forwards well to the rear of the fire. At last, when we did reach the lines, not a *sepoy* was to be found.'[84] Others, such as Lieutenant Eckford, had been waiting throughout the night to be relieved by the British troops whom they knew were close, but who never came.[85]

Enough of the senior officers, such as Lieutenant-Colonel Smyth, had personally seen the extent of the disturbances and the beginning of the killings that there could be no confusion about the gravity of the outbreak. And perhaps this was the crux of the matter. Throughout the night of 10 May, many feared that not only the crowds but the more than 2,000 mutinous *sepoys* might attack the European lines. It thus seemed advisable to move with caution and secure the defence north of the Abu Nullah. If the senior officers had previously made light of the threat posed by the discontented *sepoys*, they now seemed only too ready to exaggerate the imminent danger that faced them. When Lieutenant Möller informed Hewitt the following morning that all the native troops had left and that there were no armed crowds roaming around, the Major-General told him he was 'romancing'.[86] Even more indicative of the prevailing frame of mind amongst the commanding officers is the fact the British remained huddled up in the ammunition depot in the European lines more than three weeks after the native troops had left Meerut. On 14 and 15 May, reports went out from Meerut simply that 'The fort [the Dumdumma] and treasury are safe, and the troops ready for any attack.'[87]

Major-General Hewitt was subsequently removed from the command of the Meerut Division – a decision he appealed against by stating that Brigadier-General Wilson and not he had been in charge of the military arrangements.[88] When Wilson was later called upon to explain the 'inaction of the European troops at Meerut', he similarly disavowed any responsibility by arguing that Hewitt, as the commander of the division, had been in command. Furthermore, Wilson stated, half the Carabineers had been recruits unable to ride, and a large part of the artillery had also been untrained recruits. Once the British troops reached the native lines and realised that the mutineers had left, Wilson had asked Hewitt for further orders and, as he later stated: 'At the same time I gave my opinion that from the hubbub and noise proceeding from the *Sadr* and city, the *sepoys* had moved round in the direction of the European portion of the cantonment (this was my firm conviction at the time), and recommended that the brigade should march back for its protection, it being so weakly guarded.'[89] In the event, Hewitt's appeal was unsuccessful and he was removed from his position.

During a situation that demanded decisive action, both Hewitt and Wilson had refused to assume responsibility and had largely ignored the advice offered by the younger officers under their command. Afraid of making a 'wrong decision' for which they might later be blamed, the senior officers made none at all – with devastating results. Sending the Carabineers and Rifles into the labyrinthine streets and alleys of the Sudder Bazaar or native city after dark would indeed have been foolhardy, but many lives might have been saved by the presence of even a few companies of British troops south of the Abu Nullah at an earlier time. And there can be no doubt that, had the British at Delhi been formally warned on the evening of 10 May, many more lives, both British and Indian, might have been saved in the days, weeks and months that followed.

# 11

# Meerut Aftermath

The full scale of the outbreak and the carnage which had accompanied it only became fully apparent to the British as a strong force moved down from the European lines in the early morning of 11 May. One search-party went to Mrs Law's house to look for her husband:

> and found him lying about forty yards in front of his dwelling, with his body ripped open and his head cut off; and one of his children, a girl aged six years and a half, lying dead a few yards from him. In the house, two children were found alive; one, Eliza, aged nine years and ten days, had her arms hacked off the shoulders, and left hanging only by the skin, besides having both of her cheeks cut off so that no fluid could be retained in the mouth; the other, a boy upwards of five years of age, had a part of his ear cut off, besides being otherwise severely wounded. These two children were conveyed in a litter to the artillery hospital, where the girl died the next day.[1]

Captain Chambers himself rushed down to the site of his bungalow to look for his wife; as Harriet Tytler later described it: 'What did he behold but his poor young wife lying dead in the compound, perfectly nude, with her unborn babe lying on her chest.'[2] Captain Earle of the 20th BNI left a slightly more detached account of the gruesome scenes that met the troops:

> Early next morning, Mrs. Chamber's body was found in her compound, I saw the body covered up, consequently cannot say in what state it was; just by the old jail, we found the bodies of some fourteen or fifteen European soldiers and their wives, all these were perfectly naked and frightfully mutilated. One man had one of his hands entirely cut off, another had the whole of his stomach laid bare with the entrails hanging out. Mrs. Macdonald was so much disfigured from

the cuts about her face, that although I had known her intimately for upwards of nine years, I did not recognize her.[3] ... Captain MacDonald, 20th regiment native infantry and Mr. V. Tregear, were killed in the lines by the *sepoys* [of the] 20th native infantry, both these gentlemen were shot, when the bodies were found next day, they were dressed.[4]

While these killings hardly needed embellishment, a British official warned of the tendency to sensationalise the violence: 'The statements which appear in the English newspapers regarding the atrocities perpetrated by the rebels here and elsewhere are, in many instances, grossly exaggerated, as in the case of Riding-master Langdale's child of the 3rd Cavalry, who was actually killed with one blow of a *tulwar* while sleeping on the *charpoy*; whereas she is stated to have been cut in pieces by little and little, with every refinement of gradual torture.'[5]

The mutilation and nudity of some of the British victims of the outbreak attracted considerable attention, and the treatment of British women in particular proved to be a central concern right from the very beginning of the Uprising. One British woman's body was described by eyewitnesses as 'much cut about the body and breast', another as having been 'shamefully treated'.[6] Revd Rotton, who probably saw most of the dead bodies as they were prepared for burial, later wrote that those of the women were 'shamefully dishonoured in death'.[7] Later investigations reached the conclusion that generally British women had not been raped before their death, although there were some exceptions.[8] At Meerut, Major Williams mentioned one such case: 'Generally the ruffians seem to have been too intent upon the destruction of Christians, too eager to kill, to think of any other atrocities till life was extinct, but in one case there is no doubt of the infliction and repetition of the deepest dishonour, and acknowledgement was publicly made that this was attempted in another case on a Christian female, though these were exceptional cases.'[9] The identity of the woman referred to by Williams is not known.

The British men, women, and children who were murdered at Meerut paid with their lives for the humiliation suffered by the skirmishers and, perhaps more importantly, the general resentment against colonial rule. The extreme brutality of several of the attacks during the riot, in which Europeans were set upon and cut, stabbed, and clubbed to death, reflected the vengeful anger of crowd. The mutilation of Mrs Macdonald and Mrs Chambers, for instance, was not merely the result of a desperate struggle but a deliberate effacement or ritual of desecration. The bodies of the British were disfigured and dishonoured, dehumanised and humiliated, at the hands of angry crowds or vengeful *sepoys* and *sowars*. During the night of 10 May, some natives were bragging about the murders they had committed and one eyewitness described the scene where several Europeans had been killed: 'I saw almost every lodha ... standing armed near the police chowkee. I saw a corpse lying there, which I believe was that of Mrs.___, the natives were laughing, and about seven paces from there, was poor Mr. Hughes ... lying dead in native clothes ...'.[10] Having vented their anger and frustration, the violent impulse of the attackers was spent and their initial fear and panic was replaced by a sense of elation and euphoria.[11]

Those Europeans who lived isolated in Indian neighbourhoods near the bazaar or native city had been amongst the first targeted by the crowds, and in most instances they never stood a chance. Captain Muter's wife left a highly sensational account of her husband's discovery of more than a dozen bodies in a house near the old jail (also mentioned by Earle), with the added drama of imagining the manner in which the occupants had been killed:

Near the gaol stood a neat brick chunammed [plastered] bungalow ... It was Sunday evening and, I believe, a few friends had assembled in this house. They must have been surrounded and every hope of escape lost before even a conception of what was impending had entered their minds. The conclusions Colonel Muter formed from what he saw.[12] It seemed that they had fled to their bed and bathrooms, seeking any hiding-place in their desperate extremity.

Attempts had been made to burn down the bungalow, which were defeated by the nature of the materials, and the volumes of smoke had only blackened the walls and the ceilings, as if to throw a pall over the tragic acts the fire refused to obliterate, leaving the place a charnel-house black with crime. The doors and window-frames had been torn from their positions, the furniture was gone, the matting in shreds and tramped by a thousand feet, the plaster soiled and broken.

Following in the flights of the inmates a bedroom was entered, where a pile in the centre attracted attention, requiring inspection to understand what it was. The proceedings, of which the proofs lay here, were difficult to realize, and took some time to comprehend. Men and women dying from sword-cut wounds must have been heaped upon their own broken furniture, till the vestiges left by the fire applied to the pile did not even tell the number of the victims. The walls were dark with smoke, the floor stained with blood, and the air tainted with the smell. It was easy to trace the rush of desperate men into the small adjoining apartments, where their bodies lay just as they had furnished subjects for the brave swords of the rabble to hack at and to hew.[13]

The bodies that were found in various locations in Meerut, in the smoking ruins of bungalows, or in ditches along the roadside were all taken up to the theatre in the European lines, where they were laid out.[14] The exact number of Europeans killed at Meerut on 10 May has never been fully established; of the twenty-nine Europeans who were buried in the cemetery of St John's on 11–13 May, only twenty-two were clearly identified.[15] It seems that at least twenty more were killed, including those found in the bungalow near the old jail. At least half of the British victims of the outbreak at Meerut were thus never formally identified. Apart from the *sepoys* and *sowars* killed during the sporadic fighting of 10 May, a substantial number of native civilians probably perished in the conflagration as well. The fact that they were never mentioned in the British accounts, and their fate went unrecorded, should not make us insensitive to their suffering. The silence in the archives is a poignant reminder of the many stories of the Uprising that will never be told.

## 'They were but too ready for the work of blood'

For several days after 10 May, chaos reigned supreme in Meerut south of the Abu Nullah.[16] Only small detachments of British troops ventured down into the empty bazaar or through the rows of burnt-out bungalows near the native lines. Order was not reinstated in the native city for weeks, and when people realised that the British were still in power, the streets and alleys soon became littered with plundered goods. The British civilians who had survived the horrors were crammed together behind make-shift barricades around the artillery magazine building known as the Dum-Dumma in the very northern part of the European lines. Living in tents for weeks along with the few possessions they had saved from the fires, they nevertheless enjoyed a far more comfortable life than their compatriots elsewhere were soon to endure.[17]

On 14 May, a servant recognised the Muslim butcher, named Mowla Baksh, who had murdered Mrs Chambers.[18] The butcher used to go round to the bungalows and sell meat at the door, and Mrs Chambers had allegedly reprimanded him a few days previous to the outbreak, telling him 'that if he brought such bad meat again she would tell the other ladies not to buy from him again'.[19] Lieutenant Möller personally rode into the Sudder Bazaar and caught the man, who was trying to escape in a bullock cart, covered by a *chador* or woman's shawl.[20] Lieutenant Stubbs recalled the scene when the man was brought in before Major-General Hewitt:

> The Native Infantry officers asked General Hewitt to try him at once, but the General declined, saying he was not under military jurisdiction. They got into a state of excitement … Lieutenant Chambers, coming into the barracks, went into hysterics; revolvers and swords were taken out. Hewitt sent for Colonel Harriott, Judge Advocate, who said that martial law should be proclaimed in cantonments and civil district, if civil law was powerless. Mr. Greathed was sent for, and said he had already reported the civil law powerless. So martial law was proclaimed outside the barracks, to the wondering amusement of the men, and a few minutes after Harriott and some five officers were seated at a table trying the case.[21]

Given the circumstances, the outcome of the 'trial' was already certain, and soon after the butcher was hanged from a tree just outside the Dum-Dumma.[22] The butcher was not the only native to be executed at Meerut, and Mrs Muter later described the punishments inflicted on natives in the aftermath of 10 May:

> The most ferocious who had assisted in the fire and bloodshed that had desolated the station were to be found among our own camp followers. The butchers led, and it is said the tailors strove to vie with them; then came masons, carpenters, bakers and all the rabble who had rushed into the streets on that fatal evening to destroy the unarmed soldier in his afternoon stroll. The butchers followed the *Sepoys* to Delhi and perhaps took part in the crimes there perpetrated.
>
> When this engrossing pursuit ended, they returned to Meerut to resume their avocations, where they were seized and compelled to undergo an ordeal which blanched the cheeks and shook the limbs of many who had been the loudest in cry and foremost in cruelty and exposed them to each other as the cowardly ruffians they were. It was difficult to obtain evidence, and they were sent round the garrison, drawn up in a row; while company after company and troop after troop was halted before them, and the men asked if they could recognize any of the number as having been engaged in the riots. Most of their faces wore a

deadly hue – some could scarcely stand and all their lips muttered prayers, the name of Allah alone being distinguishable.[23]

In the event, retribution was completely indiscriminate, and the blacksmith who had saved Mrs Cahill and hid her and Mrs Millar in his house was hanged for having set fire to Mrs Markoe's bungalow.[24] The eager brutality with which vengeance was exacted in part reflected the belief prevalent amongst the British that they had but narrowly escaped a vast, treacherous plot.

*

Most of the British residents of Meerut who had lived through the outbreak could not bring themselves to believe that it was anything but the result of a plot. According to Mrs Muter, 'It was not a local disturbance, but one planned with elaboration throughout the country.'[25] Although no evidence ever emerged of a conspiracy at Meerut, the surgeon of the 11th BNI, O'Callaghan, described it in great detail:

> From the day when the 3rd Light Cavalry troopers were placed in arrest, the men of that regiment and those of the 20th Regiment of Native Infantry had drawn closer in their mutinous compact and designs than before, and held meetings in their lines both by night and by day, at which they pledged and encouraged each other to revolt, and accept the commencement of the mutiny, which, it now appeared probable, would be cast upon them. There was not much dissent or disunion amongst them; they were but too ready for the work of blood. On the 1st of May … the 11th Regiment of Native Infantry reached Meerut; and they were at once taken into the brotherhood of conspiracy; but they did not take the poison as deeply as the other two corps, nor afterwards distinguish themselves so prominently in the cruelties that were perpetrated.[26]

The absence of evidence in support of the existence of a conspiracy in the minds of many served only to prove how deviously successful the plotters were and how completely they had managed to deceive the British; as Mrs Muter pointed out, 'So complete and so secret were their plans that Mr. Greathed, the Commissioner, to whom all looked for the first intimation of danger, was wholly unaware of the proceedings, and therefore was unable to give a hint to the military. This has always appeared to me surprising, as for many months a feeling of unrest had existed among the Hindoos, a feeling that should not have been overlooked or minimised.'[27] As Cave-Browne had suggested at Ambala, many of the British residents of Meerut imagined that the *sepoys* had planned a general massacre of the Europeans when they gathered for church on Sunday.[28] The civilians would all have been easily surrounded during the service, while the European troops would have been parading with blank ammunition. It was also commonly believed that the outbreak at Meerut had been premature; as Revd Rotton described it:

> There was a deep-laid scheme; and a simultaneous and universal outburst of popular vengeance was intended. A day was fixed upon, in the counsels of the mutineers, for the massacre of every European and Christian person in India; some say, from Calcutta to Peshawur. That day was drawing near at hand. The mutineers of Meerut simply anticipated it. It was this act of anticipation which brought to light the hidden works of darkness, and made manifest that which would not otherwise have been revealed.[29]

According to Mrs Muter, who believed that the massacre had been planned for Queen Victoria's birthday on 24 May, 'The scheme was simple and practicable in the highest degree, and if carried out with secrecy and resolution, would have swept every European soldier in one and the same hour from the face of India. A massacre more foul, more widespread, more disastrous, had never before been in the power of a people.'[30]

After 10 May, there was no shortage of horror stories of the massacres which had occurred at the station and the sense of betrayal felt by the Europeans. Kate Moore, for instance, recounted how many of the NCOs of the native regiments lived near the *sepoys'* lines, adding that 'Most of these were murdered, with their wives and children, some while sitting at dinner, stabbed by their own servants with their own knives and carvers.'[31] Although O'Callaghan exonerated the native servants at Meerut, he evoked a similar scenario of paranoia: 'We were surrounded by treachery on all sides, and off all kinds, active and passive, and concealed, kept secret, and carried out with such consummate perfection and wonderful calmness and placidity, as can never fail to command the admiration of those who lived in the midst of it, and survived its murderous outbreak and results.'[32] One of the most central themes in the British trauma following the outbreak was precisely the betrayal by their native servants and *sepoys*, with whom they had lived for years and whom they treated (it was often noted) as their own children. The Revd Rotton later recalled the panic that seized the British civilians who were huddled up in the Dum-Dumma at Meerut long after the mutineers had left and order had been restored: 'The reports and rumours circulated at our place of refuge were most bewildering: one day we were all to be poisoned by the native servants; the next we were all to be murdered on the anniversary of some Mahomedan feast; indeed every sort of unfortunate prediction was promulgated.'[33]

## 'Our regiment never conspired, nor intended to mutiny'

The outbreak at Meerut was not the result of a carefully laid plan, nor an event simply orchestrated by a few conspirators. There were undoubtedly some among the native troops who had been sufficiently aggrieved to talk of killing their officers and liberating the eighty-five skirmishers; they may also have been in correspondence with *sepoys* at Delhi and expected at least some degree of support in case of a mutiny. *Sowars* of the 3rd BLC most likely cut the telegraph line to Delhi during the early afternoon of 10 May, before the disturbances broke out, and once the infantry broke out in mutiny, they immediately set off to free their imprisoned comrades. That, however, hardly amounts to a conspiracy of the sort that Malleson and other historians have invoked. One looks in vain for evidence of a sinister hand pulling the strings from behind the curtain. No traces of the sinister machinations of native rulers may be found, nor of their messengers or foreign agents spreading sedition or instigating anti-British resentment.

The Superintendent of Police at Meerut, Major Williams, later made an investigation into the supposed existence of a conspiracy, but the response he received from the local officials and the native troops, who had remained loyal, was inevitably the same: 'Nothing was conspired beforehand.'[34] The native deputy collector stated that 'Nothing was preconcerted; though the new cartridge question was generally discussed in the districts, yet the mutiny was not plotted beforehand, and no one conceived such a thing would ever come to pass.'[35] While there may have been some vague expectation that something might happen following the parade on 9 May, the actions of the native troops prior to the outbreak does not suggest that they were actively planning to mutiny. According to a *havildar* of the 3rd BLC, who had talked with one of the eighty-five skirmishers after the outbreak, the native troops 'did not plot any thing before hand. Had they done so, they would not have kept their wives and children with them as they did; these had to wander about the town for several days, and afterwards went wherever they could.'[36] A *havildar* of the 20th BNI similarly stated that 'there was no conspiracy beforehand, had there been any, the men would not have left their wives and property behind'.[37] Although there was a general expectation that something might happen, the local Indian population did not show any signs of preparation either, as Major Williams argued:

> their ignorance of, and unpreparedness for, coming events, is palpably evident from the following facts: their shops were all open and goods unprotected; men were passing to and fro, paying, realising, and carrying about with them money; vendors of goods hawking about their wares as usual, and travellers journeying unarmed both to and from the City and District; in fact the usual routine of business and of pleasure flowing on in apparent peace and security.[38]

The outbreak originated in the complete breakdown of trust and communication between the British and their native troops; the interaction between the *sepoys* and their superiors was in fact defined by consistent mutual misunderstandings. British attempts to allay the *sepoys*' worries regarding the contentious cartridges failed conspicuously, and it is deeply ironic that the very event that precipitated the outbreak, namely Smyth's order for a firing-parade on 24 April, was intended to put the issue to rest. In a highly volatile situation, the imagined threat of British subversion brought latent conflicts to the surface, and the outbreak at Meerut thus has to be understood in the contingencies of the moment. The imprisonment of Hindu and Muslim troopers during the holy month of Ramadan, for refusing to use cartridges that many alleged would compromise their religious status and purity, was always likely to provoke discontent ranging even beyond the ranks of the army itself. A situation of acute tension escalated, and the outbreak was an improvised response to an opportunity that offered itself. The causes of the immediate involvement of the *sepoys* and crowds lay in a conjunction of factors – looting, rioting, and murder were expressions of the bewilderment, panic, and anger felt by many Indians.[39] Similarly, the violence derived from the condition of the outbreak itself.[40] The layout of the city and cantonment of Meerut, with a number of isolated bungalows far from the European lines, combined with the inaction of the British commanders, allowed the disturbances to spread unhindered. Ultimately, the outbreak derived its expression from the pattern of crowd behaviour characteristic of sectarian urban riots.

Contrary to what many histories of the Uprising claim, the native troops at Meerut did not mutiny because they were ordered to bite greased cartridges; the *sepoys* of the 11th and 20th BNI and the *sowars* of the 3rd BLC had not been issued with the new Enfield rifle, nor were they receiving any drill in its use. The facts that no greased cartridges were distributed, at Meerut or elsewhere, that no bone-dust was mixed in the flour, that no shackles were being prepared or any plans made to disarm the native troops at the station were, however, entirely irrelevant. Following several months of disturbing rumours and increasing tension, the *sepoys'* mistrust of the British was so pervasive that all it took for a mutiny to break out was a panic in the bazaar. The rumours may not have been technically true, but they were acted upon as if they had been, and the consequences certainly were real enough. The Deputy Collector of Meerut, Mohur Singh, was succinct in his analysis of the outbreak:

> Previous to the outbreak, rumours to the following effect very generally prevailed:
>
> 1st: That 2.000 sets of irons were being made for the *sepoys*.
> 2nd: That by order of government, attah mixed with bones was to be sold.
> 3rd: That the *sepoys* were to be deprived of the charge of their arms and ammunition.
>
> These reports caused the disturbance.[41]

A *havildar* of the 11th BNI similarly stated that 'Nothing was premeditated, or I should have known it, the mutiny occurred from hearing that the soldiers were coming to take away the magazine.'[42] The rumours of the greased cartridges, or rather the fear of being ostracised, first led the eighty-five skirmishers to refuse the cartridges for their old weapons during the parade on 24 April. Subsequently, the parade of 9 May, during which the skirmishers were publicly humiliated, brought the fear and anger of the native troops to boiling point. The final rumour that the British troops were coming during the late afternoon of 10 May thus acted as a trigger which set the outbreak in motion. It is, however, important to remember that the rumours could only ever have been considered credible in a prevailing atmosphere of intense distrust of the colonial state. The very impact of the rumours should thus be considered against the background of a deep-seated resentment of British rule, which had built up over decades and permeated substantial parts of Indian society. Native accounts of the outbreak nevertheless focused almost exclusively on the causal significance of the rumours. Sometime after 10 May, a native of Bolundshahr wrote to his brother at Rawalpindi, explaining what had occurred at Meerut:

The foundation of the quarrel was this: that thousands of maunds [measure of weight, 1 maund = 37 kilos] of atta was taken into every ressalah [cavalry regiment] and regiment; and with this atta was mixed the ground bones of the cow and pig; and the cartridges were also made with the fat of the cow and pig. The shopkeepers in the city were ordered to purchase 'atta' from Government and sell it in all the villages. It was ordered by beat of drum that atta be not ground in any village, and that in every district all the mills should be confiscated to Government. It was also ordered that ten maunds of atta be thrown into every well, kuchcha or pukka [mud or brick], in every village and town. The troops at every station with one accord said, that if the troops at Meerut should receive the atta and cartridges, they would receive them without objection. A few European officers assembled at Meerut, and having collected the officers of the pultun [infantry regiment] and ressalah, ordered them to take the atta from the Government and to bite the cartridges with the mouth. A few Sirdars objected to do so; but two, one a Hindoo and the other a Mussulman, bit the cartridge with the mouth. A reward of one hundred rupees was immediately paid to both. The rest said that they would consult each other during the night, and intimate the result the next morning. There were about eighty-four men. They were instantly sent to jail in irons. One among them, a Syud, who was fasting, struck his head on the ground and died. About two hours before sunset the troops girded up their loins and killed all the European soldiers and officers that were present. Only the Commissioner and the District Officer escaped. The rest of the principal Europeans were killed – women nor even children, all that were Europeans, escaped. Afterwards they went to the jail. There was a sentry at the gate, whom they asked to open it. The sentry refused, upon which a Sowar, who was a Syud, advanced, and, with the name of God in his mouth, forced open the gate with a kick. They then collected blacksmiths from the city, and, taking them to the jail, unfettered several thousand prisoners. Both the jails were broken through. Then they went to and sacked the treachery. This state of things continued for two days. The people of the city of Meerut also joined

them, as also the Syuds of Ubdoollapoor, a village near Meerut. The whole of
the cantonment was fired; not a single bungalow escaped. The 'Dewanee Duftur'
was also burnt. On the third day they went away to Delhi …[43]

In this retelling of the events, the supposed plan of the Government secretly to
subvert the caste and religion of the native troops was simply taken for granted.
The outbreak was accordingly legitimate and, due to the alleged strength of
the Muslim troopers' faith, it was also ascribed religious sanction.

The outbreak at Meerut was as unexpected as it was unprecedented;
and yet it was indicative of a latent conflict that few could have imagined
even a few days prior to 10 May 1857. During the outbreak British officials,
troops and officers, in particular, were targeted by the mutineers and crowd.
Some even believed that only the British troops who had been present
at the shackling parade of 9 May, and who had escorted or guarded the
eighty-five skirmishers and had ultimately been rumoured to prepare for
the disarmament of the *sepoys*, would be attacked by the vengeful *sepoys*.[44]
This was obviously not the case, and the truly remarkable thing was how
many of the attackers knew their victims personally. Mrs Law claimed that
she recognised the son of the man who usually brought her family milk
and butter as one of her attackers, and Mowlah Baksh, who murdered Mrs
Chambers, was similarly a local butcher whose victim was amongst his
daily customers.[45] Mackenzie's own *chaukidar* or watchman attacked the
Quartermaster of the 3rd BLC, while another of the men who wounded Mrs
Law was a *chaukidar* at the school where her husband was employed.[46] The
most revealing example is that of Mrs Markoe, who was maltreated by the
neighbour's watchman, who told her: 'I only get four rupees as a chuprassie,
is that enough to feed and clothe me[?], but we will now kill the kafirs …'.[47]
Another obvious case is that of the *sowar* of Craigie's party who had recently
been demoted and who repeatedly tried to kill the officer during their chaotic
return from the new prison.[48] A certain level of intimacy between the crowd
and its victims thus informed, and in some instances exacerbated, the level of
violence at Meerut, as Indian servants took revenge on their British masters.
As at Barrackpore in 1824 and in February of 1857, personal animosity played
a significant role in shaping the outbreak. Local grievances converged with
general conflicts and personal antagonism might easily have been subsumed
under anti-British sentiments – or vice versa. The events of 10 May 1857
cannot simply be reduced to an assertion of Indian identity in opposition
to colonial rule.

For every personal grievance there were also examples of personal friendship and loyalty, and most of the Europeans who survived the riots owed their lives to native servants and friends or even locals willing to risk their lives to save them.[49] Most of the officers of the 11th BNI were helped to safety by the native officers of the regiment, and a *havildar* of the 20th BNI hid one of his officers in the regimental lines, thus preserving him from the fate that befell Captain Taylor and many others.[50] Even as Mrs Macdonald was cut down by the crowd, native servants whisked away her children to safety and a local Muslim dignitary put his own family at risk by hiding his British neighbours in his own house.[51] Clearly not all Indians reacted to the outbreak by joining the crowds; some spontaneously sought to help the British. The fact that a street-sweeper laid down his life to save the Quartermaster of the 3rd BLC also shows that it was not only the native elite, who had benefited from British rule, who remained loyal.[52] It must remain unknown exactly what made one servant risk life and limb to protect his European employer, while another seized the opportunity to kill and rob. Perhaps the attitude exhibited by the British themselves might have determined how their Indian servants reacted; a servant who felt his master had complete faith in him might be more inclined to honour that trust than someone who knew he was being suspected and held at arm's length.

It is indeed noteworthy how many of the British officers went to the lines to reason with their men rather than run away from the epicentre of the outbreak. In the face of a complete collapse of order, the British officers still thought it possible to talk with their men, and as the case of Craigie shows, it did succeed in a few instances. When Colonel Finnis rode across the parade ground and into the crowd of excited *sepoys* of the 20th BNI, however, the supreme confidence he placed in his own authority and in the loyalty of the men was dangerously misplaced. The situation at Meerut was one of complete confusion, and even the extent of the mutiny was uncertain and constantly changing. Officers like Craigie could rely on the loyalty of *some* of their men *some* of the time, but no one could say who would remain loyal or for how long. Of the 320 *sowars* and native officers of the 3rd BLC who were in the regimental lines on the evening of 10 May, eighty-five remained with their British officers while 235 deserted along with the eighty-five skirmishers they released.[53] After the outbreak, Ensign Phillipps also described how 'about 200 of the 11th *sepoys* have come back, as they did not fire on their officers, and as some of them did their best to save us, are with those who came in by Sunday pardoned'.[54] That is to say that more than 20 per cent of the native troops at

Meerut did not mutiny but, due largely to the personal bonds maintained with some of the British officers, chose to stay behind.

Any pretence that relations between the British and their native troops were mended, however, were short-lived. On 16 May, several companies of Bengal Sappers and Miners mutinied at Meerut, killing their British officer before deserting. In the stilted style of a diarist, a fellow officer described the murder of Captain Fraser of the Sappers: 'Poor fellow, we buried him yesterday, and, please God, will soon avenge him … I will never trust natives again. It is a religious panic has seized the whole army … We are about 2,000 Europeans strong here. How we wish they would attack us. A native was shot by his own men protecting Fraser. I never knew what a wound a bullet could make before I saw him. His head was blown to pieces.'[55] With an acute sense of confusion and insecurity, this brief account reflects the utter shock of the sudden violence that had been unleashed. Faith in the loyalty of Indian troops had forever been shattered.

Amongst the *sepoys* who mutinied, the situation was at least as ambiguous. After the *sepoys* had killed or chased away their officers, a *havildar* of the 20th BNI described the scene in his regimental lines: 'I saw the *sepoys* weeping, they were very sad and said the recruits had ruined them, but they had killed the *sepoy* who fired the first shot.'[56] Gough also claimed that it was new recruits of the 3rd BLC who had fired at him on the parade ground.[57] One possible explanation for the role of recruits in the outbreak may be found in the petition submitted by the senior officers of the 19th BNI after the mutiny at Berhampore, in which they claimed that they were unable to give up the names of those responsible: 'The men who are acquainted with the names and ranks of those instigators are at enmity with us and friendly with them, because, being young, they are independent of the Hon'ble Company's service, and they began with this mutiny with a view to our ruin only, and this is the reason they do not tell us.'[58] It thus seems likely that older *sepoys* and native officers were less inclined to mutiny, while the younger *sepoys* or recent recruits were much less attached to the British and more willing to take things into their own hands.

Group pressure probably also played a role, as some *sepoys* were forced to join the mutiny. A *sepoy* of the 11th BNI later claimed that 'our regiment never conspired, nor intended to mutiny'.[59] Once Colonel Finnis had been shot, however, there was no going back and the *sepoys* 'were much afraid, thinking they would not be spared, and consequently fled'.[60] Once the mutiny was under way, anyone who hesitated to join risked being killed by his comrades, as a mutiny necessitated complete solidarity amongst the troops. Not everybody who joined the mutineers did so willingly. An Indian traveller who met some of the Meerut jail guards outside the city asked where they were going, and 'one of them sorrowfully replied, the troops at Meerut have mutinied, the *sowars* joined by the city budmashes, and those of the sudder bazaar, have broken the jail, and released prisoners; had we remained at Meerut, we should have been punished, we have therefore joined the rebel troops, and must now take whatever Providence has "in store for us."'[61] There was also an element of sheer bewilderment – a native officer of the 11th BNI stated that the mutiny 'originated with the 20th regiment, who raised a tumult, our regiment being confused, ran to the bells of arms'.[62] As darkness descended over Meerut, and fires and riots broke out on all sides, many of the *sepoys* would have been as confused and scared as were the British.

# 12

# To Delhi!

After the British officers of the 11th and 20th BNI had either been killed or chased away, the agitated *sepoys* found themselves unexpectedly in control of the parade ground and regimental lines. Instead of pursuing their officers up to the European lines, however, the initial impulse of the bulk of the *sepoys* and *sowars* was to flee the station. Some of the native troops joined in the rioting and plunder, and a significant number of *sowars* went to free their comrades from the new jail. Yet by the time the British troops moved down, around 8 p.m., most of the native troops had already left Meerut. An Indian clerk later described how he and his brother, soon after the disturbance broke out, 'encountered crowds in the bazaar all very excited and noisy, and, hurrying on we found many *sepoys* in plain clothes running up Railway Street with their rifles and *toshdans* (pouches) and turning off past the Old Jail to the Delhi Road. Much larger numbers of Sepoys who were in the Sadr Bazar also ran past our house down Railway Street to their Lines to arm themselves.'[1]

When Lieutenant Möller rode across the native parade ground, before the British troops moved down, some of the mutineers who had not yet left 'were then plundering my regimental magazine; some on their knees, and all crying, "Quick, brother, quick! Delhi, Delhi!" and I saw a stream of Sepoys and troopers going off towards the Delhi road'.[2] The fact that most of the mutineers took the road to Delhi need not imply that there was a prearranged plan to do so; with the European lines to the north, and the expectation that a British force might pursue them at any moment, the road leading south-west to Delhi was the most obvious escape route. The British authorities were nevertheless suspicious. If there had been no prior communication between the regiments, Major Williams later questioned a native officer of the 11th BNI, 'How did they then at once unanimously decide on going to Delhi?'

The officer replied that 'Nothing was preconcerted before the outbreak, after which, they went off wherever they liked.'[3]

Indeed, not all troops from Meerut went to Delhi, and many scattered and returned to their homes; several horses belonging to *sowars* were found near Gulaoti some days later, evidently left behind by troops who had gone east towards Bolundshahr. One *sepoy* on a cavalry horse was actually apprehended at Bolundshahr on 11 May; two days later, five *sepoys* of the 11th and 20th BNI were apprehended at Aligarh.[4] Another large body of mutineers was said to have continued southwards from Delhi towards Agra, and as far away as Cawnpore, *sepoys* from Meerut were apprehended by the British as they were returning home laden with plunder towards the end of May.[5]

Despite the numbers found to be heading in different directions, often towards their homes, the majority of mutineers went along the road to Delhi with the mounted *sowars* in the front, followed at some distance by the infantry and civilians on foot.[6] As early as 7 p.m., streams of camp-followers of the 3rd BLC were fleeing Meerut and chained prisoners were seen hurrying away, their irons around their ankles jangling.[7] Around 10 p.m., the main body of fleeing troops reached the village of Rethanee, just a few miles south of Meerut, where they halted in order to decide which route to take.[8] The Indian scribe Mohun Lal actually overheard a conversation between two of the Meerut mutineers describing the deliberation:

> One was a Mohamedan Trooper of the 3rd Cavalry, and the other a *sepoy* who was an orderly of the late Sir William Natt in Candhar. They said that before they broke out and released their comrades & prisoners from the jail, they had no idea of coming to Delhie. It was after they had destroyed & burnt the houses of the 'Sahib logues' they all assembled on the south side of Meerut city. Here the point of refuge was discussed. To go Rohelcund, and in the direction of Agra, without a gun and other necessities for the hostile operations seemed pregnant of deadly consequences. After a calm and deliberate consideration, Delhie was named and resolved to make their head quarters, adding that if the city were once in their hands, the annihilation of the few English and Christian residents, were easy, and the possession of the magazine, and the person of the King, for future operations, were highly beneficial. They continued, they would hold Delhie against the English for months, during which time, the name of the King will work like a magic and induce the distant stations to mutiny and the disaffected chiefs to rebel against the English.[9]

The choice of Delhi as the mutineers' destination was accordingly prompted by largely strategic considerations, and probably promoted by those who had been in contact with the regiments there. The King's physician, Ahsan Ullah Khan, later explained the choice of Delhi:

> In my opinion the mutineers had several inducements for throwing themselves into the city of Delhi:

> First:    Delhi was close to Meerut, where the mutiny commenced, and the Meerut troops were of one mind with those of Delhi,
> Second:  There was considerable treasure and abundance of magazine stores at Delhi,
> Thirdly:  There was a wall round Delhi, and the city could be well defended,
> Fourthly: The King of Delhi had no army, and was defenceless; and
> Fifthly:  The King was a personage to wait upon whom all Chiefs, Hindu or Mahommedan, would have considered an honour to themselves.

> The troops did not inform the King previously of their intention to go over to him, nor had the King any knowledge of the Volunteer regiment [38th BNI] having made common cause with the Meerut troops.[10]

The harried crowds of *sepoys, sowars* and camp-followers streaming southwards from Meerut during the night of 10 May 1857 were neither revolutionaries nor peasant ideologues. They were a muddled body of mercenaries and civilians who had thrown off their allegiance to their masters and were now searching for a new employer. The troops would traditionally have changed their allegiance and found another employer who would provide better terms of service and respect their rights and religion; but there were no such employers – the *sepoys* had themselves helped defeat all remaining independent rulers and set up the Company Raj. By following the ways of the past, in a world that was no longer the vibrant military labour market it had been, they were displaying a certain anachronistic naivety.

And yet, by rising at Meerut, they had inflicted a humiliating blow against the British, and thus achieved something momentous. They had pulled the British from their pedestal and shown that they were not invincible. The *sepoys* were the real power of the colonial state. Now, they had now taken that power into their own hands. The only potential leader who could provide the legitimacy they had enjoyed as servants of the Government was an employer who wielded a similar level of authority; in other words, a native ruler who could challenge the British. And he was to be found at Delhi in the person of the once-powerful Mughal Emperor, Bahadur Shah.[11]

As long as they remained near Meerut, the mutineers were far from safe, and so they dashed along the road in the darkness of the night. Locals in the villages they passed were roused, and observed that the troops were 'evidently in a hurry, for they threw their arms and property all along the road'.[12] Several hundred *sowars* of the 3rd BLC, probably including the released skirmishers, made several stops in villages along the way, where they paused only to grab provisions and plunder official buildings, leaving a trail of burning travellers' sheds, bungalows and telegraph poles in their wake.[13] As the night progressed, the mutineers became increasingly spread out along the 40-mile road to Delhi: first came eight *sowars* in uniform, who must have left Meerut very early, and 4 miles behind them came some two dozen more *sowars* with pistols and drawn swords, some in uniform and some without. Then came the main body of cavalry, several hundred strong, and finally, tagging along far behind, the infantry and camp-followers, struggling to keep up.[14] Several Indian travellers going northwards by the *dak* had the misfortune of running straight into the *sowars* and were plundered of their possessions.[15] But the fleeing mutineers never took the time to halt for long; throughout the night they would have been looking over their shoulders, expecting British troops to catch up with them at any moment. None of the *sepoys* or *sowars*, however, could have envisaged the consequences of what they had done. By seizing the opportunity to face their superiors during the twilight hours of a Sunday in May, they had defeated the Company Raj, if only for the moment, and there were no troops in pursuit.

## 'We pray for assistance in our fight for the faith'

While some of the *sepoys* in Delhi probably expected mutineers from Meerut to arrive following the court martial of 9 May, the tense atmosphere prevailing in the Mughal capital was the result of rather different apprehensions.[16] Since April it had been widely anticipated that a Russian army was about to invade and dispel Company rule.[17] In 1855, one of the King's servants had gone on a pilgrimage to Mecca, but this had supposedly been no more than a cover for his real mission: to garner the support of the Ottoman Sultan, the Persian Shah and the Russians. The emissary had said that he would return after two years, and during the spring of 1857, many of the courtiers at Delhi 'said they expected the Russians this hot season'.[18] One of the Mughal princes actually warned a British woman that the Persians would soon be coming to Delhi.[19] The frequent invocation of Russia or Persia as a political ally and saviour of the Mughal throne was a natural ripple effect from the Crimean War and the more recent British campaign in Persia. It was not, however, the invasion of foreign troops that was to change the fate of Delhi.[20]

At the telegraph office at Delhi, the signallers had been receiving news during the morning of 10 May as they were gossiping with their Meerut counterparts. The reports from Meerut mentioned the excitement caused by the passing of the sentences, and the signallers made an (obviously exaggerated) claim that the eighty-five skirmishers were to be blown from guns.[21] On Sundays, the telegraph offices were closed between 9 a.m. and 4 p.m., and when the Delhi office opened for the afternoon its staff found that the connection to Meerut was dead. The initial suspicion was that the cable taking the line under the Jumna had been damaged, but when the two assistants crossed the river, they found that they could signal back to Delhi but not onwards to Meerut.[22] George Todd, the telegrapher in charge, decided to check the line to Meerut first thing on Monday morning. By this time, various reports about the events at Meerut seem to have spread throughout the city. On the evening of 10 May, a British family at Delhi was warned by a local nobleman who had heard of the imprisonment of the troopers at Meerut and been told that the Government would have reason to regret this.[23] The warning made such an impression that they immediately sent a note to Sir Theophilus Metcalfe, who nevertheless ignored it.

The same evening, further news of the events at Meerut reached the Mughal capital. Although the commanders at Meerut refused to allow any of their officers to ride to Delhi to warn the British there, express messengers were actually dispatched to both Ambala and Delhi.[24] These were probably some of the loyal *sowars* of the 3rd BLC, who must have been sent off soon after the disturbances broke out and before the bulk of the mutineers had left Meerut. Somewhere along the route, the patrol that went towards Delhi passed on the letter to another *sowar*, who reached the city late at night on 10 May and delivered the message at the house of the Commissioner of Delhi, Simon Fraser.[25] Fraser, however, had fallen asleep in his chair after dinner, and when his servants woke him up and gave him the letter, the Commissioner simply put it in his pocket and went back to sleep. The curious servants asked the *sowar* what the message was, but all he could say was 'that he had learned from the patrol who had given him the letter that there was a great *goolmal* (confusion) at Meerut, and he had been urged to gallop at speed with the letter'.[26] From this it seems that the message did not contain any detailed information, such as the murder of British officers and civilians, but did give intimation of the outbreak of disturbances. In the absence of more urgent warnings, the British authorities at Delhi either overlooked or ignored the signs and warnings that reached them from Meerut. One British officer later described how at Delhi 'the same spirit which actuated those who attended morning church at Meerut, or went for their afternoon drive as usual, led to the customary Sunday routine being carried out, and consequently to nothing being known that day in Delhi of the terrible events at Meerut'.[27]

Early in the morning, as the first *sowars* from Meerut were rapidly approaching the Mughal capital, the three native regiments of Delhi were paraded in their lines just north of the city. The 38th, 54th and 74th BNI, as well as a battery of native artillery, were gathered on the parade ground to be informed of the execution of Isuree Pandey, who had been hanged at Barrackpore three weeks earlier.[28] Captain Tytler of the 38th BNI was surprised at the response of his men: 'I remarked a murmur of disapprobation throughout the whole regiment. Though it lasted but a few seconds, it struck me forcibly as something extraordinary, never having witnessed anything like it before.'[29] It was indeed ironic that this order, intended as it was to dissuade any further disturbance amongst the *sepoys*, should be read to the Delhi regiments at the very same time as the Meerut mutineers were about to enter the city. The response of the Delhi *sepoys*, who 'hissed and shuffled their feet', was also indicative of the fact that the executions did nothing to alleviate their fears and resentment – something that the British would soon realise.[30] After the parade, the officers returned to their quarters and had breakfast with their families as usual.

Some time before 7 a.m. on 11 May, the first group of thirty *sowars* from the 3rd BLC arrived at the Bridge of Boats before Delhi, sweaty, dusty, and tired after the long ride from Meerut. They cut down the toll collector and set his bungalow on fire, but left his hapless wife alone.[31] As George Todd came riding up in a pony-drawn *gharry*, on his way to repair the telegraph lines, he, too, was killed by the troopers.[32] With the smoke of the burning bungalow billowing in the air behind them, the *sowars* slowly crossed the bridge and approached the imposing city walls. Reports had preceded the troopers and in Delhi it was already rumoured that 'the mutineers were making for the city, killing people here and there'.[33] The *sowars* were also being observed from the palace, where it was noted that 'They were dressed most of them in uniform, but a few had Hindustani clothes on.'[34] Inside the Red Fort, the King's physician noted that 'a Hindu *sepoy* of the 38th Regiment of Native Infantry came up to the door of the Hall of Special Audience in the palace, and said to some of the doorkeepers that happened to be on the spot, that the native army at Meerut had mutinied against the State, and were now on the point of entering Delhi; that he and the rest of them would no longer serve the Company, but would fight for their faith'.[35] Only a few days before, Ahsan Ullah Khan had of course heard the very same *sepoys* state that if the British tried to force the greased cartridges upon them 'the Meerut Troops were to come here, where they would be joined by the Delhi Troops'.[36] For some of the *sepoys* at Delhi, the arrival of the mutineers was certainly not unexpected.

One of the *sowars* entered the city through the Calcutta Gate and went around to the main entrance of the palace, the Lahore Gate. Here he made his arrival known and called out for the gate to be open; he was tired and had come to the guard for a pipe and drink of water. The Commander of the palace guard, Captain Douglas, came out and asked what the *sowar* wanted. The man replied:

> We have come from Meerut, where we have killed our officers, because they insisted on our using cartridges smeared with the fat of cows and pigs, and an attempt has been made to destroy our caste. Hindus and Mahommedans conjointly have created a mutiny (*bulwa*). There has been a fight, both Europeans and natives have fallen, and we have come here as complainants, seeking justice from the King. Advise us what we shall do, otherwise as we have been ordered, so we must do.[37]

On hearing this, Douglas ordered his men to seize the *sowar*, but the man simply galloped off to join his comrades.[38]

The other *sowars* had taken a different route and had arrived on the sandbanks directly beneath the King's quarters, at a place called *Zerjharokha*, meaning 'under the lattice', where the Mughal emperors traditionally showed themselves to their subjects and could be petitioned. In accordance with convention, the *sowars* called out: 'Dohai Badshah' or Help O King! We pray for assistance in our fight for the faith.'[39] One of the servants of the palace later described the assembled troops: 'Some had their swords drawn, others had pistols and carbines in their hands, more were coming from the direction of the Bridge, accompanied by men on foot, apparently Grooms with bundles on their heads.'[40] If the Meerut troops had expected a warm welcome from the King, they were sorely disappointed. As soon as the troops had been observed approaching, the King had ordered for the gates leading into the palace to be locked. Bahadur Shah was befuddled and dared not respond to the troops or even show himself at the window. Although persistent rumours of unrest had been circulating for some time, the arrival of the *sowars* was not expected at the palace. When the possibility of a mutiny among the *sepoys* had been discussed at court, it had been assumed that the mutineers would go to Nepal or Persia; no one thought they would come to Delhi and seek the King's assistance, 'because he had neither money nor troops.'[41]

The old King sent for Douglas, who soon returned from the Lahore Gate, already acquainted with the progress of events. When the officer showed himself on the balcony overlooking the sandbank, the *sowars* saluted him and called out: 'The English tried to make Christians of us, and gave us these cartridges with that object; for this reason we have come to the King for protection, as we have been attacked, and some of us killed by the English soldiers.'[42] But Douglas simply told them to leave as they were being a nuisance to the King.[43] This must have felt like a slap in the face for the *sowars*, who had ridden all night to reach the sanctity of the King's city, but they nevertheless complied and rode off. Immediately to the south of the palace, the Rajghat Gate led into the city, but the troopers found that it had just been closed by the watchman.[44] In their frustration they demanded it be opened, and soon after the Muslims of the nearby bazaar opened the gate and let in the *sowars*.[45] This became the signal for the gathering crowds, along with the *sowars*, to attack and plunder both Europeans and Indian Christians in the Daryaganj area south of the palace.

In the meantime, the British officials of the city were becoming alerted to the rapidly developing situation, although few of them suspected how serious it was. At the court house, Metcalfe, the Joint Magistrate, was informed that mutineers were hastening towards the city. He immediately went to the magazine, which was situated on the riverside and overlooked the Bridge of Boats. Metcalfe's plan was to place two guns to sweep the bridge and prevent the rebels from crossing, but it was too late, and together with the assembled officers he 'could distinctly see the mutineers marching over in open column, headed by the cavalry. A body of the cavalry had previously taken possession of the Delhi side of the bridge.'[46] Unprepared for any such emergency, there were neither bullocks at the magazine, nor any artillerymen to operate the cannon. Lieutenant Willoughby, the commanding officer, simply decided to close the gates and defend the magazine as best they could.[47] Metcalfe hastened to the Calcutta Gate, where it appeared the rebels might try to force an entry.

At the Calcutta Gate, Metcalfe found several of his colleagues already present, including Captain Douglas, Fraser and the two magistrates, Hutchinson and Le Bas, along with a number of native police officers and armed guards. The gate had been closed at the very last moment, and the rebels could be heard clamouring just on the other side before they eventually marched off to find another entrance. The closure of the gate had disrupted the busy morning traffic, and soon a large crowd of restive locals gathered around Metcalfe and the others, who were getting increasingly nervous.[48] It was quickly decided that the Magistrate should ride down to the city gates south of the palace and if possible prevent the rebels from entering from the side. At the same time, a message was sent to the regimental lines just to the north of the city with a request for troops and artillery to be sent down immediately. Fraser had finally found and read the note he had received the night before as well as a letter from the toll collector's wife asking for help to bury her husband.[49] There could no longer be any doubt as to the threat that the British residents of the city faced.

No sooner had Metcalfe left the gate and proceeded past the main entrance of the palace than he was confronted by a group of *sowars* charging right at him from the opposite direction. Driving on, the Magistrate made it past the *sowars*, and when later forced to leave his carriage, he escaped dressed only in his underwear.[50] After Metcalfe had disappeared, the *sowars* galloped down to the Calcutta Gate at full pelt, their swords raised. One trooper rode straight up to Fraser's buggy and fired his pistol at him at point-blank; Fraser, however, dodged the bullet by jumping out of the buggy. Grabbing a musket from the guards, he shot the *sowar* down.[51] The handful of rebel troopers were thrown into disarray, and after making a few lunges at the officials, one of which wounded Hutchinson, they rode off. This overt attack on the British was also an attack on their authority, and the crowd, which was quickly growing, now became openly aggressive. The native guards and Fraser's bodyguards had remained impassive during the attack and were seen to slink away.[52] Surrounded and vastly outnumbered by an unruly gathering, Douglas jumped into the ditch of the palace to get away, but landed wrong and sprained his foot.[53] Hutchinson followed the Captain and they both managed to get up to the Lahore Gate of the palace, where shortly afterwards Fraser also turned up. None of them was actually assaulted by the crowds that had gathered at the Calcutta Gate, but they all thought they might have been mobbed at any moment.

Once inside the palace, Douglas was immediately taken to his apartments, located just above the gate, where Revd Jennings and two young women, Miss Jennings and Miss Clifford, had taken shelter. Ahsan Ullah Khan was called upon, and after he had attended to Douglas and Hutchinson, the former asked him to get two palanquins to take the two women to the Queen's quarters, while Fraser requested that two cannon be placed in the gateway to defend the palace. The King immediately gave instructions for the conveyance and guns to be brought out, but the orders went unheeded.[54] The servants and retainers of the palace had seen the King repeatedly humiliated by the British, who had steadily eroded his status and privileges, and they had no inclination to help them now that the fortunes of the foreign rulers appeared to have been reversed. Fraser was waiting for the conveyance for the women at the foot of the staircase leading to Douglas' quarters and soon noticed how the assembled crowd of royal retainers and locals was becoming threatening. As the Commissioner, Fraser had spoken against the recognition of the King's heirs and was known to advocate that the Red Fort be vacated by the court.[55] The aggressive proselytising of Revd Jennings was also common knowledge among the Muslims of Delhi, and the small group of Europeans sheltering above the Lahore Gate were thus unknowingly at the mercy of the royal retinue, from whom they could expect little sympathy. Exasperated, Fraser ordered the guards of the 38th BNI to close the gates, but they refused to act.[56] What followed was described by a native news-writer:

> … a great crowd of men and boys of all ages having collected, began clapping their hands as a kind of insolent bravado at what was occurring. Mr. Fraser, seeing such marked feelings of hostility, began to return to Captain Douglas' quarters, and as he reached the foot of the stairs, Haji lapidary raised his sword to make a cut at him. Mr. Fraser who had a sheathed sword in his hand, turned sharply round, and thrust at him, with the sword in its sheath, saying to the Havildar of the Gate Guards 'What kind of behaviour is this?' Upon which the Havildar made a show of driving off the crowd; but no sooner was Mr. Fraser's back turned, than the Havildar nodded with his head to the lapidary, to signify

to him that now he should renew his attack. The lapidary, thus encouraged, rushed upon Mr. Fraser, and inflicted a deep and mortal wound on the right side of his neck. Mr. Fraser at once fell, when three other men … who had been concealed in an outhouse adjoining, rushed out and cut him with their swords, over the head, face and chest till he was quite dead.[57]

Douglas' servant locked the doors to the apartments as the King's servants rushed up the stairs, shouting '*Din, Din*' ('the faith, the faith'), but they eventually forced their way in and attacked the British.[58] Douglas' native attendant ran down the stairs but, as he later described, was stopped by one of the King's bearers named Mamdoh, who said:

'Tell me where Captain Douglas is, you have concealed him.' He forced me upstairs with him. I said, 'You have yourselves killed all the gentlemen already'; but on reaching the room where Captain Douglas was, I saw that he was not quite dead. Mamdoh perceiving this also, hit him with a bludgeon on the forehead and killed him immediately. I saw the other bodies including those of the two ladies. Mr. Hutchinson was lying in one room, and the bodies of Captain Douglas, Mr. Jennings and the two young ladies in another, on the floor, with the exception of that of Captain Douglas which was on a bed.[59]

And so it was that, as Mainodin, the chief of police in the Parhaganj area, stated laconically, 'By nine o'clock of that fatal morning the principal executive officers of the Government were dead.'[60] Circumstances had placed Fraser and the others in the hands of the King's retainers, who did not need any encouragement from mutinous *sepoys* to turn their swords against the British.

Elsewhere in the city, the example was set by the troops who had come straight from the murder and riot of Meerut, and soon the scenes of the preceding night played out again in the streets of Delhi. Unhampered by the fear of British troops, the crowds gave free rein to their anger. The preaching of revivalist *maulavis* had fallen on ready ears amongst the merchant communities of the city, who, similarly to Meerut, were joined by weavers and other Muslim artisans in attacking British and native Christians. In the Mughal city, the British were very clearly regarded as foreign invaders, and now their time had come. One British woman described the scene at her house in Daryagangj: 'About this time one of the city people, a Mahommedan and a dyer by trade, rushed into our grounds with a drawn sword in his hand, reeking with blood, repeating the *Kalima* [Islamic declaration of faith], and calling out to know where the Europeans were.'[61]

James Morley, who lived with his family in Daryaganj along with the Clark family, had been chased away from their house by a crowd and forced to hide for several hours. By the time he made it back, the streets were deserted and he found his home completely ransacked:

> Everywhere things were lying about that had been most wantonly destroyed. Tables had been split to pieces with hatchets, cupboards had been emptied out and every thing strewn on the floor, jams and jellies were lying in heaps; biscuits were thrown about, and there was an overpowering smell from the brandy and wine that had ran out from the broken bottles.
>
> Every minute detail is distinctly imprinted upon my mind, for with that cowardly shrinking from a knowledge of the worst, which is common to us all, I lingered in the outer room and kept looking round it. At length I nerved myself and stepped into the next room which was the hall. Oh! I had indeed to nerve myself. Just before me pinned to the wall was poor Clark's little son with his head hanging down, and a dark pool which lay near his feet. And this cruel death they must have inflicted before the mother's eyes. I closed my eyes and shuddered, but I opened them upon, even as yet, a more dreadful sight. Clark and his wife lay side by side. But I will not, I could not, describe that scene. I have said she was far advanced in pregnancy.[62]

When it came to entering the room where he knew his family lay murdered, Morley's nerves failed him and he collapsed. Later, while in hiding, Morley overheard some of his servants talking: 'One man said it was very wrong to kill the Mem Sahib and the children, and that how were they to get "rozgar" [reward]. But another said that we were kaffirs [infidels], and that now the king of Delhi would provide for every one.'[63] James Morley eventually escaped from Delhi with the assistance of faithful servants.

The entire city of Delhi was given up to plunder and riot; Mainodin described the chaos: 'On every side the scum of the population was hurrying to and fro, laden with the plunder of European houses. Arriving at the central police station I found it plundered even to the doors, which had been carried off.' Inside he found only two scared policemen who had been hiding:

> … from them I learned that the convicts who had been working on the roads had been taken to the station house that morning for custody as soon as the

disturbance had commenced. Shortly, afterwards two Mahommedan sowars had ridden up, and called out, 'Are you all here for your religion or against it?' The Kotwal had replied, 'We are all for our religion.' The convicts then made a rush for a blacksmith's shop, and assisted each other to cut off their irons. After this, two men mounted on camels and dressed in green with red turbans rode by at a trot, calling out, 'Hear, ye people, the drum of religion has sounded.' Whence they had come or whither they went, my informant knew not, but the excited and terrified crowds in the streets believed they were heavenly messengers. The convicts, freed from their fetters, returned and stormed the police station. The doors had been closed, but they forced them open with the assistance of some *Sepoys*.[64]

As the poorer classes of Delhi's population eagerly joined in the plunder, the local bankers and wealthy merchants looked on in shock. The destruction and rioting that engulfed the city was practically identical to what had taken place in Meerut the day before. A native resident of the Sudder Bazaar in Meerut thus described the pillaging crowds of 10 May: 'The tumult increased, I saw a crowd of about 150 budmashes [ruffians] coming from the direction of the bazaar, headed by 2 or 3 *sepoys*, with torches in their hands, 8 or 10 rushed into the gunge [market], and passed through the south gate, seeing this, I went inside the shop. I recognized Mowla Buksh, butcher, Kalundar, dyer and Khoda Buksh, pulladar, who were shouting, maro, maro [kill, kill], breaking to pieces the lanterns.'[65] Years later, the poet Zahir Dehlavi remembered similar scenes from Delhi on 11 May:

> Soon after I saw a mob of *badmashes* led by a big man who looked like a wrestler. He was wearing *kurta dhoti* [common Muslim dress], a cap on his head, a long bamboo *lathi* [metal-studded stick] on his shoulder, and he was leading a large number of men dressed in the same way. Near the house of Ashraf Beg, the leader hit the road lantern with his bamboo stick and it broke and shattered on the road. He laughed to his friends, and said 'Hey look I have just killed another *kafir* [infidel]'; then they started breaking the lock of a cloth merchant's shop.[66]

Although these two accounts of chaos and tumult may have reflected a common stereotype of lower classes running amok, they also indicate that the outbreaks at both Meerut and Delhi followed very similar, and quite common, patterns of urban rioting.

At the magazine, Lieutenant Willoughby and the other officers could only guess at what was happening in the city. Some time after 9 a.m., a native official, claiming to be from the palace, appeared outside the magazine and told the guards of the 38th BNI that the King was taking possession of the stores.[67] Soon after, a detachment of palace guards turned up and the British officers were told that they were to be relieved of command of the magazine, and had to assemble at the Red Fort. Willoughby ignored this and for several hours nothing further happened apart from continued attempts from the people outside to make the native troops of the magazine leave. Finally, the officers were told that scaling ladders were being brought down from the palace, and Willoughby and the others prepared to defend the magazine. As soon as the ladders were thrown up against the walls, the native soldiers inside the magazine deserted their officers, who were left to fight off the attackers and man the cannon themselves. After a long and desperate defence, Willoughby realised that they could no longer keep the attackers out, and ignited the gunpowder lest it should fall into the hands of the rebels.[68] The entire neighbourhood was flattened by the massive explosion, which could be heard for miles. Lieutenant Willoughby and several of the others miraculously survived the explosion and fled from the city, even though they were heavily wounded. Willoughby, however, was later killed by villagers as he was making his way to Meerut.

# 13

## The Fall of Delhi

Before being killed, Fraser and the other officials had sent a message up to the military lines, requesting that troops be sent down to prevent the mutineers from Meerut from crossing the river and entering the city. Even so, the officers in the cantonment had little idea of the extent of the disturbance, and when Harriet Tytler asked her husband what was going on as he rushed from the breakfast table, he simply told her: 'Oh! nothing. Only those fellows from Meerut have come over and I suppose are kicking up a row in the city. There is nothing to be frightened about, our men will be sent to coerce them and all will very soon be over.'[1] Captain Tytler nevertheless found his troops to be very agitated, and when ammunition was served out, many of them grabbed more than they were supposed to.[2] His colleague also noted that the men were behaving strangely: 'Both Captain Gardner and myself remarked the excited manner in which the men left the lines, shouting vehemently every now and then, and which neither of us could prevent.'[3] Tytler and Gardner's companies were ordered to take up position at a small magazine located further away from Delhi, a position that commanded the river to the north of the city. Here they waited for several hours in the sweltering heat, watching as the smoke from fires could be seen spreading throughout the city, where cannon shots resounded from time to time. Remembering the reports of fires at Ambala, the two officers were worried that something serious was afoot, and they were relieved that their men seemed so well disposed. But this was not to last, as Tytler recalled:

> We now remarked that our men were forming small groups in the heat of the sun. I ordered them to come in and not expose themselves thus. They said 'We like being in the sun.' I ordered them in again. When I went into one of the rooms I remarked, for the first time, a native, from his appearance a soldier, haranguing

the men of the companies, and saying that every power or government existed their allotted time, and that it was nothing extraordinary that the English had come to an end, according to what had been predicted in their native books. Before I could make a prisoner of him the Magazine in the city exploded, and then the men of the two companies with a tremendous shout took up their arms and ran off to the city, exclaiming, 'Prithvi Raj Ki Jai' or 'Victory to the Sovereign of the World.'[4]

Tytler and Gardner managed to keep back a few of their men, but were powerless as the majority of them joined the mutineers inside the city.[5] It seems that, as at Meerut, it was mainly the younger *sepoys* and more recent recruits who mutinied, while veterans remained loyal to their officers. The troops that remained loyal were thus, as Tytler stated, 'chiefly old soldiers that had served with me in Afghanistan'.[6] It is noteworthy that the *sepoy* who instigated the desertion was doing so with reference to the well-known prediction of the Company's demise 100 years after the Battle of Plassey.

Not long after her husband had left with his troops, Harriet Tytler realised that the situation was rather more serious than he had let on, as she later remembered:

> Servants running about in a wild way, guns tearing down the main street as fast as the oxen could be made to go, and Mrs Hutchinson the judge's wife, without a hat on her head and hair flowing down loosely on her shoulders, with a child in her arms and the bearer carrying another, walking hastily in an opposite direction to the guns. What could it all mean? My two little children left to themselves were getting troublesome, which made me call out to [the maid] Marie, 'Oh! Marie, do look after the children.' She replied, 'Madame, this is a *revolution*, I know what a revolution is.'[7]

Harriet, her children and the maid then made as fast as they could to the Flagstaff Tower north of the city, which served as a rendezvous for the crowds of Europeans fleeing the conflagration in Delhi.

At the nearby telegraph office, the two assistants were informed by local messengers of the developments inside the city walls, and they passed this on to their colleagues at Ambala. As the day progressed and the situation became increasingly untenable, the two assistants finally convinced the telegrapher's wife to abandon the house and flee along with the other British civilians gathered at the Flagstaff Tower. Before leaving, one last message was sent off to Ambala: 'We must leave office, all the bungalows are on fire, burning down by the *sepoys* of Meerut. They came in this morning. We are off. Mr. G. Todd is dead, I think. He went out this morning and has not yet returned. We learned that nine Europeans are killed.'[8] A few hours later, before the Flagstaff Tower was finally abandoned, one of the assistants was sent back to send a final telegram. Even though this message did mention that the Delhi *sepoys* had refused to engage the mutineers, the tone of the telegram was strangely subdued. Scores of British men, women, and children had by then been murdered, and Delhi was no longer in the possession of the British, but this last telegram ended by simply stating: 'Several officers killed and wounded. City is in a state of considerable excitement. Troops sent down, but nothing known yet. Information will be forwarded.'[9] The two telegrams were the only indications to the outside world that something was wrong at Delhi, but they hardly conveyed the seriousness of the situation.

Meanwhile, Colonel Ripley had marched down with eight companies of the 54th Bengal Native Infantry to the Cashmere Gate, where a detachment of the 38th BNI was positioned at the Main Guard in the inner court between the gate and the streets leading on to the city. As they marched into the city, entering the square in front of St James's Church, they were suddenly faced with a large body of *sowars* from Meerut, approaching from the direction of the palace. The survival of the Meerut mutineers depended on the support of the Delhi regiments, and they had so far only joined up with the smaller detachment at the Red Fort. As the *sowars* approached the 54th BNI with drawn swords, they called out to the *sepoys* 'that they had no intention of hurting them, but had merely come to slaughter these accursed Feringhees.'[10] The handful of British officers frantically called upon their men to charge the troopers, but the *sepoys* either fired into the air or ran away in the ensuing confusion. Without the assistance of their men, the officers were soon cut down by the *sowars* and to their horror found that some of the *sepoys* were turning on them. On his deathbed, Colonel Ripley later told a friend what had happened: 'on reaching the city with his regiment, a trooper fired at him, but missed his aim, whereupon he returned the compliment and killed the sowar with one shot. The men of his own corps then set upon him with their bayonets and inflicted several wounds, but the most severe were received from the sabres of the cavalry.'[11] Just inside the Main Guard, the *sepoys* of the 38th BNI stood passively by and even taunted their officers 'that now the time had arrived to take their revenge on people who had tried, as they asserted, to subvert their caste and religion.'[12]

The sudden charge by the Meerut troopers had scattered the *sepoys* of the 54th BNI, but later some of them returned; Major Patterson remembered that at around noon, a *sepoy* came up to him at the Main Guard:

> and said that the Havildar Major had sent him to ask where the regiment was to go. I then enquired where it was, and he told me at Sabzi Mandi [outside the city walls]; that on the troopers shooting down the officers, the men had run away and assembled there. I directed him to go and order them up to the Cashmere gate. They came up without any European officer, and the Havildar Major told me that they had been followed the whole way by some of the troopers who were inciting them to join in the mutiny.[13]

Even after they had seen their officers cut down, or had themselves attacked them, some *sepoys* wavered, and although they eventually did join the mutineers, this was no unequivocal action.

In spite of their precarious situation, the Main Guard at the Cashmere Gate now became the last rallying point of the British in the city of Delhi. Motley groups of Europeans fleeing the carnage passed through the gate on their way to the Flagstaff Tower, all of them with stories of the plunder and killings that were going on. Many had a hair's breadth escape:

> … some had hidden in the servants' houses while their bungalows were being looted and set on fire by the city rabble, whilst others, less fortunate than themselves, were savagely cut to pieces by the infuriated mutineers ere they could quit their burning houses. Prominent among those ruthlessly massacred were Mr. Beresford, the manager of the Delhi Bank, his wife, and entire family. On the premises being rushed by the insurgents it was reported that these poor people, accompanied by a few clerks, had ascended to the upper balcony of the house, where, after a gallant and desperate resistance, they were all eventually overpowered, and not one of the party escaped.[14]

The officers had great doubts as to the loyalty of the remaining *sepoys*; they suspected that only the fear of British reinforcements arriving from Meerut prevented them from killing the officers then and there. Lieutenant Vibart noticed the men's demeanour: 'Indeed, the *sepoys* themselves were very anxious to be informed on the latter point, and kept repeatedly inquiring when we thought the *Gora Log* [the British] would arrive. We tried to be cheerful and said they would come soon which we believed.'[15] And so the hours dragged on while the officers and men at the Main Guard upheld an unspoken and uneasy truce. The bodies of the dead officers, 'their faces distorted with all the agonies of a violent death, and hacked about in every conceivable way', were lying nearby as a constant reminder of the fickle nature of the *sepoys*' loyalty.[16] No one was certain what was going on, and there was nobody in charge to give orders. Some of the officers took the opportunity to talk to the assembled *sepoys*, the jumbled remnants of all three Delhi regiments: 'an officer asked a non-commissioned officer why the native troops at Meerut had risen in rebellion against the Sirkar (Government), on which he replied, 'Why not? The Commander-in-Chief is up at Simla, eating his dinners, and pays no heeds to our complaints.'[17] Lieutenant Vibart reached the worrying conclusion that 'it was evident from this reply that the men's minds were rankling under some fancied sense of injustice', and that the officers could not ultimately rely on their men.[18]

Eventually, around 5 p.m., it was decided to retreat. They would follow the civilians, who had started to leave the Flagstaff Tower, and make their way to the assumed safety of Meerut and other stations in the region. At the Flagstaff Tower, the situation was one of complete chaos; apart from the gathering of women and children and their servants and belongings, the officers also had to keep an eye on the restless detachment of *sepoys* of the 38th BNI who had so far remained at their posts. These *sepoys*, however, were overheard saying that 'in the event of a single shot being fired, they would immediately turn on the Europeans and murder every one'.[19] As soon as the magazine blew up, these *sepoys* cheered and left for the Cashmere Gate, firing on several officers along the way. Before the officers and troops at the Main Guard started moving out, the *sepoys* of the now openly mutinous 38th BNI started entering the Main Guard. Lieutenant Vibart witnessed the situation as it unfolded:

> At this critical juncture, and just as Major Abbott had passed through the Cashmere gate with about half his, and the guns were about to follow, some of the 38th sepoys rushed at the gate and closed it; their next act was to discharge a volley right amongst a group of officers, and their example was, as far as I could see, rapidly followed by all the other sepoys inside the enclosure. A scene now ensued that baffles description, and of which I can convey but a faint idea. Almost at the first discharge I saw Captain Gordon fall from his horse; a musket-ball had pierced his body, and he fell without a groan within a few feet of where I was standing. The next moment I saw Miss Forrest hastily dismount from

the gun wagon on which she was seated and jump across his prostrate body. It seems some sepoys had advanced towards her in a threatening manner, and, shooting a wounded conductor, who was sitting by her side, dead on the spot, had compelled her to alight. The terrible truth now flashed on me – we were being massacred right and left without any means of escape![20]

Many of the officers and civilians who had been gathered at the Main Guard got away by jumping into the deep ditch on the outer side of the wall, and alone or in small groups made their escape as best they could. The old and infirm had trouble keeping up, and Vibart's party had to leave behind the elderly and corpulent Mrs Forster.[21] Similarly, those leaving from the Flagstaff Tower had to leave some of the wounded behind, including Colonel Ripley who was still lamenting the fact that his men had bayoneted him.[22] Captain Tytler tried in vain to get some of his men from the 38th BNI to accompany the Europeans on their flight, but the *sepoys* were told that the magazine had been blown up on purpose to kill their brethren. Tytler tried to reason with them, but even the most loyal *sepoys* remained suspicious of their superiors, telling him: 'Sir, we cannot follow you, we spill our blood for you, and you treat us in return by blowing up our brothers with gunpowder, go, Sir, go, you have been our father and mother, always kind to us, with *bahana* (misleading) we will prevent the cavalry from following you; but we cannot come ourselves.'[23] And so Tytler had to leave his men and join his family and the long train of refugees slowly making its way along the road, leaving behind the city of Delhi in the hands of its population.

## 'Go that way, and you will get murdered! Come this, and you will meet the same fate!'

Long after the main body of fleeing civilians had left the Flagstaff Tower, several officers of the Delhi regiments remained in their lines, unsure of what to do.[24] As darkness was falling, groups of *sowars* and *sepoys* and villagers started plundering the cantonment and setting the bungalows on fire. Lieutenant Peile of the 38th BNI was very ill and had been about to proceed on medical leave when the outbreak caught up with him.[25] Having seen off the refugees, Peile managed to save the regimental colours with the assistance of some loyal *sepoys*. He later described the scene as he was leaving the desolated cantonment:

> … on taking [the colours] outside what was my horror and disgust to find that my *syce* had decamped, taking my horse and a large quantity of cheroots with him. As I could not, particularly in my weak state, carry it on foot, my only remaining course was to replace the standard and flee. On again coming into the open air a trooper took a deliberate aim at me with his carbine, but the ball passed harmlessly through my basket helmet, and as the man was so close to me I drew my pistol from my belt and shot him dead. Another man levelled his musket at me, but it was instantaneously knocked aside by a sepoy of my regiment, who immediately after ran his bayonet through his body, at the same time calling him by a name which it is not necessary to repeat. Several men then crowded round me, telling me to run across the parade ground, but not to venture near the lines, as the cavalry, 74th and 54th sepoys were murdering every Christian they came near.[26]

Making his escape, Peile was nevertheless set upon soon after by a group of Gujars, who stripped him of all his possessions and clothes. Like the other parties of refugees making their way to the safety of Kurnaul or Meerut, he was alternately helped and plundered in the villages he passed and by the locals he met. The loyalties of people in the environs of Delhi and the Meerut district were largely determined by contingent circumstances and fear of either the British or the mutineers exerting their authority. The greatest threat to the parties of fleeing Europeans leaving Delhi were in fact the local villagers and not necessarily the rebel troops; one British woman was so desperate that when she met what was obviously a rebel *sowar* from Meerut, she still stopped him to ask for directions: 'The answer I received was – "Go that way" (pointing to Kurnaul), "you will get murdered! Come this" (pointing to Delhi), "and you will meet the same fate!"'[27] Lieutenant Peile had an even more peculiar encounter: in a small village some distance from Delhi, he was allowed by the headman to take some rest on a *charpoy* and he soon fell asleep. But his rest did not last long:

> I had not been in the arms of Morpheus more than an hour or so, when I was awakened from my slumbers, by some one tugging violently at one of my legs, and on raising myself up I saw an old hoary man, with a fiendish countenance standing at the foot of the charpoy, who asked me what business I had there.

I told him I was the guest of the zemindar, and on his requesting me to get up and go outside, found that my limbs refused to do their accustomed duty. He then went to the door and called to some one, and immediately after two 3rd cavalry sowars rushed in with their sabres drawn and a lathee in their hands. They threatened to kill me, but on one taking me by the hand, to drag me up he found that what I had told them was correct, and that really I could not stand. Whether from compassion at my helpless state or from what other cause I am unable to judge, they relented and said I should not be injured and having called for hookahs sat down by my bed side conversing with me. They informed me that they had been imprisoned by sentence of the court martial at Meerut, at the same time corroborating their assertions by showing me the marks of the shackles, but had been released by their brother mutineers, had arrived at Delhi on the day previous, and had been instrumental in placing the king on his throne, and finished off by relating with *gôut*, how they had butchered several Europeans. They honoured me with their agreeable society for about one and half hours when they returned to Delhi, having given me to understand that they had come thus far in search of two officers, who I conclude must have been Brigadier Graves and Capt. Nicoll.[28]

Peile had to flee the village the following morning when parties of *sepoys* came by searching for refugees, but he later made it to safety. In the days and weeks that followed, ragged refugees from Delhi wandered into the stations at Meerut and Karnaul, many having been plundered of all their possessions. The Tytlers had an eventful journey, with Harriet giving birth to a son along the way, but they eventually reached Meerut, as did Lieutenant Vibart. The exact number of Europeans killed at Delhi on 11 May and during the following weeks will never be known, but a rough estimate of more than 200 would not seem to be unwarranted. At least as many native Christians must have been killed as well.

## 'Unless you the King join us, we are all dead men'

Inside Delhi, the combined troops of the Meerut and Delhi regiments were getting restless and frustrated with the King's refusal to meet with them. They had successfully overthrown British rule, but still needed the sanction of an appropriate authority; without the King's blessings and symbolic leadership, their possession of Delhi would be no more than nominal. Finally, during the late afternoon, the mutineers lost their patience, as the royal attorney, Ghulam Abbas, described:

> … two companies of infantry which were on guard at the Palace Gates, followed by the mutinous Cavalry that had come from Meerut, marched into the courtyard of the Hall of Special Audience, and commenced firing their muskets, carbines and pistols into the air, at the same time making a great clamour. The King hearing the noise came out, and standing at the door of the Hall of Special Audience, told his immediate attendants to direct the troops to discontinue the noise they were making, and to call the Native Officers forward, that they might explain the object of such proceedings. On this the noise was quelled, and the Officers of the Cavalry came forward mounted as they were, and explained that they had been required to bite cartridges, the use of which deprived both Hindus and Mahommedans of their religion, as the cartridges were greased with beef and pork fat, and they accordingly killed the Europeans at Meerut and had come to claim his protection. The King replied 'I did not call for you, you have acted very wickedly.' On this about one or two hundred of the mutinous Infantry, the Infantry from Meerut having also arrived by this time, ascended the steps and came into the Hall, saying, 'That unless you the King join us, we are all dead men, and we must in that case just do what we can for ourselves.'[29]

Bahadur Shah Zafar was in a real predicament – if he openly sided with the mutineers, his fate would be sealed along with theirs, and he was reluctant to make such a momentous decision on the spur of the moment. The King had in fact already sent a messenger to the British authorities at Agra, 222 miles to the south, to inform them of what had happened at Delhi.[30] Faced by several thousand excited troops clamouring for his support, in a city engulfed in flames and riots, the King nevertheless had to make up his mind very quickly. The courtiers argued with the troops, and the royal physician said: 'You have been long accustomed under the English rule to regular pay. The King has no treasury. How can he pay you?' The officers replied: 'We will bring the revenue of the whole Empire to your treasury.'[31] Uncertain of the real situation, yet sure of the devastating consequences an ill-considered decision would have, the King finally gave in. He seated himself on the throne, according to an eyewitness, 'and the Soldiery, Officers and all, came forward one by one, bowed their heads before him, asking him to place his hand on them. The King did so, and each withdrew saying just what came into his mind.'[32]

Within twenty-four hours of turning on their officers at Meerut, the mutinous *sepoys* and *sowars* were in possession of a heavily fortified city and had the blessing and nominal leadership of the symbolically most powerful man in India. The remarkable sequence of events, which had begun with a panic in the Sudder Bazaar at Meerut, came to an end at midnight on 11 May, as a formal salute of twenty-one cannon was fired over the bastions of the Red Fort in Delhi, heralding the defeat of the British and the restoration of Mughal rule.[33] No one could have foreseen this outcome, even if there were those who had hoped for it.

*

The closest we come to identifying a ringleader of the outbreak at Meerut is one Gulab Shah, an officer of the 3rd BLC, who is later described as the leader of the Meerut mutineers at Delhi.[34] On 16 May he also appears as one of the main perpetrators of the massacre of Europeans kept inside the Red Fort, thus irrevocably implicating the King and the royal household in the uprising.[35] This Gulab Shah is likely to have been the same *Subadar* Golaub Khan of the 3rd BLC, who was one of the judges in the court martial of the skirmishers, and probably the only one who opposed a guilty sentence.[36] Of the two *subadars* of the regiment, one is explicitly mentioned as having deserted on 10 May, and the one who remained loyal was identified as *Subadar* Ram Chum Sing.[37] Accordingly, there are very strong indications that *Subadar* Golaub Khan went to Delhi as the only senior native officer at the head of the mutinous 3rd BLC. Although we cannot be certain, Golaub Khan may have corresponded with the Delhi troops, may have been implicated in the cutting of the telegraph line to Delhi, and may have initiated the rescue of the skirmishers and subsequently led the *sowars* to Delhi.[38]

At Delhi there was said to have been a 'perfect union of mind between the Delhi and Meerut troops', but even so, the events on 11 May were not the result of a plot.[39] Despite the existing tension in the Mughal capital, and the fact that the *sepoys* there were informed of the execution of Isuree Pandey that very morning, the Delhi regiments were not standing at the ready to receive the mutineers from Meerut. The bulk of the Meerut troops arrived in a trickle throughout the morning and midday of 11 May, but most of the *sepoys* of the Delhi regiments did not openly join them until late in the afternoon.

Even then they were wavering in their actions. And even though a number of the Mughal princes and other members of Bahadur Shah's household soon became heavily involved in the Uprising, there had been no conspirators to open the gates of Delhi for the mutineers on the morning of 11 May. On the contrary, everybody in the Red Fort was taken by surprise by the arrival of the Meerut mutineers, and one of the princes stated that 'On the 11th of May when the Rebel Army came, I thought at first that the Russian Army was come ….'.[40] The fall of Delhi was as unexpected as the outbreak at Meerut.

Yet for all the similarities between the events of 10 and 11 May at Meerut and Delhi, there were some noteworthy differences worth keeping in mind. The outbreak at Meerut was a more or less spontaneous event, precipitated by the court martial of the skirmishers and determined in large part by contingencies. Panic and rumour played an absolutely decisive role at Meerut, whereas the *sepoys* and local population of the Mughal capital did not act out of fear or desperation. The Uprising of 1857 thus arrived at Delhi, as it were, in the shape of the Meerut mutineers crossing the Bridge of Boats. Widespread resistance to British rule would not have emerged at Delhi, nor would the city have exploded in violence and plunder, were it not for the invasion of the Meerut mutineers with bloodied swords, claiming they had killed all the British. Moreover, at Delhi there was a local power structure capable of replacing the British, and few inside the Red Fort harboured any sympathies for the foreign rulers. The general population of the city, where British rule had never been fully established, was similarly resentful – in part due to the intrusion of Christian missionaries and the disrespectful treatment of the King and royal family by Company officials.[41] Persistent reports of disaffection and arson amongst the *sepoys* at cantonments across northern India, and alarmist news from Persia, had further brought the situation to the boil. The influx of the Meerut mutineers thus provided the spark and impetus for local leaders at Delhi, notably members of the royal household, to take charge and lead the crowds and *sepoys*. There were no European troops at Delhi, which meant that the mutineers and locals could topple British rule with relative ease – in contrast to Meerut, they did not have to fear any immediate reprisals. The rumours that had been circulating in the capital about the end of Company rule and the imminent invasion of Persian and Russian armies thus became self-fulfilling prophecies as the *sepoys* and civilians themselves brought about this momentous event.

# 14

## The Uprising

The Uprising of 1857 really began on 12 May, after the outbreak at Meerut and the fall of Delhi. Until then, *sepoys* had merely been voicing their discontent and sharing their fears and aspirations with each other. These mutterings, however, had no clear aim, nor a notion of what might happen if the troops acted on their panic and opposed their superiors. The fate of the 19th and 34th BNI, and the executions of Mangal and Isuree Pandey, certainly did not provide a model for future action.[1] Across northern India, *sepoys* and civilians had expected something to happen for months. Now the threshold had been crossed and the outbreaks of 10 and 11 May created a powerful precedent and set in motion a series of events that were neither planned nor foreseen. With Delhi in the hands of mutinous *sepoys* under the leadership of Bahadur Shah, the widespread disaffection had attained a definite goal and had been given a distinct direction.[2] Once under way, the outbreak thus assumed a momentum of its own – an apparently self-perpetuating dynamic. The initial scope and character of the Uprising was thus shaped by contingencies and the initial success of the rebels, irrespective of the minor plotting among the *sepoys* prior to 10 May 1857.

There was never a question of Meerut having been chosen as the strategically most suitable place for an outbreak; there were any number of cantonments with no European troops at hand to quell an outbreak, and several other cities where one might have expected a disturbance, but where none occurred. At Ambala, for instance, the situation was obviously volatile, and by all accounts a mutiny was only just averted there during the morning of 10 May. Another hot spot was the recently annexed city of Lucknow, where Company rule was massively unpopular and where the *sepoys* had been showing alarming signs of unrest during the first week of May. After a British doctor offended the *sepoys* of the 48th BNI by drinking directly from a bottle of medicine in the regimental hospital, his bungalow had been set on fire in April.[3] Some of the troops stationed at Lucknow also began practising with the Enfield during that month, and it was widely rumoured that their discontent was growing.[4] As Lucknow was the old seat of the ex-King of Oudh, and the *sepoys* were thought to be corrupted through contact with the locals, the Governor-General had even been considering removing all native regiments from the city.[5] On 2 May, the native troops of the 7th Oudh Irregulars had refused to drill with the (ungreased) Enfield cartridges, and they sent a secret letter to the *sepoys* of the 48th BNI, stating that 'We are ready to obey the directions of our brothers of the 48th in the matter of the cartridges, and to resist either actively or passively.'[6] The Irregulars were disarmed the very next morning, in the presence of European troops, but it was clear that all the *sepoys* at Lucknow were then on the brink of mutiny.[7] And yet nothing happened at Lucknow until some three weeks after the outbreak at Meerut.[8] That the outbreak happened at Meerut, rather than anywhere else, was entirely accidental. Caused initially by Smyth's decision to demonstrate the new drill, it was only due to the proximity of Delhi that this relatively minor event had such massive repercussions.

As news of the outbreak spread beyond the environs of Delhi, it sent ripples throughout northern India; at Lahore, a telegram informing the authorities of the outbreak led to the prompt disarmament of the native regiments on 13 May. When European troops took charge of the magazine at the nearby station of Ferozepore the same evening, the *sepoys* tried to prevent this, and several hundred of them subsequently deserted. Elsewhere, the thoughtless acts of panicking officials provoked *sepoys* to join the rebels. Many Indians who had no previous intention of turning against the British now found themselves under constant suspicion and being accused of conspiracy. At times, official reports of the outbreak, printed in the British press, filtered through to the Indian troops and resulted in their desertion or actively joining the mutiny.[9] The mere news of the outbreak was sometimes sufficient, and a *sowar* of the 2nd Oude Irregular Cavalry thus stated that his regiment only started plotting 'after hearing of the Meerut mutiny'.[10]

The thousands of *sepoys* stationed all over northern India provided the Uprising with a sense of unity. The outbreak was initiated by the *sepoys* and it was through their networks of communication, which predated 10 May 1857, that news of the outbreak was transmitted and the diffusion of the Uprising was sustained. The *sepoys* of the Bengal Army constituted a uniquely coherent group, cutting across religious and social divides, and as such they added a sense of organisation and unity to the outbreak that was not to be found anywhere else in India at this time.[11] The correspondence between the different native regiments, which had been carried on ever since the first rumours at Dum Dum and Barrackpore in January, now assumed a more serious character. On 18 May, loyal *sepoys* of the 64th Bengal Native Infantry at Shabqadar handed over a letter to their commanding officer, which had been sent to them by the 51st Bengal Native Infantry stationed at Peshawar. The letter contained a warning that the greased cartridges would be distributed to them on 22 May and exhorted the 64th BNI to come to Peshawar the day before: 'O brother! the religion of Hindoos and Mahommedans is all one – Therefore all you soldiers should know this. Here all the sepoys are at the binding of the Jemadar, Soobadar Major, and Havildar major. All are discontented with this business, whether small or great. What more need be written? Do as you think best.'[12] Being forewarned, the British moved quickly to disarm the affected regiments, but across northern India plotting amongst the *sepoys* was now proliferating at an exponential rate.[13] The Uprising was further disseminated by mutineers and released convicts returning to their villages, and at Lucknow, a British officer thus noted in his diary that on 16 June 'twenty-two conspirators, emissaries from Benares and elsewhere, who had been sent to corrupt the troops at this place, were captured'.[14]

After Delhi had been taken by the mutineers, the letters sent out to the various *sepoy* regiments could be very effective.[15] A *sepoy* at Jhansi described how the mutiny there came under way when a servant:

> brought a chit from Delhi station that the whole army of the Bengal Presidency had mutinied and as the Regiment stationed at Jhansee had not done so, men composing it were outcasts or had lost their faith. On the receipt of this letter, the four ring leaders … prevailed upon their countrymen to revolt and to carry out their resolution; it was out that the station was going to be visited by Dacoits. On this the whole force getting under arms went to the Magazine, but finding that such was not the case, all those who were not disaffected went back to their lines and the disaffected resolved to kill their officers. They did so, and taking the two guns that were there, they went to Delhi.[16]

This did not necessarily imply that the *sepoys* at Jhansi had been part of previous plotting, and the *sepoy* specifically added that 'No answer was returned to the letter received from Delhi nor was ever correspondence kept open with the Cawnpore or other quarters.'[17] In the Mughal capital, the local head of police Mainodin described how 'In every instance the King's *perwanah* had the effect of causing the soldiers to mutiny and make their way to Delhi. At the sight of the King's *perwanah* the men who had fought for the English forgot the past, in the desire to be re-established under a native Sovereign; thus, daily, the city became more and more the centre of the rebellion.'[18] As news of the Uprising spread, it caused panic and led to further outbreaks; often fear and group pressure played an active role and *sepoys* at Moradabad mutinied on account of 'the upbraiding and taunts of the artillerymen and city people, and the constant reports circulated by them of Europeans coming from Meerut to blow them away from guns, and their resolve not to spare one, which kept the men in a state of perpetual fear'.[19] The significance of the initial outbreaks may be discerned in the manner in which the mutinies spread outwards from Meerut and Delhi – not entirely unlike the transmission of the *chapattis* a few months earlier.[20] During May and June, the early outbreaks thus followed a clear pattern, spreading outward from Delhi, and for each new regiment or station that mutinied, the Uprising and its transmission were further energised.

Major Williams, who had undertaken the inquiries into the outbreak at Meerut, made the following summary of the sequence of events following 10 May:

> A few Native troops suddenly mutiny; burn, plunder and murder; release prisoners, and completely subvert all order and authority, and this with scarce any opposition, in the face of a large European Force. Thence passing on unchecked to a large and important City, with the uncontradicted boast that they had exterminated the British and overthrown their rule; gain possession of it; winning over their fellow soldiers cantoned there; enact over again the same scene of anarchy, bloodshed and riot; proclaim a rebel King, issue proclamations and exact revenue in his name; cut off all communication and overrun the surrounding country. Their example is rapidly followed: whole Regiments tread eagerly in their steps; entire Districts pass away from our hold; petty Chiefs and Princes exercise, undisputed, the rights of sovereignty; while their late lordly Rulers are no where to be seen, or beheld only as way-worn, travellers, soiled, famishing, and often sore-wounded fugitives; pleading for food, shelter and concealment, and at times repulsed as the offscouring of earth, by those who lately would have kissed the dust under their feet! The few Provinces still held by us, kept only by the self-devotion of their Civil and military Officers, and gallant bands of

Volunteers, here and there assisted by a handful of troops. Seeing us powerless to help or protect our friends, or to chastise our foes, can we wonder that the timid, wavering, and weak fell in with those who, for the time being at least, best made the weight of their vengeance known; or can we wonder that the masses of people, losing sight of all signs of our power and authority, and witnessing only the evidences (temporary though they were) of the rule of our enemies, should really credit their reports of our subversion and utter annihilation; and all this occurring at the end of the foretold 100 years, during which our rule was to last, should fancy they saw the finger of God in the exact fulfilment of the prophecy?[21]

Though written from a distinctly British perspective, Williams' account nevertheless captures some of the main elements that characterised the spread of the Uprising.

As the Uprising spread, it became a series of localised conflicts stimulated by neighbouring examples of revolt. Popular rebellion grew out of a longstanding climate of dissatisfaction that was provided with an impetus by the *sepoys*' mutiny. But it assumed widely different characteristics in different locations, and was by no means universal across northern India. Some dispossessed rulers and landowners seized the opportunity to regain their lost possessions, while others engaged in long-standing feuds over land and power. In some instances, *sepoys* assumed the role of leadership, but generally, the absence of colonial authority meant the reimposition of pre-colonial authority based on traditional systems of governance. At the front of the rebels in Oudh were the landowners and petty rulers who had recently been dispossessed by the British. Their aims were simply to regain their possessions, but in their opposition to British rule their aims converged with those of the *sepoys*. In many places the Uprising was a purely local affair, and some rebels merely drove out the local British authorities and assumed control of districts without otherwise becoming involved in the conflict. Similarly to Bahadur Shah, Indian rulers like Nana Sahib and the Rani of Jhansi were forced by circumstances to become rebel leaders. Those who fought the British did not do so for some abstract notion of Indian independence, but to free their own territory or area from foreign rule. Others were hedging their bets, waiting to see the outcome of the struggle, before they decided which side to join.

To the British it seemed as if their defeat heralded a return to the old days of supposed 'Oriental' anarchy:

In the Pergunnahs [districts] the news spread like wild fire, and the villagers rose in every direction and plundered and murdered each other promiscuously. Old enmities and the long smothered wish for revenge were forthwith satisfied. Auction purchasers and decree-holders were ousted, travellers and merchandize plundered, and the servants of Government compelled to fly for their lives; and in all instances Government buildings and property of every description were plundered and destroyed. Every man's hand was against his neighbour, and the natives revelled in all the license and madness of unchecked anarchy and rebellion, in a manner such as only Asiatics can revel in those pleasures. Tulwars and matchlocks were scarce in Bundelkund; but armed with spears and scythes, and iron-bound latties, and extemporary axes, formed of chopping knives fastened on sticks, they imagined themselves to be warriors, chose their own Kings, and defied all comers. Never was revolution more rapid – never more complete.[22]

For all its prejudice, this account nevertheless reveals how some British officials recognised the fact that the Uprising was more than just a mutiny amongst disgruntled soldiers. In certain parts of northern India, the events of 1857 did in fact turn the world upside down.

While the sequence of events generally followed the pattern of Meerut and Delhi, the outbreaks at individual stations and towns assumed a momentum of their own, derived from the contingencies of specific events and places. 'Risings or revolutions have dynamics of their own,' as one historian has noted, 'independent of the social structure, economic grievance or political thought of the subject people or lower orders who take part in them.'[23] Indians rose for different reasons, but local grievances and idiosyncratic causes converged around general issues, among which the defence of religion and the social order assumed a central and unifying role.

However, a rebel movement born out of a sequence of contingencies and seized opportunities, united only through diverse grievances against colonial rule, and held together by the knowledge that survival depended on the defeat of the British, could not last long. What amounted to local forms of patriotism did arguably emerge in certain areas and motivated a desperate resistance against British forces, most notably in Oudh and Bihar, under leaders such as Kunwar Singh and in Bundelkhand the Rani of Jhansi. Similarly, there was a certain level of cooperation between Hindus and Muslims, together facing a Christian enemy. But the fact remains that more Indians fought alongside the British to suppress the Uprising, which never extended much beyond a limited northern portion of the subcontinent within the Indo-Gangetic plain. Many *sepoys* of the Bengal Army may have maintained close ties to their kinsfolk and villages, and this undoubtedly played a significant role in places like Oudh and Bihar during the Uprising. The regiments that mutinied at Meerut and Delhi, however, had no such connections or attachment to the local population of the region. To claim that the *sepoy* was merely a peasant in uniform does not establish the existence of a bond between the first mutineers and the urban populations of those cities, or even the Gujars and Jats of the rural areas.[24]

The proclamations issued from rebel-held strongholds such as Delhi and Lucknow do indicate that there was a conscious effort to mobilise Hindu–Muslim unity, but the very need to do so suggests that this solidarity was in practice wanting. If Hindus and Muslims had been fighting side by side, in complete secular harmony, there would have been no need for the repeated calls for sectarian unity. Events at Delhi further suggest that the united rebel front against the British had many weak spots: in July, the Hindu *sepoys* executed five Muslim butchers for slaughtering cows. In the absence of colonial rule, the religious communities did not simply embrace one another and put former strife aside; during the Uprising of 1857, sectarian cooperation amongst the rebels succeeded in some places and failed in others. The geographic scope of the Uprising, and sense of brotherhood amongst the native troops, did engender a broader notion of Hindustani patriotism *vis-à-vis* the displacement of British rule. Yet these attempts to establish a single overarching Hindu–Muslim rebel identity were simultaneously counterbalanced by local loyalties that fragmented rebel cohesion.

The *sepoys* had originally mutinied without any grand strategy, beyond removing Company rule, and by the late summer of 1857, the British had regained the initiative by launching several parallel campaigns to resume control of northern India. After the British retook Delhi, in September 1857, the theatre of war changed to Oudh and central India, and coalesced around a few rebel strongholds. The momentum of the initial outbreak, in the end, proved insufficient to sustain the uprising, and the collusion between the different rebel parties proved to be short-lived. There was no unified rebel command to pursue common strategies, and after a number of decisive defeats at the hands of the British, the Uprising eventually came to an end. Scattered bands of rebels and local groups kept up a sporadic guerrilla resistance until 1859, but all organised resistance to the British had by then subsided.

## 'The English tried to make Christians of us'

The outbreak in some places gave birth to what amounted to patriotic feelings and a reconceptualisation of the political map of northern India, which had simply been inconceivable prior to the collapse of Company rule.[25] Prior to 10 May, no Indian ruler, landlord, *sepoy* or peasant could have envisaged what an India without the British might look like. Events at Meerut and Delhi, however, opened up a range of unexpected opportunities – for the old order to be restored or a new society to be imagined. The very process of rising against the British was thus constitutive of a political rebel consciousness, which did not precede the outbreak.[26] During the early months of 1857, there was no formulation of an alternative to colonial rule, only vague rumours of Persian or Russian invasions and the imminent collapse of the East India Company. The *sepoys* and *sowars* who fled from Meerut to Delhi certainly had no fully fledged political programme, and it is in fact notable how apparently helpless they were once they had taken over the Mughal capital. Although they had reached Delhi on their own initiative, the vast majority of them relinquished all responsibility after 11 May. They had transferred their allegiance and expected the new Government to look after them as a formal employer would.[27] It was thus a throwback to the old days when the *sepoys* expected leadership and support from the Mughal Emperor, calling out to him: 'Help O King! We pray for assistance in our fight for the faith.'[28] The mutineers nevertheless saw in Bahadur Shah a figure of authority who could redress their grievances, which they voiced (as was the habit of the times) in exclusively religious terms: 'The English tried to make Christians of us, and gave us these cartridges with that object; for this reason we have come to the King for protection ….'[29] When captured *sepoys* were later interrogated by the British, they unanimously cited the cartridge, or 'cartouche' as they referred to it, as the main reason for the mutiny.[30]

It must be obvious that the cartridge issue by itself was not the sole cause behind the outbreak; at the same time, however, it cannot be dismissed as a mere pretext for the Uprising of 1857. The cartridges were a highly evocative symbol that encapsulated the most basic fears of many Indians: having firmly established their paramount rule, the British would irrevocably change Indian society, ultimately depriving Indians of their religious and social status in order to make them Christians. This was the only purpose that the East India Company appeared to serve, and few Indians would have been aware of the global network of trading stocks, and shareholders, which actually motivated the Company's acquisition of territory. Even when rebel proclamations cited a wide range of political, economic and social grievances against the British, the perceived attack on religion loomed large and was the one thing that affected Hindus and Muslims alike. When the British Prime Minister, Disraeli, dismissed the cartridges as the real cause behind the uprising and famously told the House of Commons that 'the decline and fall of empires are not affairs of greased cartridges', he was correct.[31] However, the rumour of the greased cartridges evoked the collective fears of Hindu and Muslim *sepoys* in a very tangible manner. Whether the objection to the cartridges should be attributed to an actual belief that the grease was polluting, or whether group pressure and the fear of being ostracised by friends and kin weighed more heavily, the cartridge issue constituted a unique symbol around which *sepoy* disaffection consolidated. The prominent Muslim scholar Fazl Ul Haq, who was deported by the British for his role in the Uprising, described the outbreak in the following terms:

> [The British] started their machinations by making the Hindu and Muslim sepoys give up their (religious) rites and practices and leading them astray from the path of their religions and faiths, because they were under the impression that if the brave sepoys would agree to denouncing and changing their religion and obeying their orders then the others (civil population) would not dare to recoil (disobey) because of the fear of chastisement and punishment.
>
> (Accordingly) they forced Hindu soldiers, who were in overwhelming majority to taste the fat of the cow and the Muslims who were in minority to taste the fat of the pig. Thus each of the two peoples (fariqayn), in order to safeguard their faith and religion left the path of obedience. They began to murder, loot and kill their officers (tarkhan) and chiefs …[32]

The cartridges epitomised broader fears of British intervention, and the *sepoys'* response to the cartridges may be seen as an index of these wider concerns. Given that no single greased cartridge was ever distributed to *sepoys* anywhere, the significance of the issue is testament to the immense power of rumours.

If, however, the native troops were mistaken in seeing the cartridge as a tool for conversion, their British officers were no more clear-sighted in their assessment of the *sepoys'* objections. In late April and early May, *The Delhi Gazette* published two letters, written by British officers pretending to be *sepoys*. The first was by 'Sepoy Ram Sing' and explained the importance of caste pride to the Indian troops and the obnoxious smell of the greased cartridges, which had supposedly gone bad in the hot climate of the subcontinent.[33] The remedy for the discontent amongst the *sepoys*, the anonymous author suggested, was to treat them like men and convince them in a calm manner that the Government would never do anything to ruin their caste. Two weeks later, 'Ram Sing' received a response from the 'Ghost of Mungul Pandy'.[34] In his humorous attempt to reveal the hypocrisy and irrationality of the *sepoys*, the British author inadvertently revealed his own and his fellow countrymen's complete lack of understanding of Indian religious beliefs and of the long-standing relationship between religious practice and governance within the subcontinent. Without respect for religion, which legitimised their rule, no *raja* or *zamindar* had ever governed peacefully for long during pre-colonial times. Local rulers patronised temples and shrines, to which they personally owed no allegiance, and the most successful of the Mughal and Rajput rulers enjoined their subjects to celebrate and respect Muslim, Hindu, and other religious festivals alike.[35] This reality was lamentably misunderstood by the British. The letter in *The Delhi Gazette* ended with an exposition of Indians' treatment of cows (written from the assumed perspective of the Brahmin Mangal Pandey) and a stern note of warning:

> Two calves are born, one they emasculate and put it into a cart and work it and wallop it. The other grows up a brahminee bull and they fall down before and worship it – and you feed upon the milk and the ghee, the produce of the live cow, and grow fat and thrive upon it, and you put the hide of your dead god on your shoulders, on your back and breast; and you wear it on your feet, and you think no harm in this. But if you are asked to touch the fat of your dead deity, AND IT SUITS YOUR PURPOSE, then and not otherwise, the touch of your god becomes pollution! – Verily, RAM SING, this is, believe me, all rot and the sooner you get rid of such rubbish out of your foolish heads the better for you. I now clearly see that I made an ass out of myself and I deserved what I got and I can see with equal clearness that if you go on as you seem to think many are inclined to go on, they will be served as I was served, and deservedly too! Depend upon it, RAM SING, that if you merit hanging, the Sirdar Buhadoor [the Government] will not only have the heart, and the pluck, to hang you, but will also find the rope.[36]

> THE GHOST OF MUNGUL PANDY BY KOONT
> The Paradise of Fools, April 21, 1857.

Most Britons never grasped the real issues behind the *sepoys'* fears until it was too late – if at all. Applying a distinctly Western interpretation to a religion they despised, they found it impossible to believe that the grievances of the Indian troops were sincere. The outbreak of 1857 thus constituted a catastrophic intelligence failure on the part of the British authorities; most of the disaffection steadily developed into a deadly hatred right in front of their eyes, and amongst the very *sepoys* with whom they worked daily. Similarly, the authorities did not register the increasing resentment amongst a wider proportion of the Indian population – the background noise of anti-British sentiments, as it were. It was thus the consistent misreading of the abundant information and unmistakable signs that something very serious was happening, which led to the failure to anticipate an outbreak. There were a few exceptions, like Martineau at Ambala or Greathed at Meerut, who recognised the signs all too clearly. In general, however, senior commanders such as Hearsey, Mitchell, Anson and Smyth did not realise the seriousness of the situation that was slowly emerging. For all their thick-headedness, however, it must be acknowledged that the military authorities did try to to resolve the cartridge issue and dispel the fears of the *sepoys*. The Commissioner at Jabalpur, Major Erskine, thus described the official response to the rumours of bone-dust that circulated in May 1857:

> Every care was taken by the Military Authorities to disabuse the soldiers of the stories they heard, and it was early in May that stories were spread in Saugor, Dumoh and Jubbulpore, to the effect that the ghee, atta and sugar had been adulterated by order of Government with pig's and cow's blood and bone-dust, in order that all Hindoos and Mohametans partaking of them might lose their caste or religion.
>
> I issued a proclamation explaining that all reports of the kind were false, and I recommended Commanding Officers to have their men's provisions purchased and examined by Committees of Native Officers, and the atta to be ground in their presence.[37]

The problem was, however, that the rumours merely reflected wider problems between rulers and ruled. Erskine's following sentence in that regard is very revealing: 'This had a good effect, and two or three persons having been caught spreading false reports were well flogged.'[38] No amount of understanding between individual officers and their men could hide the fact the British were alien to India and in large part maintained their rule through brute force.

Preceding decades had witnessed an increasing distance between the British and the Indians, exacerbated by the advent of Evangelicalism and increasing social segregation. The days when British officials adopted local customs and openly married Indian women were definitely a thing of the past.

On 10 and 11 May 1857, the shortcomings of the relationship between the British and their Indian subjects were made devastatingly explicit. The British had been taken unawares by what they perceived to be a widespread Indian conspiracy to overthrow the Company's rule and revive the idolatry and anarchy of the past. The *sepoys*, however, and with them many Indians, believed that they had only just averted an extensive conspiracy on the part of the British Government to undermine the social order and their faith – either by force or by treachery. As the Uprising progressed, the dual nature of the great fear of 1857 thus became plainly evident. Amongst the native troops, the panic inspired by stories of the greased cartridges and polluted flour were augmented by the old bogey of European troops turning against them. Following the events of 10 May, this scenario became increasingly likely. Less than a week after the outbreak at Meerut, a *sepoy* thus attempted to incite the *sowars* of the 2nd Bengal Light Cavalry at Cawnpore 'by stating that they would all be blown away from guns'.[39] Similarly, a British official at Faizabad noted how 'The disarming and massacring story, which was industriously promulgated all over the country, was almost universally believed, and may have had most injurious effect. A native, in whom I placed considerable reliance, assured me that it was the immediate cause of the mutiny and cruel murders [of Europeans] at Allahabad.'[40] After the outbreak at Meerut, British officials in many instances panicked, which exacerbated an already deteriorating situation. At Benares, for instance, the British officers facing a crowd of mutinous *sepoys* accidentally opened fire on a loyal regiment of Sikh soldiers, which prompted these to join the mutineers.[41] Even in the safety of Calcutta, the British community fell prey to extreme paranoia, as described by the Revd Alexander Duff:

> The hundred and one rumours – rumours of secret night meetings of the Mohammedans – of fanatic devotees rousing the ignorant multitude to rise up and murder the enemies of their faith – of hundreds of disbanded sepoy mutineers in the native town panting for revenge – of thousands of desperadoes from the neighbouring districts swarming in the bazaars thirsting for plunder – of numbers of the native police, weak, cowed, and disaffected – of suspicious-looking characters prowling about the houses of Europeans in the dark – of the insolence,

and strange glances, and mysterious whispering of native servants – of regiments on the plain detected in treasonable correspondence with those in the fort – of the personal danger of the Governor-General, and of the Government-house being actually in possession of traitorous native guards – of intercepted letters, said to specify the plan to be adopted, and the very hour when all Europeans were to be swept away in a deluge of blood – these, and such like rumours, some more or less exaggerated, and some, it may be, wholly unfounded, but all in succession momentarily believed, tended to raise the public terror to fever heat.[42]

Both *sepoys* and British officers consistently failed to grasp the nature of their antagonistic encounter, and instead reverted to preconceived notions about the opponent. In virtually simultaneous proclamations, Governor-General Canning warned the *sepoys* of 'designing and evil-minded men' stirring them to mutiny, while a rebel proclamation issued in the name of Bahadur Shah warned Indians of the 'designing plans' of the British Government trying to convert them to Christianity.[43] The events surrounding the outbreak were thus characterised by a dynamic of mutually enforcing misunderstandings, or what one Indian historian has described as 'a dialogue in which neither of the interlocutors understood the other's language'.[44] This deep-seated inability to understand each other inextricably led towards an eruption that was based, ultimately, on cultural miscognition. Violence thus bred violence on an unprecedented scale. The *sepoys* and locals initially lashed out with extreme violence in defence against the perceived assault on their religion. As colonial authority collapsed, general resentment of Company rule was expressed through indiscriminate attacks on British and native Christian men, women, and children. Once the initial shock had passed, and the implications of the outbreak had become apparent, the British responded in kind. In retribution for the often sensationalised stories of white women and children slaughtered by the savage rebels, the British exacted an unbelievably brutal revenge; tens of thousands of Indian men, women, and children were indiscriminately shot, hanged or blown from cannon in an unbridled assertion of colonial power and authority.

# 15

## The Great Conspiracy

The British found it hard to comprehend that the *sepoys* along with large parts of the Indian population had risen against them. Having effectively ruled the Indian subcontinent for generations, they believed they knew everything that went on amongst their native subjects. They had successfully penetrated even the darker corners of the native underworld and supposedly established a solid base of loyal supporters amongst the local population. Thus it came as shock for the British to realise that even their most trusted soldiers and servants harboured feelings of resentment and were capable of such violence. Kaye very succinctly expressed this:

> There was not an English gentlewoman in the country who did not feel measureless security in the thought that a guard of Sepoys watched her house, or who would not have travelled, under such an escort, across the whole length and breadth of the land. What was lurking beneath the fair surface we knew not. We saw only the softer side of the Sepoy's nature; and there was nothing to make us believe that there was danger in the confidence which we reposed in those outward signs of attachment to our rule.[1]

The British were further appalled by the readiness with which some local officials adapted to the situation following the collapse of colonial rule. One magistrate noted that 'They changed masters as they would change their clothes, and thought nothing of it. Their conduct was disgraceful.'[2] The British had erroneously assumed that because local people had worked for them, they would then also entertain a sense of loyalty, and even prefer Company rule to that of their own.

The belief in a great conspiracy became conspicuously pervasive amongst the British during the suppression and in the immediate aftermath of the

Uprising. After the outbreak, the events of the preceding months were suddenly seen in a new teleological light, or, as the Delhi police officer Mainodin expressed it, 'When the rebellion had begun, the full force and significance of all that had preceded it became apparent, and men understood what it meant.'[3] The rumours and *chapattis* could now be recognised as the vehicles of the planned uprising, while the cartridge issue was revealed as a mere ploy to mislead the gullible *sepoys*. This new interpretation emphasised the treachery and villainy of the native conspirators, but at the same time also hinted at the negligence of incompetent officials, who had ignored the warnings of experienced officers with a real knowledge of the land. Ultimately, the blame was placed squarely on the insidious Indian plotters; as the Revd Duff described it:

> Throughout the ages the Asiatic has been noted for his duplicity, cunning, hypocrisy, treachery; and coupled with this, – and, indeed, as necessary for excelling in his accomplishment of Jesuitism, – his capacity of secrecy and concealment. But in vain will the annals even of Asia be ransacked for examples of artful, refined, consummate duplicity, surpassing those which have been exhibited throughout the recent mutinies. In almost every instance, the *sepoys* succeeded in concealing their long-concocted and deep-laid murderous designs from the most vigilant officers to the very last …[4]

One curious aspect of British paranoia following 1857 is the extent to which it owed its origins to the rumours that had circulated amongst the local population at places like Delhi. The prevalent belief that foreign powers, and especially Russia, had played an active role in instigating the Uprising was thus derived as much from native newsletters and proclamations as it was from any real grasp of international *realpolitik*.[5] Like the indigenous conspiracy, Russian influence was never proven but rather assumed, and this indeed became a standard trope in British India.[6]

The British authorities were nevertheless very prone to see a guiding hand and design behind the Uprising, as when Special Commissioner J. C. Wilson famously described the *sepoy* conspiracy:

> Carefully collating oral information with facts as they occurred, I am convinced that Sunday, 31st March, 1857, was the day fixed for the mutiny to commence throughout the Bengal Army; that there were committees of about three members in each regiment, which conducted the duties, if I may so speak, of the mutiny;

that the sipahees [sepoys], as a body, knew nothing of the plans arranged; and that the only compact, entered into by regiments, as a body, was that their particular regiment would do as the other regiments did. The committee conducted the correspondence and arranged the plan of operations, viz., that on the 31ˢᵗ May, parties should be told off to murder all European functionaries, most of whom would be engaged at church, seize the treasure, which would then be augmented by the first instalment of the rubbee harvest, and release the prisoners, of which an army existed in the North Western Provinces alone, of upwards of twenty-five thousand men. The regiments in Delhi, and its immediate vicinity, were instructed to seize the magazine and fortifications; but the massacre being complete and thoroughly carried out, and all opposition thus rendered impossible, it was arranged that all other brigades and out-posts should remain at their respective stations.[7]

While this account of the *sepoys'* plotting may not seem too ill-informed, it still attributed the outbreak to the work of committees that planned operations, dispatched instructions, and conducted the mutiny. Even Major Williams, who made extensive investigations into the causes of the outbreak, claimed that at Meerut, 'there were secret Agents, and those Mahomedans, watching, if not guiding events; it seems impossible in this part of the country to doubt'.[8]

Bahadur Shah had in fact been 'identified' as the main force behind the outbreak as early as 13 May – mere days after he had been forced to give the mutineers his blessing. In the first official account of the outbreak at Delhi, Major Abbott of the 74th Bengal Native Infantry stated that:

From what I could glean there is not the slightest doubt that this insurrection has been originated and matured in the palace of the King of Delhi, and that with his full knowledge and sanction in the mad attempt to establish himself in the sovereignty of this country. It is well known that he has called on the neighbouring States to co-operate with him in thus trying to subvert the existing Government. The method he adopted appears to be to have gained the sympathy of the 38ᵗʰ Regiment, Light Infantry, by spreading the lying reports now going through the country of the Government having it in contemplation to upset their religion, and have them all forcibly inducted to Christianity.[9]

From the very outset of the Uprising, the British accordingly operated from the assumption that the Mughal Emperor had played a key role in its instigation. This had not changed by the time Bahadur Shah was captured following the fall of Delhi on 16 September 1857.

*

The trial of the last Mughal Emperor, Bahadur Shah Zafar, produced the very first and single most elaborate account of the great conspiracy of 1857. As an official record, the trial proceedings thus provided a veritable blueprint for later influential conspiracy theories such as that of Malleson. Yet, like so many other events of this fateful year, the trial was by no means an ordinary affair.

When Captain Hodson famously apprehended Bahadur Shah after the fall of Delhi, he had, contrary to his orders, promised the old Emperor that his life would be spared. The same pardon did not apply to the two princes Mirza and Bakht, whom Hodson simply gunned down while they were in his keeping. This left the British with the ailing Bahadur Shah, who had played only a nominal role in the Uprising, but who was nevertheless generally perceived as the figurehead of this most serious challenge to British rule.[10] The technical legality of putting Bahadur Shah on trial was highly dubious, as the East India Company was still formally a vassal of the Mughal Emperor, as had been established after the Battle of Buxar in 1765.[11] This was, however, purely a formality, and at no point during his reign had Bahadur Shah been anything but a titular ruler dependent upon the Company for the maintenance of his position. By the time of his ascension to the throne in 1838, for instance, the British had long since ceased acknowledging the Mughal Emperor on their coinage.[12] Even the symbolic significance of Bahadur Shah during the Uprising, and the brief resurgence of his status, could not hide the fact that by 1857 he was the pensioner of the East India Company in everything but name. Accordingly, there were many in the British administration who saw in the trial the perfect opportunity finally to put to rest what they considered to be the anachronistic pretensions of a decrepit dynasty belonging to a bygone era.

What has hitherto not been recognised, however, is the controversy within the British administration as to the nature of the trial. Martial law had first been declared at Meerut on 14 May 1857 when Deputy Judge Advocate Major F. J. Harriott summarily sentenced the butcher Mowla Baksh to death for the murder of Mrs Chambers.[13] The following day, martial law was formally declared, and it was still in place after the fall of Delhi, which meant that, as a prisoner, Bahadur Shah would be dealt with by a Military Commission.[14] Captain Hodson's unauthorised promise to the Emperor was upheld as legally binding, and Bahadur Shah could accordingly not be given the death sentence, as had so many of the other rebel leaders tried at Delhi. Given this situation, the civil authorities were in favour of 'a political enquiry rather than a trial' and the Chief Commissioner of Punjab, John Lawrence, stated: 'I do not think it would be expedient to prepare any specific charges against the King of Delhy on which to try him. I would propose that the Commission be at liberty to hear and place upon record all evidence bearing against the King and connected with the late insurrection. This is simply for record. He is not being tried for his life.'[15]

The man put in charge of the case was none other than Judge Advocate Harriott of the 3rd BLC, who had been part of the original inquiry of the eighty-five skirmishers at Meerut as well as their subsequent trial. The same man who had played an active role in the events surrounding the outbreak at Meerut was thus to head the legal case formally marking the suppression of the Uprising at Delhi.[16] Harriott did not concur with Lawrence and simply assumed that the Mughal Emperor was to be tried. If a trial of Bahadur Shah was to be considered fair, Harriott further argued, specific charges had to be made and a verdict reached. The Judge Advocate's rationale smacked heavily of legal sophistry: unless the Emperor was given the purely hypothetical opportunity to clear himself, the British might incur accusations of being unjust. A mere inquiry would not provide the legal opportunity for this, and accordingly Harriott wrote up the charges against Bahadur Shah on 5 January 1858. As the Emperor's health was rapidly deteriorating, there was a general concern to avoid any further delays, and the Commissioner in Delhi simply agreed with Harriott's proposals and so the trial went ahead. When Lawrence learnt of this new development, he strongly objected:

> The fact is, however, that the object of the enquiry is really rather with the view of elucidating important facts connected with the rebellion than to determine the precise nature and extent of the ex-King's complicity. From the moment that his life was guaranteed there ceased, in the Chief Commissioner's judgement, to be any advantage in bringing him individually to trial. His complicity in the rebellion was open and notorious, and under no circumstances could he ever obtain his liberty or be restored to his former status.[17]

Set to begin on 9 January, the trial was nevertheless postponed for almost three weeks due to Bahadur Shah's health. Fearing that this delay might allow time for a change in the proceedings, Harriott took the unprecedented step of publicising the charges in the English-language newspapers. This effectively committed the Government to the type of trial he had planned.[18]

The case against Bahadur Shah, which to all intents and purposes was directed by Harriott single-handedly, finally began on 27 January and lasted until 9 March 1858. With great symbolic poignancy, the proceedings were held in the Red Fort in the Great Hall of Audience – where Bahadur Shah had given the mutineers his blessings, and thus sealed his own fate, on 11 May 1857. Even at this late date, there was no consensus amongst the authorities, and prompted by reports of the Emperor's continuing poor health, Lawrence's secretary wrote to the Commissioner of Delhi stating that 'The Chief commissioner considers that under the circumstances you have reported it will perhaps be better to postpone the trial until the ex-King either dies or recovers. If he should die, the charges will naturally drop and a mere political enquiry be made. If he should recover, the trial can proceed.'[19]

Bahadur Shah did recover and the trial thus did proceed. The Emperor was formally charged with having, between 10 May and 1 October 1857, encouraged, aided, and abetted the various rebel leaders and royal princes to mutiny, rebel, and wage war against the state. As a subject of the British Government, he was also charged with being 'a false traitor' for seizing the throne and taking possession of Delhi. During the period when Delhi was in his hands, he conspired and consulted with the rebel leaders and furthermore, 'to fulfil his treasonable design of overthrowing and destroying the British Government in India, did assemble armed forces at Delhi, and send them forth to fight and wage war against the said British Government'. Finally he was charged with having caused and been an accessory to the murder of those Europeans killed in the Red Fort on 16 May 1857. Bahadur Shah pleaded not guilty.[20]

It is notable that not a single charge referred to events predating 10 May 1857, which in effect implied that Bahadur Shah was *not* charged with conspiracies preceding the outbreak at Meerut. And as John Lawrence had previously argued, there was little doubt as to the actual role of the Emperor between May and October 1857. The peculiarity of the trial was thus a result of its contested origins, and it was in fact little more than an inquiry with a purely nominal trial attached in the most perfunctory manner. Even though Harriott had managed to press the charges he wanted, he would have to pursue them through a very general investigation. An extensive amount of evidence, including royal orders, proclamations, letters and native news reports, was produced to prove that the Emperor had indeed been the ruler of Delhi during the Uprising. Numerous witnesses were also brought forward to give testimony, including the Emperor's own physician and servants, as well as Europeans who had survived the fall of Delhi. Following weeks of lengthy testimonies and examinations, Harriott made his final address to the Court, stating that:

> the questions, which as far as I am aware of have not as yet found a satisfactory solution, are, by what circumstances was this most atrocious revolt, with its series of massacres brought about, and who were its prime original instigators? … To throw the fullest light on a subject like this, is not the work of a day, or of a month … That we have been able to unravel many of the secret workings of the conspirators, will, I believe, be conceded …[21]

Harriott thus presented the trial as his own unravelling of the great conspiracy of 1857 and went on to discuss the various aspects of the wider networks of conspirators. *Sepoys* from Meerut had brought news of the trial of the eighty-five skirmishers on 10 May, according to Harriott, who stated that 'although we may not possess positive evidence to the fact, yet it may fairly be presumed that Sunday evening was not the first occasion that these plotters of evil held their secret and sinister councils together'.[22] The outbreak at Meerut was similarly planned, he stated, and bore 'the impress of cunning and of secret combination'.[23] The outbreak at Meerut was thus carefully planned, and the conspirators there waited until the troops at Delhi had been warned and meticulously timed the outbreak so that they could operate under the cover of darkness. Echoing official sentiments on the *sepoys'* objections to the cartridges, Harriott dismissed them as 'transparently false' and erroneously claimed that the mutineers had used the greased Enfield cartridges against the British once the Uprising began without any compunction.[24] Further, he added, the *sepoys* could simply have left the service of the Company if they had been so dissatisfied with their employment. The conclusion was that the cartridge issue was a mere pretext:

> Does it appear consistent with the natural order of events, that such intense malignity should start into existence on one single provocation? Or can it be reconciled with the instincts, the traditions, or the idiosyncrasies of the Hindus,

that they should, recklessly, without inquiry, and without thought, desire to imbrue their hands in human blood, casting aside the pecuniary and other advantages that bound them to the cause of order and of the Government? Or, more than this, can it be imagined that the three regiments at Meerut, even when joined by those at Delhi, could have conceived an idea so daring as that of overthrowing, by themselves, the British Government in India?

I think Gentlemen, even if one must allow that if we had no other evidence of a plot, no testimony indicative of a previous conspiracy, the very nature of the outbreak itself must have convinced us of the existence of one. In the moral, as in the physical world, there must be cause and effect; and the horrible butcheries of the past year would remain an anomaly and a mystery for ever, could we trace them to nothing more occult and baneful than a cartridge of any kind.[25]

Here the Judge Advocate invoked what amounted to a naturalist perception of conspiracies; it was a highly mechanistic notion of cause and effect that was little different from the epidemiological and geological terminology used by later historians. The fact of the outbreak was in itself proof of a prior conspiracy – things happened because someone had made them happen, and the cause of events could be inferred from their effect. Following this line of reasoning, it was inconceivable that a mutiny could occur without previous planning. Moving on to an elaboration of the wider causes of the Uprising, Harriott argued that 'there must have been some other and more latent power at work to have thus operated on a whole army scattered in different cantonments from Calcutta to Peshawar. I think that such could not have been accomplished without some secret mutual understanding, and some previous preparation, the establishment of which may appropriately be termed conspiracy.'[26] With theatrical grandiloquence, the Judge Advocate described how he uncovered the secret machinations, explaining that 'I should be more than blind to all that has appeared in these proceedings and elsewhere, if I failed to recognise in the cartridge question, the immediate means or instrument adopted for bringing about a much desired end. It seems to have been the spark, not accidentally shot forth, but deliberately chosen to explode a mine previously prepared.'[27]

Ultimately, the Muslims were identified as the main conspirators, and in Harriott's assessment, 'the revolt has perhaps assumed many of the features of a Mussulman conspiracy, and it is, I think, probable that to Mussulman intrigue may eventually be traced those false and fabricated rumours, which, adroitly mixed up with some small portion of truth, have been so instrumental in effacing the last vestiges of fidelity in an army whose faithfulness was at one time perhaps its very chiefest pride and boast'.[28] Already disaffected by the conditions of service, the *sepoys* had been easy prey to manipulation by the wily Muslims:

> Among such a body as this there must always be some discontented intriguers, and who that knows anything of Asiatic character will readily admit, especially with reference to Hindus, that the few are more potent for evil than the many for good? Let but three or four leaders come forth in all the open audacity of crime, or mix themselves up in the secret intrigues of sedition, and the rest, if not immediately panic struck, never think it their duty to check or oppose them.[29]

Harriott further reasoned that the conspirators were responsible for the spread of discontent prior to the outbreak, especially through the circulation of *chapattis*. 'This and the false rumour about mixing ground bones with the flour had doubtless one common origin, and it is not going beyond the bounds of fair indication or reasonable inference, to attribute both one and the other to the unceasing wiles of Mahommedan conspiracy.'[30] Even the stories about Persian and Russian invasions of India had been part of the conspiratorial propaganda, and although these rumours appeared silly to Europeans, Harriott warned that 'we should commit a grievous and most fatal error, if we were to gauge Asiatic thought and understanding by the same measure that would be applicable to our own'.[31] Tracing all the different strands of native discontent to the same insidious source, the Judge Advocate could not help but admire the evil genius behind the plotting: 'I must own that to me this apparently natural transition from the chapaties to its component parts, seems a masterstroke of cunning, and evidenced most able leadership in the cause the conspirators were embarked in.'[32]

Having established the existence of a vast conspiracy, it was only left for Harriott to establish the role of Bahadur Shah, which he did by asking the court a typically rhetorical question:

> … has he in these transactions been the leader, or the led, has he been the original mover, the head and front of the undertaking, or has he been the consenting tool, the willing instrument in the hands of others, the forward, unscrupulous, but still pliant puppet, tutored by priestly craft for the advancement of religious bigotry. Many persons, I believe, will incline to the latter. The known restless

spirit of Mahommedan fanaticism has been the first aggressor, the vindictive intolerance of that peculiar faith has been struggling for mastery, seditious conspiracy has been its means, the prisoner its active accomplice, and every possible crime the frightful result.[33]

The Uprising had been a Muslim conspiracy through and through, the Judge Advocate concluded, and the Hindus had been entirely subservient to their 'ever-aggressive neighbour'. Harriott had by then already asked for the court to pass a guilty verdict, 'which shall record to this and to all ages, that kings by crime are degraded to felons, and that the long glories of a dynasty may be for ever effaced in a day!'[34] The court readily complied with Harriott's pompous request and Bahdaur Shah was found guilty on all the charges; the last Mughal Emperor was deported to Rangoon, where he died in 1862.

The case against Bahadur Shah was nothing if not a show trial, and few within the British administration failed to notice the glaring shortcomings of the proceedings: *none* of the testimonies or evidence produced during the trial had actually corroborated Harriott's lengthy exposé of the great conspiracy.[35] The Judge Advocate had been forced to admit as much himself: 'In alluding to the existence of a conspiracy, I do not mean to imply that we have come upon traces of a particular gang of men specially banded together for the fixed definite object of causing the late rebellion in the native army…'[36] Yet this did not prevent Harriott from pursuing his line of enquiry, ignoring whatever evidence contradicted his argument and mobilising a host of Orientalist stereotypes to invoke a timeless Islamic fanaticism as the prime mover of the conspiracy.

As he had been opposed to a trial, rather than an inquiry, right from the beginning, John Lawrence's formal opinion was highly pragmatic. He concurred with the conviction, but added an important comment several pages long.

I do not however consider that there is satisfactory evidence to show that the ex-King was connected with a conspiracy, previous to the 10th of May 1857, to induce a mutiny in the Bengal Native Army. Indeed, it is my decided impression that that mutiny had its origin in the Army itself, and was simply taken advantage of by disaffected persons in the country to compass their own ends. It is, moreover, my belief that the cartridge question was the immediate cause of the mutiny.[37]

While dismissing the existence of any greater conspiracy, Lawrence did add that:

> It is very possible, indeed probable, that the native soldiers of the regiments of Infantry at Delhy were so far in the scheme that they had engaged to stand by their comrades at Merutt. Such indeed was the case all over the Bengal Presidency. The men consisted of a common brotherhood, with feelings, hopes in common, and whether they had actually engaged to stand by each other or not, all well knew that as a body such would prove the case …
>
> Had there been a general conspiracy in the country, or even in the Army as unconnected with the cartridge question, how is it that the people and soldiers did not rise simultaneously in insurrection? I am told that the time fixed for it was anticipated by the Merutt outbreak. But if such were the case, how came it then that the news of the outbreak was not followed by immediate insurrection? No preparation was necessary. But nothing of the kind occurred. It was only when the Native Troops saw how powerless we were that they resolved to convert what was a mere combination against what they fancied to be gross oppression into a struggle for empire.[38]

The trial of Bahadur Shah thus resulted in two inherently opposed interpretations of the events of 1857. According to Harriott, the Uprising could only have been the result of a vast conspiracy; while in Lawrence's opinion, there was no evidence for such a conspiracy and the events of 1857 were shaped by several different and rather more complex issues. In the end, however, it was Harriott's account that won out; it provided the simplest explanation that linked all the different aspects and events of the Uprising together in a neat narrative. It was furthermore the account most in tune with popular perceptions of indigenous conspiracies, and confirmed the panic and paranoia that had gripped the British public both in India and in Britain during 1857:

> Stunned and shocked, the British saw the complaisant *sepoy* suddenly revealed as a rapacious murderer, the faithful bearer a treacherous villain. Safety, they discovered, could be found only among their own countrymen. Once betrayed by those whom they had trusted, the British could no longer bring themselves to trust anyone with a brown face: all alike were tainted. Hence the bonds of race were quickly tightened, for survival itself was seen to depend on it; and the British from their entrenchments looked upon the Indian people with increasing

bitterness and hatred. This growing racial antagonism was exacerbated beyond measure by the reports of massacres and atrocities in which English women and children were murdered in cold blood. Nothing could arouse such a frenzy of hatred in the Victorian Englishman as to see his womenfolk, so long safe from foreign invaders and hedged round by sentiment and chivalry, hacked to pieces by barbarous ruffians.[39]

Just as the conspiracy of Nana Sahib was intrinsically linked to his betrayal and murder of British civilians, so too did the trial of Bahadur Shah connect the notion of indigenous conspiracy with the brutal massacre of white-skinned women. The trial thus elicited detailed eyewitness accounts of the murders of Miss Jennings and Miss Clifford as well as the forty-eight prisoners on 16 May.[40] If the earliest atrocities at Meerut had been exaggerated and sensationalised, this was even more so in the case of Delhi as these stories were disseminated. Whenever the exact circumstances were unknown, the imagination was given free rein; in that respect Harriet Tytler's account of the deaths of Miss Jennings and Miss Clifford was rather sober: 'The one generally believed was that when Captain Douglas and Mr Jennings had been murdered, the two poor girls in their terror hid themselves under their beds and were dragged out and thrown out of the window on the pavement below, a merciful death compared to what might have been their fate.'[41] Others did not hesitate to describe what that fate actually was: 'Two ladies, both young, and described as "very pretty," were seized at Delhi, stripped naked, tied on a cart, taken to the Bazaar, and there violated. They died from the effects of the brutal treatment they received.'[42] The actual massacre of the British prisoners at the Red Fort also lent itself to gratuitous embellishment, and in one account the fate of the two girls was combined with that the of the palace prisoners:

> [The *sepoys* at Delhi] took forty-eight females, most of them girls of from ten to fourteen, many delicately nurtured ladies, violated them, and kept them for the base purposes of the heads of the insurrection for a whole week. At the end of that time, they made them to strip themselves, and gave them up to the lowest of the people, to abuse in broad day-light in the streets of Delhi. They then commenced the work of torturing them to death, cutting off their breasts, fingers, and noses and leaving them to die. One lady was three days dying. They flayed the face of another lady, and made her walk naked through the streets.[43]

These stories were not merely produced to feed the hysteric outrage of the British public; the horrors became an intrinsic part of 'understanding' the Uprising and what indigenous conspiracies entailed. Native treachery constituted not only an attack on British authority but also a very tangible attack on British women, and that is what made the conspiracies of 1857 such potent sources of fear in the colonial psyche.[44] The outbreak of the mutinies at Meerut and Delhi thus became embodied in the stories of Mrs Chambers, the Law family and the Misses Jennings and Clifford.

## 'Streams of maddened natives, bent upon murder and plunder'

In spite of his efforts, F. J. Harriott had succeeded in no more than suggesting the vague outlines of the alleged conspiracy. But where the legal and historical accounts fell short, fiction stepped in to flesh out the conspiracy narrative and provide the kind of detail that was to become the hallmark of the so-called 'Mutiny' novel. The weakness of colonial rule and the traumatic events of 1857 were thus redressed through a literary reimagination. In the hundreds of fictional accounts that were produced during the decades following the Uprising, the stories of evil plotters and secret signs were thus given full expression, alongside the standard themes of betrayal and revenge, rape and interracial love, identity and disguise.[45] J. E. Muddock's *The Great White Hand* (1896) encapsulates much of the standard 'Mutiny' repertoire in its depiction of the outbreak at Meerut.[46] Following the shackling parade on 9 May, the young hero Walther, a 'greenhorn' fresh out from Britain, explains to his fiancée Flora that the example of the eighty-five skirmishers will quell all trouble amongst the *sepoys*:

> 'There you are in error, Walther; what our troops did this morning has only increased our danger manifold. There is not a *Sepoy* in all Meerut to-night, but who is nursing in his breast feelings of the most deadly hatred towards the English. The fire smoulders, and a breath will fan it into flame. If the natives should rise, may God in His mercy pity us.'

'Tut, tut, my girl; you are alarming yourself with foolish fears, and there is nothing at all to justify your apprehensions. The soldiers dare not revolt, and if they did, we have such an overwhelming force of British in the cantonment, that all the native regiments would be speedily cut to pieces.'

'The belief in our security is our danger,' she answered. 'Remember I know the country and the natives well. I have been in India from the time I was a little child. Those who are in authority seem to me to be wilfully blind to the signs which indicate coming mischief. For some days past, a man, ostensibly a Fakeer, has been riding about the city on an elephant, and visiting all the native quarters. I do not believe that man to be what he professes to be. He is an agent moving about from place to place, and stirring up the rankling hatred for the British which is in the hearts of all his country-men.'[47]

A key theme within the Anglo-Indian novel was that of the experienced India-hand who knew the land and perceived the signs of unrest, while the ignorant newcomer, relying on Western rationale, failed to heed the warnings. The knowledgeable character inevitably had a rapport with the natives and usually a Man-Friday figure who informed him, or her, of the impending trouble. In Flora's case, the native informant is a servant who is infatuated with her and who warns her of the *sepoys'* plans. The girl informs Walther of this, telling him: 'I feel sure that there was truth in what the man told me, and his leaving you on that day was part of his scheme. You may say I am nervous, foolish, stupid, what you will, but I understand the natives well. I know how treacherous they can be; and it is useless our trying to cheat ourselves into a belief that they love us, because they don't do anything of the sort.'[48]

Flora is eventually placated by Walther, who assures her of the loyalty of natives such as Nana Sahib. The girl, however, retorts: 'But what proof have you that the Nana is not playing a well-studied game; only biding his time to execute a well-planned *coup-d'état*, and strike for his home and liberty?' But Flora's worries are simply dismissed with a 'Bosh!'[49] The foolish Englishman, however, would have done well to listen to Flora:

As sleep fell upon the northern quarter of Meerut on that Saturday night, there was an unusual stir in the native part. In the lines of the native soldiery, in the populous bazaars, and in the surrounding villages, a fatal signal was passing. Five fleet-footed Indians were speeding from place to place; and as they went, they put into the hands of the principal men a small cake. It was a chupatty; and, like the fiery cross, it was the signal of a general rising.[50]

Subsequently, in yet another cliché-ridden passage, hundreds of natives assemble for a secret meeting in a ruined temple, access to which is granted by the inept password: 'Chupatty!'[51] As the meeting begins, a scene evoking all the sinister mysteries of the 'Orient' is described:

> The dark wall of the ruin appeared to be actually jewelled with gleaming eyes, which, as they caught the fitful glare of the lamp, flashed with hatred and revenge. A dull, confused sound only was heard as the swarming natives conversed with one another in subdued tones. Presently six distinct beats were given on a tom-tom. Then there was a death-like silence, as there entered, by the main entrance, a tall man, whose face was muffled by a puggeree [turban cloth]. He was followed by several other natives; and as they entered and took up their position at one end of the ruins, salaams rose from a hundred throats. Then the tall man threw back his puggeree, and exposed his features.[52]

The man turns out to be none other than Nana Sahib, described as a dashing Asian prince with daggers and jewels in his turban, attended by the panther-like Azimullah Khan. Finally, Nana Sahib addresses the eager crowd:

> Countrymen, I have ventured here to-night that I may, by my presence, inspire you with courage and hope. We stand on the eve of great events, and no man has the cause more at heart than I. We wait but for one signal now to decide us in the course of action we are to take. That signal is to come from Delhi. Our agents have been hard at work for some days, and if the regiments there will join us, and give us shelter if needed, all will be well. Though I must hurry back to Bithoor to-night, that it may not be known, until the proper hour arrives, that I have shaken off allegiance to the hated Feringhees, I shall be with you in spirit; and, in the name of the prophet, I invoke success on your arms.[53]

By having Nana Sahib present in Meerut on the eve of the outbreak, Muddock drew upon the well-established figure of the arch-fiend of 1857 to create the impression of a massive plot. The very setting for the meeting, and the religious invocation, further emphasise the superstitious and fanatical nature of the Indian plotters. When the awaited signal from Delhi arrives, it is in the shape of a *chapatti*, on which there is written in red the following message: 'We fight for the King. We fight for the restoration of the Mogul throne. We fight for the Prophet.'[54] The vagueness of the original transmission of *chapattis* is thus transformed into a clear written message, however occult the medium, and the aims of the mutineers are quite literally spelled out. Assured of the assistance of their brethren at Delhi, the meeting comes to an end and Nana Sahib hurries back to his palace to finalise the plot:

> Then the crowd of natives quietly left the ruined temple, and soon the roofless halls were silent and deserted, and the slimy things that had sought shelter from the trampling feet, in the nooks and crannies, timidly came forth now, in search of prey, upon which they might feed so that they might live in accordance with the instinct planted by a Divine hand. But the hundreds of human beings who a little before had held possession of the temple had also gone forth in search of prey, thirsting for blood – blood of the innocent and guilty alike – not that they might live thereby, but to gratify a burning feeling of hatred and revenge.[55]

Driven by a gratuitous impulse to kill, the Indian conspirators are not even granted the rationale of hungry animals. The months of rumours and increasing panic amongst the *sepoys* and the subsequent confusion and chaos of the events of 10 May are thus transformed into a single linear and logical narrative. The Uprising of 1857 had been planned and executed by the conspirators, with Nana Sahib and Bahadur Shah at the head; *fakirs* and mendicants had spread sedition and manipulated the native troops, who broke out in mutiny only when the requisite signal was given in the form of the mysterious *chapatti*. The resemblance between the basic plot of Harriott's account and Muddock's novel is indisputable. It is certainly no coincidence that Muddock, and with her many other writers using the 'Mutiny' as a backdrop for their fiction, explicitly invoked the 'authority of history' to assert the truthfulness of her story.[56] The line between historical account and fiction was indeed blurred, and by the time Malleson wrote his history of the Uprising, the two had in effect become indistinguishable. As Muddock's story continues, the *sepoys* turn against their officer on the parade ground at Meerut and the general population joins in:

> From every street, and corner, and hole, and alley – from the bazaars and the villages – poured forth streams of maddened natives, bent upon murder and plunder. And 'death to the Feringhees!' was the one cry heard above all others. Like wild beasts from their lairs, seeking whom they might devour, came the hordes; and as the European officers rushed from their bungalows, they were shot down, and fell riddled with bullets.[57]

The outbreak at Meerut is thus described as a completely meaningless slaughter, an attack by bloodthirsty natives, without any recognisable grievances whatsoever. To the British public, this was what had happened on 10 May 1857 – and what could so very easily happen again.

*

The Uprising of 1857 cast a long shadow and its memory remained alive until the last days of the Raj. The most significant legacy of the Uprising was arguably the manner in which the British henceforth perceived any kind of anti-colonial sentiments amongst Indians. Superstition and fanaticism were thus seen to be the prime motivation behind the Uprising, and the same interpretation was later applied to the Indian nationalist movement – as became obvious in 1907. But the reverberations of the great fear of 1857 did not stop there. When Brigadier-General Dyer ordered his troops to open fire on thousands of unarmed civilians at Jallianwala Bagh in 1919, it was the spectre of the 'Mutiny' which spurred him on.[58] British paranoia, and the failure to understand the outbreak of the Uprising in 1857, were not simply caused by the momentary collapse of the information order, but were in effect key features of colonial rule in India.

# Epilogue: 1857 Today

On 10 May 2007, some 10,000 people, representing all the states and regions of India, participated in a symbolic march to celebrate the 150th anniversary of 1857. Accompanied by the familiar rallying call: '*Dili Chalo!*' ('To Delhi!'), the procession followed in the footsteps of the first mutineers, from the site of the new jail at Meerut to the erstwhile Mughal capital of Delhi. Before the departure, *chapattis* were served out to the crowds. At Meerut, the Uprising is today commemorated by the Shaheed Smarak, or 'Martyr's Memorial', which is located just south of the Sudder Bazaar. Portraits of celebrated rebel leaders such as Nana Sahib and Tantia Tope adorn the walls of the memorial museum, which also has dioramas of the outbreak at Meerut.[1]

Although his actions were historically confined to Barrackpore, the *sepoy* Mangal Pandey is also represented in both a bust and a life-sized statue at the memorial in Meerut. Thanks to the hagiographic efforts of V. D. Savarkar, whose account *The Indian War of Independence* first appeared in 1909, Mangal Pandey has emerged as one of the most popular Indian national heroes, and in popular history his name has come to be inexorably associated with the events of 10 May 1857. According to some oral accounts, it was Mangal Pandey who was first informed by a low-caste magazine labourer that the cartridges were smeared with the fat of pigs and cows.[2] This makes Mangal Pandey the original author of the rumour of the cartridges and provides a further context for his subsequent attack on the British officers of the 34th BNI at Barrackpore. Mangal Pandey is thus remembered as the first nationalist who sacrificed his life to spark off the Uprising, and the outbreak on 10 May is commonly believed to have been inspired by the news of his execution.

But Mangal Pandey also plays a key role in the somewhat surprising revival of the history of the great conspiracy of 1857. In his book, Savarkar extolled the anti-colonial plotting carried out by the secret leaders of the conspiracy:

> Of all the surprising incidents connected with the Revolution of 1857, the most striking was the secrecy with which the vast movement was organised. The clever English administrators had so little information about the source of the movement, even after the tremendous revolutionary upheaval all over Hindustan, that, even a year after the mutiny had broken out, most of them still persisted innocently in the belief that it was due to the greased cartridges![3]

In Savarkar's nationalist epos, however, Mangal Pandey was not one of the ringleaders but an inspirational martyr. By boldly attacking the British officers, and killing one according to Savarkar, the *sepoy* fulfilled his duty as a Brahmin and aroused the nationalist pride in his comrades through his example.[4]

Savarkar's nationalist conspiracy theory has proven resilient to the passing of time, and it has recently been resurrected by the journalist Amaresh Misra, who has written extensively on 1857.[5] For Misra, Mangal Pandey was *the* great conspirator of 1857 and allegedly orchestrated most of the unrest at Barrackpore and Berhampore, where the 19th BNI only mutinied in February after 'Mangal gave his approval.'[6] Following Savarkar, Misra's Mangal Pandey provides the spark that will set off the rebellion, and when he is court-martialled, he declines his comrades' offer to free him: 'Let them try me – the British make a great deal out of their system of justice. I want to show the world the farce of the British judicial system.'[7] The *sepoy*'s sacrifice bears fruit; the *fakir* who was reported at Meerut in April was, in Misra's account, actually spreading a revolutionary message and would 'often offer water to the *sepoys* and then utter the name Mangal Pandey – seizing upon the allusion the *sepoys* would listen to him more'.[8] When the eighty-five skirmishers of the 3rd BLC subsequently refused the cartridges, it was thus a 'conscious revolutionary act'.[9] Misra even provides the name of the 'leader of the Meerut revolutionary committee', namely one Basharat Ali, who started the rumour in the Sudder Bazaar and thus triggered the outbreak.[10] The events of 10 May at Meerut were accordingly not spontaneous and the *sepoy* army was both 'the actor and the director'.[11]

Writing the history of 1857 becomes the occasion for Misra to reinvent the history of modern India according to his own ideals: 'The fact that even 1857, hitherto seen as a mutiny or at best a national war, was actually an armed mass movement, wider, deeper and more nationalist than the Gandhian initiative is truly unusual.'[12] During an interview in 2007, Misra was asked how his book differed from the existing literature on the subject, to which he responded: 'It is radically different because no one has ever accepted that there was a plan.'[13] This not only obscures the fact that the notion of a great conspiracy originated with colonial authors such as Malleson, but also ignores Misra's indebtedness to Savarkar.

It is further worth noticing that the same basic plot-line is followed in Amir Khan's celebrated film, *The Rising – Ballad of Mangal Pandey* (2005), which popularises the revisionist vision of a proto-nationalist conspiracy.[14] In a key scene, the incredulous *sepoys* are shown the factory where the grease for the Enfield cartridges is made: the imagery appears taken from Dante's *Inferno*, with boiling cauldrons and slimy carcasses of pigs suspended from hooks in a dark, cavernous room full of nauseating steam. The issue of the greased cartridges is thus reduced to a simple story of the evil and arrogant British bent on ruining India. Between love affairs and dancing scenes, a dashing Mangal Pandey finds time to organise the Uprising along with Azimullah Khan and Tantia Tope. Gathered with his men around a map of India, the blueprint for the revolt, it is in fact Mangal Pandey who decides on the date, 31 May 1857, when 'all of India will rise and become free'.

Needless to say, there is little historical evidence to back up any of these revisionist interpretations of the events of 1857, which illustrates how the history of the Uprising continues to be rewritten to match modern sentiments.[15] As *The Rising* comes to an end, the image of Mangal Pandey fades into archive footage of Gandhi and other twentieth-century Indian nationalist leaders. The voiceover reiterates the patriotic message: 'Mangal Pandey in his death became a hero, a legend who inspired a nation to fight for freedom. The dream of freedom ignited by Mangal finally came true 90 years later on 15th August 1947, when India became free.'

*

A number of Indian historians have recently argued that it should be the prerogative of Indians to write about their own past.[16] Quoting Hiren Mukherji, the historian K. C. Yadav states: 'The "mutiny", more than any other event of the 19th century, shook our people's minds and hearts, and its real story can be told only by ourselves.'[17] This project has not fared well. In their attempt to reappropriate the history of 1857, to reclaim Indian history for Indian audiences, writers like V. D. Savarkar and Amaresh Misra have achieved little more than the perpetuation of the most staid tropes and crassest stereotypes of colonial historiography. This may provide India with a pantheon of proto-nationalist revolutionary heroes, amongst whom Mangal Pandey assumes the seat of honour, but this type of anachronistic hagiography pays a disservice to history. Perhaps more importantly, it is a version of the past that appeals to the ideals of a generation that is now itself passing. It provides little encouragement or direction to the historians of the future, who in the twenty-first century might wish to look for very different lessons to be learnt from India's past, to guide the nation toward its increasingly globalised, internationalist, and hopefully prosperous future.

# Notes

## Prologue

1 I owe the initial idea for this prologue to an article by my friend Deep Kanta Lahiri Choudhury, 'Sinews of Panic and the Nerves of Empire: The Imagined State's Entanglement with Information Panic, India c. 1880–1912', *Modern Asian Studies*, 38, 4 (2004), 965–1002. The work of my former supervisor, C. A. Bayly, and in particular *Empire and Information: Intelligence Gathering and Social Communication in India, 1780–1870* (Cambridge: Cambridge University Press, 1996), has also provided a constant source of inspiration.

2 See *The Times*, 9 May 1907; and *The Golden Commemoration of the Indian Mutiny at the Royal Albert Hall, Decr 23$^{rd}$ 1907* (London: W. H. Smith and Sons, 1907).

3 *The Golden Commemoration*, 12.

4 When referring to the Indians who rose against the British in 1857, I use the term 'rebel' in a purely descriptive manner without any suggestion of illegitimacy.

5 Savarkar Newsletter, 5 June 1908, <www.satyashodh.com/Savarkar%20 Newsletters1A.htm#d14> (accessed 1 Mar. 2008).

6 *The Times*, 24 Sept. and 2 Oct. 1907.

7 Savarkar Newsletter, 10 June 1907, <www.satyashodh.com/Savarkar%20 Newsletters1A.htm#d14> (accessed 1 Mar. 2008).

8 *The Times*, 24 Sept. 1907.

9 See Peter Heehs, 'Foreign Influences on Bengali Revolutionary Terrorism 1902–1908', *MAS*, 28, 3 (1994), 533–56: 534–5.

10 See for instance ibid., 537; and James Cambell Ker, *Political Troubles in India 1907–1917* (Calcutta: Superintendent Government Printing, 1917), 57.

11 *The New York Times*, 5 Jan. 1908. See also Ker, 17–18, 52 and 54; and Valentine Chirol, *Indian Unrest* (London: Macmillan, 1910), ix and 3.

12 See Lahiri Choudhury, 978.

13 Ibid., 978–9. See also Harrison to Sands, 6 May 1907, Minto Papers, MS 12756, NLS, 493.

14  See Martin Gilbert (ed.), *Servant of India* (London: Longmans, 1966), 93 and n. 1.

15  See N. Gerald Barrier, 'The Punjab Disturbances of 1907: The Response of the British Government in India to Agrarian Unrest', *Modern Asian Studies*, 1, 4 (1967), 353–83.

16  See Countess of Minto, *India: Minto and Morley 1905–1910* (London: Macmillan, 1934), 122–5 and 150–1. See also Barrier (1967), 365.

17  Minto to Morley, 8 May 1907, in *Minto and Morley*, 124.

18  See 'The Effect of the Present Unrest on the Native Army', 12 May 1907, Minto Papers, MS 12756, 433, NLS.

19  Gokhale was, however, a moderate and did not encourage the soldiers; see Holmes to Risley, 23 May 1907, Minto Papers, MS 12756, 494.

20  Para. 5–6 in ibid.

21  Para. 6 in ibid.

22  See below.

23  'Political Activity of the Sadhus up to 1909', History of the Freedom Movement Papers, II, R–I, 3/2, 80–89.

24  George MacMunn, *The Underworld of India* (London: Jarrolds, 1933), 111.

25  Harrison to Sands, 6 May 1907, Minto Papers, MS 12756, NLS, 493. See also Chirol, 194.

26  Ibid.

27  *New York Times*, 10 May 1907.

28  Barrier (1967), 365.

29  Pandit Rajani Kanta, *Swadeshi pallisangeet* (Mymensing, 1907); translated and reproduced by Lahiri Choudhuri, 983. In the colonial administration, however, some also feared that the Muslim tribesmen of the North-West Frontier might attack the Hindu population; see Minto to Morley, 8 May 1907, in *Minto and Morley*, 126.

30  Minto to Morley, 9 and 16 May 1907, in *Minto and Morley*, 128 and 131.

31  Minto to his wife, 15 May 1907, in *Minto and Morley*, 136.

32  See *Daily Hitavadi*, 8 Mar. 1907, Minto Papers, MS 12756, 265, NLS.

33  Minto to Morley, 8 May 1907, in *Minto and Morley*, 124–5.

34  Minto to Morley, 29 Aug. 1907, in *Minto and Morley*, 151–2.

35  Diary of Sir James Dunlop Smith, 4 June 1907, in Martin Gilbert (ed.), *Servant of India: A Study of Imperial Rule from 1905 to 1910 as Told through the Correspondence and Diaries of Sir James Dunlop Smith* (London: Longmans, 1966), 87.

36  Barrier (1967), 373.

37  The protests in Punjab eventually subsided, though *not* because Raj and Singh were deported, but because the contested regulation was annulled; see Barrier (1967), 374–77.

38  See 'Review of Legislation, 1907: British India', in *Journal of the Society of Comparative Legislation*, 9, 2 (1908), 383–4; and Ker, 63–105.

39  Chirol, 99.

40  Minute by Commander-in-Chief Kitchener, 5 June 1907, Minto Papers, MS 12756, 528, NLS.

41  Lahiri Choudhuri, 979–80 and 993; and Richard Popplewell, *Intelligence and Imperial Defence: British Intelligence and the Defence of the British Empire 1904–1924* (London: Frank Cass, 1995), 107.

42  Minto to Morley, 8 May 1907, in *Minto and Morley*, 127.

43  Lahiri Choudhuri, 979; and Michael Silvestri, '"The Sinn Féin of India": Irish Nationalism and the Policing of Revolutionary Terrorism in Bengal', *Journal of British Studies*, 39 (Oct. 2000), 454–86: 465.

44  Silvestri, 465; and Lawrence James, *Raj: The Making and Unmaking of British India* (London: Abacus, 1997), 424.

45  Minto to Morley, 8 May 1907, in *Minto and Morley*, 131.

46  Minto to his wife, 15 May 1907, in *Minto and Morley*, 136.

47  See Lahiri Choudhury, 983; and S. A. A. Rizvi and M. L. Bhargava (eds.), *Freedom Struggle in Uttar Pradesh* (Lucknow: Publications Bureau, 1957–61), I, 325.

48  See also diary of Sir James Dunlop Smith, 28 June 1907, in *Servant of India*, 90.

49  John Morley, *Indian Speeches (1907–1909)* (London: Macmillan and Co., 1909), 6 June 1907. During an outbreak of bubonic plague in Poona in 1897, the head of the Plague Committee and his assistant had also been killed by a youth enraged by the Government's harsh measures to curb the epidemic.

50  Minto to Morley, 8 May 1907, in *Minto and Morley*, 126–7.

51  See for instance Minto to Morley, 23 May 1907, in *Minto and Morley*, 132–3.

52  *The New York Times*, 10 May 1908.

53  Chirol, 57.

54  John Buchan, *Lord Minto: A Memoir* (London: Nelson, 1924), 78.

55  See Chirol, 103 and n. 10, 345–6.

56  Speech by Bipin Chandra Pal, cited in *New India*, 6 June 1907; see Ker, 48.

57  See Ker, 173; and Savarkar Newsletter, 5 June 1908, <www.satyashodh.com/ Savarkar%20 Newsletters1A.htm#d14> (accessed 1 Mar. 2008).

58  Savarkar Newsletter, 5 June 1908. <www.satyashodh.com/Savarkar%20 Newsletters1A.htm#d14> (accessed 1 Mar. 2008). There had been a similar but less publicised meeting at India House the year before, which had been secretly attended by detectives from the Special Branch; see Popplewell, 128.

59  Charles Pearce, *Love Besieged* (1909; reprint Delhi: Oxford University Press, 2007), Preface, 3.

# Preface and Acknowledgements

1　Shahid Amin, 'A Hanging Twice Over', *Outlook India*, 26 Mar. 2007.

# Introduction

1　Evelyn Wood in *The Times*, 1907; and *The Revolt in Hindustan, 1857–59* (London: Methuen and Co., 1908).

2　W. Forbes-Mitchell, *Reminiscences of the Great Mutiny* (London: Macmillan and Co., 1893), 172–93.

3　Sitaram Bawa, in R. C. Majumdar, *The Sepoy Mutiny and the Revolt of 1857* (Calcutta: Mukhopadhay, 1957), 341–6. Also reproduced in S. A. A. Rizvi and M. L. Bhargava (eds.), *Freedom Struggle in Uttar Pradesh*, I–V (Lucknow: Publications Bureau, 1957–61), 376–81 (henceforth referred to as *FSUP*).

4　Ibid.

5　Martineau to Kaye, 20 Oct. 1864, Kaye Papers, H/725(2), 1020, APAC. See also W. H. Russell, *My Diary in India* (London, 1860), I, 170.

6　John Kaye and G. B. Malleson, *History of the Indian Mutiny* (London: Allen, 1888–9), I, n. 425.

7　Kaye and Malleson, I, 388.

8　Kaye and Malleson, I, fn. 421. The 'Oudh people at Garden Reach' refers to the dispossessed King of Oudh, who lived with his extensive retinue at Garden Reach, near Calcutta.

9　G. B. Malleson, *The Indian Mutiny of 1857* (London: s.n., 1891). In 1858, Malleson had also written the so-called 'Red Pamphlet' anonymously: *The Mutiny of the Bengal Army: An Historical Narrative. By one who has served under Sir Charles Napier* (London: Bosworth and Harrison, 1857).

10　Malleson, viii and 17.

11　Ibid., 33.

12　Ibid., 16 and 17.

13　Ibid., 17.

14　Ibid., 18.

15　Kaye and Malleson, I, 360.

16　Malleson, 38.

17　Ibid., 33.

18　Russell, *My Diary*, I, 3.

19   See Gordon Wood, 'Conspiracy and the Paranoid Style: Causality and Deceit in the Eighteenth Century', *The William and Mary Quarterly*, 3, 39, 3 (July 1982), 401–41.

20   Ibid., 429.

21   See for instance Norman Cohn, *Warrant for Genocide: The Myth of the Jewish Conspiracy and the Protocols of the Elders of Zion* (London: Eyre and Spottiswoode, 1967); and G. Cubitt, *The Jesuit Myth: Conspiracy Theory and Politics in Nineteenth-Century France* (Oxford: Clarendon Press, 1993).

22   Cited in Cohn, 36–7.

23   See Richard Hofstadter, 'The Paranoid Style in American Politics', *Harper's Magazine* (Nov. 1964), 77–86. Similarly, Cubitt describes alarmism as 'dramatised insecurities and systematic distrust'; see Cubitt, 314.

24   See also Albert D. Pionke, *Plots of Opportunity: Representing Conspiracy in Victorian England* (Columbus: Ohio State University Press, 2004), xiii.

25   In Britain, fear of Catholic subversion and 'popish plots' obviously had a long history; see ibid., 50–78.

26   Ibid.

27   G. O. Trevelyan, *Competition Wallah* (London: Macmillan and Co., 1866), 429.

28   See Kate Teltscher, *India Inscribed: European and British Writing on India, 1600–1800* (Delhi: Oxford University Press, 1995), 229–55.

29   W. H. Sleeman, *Rambles and Recollections of an Indian Official* (London, 1844; reprint: Westminster: Archibald Constable and Co., 1893), II, 106–25.

30   Philip Meadows Taylor, *Confessions of a Thug* (London: Richard Bentley, 1839).

31   J. Macpherson, 'Report on Insanity among Europeans in Bengal', *The Indian Annals of Medical Science*, Apr. 1854, 704–5.

32   Halhed to Perry, 10 Dec. 1812, in Perry to Dowdeswell, 15 Jan. 1813, Bengal Criminal and Judicial Proceedings, P/131/12, 30 Jan. 1813 (no. 62), APAC.

33   *The New Monthly Magazine*, 38, 1833, 285.

34   See Pringle to Barwell, 9 May 1827, in W. H. Sleeman, *Ramaseeana, or A vocabulary of the peculiar language used by the Thugs, with an introduction and appendix, descriptive of the system pursued by that fraternity and of the measures which have been adopted by the Supreme Government of India for its suppression* (Calcutta: Military Orphan Press, 1836), II, 252.

35   'Souvenirs du P. Grivel sur les PP. Barruel et Feller', *Le Contemporain*, July, 1878, 67–70, cited in Cohn, 36. In Barruel's feverish imagination, the Freemasons and Jews were part of the same conspiracy.

36   Harvey, in *FSUP*, I, 392.

37   Kaye and Malleson, I, 361.

38   H. H. Spry, 'Some Accounts of the Gang Murderers of Central India, Commonly Called Thugs; Accompanying the Skulls of Seven of Them', *The Phrenological Journal and Miscellany*, 8 (Mar. 1834), 511–24: 514.

39  Spry, 515. This was a commonly held view of Indian society, as appears from another contemporary description of the 'Thugs', who were said to be 'as much the slaves of superstition, and as much directed by the observance of omens in the commission of murder, as the most inoffensive of the natives of India are in the ordinary affairs of their lives'. 'On the Thugs', *The New Monthly Magazine*, 38 (1833), 277–87: 280.

40  *Westminster Review*, 69, 135, 13, 1 (Jan. 1858), 180–209: 197.

41  Alexander Duff, *The Indian Rebellion: Its Causes and Results. In a series of letters* (London: s.n., 1858), 18.

42  *Bentley's Miscellany*, 43 (Feb. 1858), 123. See also Jenny Sharpe, *Allegories of Empire: The Figure of Woman in the Colonial Text* (Minneapolis: University of Minneapolis Press, 1993), 60.

43  Cubitt, 81.

44  *Fraser's Magazine for Town etc.*, 56, 335 (Nov. 1857), 627.

45  See Cubitt, 182; and David Arnold, *Colonizing the Body: State Medicine and Epidemic Disease in Nineteenth-Century India* (Berkeley: University of California Press, 1993), 168. See also Ranajit Guha, *Elementary Aspects of Peasant Insurgency in Colonial India* (Delhi: Oxford University Press, 1983).

46  Kaye and Malleson, II, 231; and Malleson, 43.

47  Pionke, 87.

48  See also Cubitt, 81.

49  V. D. Savarkar, *The Indian War of Independence, 1857* (London, 1909; reprint New Delhi: Rajdhani Granthagar, 1970), 102–3. Veer Savarkar, as he is commonly known, was one of the founding fathers of Hindu nationalism as famously expressed in his political programme of 1923, *Hindutva*. See John Pincince, *On the Verge of Hindutva: V. D. Savarkar and the Historical Construction of Hindu National Identity, 1905–24* (unpublished PhD thesis, University of Hawai'i, 2007).

50  Svarkar, 1 and 101.

51  Ibid., 72–3 and 78–9.

52  Ibid., 80–2 and 85.

53  Ibid., 90–1.

54  Ibid., 82.

55  Ibid., 89.

56  Ibid., 97. See also Prologue above.

57  Ibid., 111.

58  Ibid., 103–6.

59  Ibid., 114–15.

60  Savarkar, 90–1.

61  C. J. Stevenson-Moore, 6 Jan. 1909, Home, political A, Feb. 1909, 13–13a: 'Interception of a book or pamphlet by V. D. Savakar [*sic*] on the Indian Mutiny', NAI. Thanks to John Pincince for this reference.

62  Martineau to Kaye, 20 Oct. 1864, Kaye Papers, H/725(2), 1020, APAC.

63  Forbes-Mitchell, 172–93. The book was published almost thirty years after the Uprising and yet presents lengthy 'verbatim quotes'.

64  Ibid., 190–1.

65  Sometimes British officials also engaged in public debates in the newspapers, writing under the pseudonyms of Indians; see for instance the humorous exchange between '*Sepoy* Ram Sing' and the 'Ghost of Mungul Pandy', *The Delhi Gazette*, 23 Apr. and 7 May 1857.

66  James Lunt (ed.), *From Sepoy to Subedar, being the Life and Adventures of Subedar Sita Ram, a Native Officer of the Bengal Army written and related by Himself* (Lahore, 1873; reprint London: Papermac, 1988). Patrick Cadell, 'The Autobiography of an Indian Soldier', *Journal of the Society for Army Historical Research*, 37 (1959), 3–11 and 49–56.

67  See 'Editorial note' by James Lunt, ibid., xvii–xviii.

68  Ibid., 161.

69  The original is in the Kaye Papers, but has been reproduced in Majumdar, 341–6.

70  Majumdar, 342. The fact that Sitaram Bawa and Nana Sahib's guru, Dassa Bawa, both came from the same Brahmin caste might explain why the former gave such prominence to the latter. Interestingly, Azimullah Khan is nowhere mentioned in this account of Nana Sahib's conspiracy.

71  Kaye, I, 647.

72  Majumdar, 345.

73  Ibid., 344.

74  Statement of Sitaram Bawa, Majumdar, 344. This has not prevented a number of historians from citing this source as reliable evidence of a conspiracy; see for instance Saul David, *The Indian Mutiny* (London: Viking, 2002), 385.

75  See Pramod K. Nayar (ed.), *The Trial of Bahadur Shah* (Hyderabad: Orient Longman, 2007). Henceforth referred to as *Trial*.

76  Statement of Sitaram Bawa, Majumdar, 341–4; and *Trial*.

77  Testimony of Ahsan Ullah Khan, *Trial*, 24.

78  Statement of Sitaram Bawa, 18 Jan. 1858, *FSUP*, I, 373.

79  Ibid., 375.

80  Testimony of Ghulam Abbas, *Trial*, 13; and statement of Mohun Lal, Kaye Papers, H/725, 389–422, APAC. For the receipt of the letter, see *Agra Narrative* by G. F. Harvey, Commissioner of Agra, 5.

81  See Andrew Ward, *Our Bones are Scattered* (London: John Murray, 1996), 109.

82  Ward, 118 and 125.

83  See statement of Kunhye Pershad Mahajun, *Depositions taken at Cawnpore under the Directions of Lieut-Colonel G. W. Williams* (Allahabad, 1858), no. 16.

84  Ward, 169.

85  Ibid., 170–1.

86  Duff, 2.

87  *FSUP*, III, 65–7. See also *Official Narrative of Events Attending the Outbreak of Disturbances and the Restoration of Authority in the District of Jhansie* (Allahabad, 1858).

88  See Tapti Roy, *Raj of the Rani* (New Delhi: Penguin India, 2006).

89  See Majumdar; S. N. Sen, *Eighteen Fifty-Seven* (Delhi: s.n., 1957); and Eric Stokes (C. A. Bayly ed.), *The Peasant Armed: The Indian Rebellion of 1857* (Oxford: Clarendon Press, 1986).

90  J. A. B. Palmer, *The Mutiny Outbreak at Meerut in 1857* (Cambridge: Cambridge University Press, 1966).

91  Ibid., 129–32. It was a common belief among the British that the rebels deliberately planned their attacks to fall on Sundays; see Journal of John Charles Brown, MS 15393, NLS, 32. Thanks to John Jarvis for this reference.

92  Palmer, 129.

93  David, 185. See also Ward.

94  See David, appendix two: 'The Civilian Conspiracy and Rebel Chiefs', 385–8.

95  Ibid., 385.

96  Ibid., 55.

97  David, 72.

98  William Dalrymple, *The Last Mughal: The Fall of a Dynasty, Delhi, 1857* (London: Bloomsbury, 2006).

99  Sayed Ahmed Khan, *The Causes of the Indian Revolt* (1858; trans: Benares: Medical Hall Press, 1873).

100 Eric Stokes first highlighted the significance of contingencies in the connection of the Uprising; see Stokes, 240.

101 See Marshall Sahlins, *Apologies to Thucydides: Understanding History as Culture and Vice Versa* (Chicago: University of Chicago Press, 2004).

102 George Lefebvre, *The Great Fear of 1789* (orig. 1932; trans. London: New Left Books, 1973).

103 George Rudé, introduction to ibid., xv.

104 Apart from Guha, see also S. B. Chaudhuri, *Civil Disturbances during the British Rule in India, 1765–1857* (Calcutta: World Press, 1955).

105 See S. Tambiah, *Levelling Crowds: Ethnonationalist Conflict and Collective Violence in South Asia* (Berkeley: University of California Press, 1996); Veena Das, *Life and Words: Violence and the Descent into the Ordinary* (Berkeley: University of California Press, 2007); Paul Brass, *Theft of an Idol: Text and Context in the Representation of Collective Violence* (Princeton: Princeton University Press, 1997).

106 Barbara English, 'The Kanpur Massacres in India and the Revolt of 1857', *Past and Present*, 142 (Feb., 1994), 169–78: 177.

107 Rudrangshu Mukherjee, '"Satan Let Loose upon Earth": The Kanpur Massacres in India in the Revolt of 1857', *Past and Present*, 128 (Aug. 1990), 92–116.

108 If the argument is extended to colonial warfare, it becomes even more difficult to sustain, since most of the British campaigns were fought by Indian troops: much colonial violence was actually committed by *sepoys*.

109 See Mukherjee (1990), 112.

110 Bayly (1996), 171–4.

111 Pramod K. Nayar (ed.), *The Trial of Bahadur Shah* (Hyderabad: Orient Longman, 2007); Charles T. Metcalfe (trans.), *Two Native Narratives of the Mutiny in Delhi* (Westminster: A. Constable and Co., 1898); Statement of Shaik Hedayut Ali, Kaye Papers, H/727(a), 759–66; and Statement of Mohun Lal, Kaye Papers, H/725, 389–422, APAC.

112 George W. Forrest (ed.), *Selections from the Letters, Despatches and Other State Papers Preserved in The Military Department of the Government of India, 1857–58* (Calcutta: Military Dept Press, 1893); and *Depositions taken at Meerut by Major G. W. Williams* (Allahabad, 1858). Henceforth referred to as *Selections* and *Depositions taken at Meerut* respectively.

113 Rajat Kanta Ray has done some interesting work on the ideas and beliefs of the rebels based on various sources, including Indian proclamations issued after 10 May 1857; see R. K. Ray, *The Felt Community: Commonality and Mentality before the Emergence of Indian Nationalism* (Delhi: Oxford University Press India, 2003), 360–95. I am, however, sceptical of using the later rebel proclamations to argue for the existence of a rebel consciousness prior to the Uprising.

114 Mukherjee (1994), 186.

115 For a more extensive argument of the historian's use of colonial sources, see Wagner, *Thuggee: Banditry and the British in Early Nineteenth-Century India* (Basingstoke: Palgrave, 2007), 15–24.

# Chapter 1

1 Many historians persistently and mistakenly refer to the rifle as the Lee Enfield, which, however, was only introduced in the 1890s.

2 D. F. Harding, *Smallarms of the East India Company 1600–1856* (London: Foresight Books, 1999), II, 155–66; and IV, 124–37 and 294–310.

3 Harding, II, 176–91; and Christopher Wilkinson-Latham, *Men-At-Arms Series 67: The Indian Mutiny* (London: Osprey, 1977), 34–5 (plate D).

4 Harding, II, 192–3.

5   Kaye, I, 655–6; Chester to Birch, 28 Jan. 1857, HC PP, 1857, Session 2 [2254], 13; and Abbott to Birch, 29 Jan. 1857, House of Commons, Parliamentary Papers, 1857, Session 2 [2254], 7.

6   See also Kaye, I, 380–1.

7   Harding, II, 225–47 and 302–8. See also Michael Barthorp, *Men-At-Arms Series 268: The British Troops in the Indian Mutiny 1857–59* (London: Osprey, 1994), 18.

8   It appears that two-thirds of the cartridge was dipped in the grease: that is, the bullet end and not the end to be bitten; see examination of Lieut. Currie, in *Selections*, I, Appendix D, lxv.

9   See Palmer, 13–14.

10  Kaye, I, 380.

11  Ibid., 381.

12  Ibid., 381–2.

13  Examination of Martineau, *Trial*, 84; and examination of Lieutenant Currie, *Selections*, I, Appendix D, lxii.

14  See *Selections*, I, 45–6, 57, 65 and 68.

15  It was noted that the native troops applied grease to the wheels of gun-carriages and wagons without any complaints, and that the real problem might have been that they had to bite the cartridges; see Kaye, I, 383.

16  Statement of Shaik Hedayut Ali, Kaye Papers, H/725, 759, APAC.

17  Ibid., 760.

18  Wright to Bontein, 22 Jan. 1857, *Selections*, I, 3.

19  Ibid.

20  Abbott to Birch, 29 Jan. 1857, HC PP, 1857, Session 2 [2254], 7.

21  Examination of Lieutenant Currie, *Selections*, I, Appendix D, lxvi.

22  Examination of Colonel Abbott, ibid., lxvii.

23  Cited by David, 54. Kaye himself believed that 'there is no question that some beef-fat was used'; Kaye, I, 381. The fact remains that we do not know for sure.

24  In this context a 'Hindostanee' means a Hindu.

25  Traditionally Chamars were tanners and therefore untouchable.

26  Native officers with the rank equal to a Captain.

27  Nund Singh to Nehal Singh, 10 June 1857, cited in Kaye, I, 652.

28  K. C. Yadav, *The Revolt of 1857 in Haryana* (Delhi: Manohar, 1977), 39 and n. 6, 52. The provenance of this story is unclear.

29  *The Delhi Gazette*, 26 Feb. 1857.

30  Ibid.

31  Bontein to Reid, 23 Jan. 1857, *Selections*, I, 2–3.

32  The following account closely follows that of Seema Alavi in *The Sepoys and the Company: Tradition and Transition in Northern India 1770–1830* (Delhi: Oxford University Press, 1995), in particular: 1–5, 13, 21–7, 75–6 and 83. See also Dirk

H. A. Kolff, *Naukar, Rajput and Sepoy: The Ethno-history of the Military Labour Market in Hindustan, 1450–1850* (Cambridge: Cambridge University Press, 1990), in particular 86–92.

33   Recruitment practices in the Madras and Bombay Presidencies were of a very different nature.

34   The following is based on James W. Hoover, *Men Without Hats: Dialogue, Discipline and Discontent in the Madras Army, 1806–1807* (New Delhi: Manohar, 2007), in particular: 55–7, 100–1, 127, 155 and 266–8.

35   Montresor to Sydenham, 21 July 1806, cited in Hoover, 152.

36   See Alavi, 77–8.

37   See P. Bandyopadhay, *Tulsi Leaves and the Ganges Water: The Slogan of the First Sepoy Mutiny at Barrackpore 1824* (Kolkata: K. P. Bagchi and Co., 2003), 24.

38   Ibid., 41, 52 and 99.

39   Cited in ibid., 51 and 100.

40   Cited in ibid., 101.

41   Alavi, 92–3.

42   See David, 22–3.

43   See Ian Copland, 'Christianity as an Arm of Empire: The Ambiguous Case of India under the Company, c. 1813–1858', *The Historical Journal* (2006), 1025–54.

44   One should be careful not to exaggerate the influence of missionaries – most Indians, besides a handful (predominantly elite) in urban areas, never encountered them.

45   Copland, 1049–50 and 1040.

46   Alavi, 85; and Copland, n. 28, 1032.

47   See the *Hindoo Patriot*, 30 Apr. 1857, and *The Englishman*, 6 Oct. 1857, *FSUP*, I, 294–6.

48   Wheler to Hearsey, 4 Apr. 1857, *FSUP*, I, 297. See also Copland, 1037.

49   In numerical terms, proselytising in India failed miserably; see Copland, 1048.

50   Andrea Major, *Sati: An Historical Anthology* (Delhi: Oxford University Press, 2006), xv.

51   Indians who converted to Christianity were not allowed to inherit by law, but this was also changed by the Caste Disabilities Removal Act of 1850; see Copland 1032 and 1043.

52   Statement of Shaik Hedayut Ali, Kaye Papers, H/727(a), 762, APAC.

53   Kaye, I, 304.

54   See Kaye, I, 195–9; and Clare Anderson, *The Indian Uprising of 1857–8: Prisons, Prisoners and Rebellion* (London: Anthem, 2007), 27–54.

55   Statement of Shaik Hedayut Ali, Kaye Papers, H/727(a), 762, APAC.

56   Cited in Anand A. Yang, 'Disciplining "Natives": Prisons and Prisoners in Early Nineteenth Century India', *South Asia*, 10, 2 (1987), 29–46: n. 38, 37–8.

57   Kaye, I, 305.

58    Ibid., 308.

59    Ibid., 262–4.

60    See report by Captain Armstrong, 15 Mar. 1833, Tweeddale MS 14558 (1–16), NLS.

61    Majumdar, 344.

62    Kaye, I, n. 279–80, 288 and 298.

63    Ibid., 310.

64    Ibid., 312 and 313–15. General Napier later resigned over the Company's attempts to economise on military expenditure.

65    Colonel Keith Young, Papers Connected with the Reorganization of the Army in India, HC, PP, 1859, session 2 [2541], 142 (789).

66    See Rudrangshu Mukherjee, *Awadh in Revolt 1857–1858* (New Delhi: Permanent Black, 2001), 1–63.

67    Mainodin Hassan Khan, in Charles T. Metcalfe (trans.), *Two Native Narratives of the Mutiny in Delhi* (Westminster: A. Constable and Co., 1898), 37.

68    See statement of Shaik Hedayut Ali, Kaye Papers, H/727(a), 763–5, APAC. The *subadar* was obviously a small landowner in Gaya (in Benares and not Bengal).

69    Statement of Mohun Lal, Kaye Papers, H/725, 389–422, APAC.

70    See also Kaye, I, 254.

71    Cited in G. Anderson (ed.), *The Last Days of the Company: A Source Book of Indian History, 1818–1858* (London: Bell, 1921), I, 110.

72    David, 23–4.

73    Statement of Shaik Hedayut Ali, Kaye Papers, H/727(a), 765, APAC.

74    See Alavi, 31.

# Chapter 2

1    Examination of Duriou Sing, *Selections*, I, Appendix D, lxxvii.

2    See examination of Sewbuccus Sing, ibid., lxix–lxx. It should be noted that there are different versions of the exchange.

3    Ibid., lxxi.

4    It is not clear exactly when the fear in the Sudder Bazaar occurred, but it seems to be very similar to the panic of 28 January; see below.

5    See ibid., xc, xciv and xcv.

6    *FSUP*, I, 389; and Hearsey to Mayhew, 28 Jan. 1857, *Selections*, I, 4.

7    Statement of Lieutenant Allen, 8 Feb. 1857, *Selections*, I, 18.

8    Account of Mainodin, *Two Native Narratives*, 38.

9    Hearsey to Birch, 11 Feb. 1857, *Selections*, I, 26.

10  Hearsey to Sanders, 5 Feb. 1857, ibid., 6.

11  Hearsey to Birch, 11 Feb. 1857, ibid., 26.

12  Statement of Durriow Sing, ibid., 156–9.

13  Mainodin, *Two Native Narratives*, 37–8.

14  Statement of Durriow Sing, ibid., 156–9.

15  Ibid.

16  See *Selections*, I, Appendix C, xxv–liv.

17  Michael Maclagan, *'Clemency' Canning Charles John, 1st Earl Canning Governor-General and Viceroy of India 1856–1862* (London: Macmillan, 1962), 71.

18  *FSUP*, I, 361.

19  Hearsey to Mayhew, 28 Jan. 1857, *Selections*, I, 5.

20  Ibid., I, Appendix D, lxii, lxxviii and lxxx.

21  Examination of M. E. Currie, ibid., lxv.

22  See Hearsey to Mayhew, 24 Jan. 1857, ibid., 1; and Abbott to Mayhew, 27 Jan. 1857, ibid., 3–4.

23  Hearsey to Mayhew, 24 Jan. 1857, ibid., 1.

24  Hearsey to Mayhew, 28 Jan. 1857, ibid., 4. The Dharma Sabha was an orthodox Hindu association established in 1830 to protest against the infringement on their religious beliefs and practices in connection with the abolishment of *sati*; their involvement in the events of 1857 is pure speculation.

25  Ibid., 5.

26  The possible involvement of the deposed King of Oudh had not come to light by 28 January.

27  See for instance *Selections*, I, 2, 3, 5, lxii, lxxviii and lxxx.

28  Examination of Duriou Sing, ibid., Appendix D, lxxviii–lxxix.

29  Examination of Kennedy, ibid., lxi.

30  Ibid., xcii. The description of this disturbance is very similar to that at Berhampore on 26 February, but they are separate events; see also ibid., xc.

31  Examination of Byjonath Pandy, ibid., 8; and Boswell to Grant, 4 Feb. 1857, ibid., 13.

32  Examination of Kennedy, ibid., Appendix D, lxi. Kennedy went into the lines and had native officers at his bungalow on several occasions in late January and during February; ibid.

33  Boswell to Grant, 4 Feb. 1857, ibid., 13.

34  Hearsey to Mayhew, 8 Feb. 1857, ibid., 15; and Minute on the Mutiny at Berhampore of the 19th Regiment, Native Infantry, 27 Mar. 1857, ibid., 88. See also examinations of Bontein and Mitchell, ibid., lxiii–lxvi.

35  Examination of Byjonath Pandy, ibid., 8.

36  Examination of Chand Khan, ibid., 9.

37  Examination of Ram Sing, ibid., 11.

38  Examination of Ajoodiah Singh, ibid., 12.

39  Examination of Bheekun Khan, ibid.
40  See for instance examination of Buddun Singh, ibid., 10.
41  Closing statement of the prosecutor, Colonel Kennedy, ibid., Appendix D, cxxx. The evidence against the *jemadar* was far from conclusive, and I have used the trial records to show the general concerns of the *sepoys* rather than to prove the specific acts for which he was committed.
42  Statement of Lieutenant Allen, 8 Feb. 1857, ibid., 17.
43  See also ibid., Appendix D, xcii.
44  Deposition of Jemadar Durrow, 10 Feb. 1857, ibid., 20.
45  Examination of Ramsahai Lalla, 11 Feb. 1857, ibid., 22.
46  Statement of Lieutenant Allen, 8 Feb. 1857, ibid., 18.
47  Statement of Lieutenant Allen, 8 Feb. 1857, ibid.; and Grant to Ross, 8 Feb. 1857, ibid., 19.
48  See ibid., Appendix D, xcvii–cxxxv.
49  Statement of Lieutenant Allen, 8 Feb. 1857, ibid., 18.
50  See for instance ibid., Appendix D, lviii and cxxviii–cxxix.
51  Hearsey to Mayhew, 8 Feb. 1857, ibid., 14–17. For the further measures taken to prevent fires, see Hearsey to Birch, 11 Feb. 1857, ibid., 24.
52  Ibid., 16.
53  Hearsey was obviously not aware that the Calcutta Native Militia was also involved in the various plots; see Statement of Durrow Sing, ibid., 158.
54  Hearsey to Birch, 11 Feb. 1857, ibid., 24.
55  Ibid., 27.
56  Colonel Wheler commanding the 34th Bengal Native Infantry had previously made a similar speech to his regiment; see ibid., 162.
57  Ibid.
58  Boswell to Ross, ibid., 31.
59  Statement of Ramjan Khan, ibid., 29–30. A *kossid* was a private post-runner as opposed to the official *dak*.
60  There is one significant discrepancy, namely that the *sepoy* informant stated that there were 300 present at the secret meeting, while only ten or twelve had sent a letter to the other regiments.
61  See ibid., 45–6, 57, 65 and 68.
62  Mitchell to Ross, 16 Feb. 1857, ibid., 39.
63  Ibid.
64  See examination of Lieutenant James Vallings, ibid., 70. It is unclear exactly what was sent from Calcutta: the Sergeant-Major stated that only powder in barrels had arrived, while Mitchell states that it was balled ammunition; see Examination of Shaikh Murad Bux, ibid., 63; and statement of Mitchell, ibid., xii.
65  Statement of Mitchell, ibid.
66  Mitchell to Ross, 16 Feb. 1857, ibid., 39.

67  Examination of Shaikh Kureem Bux, ibid., 55–6.

68  See Mitchell to Ross, 27 Feb. 1857, ibid., 41; and remarks of the court, ibid., 79.

69  Examination of Jemadar Lalla Dokehore, ibid., 76. The *sepoys* of the 34th BNI who made up the detachment later denied having communicated with men of the 19th BNI; see ibid., 79–81.

70  Examination of Doolum Sing, ibid., 68.

71  This is according to the Hadith Al-Bukhari.

72  Over time, the story developed even further and a *sepoy* of the 12th BNI at Jhansi later recalled how his comrades suspected 'that the cartridges newly received were covered over with dog's or cow's skin'; Statement of Aman Khan, 14 Apr. 1858, *FSUP*, III, 24.

73  Petition of 19th BNI to Hearsey, 29 Mar., *Selections*, I, 45.

74  Mitchell to Ross, 27 Feb. 1857, ibid., 41.

75  Examination of Shaikh Muden Bux, ibid., 60.

76  Ibid., 66; and examination of Doolum Sing, ibid., 68.

77  Examination of Shaikh Murad Bux, ibid., 63.

78  Ibid.

79  Ibid. Mitchell later denied this outburst, but it is corroborated by several witnesses; see Mitchell to Ross, 18 Mar. 1857, ibid., 85 (the letter is reproduced in ibid., Appendix A, i–iii); examination of Shaik Kureem Bux, ibid., 53; and examination of Lieutenant I. F. MacAndrew, ibid., vi.

80  Examination of Shaikh Murad Bux, ibid., 63.

81  Ibid., 48 and vi.

82  Petition of 19th Bengal Native Infantry to Hearsey, 29 Feb. 1857, ibid., 46.

83  The information pertaining to the supposed meeting and oath in the tank is based exclusively on hearsay; see ibid., 52, 60, 66 and 69.

84  Examination of Beharee Sing, ibid., 58.

85  Examination of Shaik Muden Bux, ibid., 50–1.

86  Examination of Havildar-Major Bijoo Sing, ibid., 57.

87  Mitchell to Ross, 27 Feb. 1857, ibid., 42.

88  Ibid., 46.

89  Abbott to Grant, 19 Feb. 1857, HC PP, 1857 session 2 (2265).

90  Examination of Shaikh Murad Bux, *Selections*, I, 64.

91  Ibid.

92  Mitchell to Ross, 27 Feb. 1857, ibid., 42.

93  Petition of 19th Bengal Native Infantry to Hearsey, 29 Mar., ibid., 47.

94  Examination of Sergeant-Major Frawley, ibid., 52.

95  Examination of Drum-Major James Renny, ibid., 58–9.

96  Mitchell to Hearsey, 3 Mar. 1857, ibid., 61.

97  Examination of Shaikh Murad Bux, ibid., 65. The cartridges that were to have been distributed on the morning of the 27 February, and to which the *sepoys*

objected, were blank cartridges; the ones that the *sepoys* seized during the night were balled cartridges.

98   Mitchell to Ross, 27 Feb. 1857, ibid., 42.
99   Examination of Lieutenant I. F. MacAndrew, ibid., 49–50; Mitchell to Ross, 28 Feb. 1857, ibid., 43.
100  Examination of Shaikh Murad Bux, ibid., 65.
101  Mitchell to Ross, 28 Feb. 1857, ibid., 43.
102  Ibid.; and Examination of Shaikh Kureem Bux, ibid., 55.
103  Examination of Shaikh Murad Bux, ibid., 65.
104  Petition of 19th Bengal Native Infantry to Hearsey, 29 Mar., ibid., 45–7. For the date of the petition, see Mitchell to Hearsey, 3 Mar. 1857, ibid., 61.
105  Petition of 19th Bengal Native Infantry to Hearsey, 29 Mar., ibid., 47.
106  Minute on the Mutiny at Berhampore of the 19th Regiment, Native Infantry, 27 Mar. 1857, ibid., 93; and General order by GG, 27 Mar. 1857, ibid., 94–7.
107  Ibid., 93–4.

# Chapter 3

1   See also G. E. Dowd, 'The Panic of 1751: The Significance of Rumours on the South Carolina–Cherokee Frontier', *The William and Mary Quarterly*, 3, 53, 3 (July 1996), 527–60: 527–8.
2   See Arnold, 171–2.
3   Much of what has been written about the *chapattis* was written after the outbreak and interpreted the circulation in light of subsequent events, thus implying a direct causal link for which there is in fact no real evidence. The most comprehensive discussion of the phenomenon is to be found in Troy Downs, 'Host of Midian: The Chapati Circulation and the Indian Revolt of 1857–58', *Studies in History*, 16 (2000), 75–107; Guha, 239–46; and Majumdar, 375–8. Many of the primary sources are reproduced in Kaye, I, 632–9; and *FSUP*, I, 389–95.
4   M. Thornhill, *The Personal Adventures and Experiences of a Magistrate during the Rise, Progress, and Suppression of the Indian Mutiny* (London: John Murray, 1884), 2.
5   Mainodin, *Two Native Narratives*, 40. The same officer also reported that pieces of goat's flesh were being distributed, but that was an isolated case and not recorded elsewhere; ibid.
6   John Cave-Browne, *The Punjab and Delhi in 1857: Being a Narrative of the Measures by which the Punjab was Saved and Delhi Recovered during the Indian Mutiny* (London: W. Blackwood and Sons, 1861), I, 2; and Erskine to Thornhill,

5 Mar. 1857, cited in Charles Ball, *The History of the Indian Mutiny* (London: Printing and Publishing Co., n.d.), 39.

7  Testimony of Metcalfe, *Trial*, 43.

8  Guha, 234–8; Kaye and Malleson, V, 63 and *Two Native Narratives*, n. 41.

9  See Sir Walther Scott, *The Lady of the Lake* (1810), canto III. It is beyond the scope of this book to examine the historical occurrence of the passing of the fiery cross in Scottish history, but by 1857 the practice would have been commonly known through Scott's work.

10  Anon., *Siege of Delhi*, cited in Kaye, I, 636–7.

11  Harvey, *FSUP*, I, 392. One officer in Oudh made a calculation of how long it would take for *chapattis* to be distributed throughout his district, but the actual circulation happened 'with such amazing rapidity' and took ten days less than the estimate; Kaye, I, 637.

12  *The Friend of India*, 5 Mar. 1857.

13  Ibid.

14  Ibid., 19 Mar. 1857, *FSUP*, I, 390.

15  Cited in W. H. Carey, *The Mahomedan Rebellion* (Roorkee: Directory Press, 1857), 10.

16  Testimony of Metcalfe, *Trial*, 43.

17  Mainodin, *Two Native Narratives*, 40; and Kaye, I, 637.

18  Thornhill, 2; Mainodin, *Two Native Narratives*, 39.

19  R. H. W. Dunlop, *Service and Adventure with the Khakee Ressalah, or Meerut Volunteer Horse, during the mutinies of 1857–58* (London: s.n., 1858), 26. See also Reade to Kaye, 10 Mar. 1864, Reade, Mss. Eur. E124, 223, APAC.

20  Palmer rejects the possibility that the *chapattis* had anything to do with disease transmission on the basis of a typically positivist argument: since no *chapattis* were recorded when the cholera was raging in 1856, their transmission in the beginning of 1857, when there was no widespread epidemic, must be unrelated; see Palmer, 2–3. There is, however, evidence for the continuation of cholera in 1857 across northern India, including Indore; see *The Delhi Gazette*, 18 and 23 Apr., and 7 and 9 May.

21  Keatinge, cited in Kaye, I, n. 572–3. See also Dunlop, 25–6.

22  See S. C. Townsend, *Report on the Cholera Epidemic of 1868* (s.n., 1869), 1.

23  See W. Crooke, *An Introduction to the Popular Religion and Folklore of Northern India* (Allahabad: Government Press, 1894), 106–10; and Arnold, 176. See also Sleeman, *Rambles*, I, 197–8 and 203–5.

24  *Official Narrative of Events Attending the Outbreak of Disturbances and the Restoration of Authority in the District of Ajmere* (Allahabad, 1858), 7–8; Captain Lloyd, *The Delhi Gazette*, 25 Apr. 1857; and *Gazetteer of the Bombay Presidency* (Bombay: s.n., 1896), I, pt. I, 433.

25  Dunlop, 25.

26 Mainodin, *Two Native Narratives*, 40; and *The Delhi Gazette*, 14 Apr. 1857. It has also been alleged that lotus-flowers were distributed at the same time as the *chapattis*; see Thomas Frost, *Complete Narrative of the Mutiny in India, from its Commencement to the Present Time* (London: s.n., 1858), 4; George Dodd, *The History of the Indian Revolt and of the Expeditions to Persia, China, and Japan, 1856–58* (London: W. and R. Chambers, 1859), 36; Mowbray Thompson, *The Story of Cawnpore* (London: R. Bentley, 1859), 24. None of these accounts provides any primary sources for the transmission of lotus-flowers, seeds or leaves; see also P. C. Gupta, *Nana Sahib and the Rising at Cawnpore* (London: Clarendon, 1963), 34. Thanks to John Pincince for these references.

27 See *The Friend of India*, 5 Mar. 1857, 219; and *The Times*, 14 Apr. 1857, 7.

28 My reconstruction of the circulation of *chapattis* in 1857 is based on the above-mentioned sources in Kaye and *FSUP* as well as Erskine to Thornhill, 5 Mar. 1857, cited in Ball, n. 39; Ternan in Kaye and Malleson, V, 62–3; Captain Lloyd, *The Delhi Gazette*, 25 Apr. 1857; Mainudin, *Two Native Narratives*; Testimony of Metcalfe, *Trial*, 43–4; Mohur Singh and Gunga Pershad, *Depositions taken at Meerut by Major G. W. Williams* (Allahabad, 1858), nos. 2 and 5.

29 It should be noted that Carey's description of the geographic distribution of the *chapattis* is in reverse and is not supported by primary sources; see Carey, 9–10. There were a number of suggestions as to where the *chapattis* might have originated, but these were all made after the outbreak; see Testimony of Metcalfe and Ahsan Ullah Khan, *Trial*, 43–4 and 182; Anon., *Siege of Delhi*, cited in Kaye, I, 637.

30 Thornhill, 3; and Mainodin, *Two Native Narratives*, 41. Thornhill's story of a transmission prior to the Vellore Mutiny is not corroborated by any other sources. The downfall of the Marathas probably refers to the Third Maratha War of 1817–18.

31 Arnold, 177.

32 John Malcolm, *A Memoir of Central India including Malwa and Adjoining Provinces* (London, 1823), 217–19.

33 Captain Lloyd, *The Delhi Gazette*, 25 Apr. 1857.

34 Ford to Fraser, 19 Feb. 1857, *FSUP*, I, 390.

35 Carey, 9–10.

36 Kaye and Malleson, V, 62.

37 See Anon., *Siege of Delhi*, cited in Kaye, I, 637; William Waterfield to his wife, 15 Jan. 1858, Mss. Eur. D680–9, APAC, BL. See also Anand A. Yang, 'A Conversation of Rumours: The Language of Popular "Mentalités" in Late Nineteenth-Century Colonial India', *Journal of Social History*, 20, 3 (Spring, 1987), 485–505.

38 Testimony of Jat Mall, *Trial*, 30.

39 Testimony of Martineau, *Trial*, 83.

40 See Anderson.

41 Cited in Tapti Roy, *The Politics of a Popular Uprising: Bundelkhand in 1857* (Delhi: Oxford University Press, 1994), 232. See also Thompson, 24; and Downs, 90.

42 Testimony of Ahsan Ullah Khan, *Trial*, 183.

43 Testimony of Chuni, ibid., 53. For references to a holy man, see Anon., *Siege of Delhi*, cited in Kaye, I, 637; and deposition of Seetaram Bawa, ibid., 647.

44 Kaye and Malleson, V, 63.

45 Carey, 27–8, *FSUP*, I, 395–6.

46 See also report from Roorkee by Lieutenant-Colonel R. Baird Smith, *FSUP*, I, 396.

47 Edward Leckey, *Fictions Connected with the Indian Outbreak of 1857 Exposed* (Bombay: Chesson and Woodhall, 1859), 77–9.

48 Letter by Mrs Keith Young, *FSUP*, I, 396–7.

49 Martin Gubbins, cited in Kaye, I, 570.

50 Report of 18 Mar. 1858, *FSUP*, II, 22.

51 Kaye, I, 248.

52 *Gazetteer of the Bombay Presidency* (Bombay: s.n., 1896), I, pt. I, 434.

53 Kaye, I, 416–17.

54 Cited in Kaye, I, 592.

55 Ibid., 594.

56 *Bengal Hurkaru*, 8 Apr. 1857, cited in Leckey, 79. See also Canning to Vernon-Smith, 23 Mar. 1857, IOR, Eur. F231, APAC.

57 See Ann Laura Stoler, '"In Cold Blood": Hierarchies of Credibility and the Politics of Colonial Narratives', *Representations*, 37 (Winter 1992), 151–89: 179 and 183.

58 See Yang, 'A Conversation of Rumours', 499.

59 See Steven Hahn, '"Extravagant Expectations" of Freedom: Rumour, Political Struggle, and the Christmas Insurrection Scare of 1865 in the American South', *Past and Present*, 157 (Nov. 1997), 122–58: 133.

60 Kaye and Malleson, I, 361–2. See also the chapter 'Bazaar Gub' in J. C. Oman, *Cults, Customs and Superstitions of India* (London: T. Fisher Unwin, 1908), 218–28. For the notion of the 'grapevine telegraph', see also Hahn, 128; and Guha, 258.

61 I. T. Prichard, *The Mutinies in Rajpootana: Being a Personal Narrative of the Mutiny at Nusseerabad* (s.n., 1860), 21.

62 Dowd, 548.

63 See Lefebvre, 73–4; and Guha, 253.

64 See also Glenda Riley, 'The Specter of the Savage: Rumours and Alarmism on the Overland Trail', *The Western Historical Quarterly*, 15, 4 (Oct. 1984), 427–44.

65 This was to be a recurring feature of panics amongst the Indian population; see Yang, 'A Conversation of Rumours', 489.

66 See Guha, 268.

67 Yang, 'A Conversation of Rumours', 500.

68 See Guha, 256.

69   See Dowd, 539.

70   See Hahn, 123–4.

71   *FSUP*, I, 342.

72   Guha, 253.

73   See diary of Waterfield, 27 June 1857, IOR, Mss. Eur. D 680/6, APAC; or *Memorandum on the Mutiny and Outbreak at Meerut in May 1857 by Major Williams* (Allahabad, 1858), 4. See also Trevelyan, 72.

74   Testimony of John Everett, *Trial*, 111.

75   Testimony of Ahsan Ullah Khan, *Trial*, 24.

76   Testimony of Ghulam Abbas, *Trial*, 16.

77   Mainodin, *Two Native Narratives*, 39–40. See also Testimony of Ahsan Ullah Khan, *Trial*, 26; and Testimony of Chuni, ibid., 50–1.

78   Testimony of Ahsan Ullah Khan, *Trial*, 180–1.

79   Statement of Mohun Lal, Kaye Papers, H/725, 389–422, APAC.

80   Testimony of Ahsan Ullah Khan, *Trial*, 65.

81   Extract from the *Authentic News*, 26 Jan. 1857, cited in *Trial*, 113–14. See also 115–25.

82   Testimony of John Everett, *Trial*, 109–10.

83   Extract from newspaper in Lucknow, 28 Mar. 1857, *FSUP*, I, 312–13.

84   Testimony of Metcalfe, *Trial*, 42.

85   See *FSUP*, 301–2.

86   Cited in Roy, 232.

87   William Butler, *The Land of the Veda* (New York: Phillips and Hunt, 1871), 226. See also Bayly, *Empire and Information*, 322.

88   G. O. Trevelyan, *Cawnpore* (1865; reprint London: Macmillan and Co., 1886), 72–3.

89   Trevelyan, *Competition Wallah*, 431; see also 430.

90   See also Hahn, 125.

91   Ibid., 125–6.

92   Mainodin, *Two Native Narratives*, 41.

# Chapter 4

1   *Selections*, I, Appendix D, lv–cxxxviii. It should be noted that the evidence in this trial, as well as the one of the two *sepoys* of the 34th Bengal Native Infantry, is contradictory and insufficient to give more than a general impression of the events at the time.

2   Ibid., cxxxv.

3   Ibid., Appendix C, xxv–liv.

4   *The Friend of India*, 19 Mar. 1857, *FSUP*, I, 293.

5   See Kaye and Malleson, I, 388–9.

6   Ibid.

7   Anonymous petition to Major Matthews, Mar. 1857, cited in Kaye, I, 639–41.

8   Ibid.

9   Ibid. The list of consequences for failing to deliver the petition is repeated no fewer than three times.

10  Hearsey to Birch, 18 Mar. 1857, *Selections*, I, 81–2.

11  Hearsey to Birch, 18 Mar. 1857, ibid., 83.

12  The best account of Mangal Pandey is Rudrangshu Mukherjee, *Mangal Pandey: Brave Martyr or Accidental Hero?* (New Delhi: Penguin Books India, 2005). The following events have been the subject of much debate and are accordingly narrated in greater detail. Unless otherwise stated, the following is based on the documents in *Selections*, I, 108–60.

13  Hearsey to Ross, 30 Mar. 1857, *Selections*, I, 99.

14  Hearsey to Birch, 9 Apr. 1857, ibid., 111.

15  Examination of Mangal Pandey, 4 Apr. 1857, ibid., 108.

16  Examination of Havildar Shaik Pultoo, ibid., 124. 'Bhainchute': sister-fucker in Hindi.

17  Examination of Lewis, ibid., 123.

18  Defence of Isuree Pandey, ibid., 205.

19  Examination of Hewson, ibid., 117.

20  Examination of Hewson, ibid., 118.

21  Ibid., 183.

22  Ibid.

23  Ibid., 144. See also 187.

24  Ibid., 119.

25  Examination of Shaik Pultoo, ibid., 134.

26  Examination of Hewson, ibid., 118.

27  Ibid., 145.

28  Both Baugh and Hewson had received severe injuries during the struggle and their statements during the subsequent trials were taken at their bedsides; see for instance ibid., 117, 120, 141 and 143.

29  Examination of Shaik Pultoo, ibid., 133.

30  Defence of Isuree Pandey, ibid., 206.

31  Examination of Sobha Sing, ibid., 194.

32  The only *sepoy* who was identified as having attacked Baugh and Hewson, namely Heeralall Tewary, deserted in the evening of 31 March and was never brought to trial; see examination of Drury, ibid., 202.

33  Examination of Atma Sing, ibid., 197.

34  Examination of Hewson, ibid., 145.
35  Defence of Isuree Pandey, ibid., 206.
36  Examination of Mookta Persaud Pandy, ibid., 138.
37  Defence of Isuree Pandey, ibid., 206.
38  Examination of Shaik Pultoo, ibid., 134. In another statement, Shaik Pultoo said that Mangal Pandey was inciting the men to mutiny, 'saying that the guns and Europeans had arrived for the purpose of slaughtering them'. Ibid., 129–30.
39  Examination of Wheler, ibid., 182.
40  Examination of Drury, ibid., 149.
41  Defence of Isuree Pandey, ibid., 206.
42  Examination of Wheler, ibid., 147–8.
43  Examination of Drury, ibid., 150.
44  Hearsey to Birch, 9 Apr. 1857, ibid., 109.
45  Ibid., 110–11.
46  Examination of Lieutenant Hearsey, ibid., 204.
47  Hearsey to Birch, 9 Apr. 1857, ibid., 111.
48  Ibid.
49  Ibid.
50  *The Delhi Gazette*, 11 Apr. 1857. According to another report, Mangal Pandey had promised to reveal everything he knew in return for a pardon, and his comrades accordingly threatened to poison him; ibid. In 1856, William Palmer was famously threatened with force-feeding with a stomach pump in Stafford Jail, hence the wording: '*a la Palmer*'.
51  Examination of Mangal Pandey, 4 Apr. 1857, *Selections*, I, 108.
52  Hearsey to Birch, 8 Apr. 1857, ibid., 107.
53  The job of executioner was often performed by unclean castes, such as the Mehtar who were sweepers and scavengers. In this particular case, the Mehtars had been brought in from Calcutta as no one in Barrackpore was willing to perform the task; see *The Delhi Gazette*, 14 Apr. 1857.
54  *The Delhi Gazette*, 18 Apr. 1857.
55  Defence of Isuree Pandey, *Selections*, I, 207.
56  Proceedings of trial of Isuree Pandey, ibid., 178–9 and 207.
57  Hearsey to Birch, 21 Apr. 1857, ibid., 211.
58  *The Delhi Gazette*, 25 Apr. 1857. 'Seeta Ram' is a Hindu invocation.
59  Hearsey to Birch, 8 Apr. 1857, *Selections*, I, 111. See for instance David, 72.
60  Hearsey to Birch, 9 Apr. 1857, ibid., 112. See also examination of Shaik Pultoo, ibid., 125; and examination of Hewson, ibid., 146.
61  Examination of Jemadar Gunness Lalla, ibid., 135.
62  Examination of Aubert, ibid., 165.

63  *The Delhi Gazette*, 9 Apr. 1857. This might have been the tank which contained Ganges water, and in which *sepoys* had taken a holy oath earlier that year and during the mutiny of 1824; see Bandyopadhay, 29–30.

64  Examination of Allen, *Selections*, I, 172.

65  Abbott to Govt, 27 Mar. 1857, Kaye Papers, H/725, 427–37, APAC. The document is in part illegible.

66  Ibid.

67  Ibid.

68  Abbott was actually mistaken on this point, as no such act had been passed.

69  Ibid.

70  Ibid.

71  *The Delhi Gazette*, 23 Apr. 1857. See also *The Friend of India*, 7 May 1857, *FSUP*, I, 328; and Kaye and Malleson, I, 399.

72  *The Delhi Gazette*, 7 Apr. 1857.

73  Hearsey to Birch, 31 Mar. 1857, *Selections*, I, 101.

74  Cited in Kaye, I, 401.

75  Hearsey to Birch, 31 Mar. 1857, *Selections*, I, 101.

76  Petition of discharged 19th Bengal Native Infantry to Hearsey, 31 Mar. 1857, ibid., 103.

77  Hearsey to discharged 19th Bengal Native Infantry, 31 Mar. 1857, ibid., 103–4.

78  Petition of discharged 19th Bengal Native Infantry to Hearsey, 2 Apr. 1857, ibid., 104.

79  See also *The Delhi Gazette*, 11 Apr. 1857.

80  Hearsey to discharged 19th Bengal Native Infantry, n.d., *Selections*, I, 104–5.

81  Canning to Lawrence, 27 Apr. 1857, *FSUP*, I, 333.

82  Birch to Secy Govt, 27 Mar. 1857, *Selections*, I, 87.

83  Canning to Lawrence, 27 Apr. 1857, *FSUP*, I, 333.

84  Deposition of Sheo Churrun Das, *Depositions taken at Cawnpore*, no. 17.

85  Statement of Shaik Hedayut Ali, Kaye Papers, H/727(a), APAC.

86  Examination of Baugh, *Selections*, I, 170.

87  Ibid., 171.

88  Examination of Wheler, ibid., 163.

89  Opinion of court, ibid., 169.

90  Examination of Aubert, ibid., 165. For the composition of the 34th BNI, see ibid., 176–7.

91  General order by GG, 4 May 1857, ibid., 222; and Hearsey to Birch, 6 May 1857, ibid., 225.

92  Inquiry into conduct of Lieutenant-Colonel Mitchell, 2–6 Apr. 1857, ibid., i–xviii.

93  *The Delhi Gazette*, 7 May 1857.

94  Ibid. See also *FSUP*, I, 328.

95    Mainodin, *Two Native Narratives*, 38.
96    According to Malleson, correspondence from Barrackpore was discovered as far north as the station of Sialkot; see *The Mutiny of the Bengal Army* (*Red Pamphlet*), 28.
97    Hearsey to Birch, 6 Apr. 1857, *Selections*, I, 106; and Birch to Military Auditor General, 16 Apr. 1857, ibid., 209.
98    *The Delhi Gazette*, 9 May 1857.

# Chapter 5

1    Examination of Martineau, *Trial*, 83.
2    Ibid.
3    Martineau to Kaye, 20 Oct. 1864, Kaye Papers, H/725(2), 1019, APAC. This letter is a fragment and some words have to be inferred from the context.
4    Examination of Martineau, *Trial*, 84.
5    Martineau to Kaye, 20 Oct. 1864, Kaye Papers, H/725(20), 1022, APAC.
6    Ibid., 1023.
7    Ibid., 1023–4.
8    Ibid., 1024.
9    Ibid., 1027. See also Cave-Browne, I, 42.
10   Cave-Browne, I, 42. It should be noted that the *sepoys* at the depot at Ambala had not yet started practising with the cartridges.
11   Martineau to Becher, 20 Mar. 1857, Martineau Letters, Mss. Eur. C571, APAC.
12   Ibid.
13   Robert Montgomery Martin, *The Indian Empire: With a Full Account of the Mutiny of the Bengal Army* (London: London Printing and Publishing Co., 1861), I, 176.
14   Cave-Browne, I, 47.
15   Ibid., 47–8.
16   Martineau to Becher, 20 Mar. 1857, Martineau Letters, Mss. Eur. C571, APAC.
17   Ibid.
18   Ibid.
19   See Kaye, I, 407–8.
20   Martineau to Becher, 23 Mar. 1857, Martineau Letters, Mss. Eur. C571, APAC.
21   Ibid.
22   Ibid.
23   Martineau to Becher, 5 May 1857, Kaye Papers, H/725(2), 1057 APAC.

24 Howard to Barnes, 4 May 1857, *Punjab Government Records*, VII–I, 8–9.

25 See Kaye, I, 409–10.

26 Bontein to Ross, 2 Mar. 1857, *Selections*, I, 36–8.

27 Ibid., 36.

28 See Palmer, 18.

29 Chester to Hearsey, 13 Apr. 1857, cited in Kaye, I, 630–1.

30 Howard to Barnes, 4 May 1857, *Punjab Government Records*, VII–I, 13–14.

31 Examination of Martineau, *Trial*, 84; and Martineau to Kaye, 20 Oct. 1864, Kaye Papers, H/725(2), 1025, APAC.

32 See examination of Martineau, *Trial*, 85; and Cave-Browne, I, 48. It appears that firing also commenced at the depot at Sialkot without any problems; see *The Delhi Gazette*, 18 Apr. 1857.

33 Howard to Barnes, 4 May 1857, *Punjab Government Records*, VII–I, 12.

34 Barnes to Montgomery, 20 Apr. 1857, ibid., 3; and Cave-Browne, I, 48–9.

35 Barnes to Montgomery, 20 Apr. 1857, *Punjab Government Records*, VII–I, 2–3; and Howard to Barnes, 4 May 1857, ibid., 10.

36 Barnes to Montgomery, 20 Apr. 1857, ibid., 3.

37 Barnes to Montgomery, 20 Apr. 1857, ibid., 3. The lancer later claimed to have been stabbed while sleeping, but the wound turned out to be self-inflicted; see *The Delhi Gazette*, 21 and 28 Apr. 1857.

38 Cave-Browne, I, 50.

39 Martineau to Kaye, 20 Oct. 1864, Kaye Papers, H/725(2), 1028–30, APAC.

40 Ibid.

41 Ibid.

42 Cave-Browne, I, 49.

43 Forsyth's narrative of events at Ambala, no date but probably Feb. 1858, *Punjab Government Records*, VIII–I, 34.

# Chapter 6

1 MacNabb to his mother, 19 Feb. 1857, Mss. Eur. F206/145, APAC, BL. See also Hugh Gough, *Old Memories* (Edinburgh: Blackwood and Sons, 1897), 2.

2 See Stokes, *The Peasant Armed*, 19.

3 D. O'Callaghan, *Scattered Chapters of the Indian Mutiny: The Fatal Falter at Meerut* (Calcutta: s.n., 1861), 4–6; and Gough, 3–4.

4 Gough, 4.

5 The numbers are based on R. S. Thring, 'Report of the Visitation of Epidemic Cholera, as it appeared in the Meerut Jail, in July and August, 1856', in *Reports on Cholera in the Meerut, Rohilcund and Ajmere Divisions in the Year 1856* (Agra: Secundra Orphan Press, 1857), 25.

6 See Dunlop 24; Gough 7; and A. R. D. MacKenzie, *Mutiny Memoirs*, 217, in Edward Vibart, *The Sepoy Mutiny, as seen by a Subaltern from Delhi to Lucknow* (Smith Elder, 1898).

7 Cited in H. H. Greathed (Elisa Greathed ed.), *Letters Written during the Siege of Delhi* (London: Longmans, 1858), x–xi.

8 Nund Singh to Nehal Singh, 10 June 1857, cited in Kaye, I, 653.

9 Francis Shester, *Depositions taken at Meerut*, no. 1.

10 Narain Dass, Mirchgee and Juggernauth Doss, ibid., nos. 6 and 8.

11 Sagur Brahmin, ibid., no. 9.

12 *The Delhi Gazette*, 7 May 1857.

13 Williams, *Memorandum on Meerut*, 2.

14 Kate Moore, 'At Meerut during the Mutiny: A Lady's Narrative of Her Experiences during the Outbreak', *The Nineteenth Century*, XIX–XX, LIV (July–Dec. 1903), 826–38: 826.

15 Colonel W. R. Cra'ster, 'A Reminiscence of the *Sepoy* Mutiny, written 8 years afterwards', Cra'ster Papers, CSAS.

16 Ibid.

17 See G. Carmichael-Smyth in N. A. Chick, *Annals of the Indian Rebellion* (Calcutta: Sanders, Cones and Co., 1859), 90–1.

18 G. Carmichael-Smyth, *Memorandum, or, A few words on the Mutiny* (Meerut: s.n., 1859), 3. See also Chick, 90–1.

19 Ibid. Italics in original.

20 Smyth to Whish, 24 Apr. 1857, *Selections*, I, 227.

21 Apart from their swords, the skirmishers of the 3rd Bengal Light Cavalry were armed with the 1842 Victoria Carbine, while it appears that the remainder of the regiment were armed with the 1842 Lancer Pistol. Both types of firearm were smoothbore, and the troopers had previously used ungreased paper cartridges to fire them; see Harding, II, 225–47 and 302–8. See also Barthorp, *Men-At-Arms Series 268*, 18.

22 Considerable confusion appears to exist amongst some historians and it is often claimed that the eighty-five skirmishers at Meerut were given greased cartridges for the new Enfield rifles; see for instance Anderson, 1, 3 and 55. This is quite clearly *not* correct.

23 Carmichael-Smyth, *Selections*, I, 232.

24 Mainodin, *Two Native Narratives*, 38–9.

25 Defence of Mattadin Havildar, *Selections*, I, cxliv.

26 Kooman Singh, *Depositions taken at Meerut*, no. 12.

27   See also Zalim Singh, ibid., no. 14.

28   See letters of the respective troop commanders in Chick, I, 92–4.

29   Craigie to Adjutant 3rd Light Cavalry, 23 Apr. 1857, *Selections*, I, 228–9.

30   Ibid., 228.

31   Carmichael-Smyth in Chick, I, 92–4.

32   MacNabb to his mother, 10 May 1857, in Patrick Cadell, 'The Outbreak of the Indian Mutiny', *Journal of the Society for Army Historical Research*, 33 (1955), 118–22, 120.

33   *The Delhi Gazette*, 30 Apr. 1857; Carmichael-Smyth, *Selections*, I, 232. It is possible that Brijmohun Sing had also been the target of an earlier arson attack on 13 April; see *Depositions taken at Meerut*, no. 12. The *tehsildar*, however, mentions only fires during the end of April; see Gunga Pershaud, ibid., no. 5.

34   Kooman Singh, *Depositions taken at Meerut*, no. 12.

35   Carmichael-Smyth, *Selections*, I, cxliii.

36   Ibid., 231.

37   Ibid.

38   See also Memorandum by Young, 21 Oct. 1857, ibid., cxlii–cxliii.

39   Carmichael-Smyth to Whish, 24 Apr. 1857, ibid., 228.

40   Defence of Mattadin Havildar, ibid., cxliv–cxlv.

41   Carmichael-Smyth, *Papers regarding the Indian Mutiny* (s.n., 1871), 9–10.

42   MacNabb to his mother, 10 May 1857, in Cadell (1955), 120.

43   Ibid., 121.

44   Gough, 14.

45   Greathed, xii–xiii.

46   Gough 12.

47   This goes some way towards explaining why the five NCOs accepted the cartridges; see Pursaud Sing, *Selections*, I, 233. See also Bhuggun, ibid., 236.

48   Saheb Deen Khan, ibid., 236.

49   Fuzzur Ally Khan, ibid., 235.

50   Moullah Bux, ibid., 236.

51   Young to Chester, 29 Apr. 1857, ibid., 238–9.

52   Chuttur Sing, ibid., 234.

53   O'Callaghan, 4–6; see also Palmer, 34–6; and *Lahore Chronicle*, 22 July, 1857. O'Callaghan gives the number of the 3rd as 504, but he does not count the *sowars* on furlough; see Carmichael-Smyth, *Papers regarding the Indian Mutiny*, 16.

54   Opinion of native court of inquiry at Meerut, 25 Apr. 1857, *Selections*, I, 237.

55   Anson to Chester, 29 Apr. 1857, ibid., 240, and Memorandum by Young, 21 Oct. 1857, ibid., cxli. The memorandum is the only source that we have for the court martial.

56   Gough, 13–14.

57   Memorandum by Young, 21 Oct. 1857, *Selections*, I, cxlvi.

58   Gough, 14.

59   Cambell to Waterfield, 30 Apr. 1857, *Selections*, I, 241–3.

60   Wilson to his wife, 4 May 1857, Wilson Letters, 6807-483, NAM.

61   Hewitt to Chester, 7 May 1857, *Selections*, I, 247.

62   Mohur Singh, *Depositions taken at Meerut*, no. 1.

63   Gough, 17; see also O'Callaghan, 12–15.

64   Mackenzie in Vibart, 218.

65   MacNabb in Cadell (1955), 121.

66   Mackenzie in Vibart, 219.

67   Gough 218; and MacNabb in Cadell (1955), 121.

68   MacNabb, ibid.

69   Ibid., 122.

70   Hewitt to Chester, 9 May 1857, *Selections*, I, 247.

71   Gough, 19–20.

72   MacNabb in Cadell (1955), 121. For references to 'our poor 3rd', see account of the outbreak by Mrs Craigie, 'The Mutinies at Meerut', *The Times*, 24 July 1857, which also refers to one native officer of the 3rd BLC as Smyth's 'victim'. The Commander-in-Chief and Governor-General were later criticised for the excessively harsh procedure; see Lord Roberts, *Forty-One Years in India: From Subaltern to Commander-in-Chief* (London: Bentley, 1897), 45.

73   Wilson to his wife, 10 May 1857, Wilson Letters, 6807-483, NAM.

74   Ibid.

75   *Official Narrative of Events Attending the Outbreak of Disturbances and the Restoration of Authority in the District of Meerut* (Allahabad, 1858), 27.

76   Mahomed Moweezodeen, *Depositions taken at Meerut*, no. 4.

77   Greathed, xiv.

78   Ibid.

79   Roberts, 48. Gough also told this story in his own *Old Memories*, 20, published a year after Roberts' book, and his version is more detailed than that given in Roberts. Gough's version, however, appears to have been written with the exact sequence of the subsequent events in mind, and I have instead relied on Roberts' earlier version; see also Palmer, 154, no. 1.

80   Roberts, 48.

81   Tytler, *Trial*, 80. See also Tytler, 114.

82   Jat Mall, *Trial*, 32.

83   Mainodin, *Two Native Narratives*, 39–40.

84   Ahsan Ullah Khan, *Trial*, 26.

85   Forrest, ibid., 37.

86   Ahsan Ullah Khan, *Trial*, 26. According to Ahsan Ullah Khan, this plan of action had been 'arranged through some native officers, who went over on Court Martial

duty to Meerut'. See *Trial*, 26. That is nevertheless unlikely since the native offic-ers of the Delhi regiments, who had presided at the trial, were still in Meerut on the evening of 10 May; see Moore, 828.

87  See also *Trial*, 183 and 187.

# Chapter 7

1   Forsyth's narrative of events at Ambala, no date, but probably Feb. 1858, *Punjab Government Records*, VIII–I, 34–5.

2   Forsyth to Barnes, 30 Apr. 1857, *Punjab Government Records*, VII–I, 6.

3   Forsyth's narrative of events at Ambala, 34–5.

4   Cave-Browne, I, 49.

5   Forsyth's narrative of events at Ambala, 35.

6   Cave-Browne, I, 49.

7   Ibid.

8   Forsyth's narrative of events at Ambala, 35.

9   Barnard to Canning, 1 May 1857, cited in Kaye, I, 428.

10  Martineau to Becher, 5 May 1857, Kaye Papers, H/725(2), 1057, APAC.

11  Martineau to Kaye, 20 Oct. 1864, Kaye Papers, H/725(2), 1030, APAC.

12  Except for Yadav, 49–50, this incident has hitherto been ignored by historians. The only documents to mention this affair are: Barnes to Montgomery, 5 Feb. 1857, *Punjab Government Records*, VIII–I, 3; and Forsyth to John Lawrence by telegram, 10 May 1857, 4.45 p.m., *Punjab Government Records*, VII–I, 15.

13  Cave-Browne, I, 186.

14  See Martin, I, 177.

15  Forsyth's narrative of events at Ambala, 35.

16  Cave-Browne, I, 188–9.

17  Ibid.

18  Barnes to Montgomery, 5 Feb. 1857, *Punjab Government Records*, VIII–I, 3.

# Chapter 8

1 Greathed, xv.

2 Gough, 23. Before he left for church, MacNabb began a lengthy and extremely interesting letter to his mother, describing the events surrounding the parade on 9 May; see MacNabb to his mother, 10 May 1857, in Cadell (1955), 120–2. He never finished the letter and it was only discovered in 1895; see unpublished manuscript, Mss. Eur. F/206/287, 31, APAC.

3 Gough, 24.

4 Ibid.

5 Sheikh Moula Bux, *Depositions taken at Meerut*, no. 19.

6 Runddeer Singh, ibid., no. 13.

7 Vibart, 253. Tying prisoners to the mouths of cannon and executing them by blowing them to pieces was originally a Mughal punishment, which, however, the British adopted and used extensively during the 1857 Uprising and even after; see Mukherjee (1994), 183–4.

8 Wilson to his wife, 6 May 1857, Wilson Letters, 6807-483, NAM.

9 J. Hawes, *Depositions taken at Meerut*, no. 20.

10 Mohur Singh, ibid., no. 2.

11 Palmer argues that the cutting of the lines about an hour previous to the actual outbreak is proof of the existence of a detailed plot, see Palmer, 71, 96, 129–30. However, if there had been an elaborate conspiracy initiated hours before the outbreak, one would expect that the plotters would have tried to isolate Meerut by cutting all the lines and not just the one; the cutting of the line does not in itself constitute proof of a pre-existing plan.

12 O'Callaghan, 16–17.

13 Moore, 827.

14 W. H. Earle, *Depositions taken at Meerut*, no. 33.

15 Ibid. Much has been made of the supposed warning of the Kashmiri prostitute Sophie, but she denied having had any previous knowledge of the outbreak or passing on such a warning; see Mussumat Sophie, ibid., no. 35. It seems more reasonable simply to suppose that there were some vague reports of an intended outbreak amongst the prostitutes of the Sudder Bazaar and that Dr Smith's mistress warned him.

16 *Official Narrative of Events Attending the Outbreak of Disturbances and the Restoration of Authority in the District of Moradabad* (Allahabad, 1858), 2; and Mackenzie in Vibart, 220. There is also the story of an English prostitute, 'Mees Dolly', who was supposedly executed by the British for egging on the *sepoys* in the bazaar at Meerut; see P. J. O. Taylor (ed.), *A Companion to the 'Indian*

*Mutiny' of 1857* (Delhi: Oxford University Press, 1996), 217–18; and G. Macmunn, 'Mees Dolly (An Untold Tragedy of '57)', *The Cornhill Magazine*, 63 (July to Dec. 1927), 327–31. Appealing as the story may be, however, it is completely unsubstantiated.

17 *Official Narrative of Events in the District of Meerut*, 27.

18 See *Depositions taken at Meerut*, no. 2, 12–16 and 18.

19 Sheikh Moula Bux, ibid., no. 19. Palmer argues that because the cook boy's rumour precedes the actual parading of HM 60th Rifles by an hour, it may be discounted as an explanation; see Palmer 129. The cook boy's report, however, need not be related to the church parade at all and was probably just a rumour, which nevertheless had a profound effect. See also Williams, *Memorandum on Meerut*, 6–7.

20 See also Alalvi, 78–9.

21 Ibid., 83–4.

22 Sheikh Moula Bux, *Depositions taken at Meerut*, no. 19.

23 Ibid.

24 Ibid.

25 Anonymous account in Chick, 115.

26 Ibid.

27 E. L. Phillipps, letter of 15 May, cited in Stuart Ryder, 'Everard Lisle Phillipps VC: First Memorandum Qualifier', Royal United Services Institute, 143, 3 (June 1998), 70–5, 71.

28 Ryder, 71; and Joygopal Singh, *Depositions taken at Meerut*, no. 17; and O'Callaghan, 22.

29 Ryder, 71; Sheikh Moula Bux, *Depositions taken at Meerut*, no. 19; O'Callaghan in Chick, 100.

30 Bukt Singh, *Depositions taken at Meerut*, no. 16.

31 Sheikh Moula Bux, ibid., no. 19.

32 Ryder, 71.

33 O'Callaghan in Chick, 99.

34 Anonymous in Chick, 116; Sheikh Moula Bux, *Depositions taken at Meerut*, no. 19.

35 Anonymous in Chick, 116.

36 Sheikh Moula Bux, *Depositions taken at Meerut*, no. 19.

37 Anonymous in Chick, 116.

38 Ibid.

39 Ibid.

40 Ibid.

41 Gough, 27–9.

42 Mahomed Ashraf Beg, *Depositions taken at Meerut*, no. 22.

43 Ibid., no. 4, 22 and 52.

# Chapter 9

1 Williams Caldwell, ibid., no. 42.
2 This *sowar* apparently made an effort to warn all the British present in the Sudder Bazaar at the time; see ibid., nos. 40–3.
3 Williams Caldwell and James McQuade, ibid., nos. 42–3.
4 Hugh McCartney, ibid., no. 40.
5 William Harwood, ibid., no. 50.
6 Mohur Singh and Gunga Pershad, ibid., nos. 2 and 5.
7 Mahomed Moweezoodeen, ibid., no. 4.
8 See Sandria Freitag, *Collective Action and Community: Public Arenas and the Emergence of Communalism in North India* (Berkeley: University of California Press, 1989).
9 Haidar, meaning 'lion', is an epithet of Muhammad's son-in-law Ali.
10 Mohur Singh and Joseph Henry Jones, *Depositions taken at Meerut*, nos. 2 and 52, see also Wuzeer Ali Khan and Hurnam Singh, ibid., nos. 3 and 56. Thanks to Markus Daechsel and Avril Powell for their help in translating these quotes and for their general comments.
11 Kooman Singh, ibid., no. 12. See also ibid., nos. 5, 13–14 and 51.
12 The fact that the rallying cries were Shi'i in character does not appear to have been particularly significant and both Sunnis and even Hindus might have joined in such processions; see J. R. I. Cole, *Roots of North Indian Shi'ism in Iran and Iraq* (Berkeley: University of California Press, 1988), 273; and P. J. Marshall, 'The Muharram Riot of 1779 and the Struggle for Status and Authority in Early Colonial Calcutta', *Journal of the Asiatic Society of Bangladesh*, 50, 1–2 (2005), 293–314.
13 See Tambiah, *Levelling Crowds*, 240 and 266.
14 See for instance Sheikh Moula Bux, *Depositions taken at Meerut*, no. 19.
15 Gunga Pershad, ibid., no. 5; but see also nos. 19, 22, 52–3, 55, 58 and 60.
16 Hurnam Singh, ibid., no. 56.
17 C. A. Bayly, 'The Pre-History of "Communalism"? Religious Conflict in India, 1700–1860', *MAS*, 19, 2 (1985), 177–203: 200.
18 See Gyanendra Pandey, 'The Bigoted Julaha' in *The Construction of Communalism in Colonial North India* (Delhi: Oxford University Press, 1990), 67–108; and Katherine Prior, 'Making History: The State's Intervention in Urban Religious Disputes in the North-Western Provinces in the Early Nineteenth Century', *MAS*, 27, 1 (1993), 179–203.
19 See *Report of the Collector of Azimgurh on the Settlement of the Ceded Portion of the District commonly called Chuklah Azimgurh* (Agra, 1837), 130.

20   Gunga Pershad, *Depositions taken at Meerut*, no. 5. See also Baboo Bunseedhur, ibid., no. 72.
21   See William Beik: *Urban Protests in Seventeenth-Century France: The Culture of Retribution* (Cambridge: Cambridge University Press, 1997).
22   Natalie Zemon Davis, 'Rites of Violence: Religious Violence in Sixteenth-Century France', *Past and Present*, 59 (May, 1973), 51–91: 90. Having written this, I subsequently realised that Rudrangshu Mukherjee has used the same quotation for his argument on the Cawnpore Massacres; see Mukherjee (1990), 112–13. I hope I may be forgiven for suggesting that his argument works much better when applied to the violence at Meerut rather than Cawnpore.
23   Ahsan Ullah Khan, *Trial*, 183.
24   Davis, 53.
25   See also Guha.
26   For the extent of plunder and looting that occurred at Meerut on 10 May, see *Depositions taken at Meerut*, nos. 3–5 and 69–70. See also Mukherjee (1994), 187.
27   Laik Ram, ibid., no. 68.
28   Ibid., nos. 56 and 69–70.
29   Soondur Dass, ibid., 63. See also Stokes, 145; and Pandey, 79.
30   See Mahomed Ashruf Beg, *Depositions taken at Meerut*, no. 22. The number of prisoners is given in James Doorit, ibid., no. 21.
31   Joseph Henry Jones, ibid., no. 52.
32   Baboo Bunseedhur, ibid., no. 72. As the Superintendent of Police, Major Williams was probably also involved in the work of the Thagi and Dakaiti Department at Meerut, hence the sobriquet.
33   Mahomed Moweezoodeen and Gunga Pershad, ibid., nos. 4 and 5.
34   See Bayly (1985), 197–8.
35   Gunga Pershad, *Depositions taken at Meerut*, no. 5.
36   Mohur Singh, ibid., no. 2. 'Religion' should in this context be understood as a broad generic concept that encompassed the social order – no less secular than a British soldier fighting for 'Queen and Country'.
37   Wuzeer Ali Khan, ibid., no. 3.
38   Mahomed Moweezoodeen, ibid., no. 4.
39   Ibid.
40   Ibid.
41   Smyth was later criticised for not having gone to the parade ground himself, but he later claimed that, as the field officer of the week, his immediate duty was with the headquarters; see Smyth in Chick, 94.
42   Ibid., 95. Smyth's active involvement in the events of 10 May ended here.
43   Mrs D. D. Muter, *My Recollections of the Sepoy Revolt (1857–1858)* (London: Long John, 1911), 24–6.

44  Moore, 827.

45  See for instance J. E. W. Rotton, *The Chaplain's Narrative of the Siege of Delhi from the Outbreak at Meerut to the Capture of Delhi* (London: Smith Elder and Co., 1858), 2–3.

46  Muter, 17–18.

47  See also Revd T. C. Smyth in Chick, 103–4.

48  Moore, 827.

49  Muter, 19–20.

50  Moore, 828.

51  Ibid.

52  The telegraph line to Delhi was accordingly cut before 4 p.m. and the one to Agra around 8 p.m.

53  Anthony Sattin (ed.), *An Englishwoman in India: The Memoirs of Harriet Tytler 1828–1858* (Oxford: Oxford University Press, 1986), 111–12.

54  Moore, 828.

55  F. W. Stubbs, *Extracts from the Diary of Lieutenant F. W. Stubbs, Bengal Artillery, in 1857–1858* (Woolwich: Royal Artillery Institution, 1894), 2.

56  Revd T. C. Smyth in Chick, 104.

57  W. H. Furnell, *Depositions taken at Meerut*, no. 29.

# Chapter 10

1   Mrs Craigie, *The Times*, 24 July 1857. It has not been possible to ascertain the first names of Mrs Craigie and Mackenzie's sister.

2   Mackenzie in Vibart, 228–9.

3   Ibid., 219.

4   Ibid., 220.

5   Ibid., 221.

6   Ibid. Later that night a street-sweeper helped the Quartermaster and two other officers escape at the cost of his own life; ibid., 241–2.

7   Mrs Craigie, *The Times*, 24 July 1857.

8   Mackenzie in Vibart, 224.

9   Ibid.

10  It is unclear who stated that Carmichael-Smyth was fleeing; see Mrs Craigie, *The Times*, 24 July 1857.

11  Among these troopers were at least two of the five skirmishers who *had* accepted the cartridges on 23 April; see Smyth, Account, 15; and Selections, I, 231.

12    There were later some questions as to the legality of Craigie leading the troopers to the jail without orders from his superiors; see Carmichael-Smyth, *Papers*, 2–3.

13    Mackenzie in Vibart 225.

14    Mrs Craigie, *The Times*, 24 July 1857.

15    James Doorit, *Depositions taken at Meerut*, no. 21.

16    Ibid.

17    Mackenzie in Vibart, 227.

18    Mrs Craigie, *The Times*, 24 July 1857. This account quite clearly depicts the relationship between Craigie and his men in rather hyperbolic terms.

19    Mackenzie in Vibart, 227.

20    Ibid., 226. It should be noted that there are several minor inconsistencies in the accounts of Craigie and Mackenzie, notably concerning the sequence of events. I have relied on Craigie's version for the chronology, as it was written mere days after the events and not decades as was the case with Mackenzie. The woman in the carriage was *not* Mrs Courteney, as is sometimes assumed; Mrs Courteney was killed along with two children, and their bodies were found the following day – see Jorawun, *Depositions taken at Meerut*, no. 39.

21    Mackenzie in Vibart, 226.

22    Ibid., 227.

23    Mrs Craigie, *The Times*, 24 July 1857.

24    Ibid.

25    Le Champion Möller to J. W. Kaye, 27 Feb. 1871, cited in Kaye, III, 680.

26    Mrs Craigie, *The Times*, 24 July 1857.

27    Ibid.

28    Mackenzie in Vibart, 229.

29    Mackenzie in Vibart, 230; and Mrs Craigie, *The Times*, 24 July 1857.

30    Mackenzie in Vibart, 231.

31    Mrs Craigie, *The Times*, 24 July 1857; and Mackenzie in Vibart, 232–3.

32    The building is referred to as a shrine by Mackenzie in Vibart, 232, but see N. T. Parker, *A Memoir of Meerut* (Meerut: s.n., 1904), 8 and 18. This little-known piece of local history has been invaluable in reconstructing events at Meerut.

33    Mackenzie in Vibart, 235. Revd Smyth states that it was Mrs Chambers who was set on fire (see Chick, 104), but he must have confused Chambers and Dawson.

34    Nusseebun and Sookha Dhobee, *Depositions taken at Meerut*, nos. 37 and 38.

35    Ibid., nos. 52–4.

36    T. C. Smyth to G. W. Williams, 16 Dec. 1857, *FSUP*, I, 32.

37    Emma Markoe, *Depositions taken at Meerut*, no. 46.

38    Ibid.

39    Mrs E. Law, ibid., no. 47.

40   W. H. Earle, ibid., no. 32.

41   Joseph Chapman, ibid., no. 31.

42   Ibid.

43   Letter by John Eckford, 4 Sept. 1857, Mss. Eur. F240/45, APAC; and John Eckford, ibid., no. 30.

44   Letter by John Eckford, ibid.

45   Ibid.

46   Ibid.

47   Ibid.

48   Ibid.; and W. H. Earle, *Depositions taken at Meerut*, no. 32.

49   Mrs. E. Law, *Depositions taken at Meerut*, no. 48.

50   Ibid.

51   William Foster, ibid., no. 49.

52   Wuzeer Ali Khan, ibid., no. 3.

53   See Stokes, 145–54.

54   Dunlop, 39.

55   *Official Narrative of Events in the District of Meerut*, 27.

56   Cited in Henry Scholberg, *The Indian Literature of the Great Rebellion* (New Delhi: Promilla and Co., 1993 ), 105. See also Pankaj Rag, '1857: Need for Alternative Sources', *Social Scientist*, 26, 1/4 (Jan.–Apr. 1998), 113–47: 124.

57   Laik Ram, *Depositions taken at Meerut*, no. 68.

58   Ibid.

59   Sauta Singh, ibid., no. 67.

60   Laik Ram, ibid., no. 68.

61   For the ambiguous role of *kotwals* during riots in the early nineteenth century, see Bayly (1983), 335–6.

62   Sauta Singh and Laik Ram, *Depositions taken at Meerut*, nos. 67 and 68.

63   James Doorit, ibid., no. 21. See also *Official Narrative of Events in the District of Meerut*, 30.

64   See also Anderson.

65   Gough, 30.

66   Ibid., 32–3.

67   Greathed, xvi–xvii.

68   Ibid., xviii–xix.

69   Ibid.

70   Gough, 38.

71   Ibid., 38–9.

72   For a detailed account of the movements of the British troops, see O'Callaghan, 23–31.

73   W. H. Furnell, *Depositions taken at Meerut*, no. 29.

74   Muter, 28–9.

75   Möller cited in Kaye, III, 680; and O'Callaghan, 25.

76   See Palmer, 97–105; and O'Callaghan in Chick, 99–101.

77   Muter 28–9.

78   See Kooman Singh and Zalim Singh, *Depositions taken at Meerut*, nos. 12 and 14. This scene is sometimes depicted as a dramatic exchange of volleys between the British troops and mutinous *sepoys*, but the primary sources do not corroborate this; see for instance Lewis Butler, *The Annals of the King's Royal Rifle Corps, vol. III* (London: John Murray, 1923), 96.

79   Gough, 45. For the mutilations of MacNabb's body, see W. H. Earle, *Depositions taken at Meerut*, no. 32.

80   W. H. Earle, ibid.

81   Gough, 43; and O'Callaghan, 29–30.

82   Möller, 680 (see also p. 678); and Meerut District Narratives, para. 181. For a discussion of this issue, see Palmer, 106–18.

83   See for instance O'Callaghan; and Carey in Dunlop, 31.

84   Ryder, 71. See also Mackenzie in Vibart, 242–4.

85   Letter by John Eckford, 4 Sept. 1857, Mss. Eur. F240/45, APAC.

86   Möller cited in Kaye, III, 680.

87   *Selections*, I, 250–1.

88   Birch to Mayhew, 24 June 1857, ibid., 258; Mayhew to Birch 6 July 1857, ibid., 259; and Becher to Wilson, ibid., 262.

89   Wilson to Becher, 18 Oct. 1857, ibid., 260.

# Chapter 11

1   Leckey, 31–2. See also deposition of Mrs Law, *Depositions taken at Meerut*, no. 48, which confirms the veracity of Leckey's account.

2   Tytler, 113.

3   This was Fitzgerald, the private of HM 60th Rifles who sought refuge in Eckford's house and later tried to escape on his own.

4   W. H. Earle, *Depositions taken at Meerut*, no. 32.

5   W. Muir, *Records of the Intelligence Department of the Government of the North-West Provinces of India during the Mutiny of 1857* (Edinburgh: T. and T. Clark, 1902), I, 375.

6   William Harwood and Joseph Henry Jones, *Depositions taken at Meerut*, nos. 50 and 52.

7   Rotton, 6.

8   See Muir, I, 370–7, where it is asserted that no women were 'violated'. Several of these sources are reproduced in *FSUP*, I, 31–3. The insistence on the absence of sexual assault, though, was based upon the assertions of district officers months after the Uprising had been suppressed. At this point a desire to bring an end to matters, to avoid further sorrow, and to re-establish British control (and honour) was likely to have been uppermost in the minds of the officials concerned. Certainly no concrete evidence either way was ever presented, nor was the definition of 'sexual assault' clarified.

9   *Official Narrative of Events in the District of Meerut*, 32.

10  Runddeer Singh and Joseph Henry Jones, *Depositions taken at Meerut*, nos. 13 and 52. Lodhas were an agricultural caste.

11  See Tambiah.

12  Captain Muter had become a colonel by the time the account was published.

13  Muter 35–7; see also Rotton, 6.

14  *Official Narrative of Events in the District of Meerut*, 31.

15  Burial Register of St John's Church, in Parker, 23. There were also some who survived the outbreak but died days later of their wounds or 'exposure'; see E. Law, *Depositions taken at Meerut*, no. 48, and Alan Harfield, *Meerut: The First Sixty Years (1815–1875)* (London: BACSA, 1992), 240.

16  Mohur Singh and Gunga Pershad, *Depositions taken at Meerut*, nos. 2 and 5.

17  See Muter, 59–60; Moore, 832; and Greathed, xx–xxi.

18  Moore, 835; and Parker, 8. The man had also been named by residents of the Sudder Bazaar as having taken part in the rioting; see deposition of Ram Nath, *Depositions taken at Meerut*, no. 59.

19  Tytler, 113.

20  Möller cited in Kaye, III, 681; and Tytler, 113.

21  Stubbs, 4. Martial law was not formally authorised until the following day; see *Selections*, I, 251.

22  For a more dramatic account of the incident, see Moore, 836. Lieutenant Thackeray of the Bengal Engineers wrote to his brother that 'We got a faker in yesterday, who murdered one of the ladies, and hanged him in front of the men.' C. B. Thackeray (ed.), *A Subaltern in the Indian Mutiny* (London: s.n., 1930–1), 2. This is probably a reference to the murderer of Mrs Chambers.

23  Muter, 63–4.

24  Elizabeth Cahill, *Depositions taken at Meerut*, no. 47.

25  Muter 44.

26  O'Callaghan, 9.

27  Muter 49.

28  See Gough, 42; and Tytler, 112–13.

29  Rotton, 5.

30  Muter, 39.

31  Moore, 830.

32  O'Callaghan, 17.

33  Rotton, 22.

34  Duljeet Singh, *Depositions taken at Meerut*, no. 15.

35  Wuzeer Ali Khan, ibid., no. 3.

36  Kooman Singh, ibid., no. 12.

37  Punchum Singh, ibid., no. 18.

38  Williams, *Memorandum on Meerut*, 6.

39  This is based on David Arnold's description of food-riots in the early twentieth century; see D. Arnold, 'Looting, Grain Riots and Government Policy in South India 1918', *Past and Present*, 84 (Aug. 1979), 111–45: 111.

40  See Bruce Berman and John Lonsdale (eds.), *Unhappy Valley: Conflict in Kenya and Africa* (London: Currey, 1992), II, 253.

41  Mohur Singh, *Depositions taken at Meerut*, no. 2. See also Runddeer Singh, ibid., no. 13.

42  Bukt Singh, ibid., no. 16.

43  Inayut-Oolah Goolaothee to Fyzool Hussan, May 1857, cited in Kaye, I, 641–2.

44  John Eckford and Emma Markoe, *Depositions taken at Meerut*, nos. 30 and 46.

45  Mrs E. Law, ibid., no. 48; Moore, 835; and Parker, 8.

46  Mackenzie in Vibart, 221, and Mrs E. Law, ibid.

47  Emma Markoe, ibid., no. 46.

48  Mrs Craigie, 'The Mutinies at Meerut', *The Times*, 24 July 1857.

49  See for instance Joseph Henry Jones, *Depositions taken at Meerut*, no. 52.

50  Pinchum Singh ibid., no. 18.

51  Nusseebun and Sookha Dhobee, ibid., nos. 37–8.

52  Mackenzie in Vibart, 241–2.

53  Carmichael-Smyth, *Papers regarding the Indian Mutiny*, 16.

54  Ryder, 71. See also *Selections*, I, 255.

55  Thackeray, 4–5.

56  Sheikh Moula Bux, *Depositions taken at Meerut*, no. 19.

57  Gough, 30.

58  Petition of discharged 19th Bengal Native Infantry to Hearsey, 2 Apr. 1857, *Selections*, I, 104.

59  Joygopal Singh, *Depositions taken at Meerut*, no. 17.

60  Duljeet Singh, ibid., no. 15.

61  Baboo Hursarun Dass, ibid., no. 23.

62  Bukt Singh, ibid., no. 16.

# Chapter 12

1   Radha Nath, cited in Parker, 30.

2   Möller, cited in Kaye, III, 680.

3   Duljeet Singh, *Depositions taken at Meerut*, no. 15.

4   Narrative of events, 19 May 1857, *Selections*, I, 267–8.

5   Ibid.; and Ward 136.

6   Kooman Singh, *Depositions taken at Meerut*, no. 12.

7   Rutton Lall, ibid., no. 58.

8   Mahomed Moweezoodeen, ibid., no. 4.

9   Statement of Mohun Lal, Kaye Papers, H/725, 389–422, APAC.

10  Ahsan Ullah Khan, *Trial*, 187.

11  Part of the mutineers took a more westerly route through Kishanpur to Bhagpat and then to Delhi; see Dunlop, 30.

12  Bidhee Singh, *Depositions taken at Meerut*, no. 26.

13  Dowlut and Thundie and Behal, ibid., nos. 25 and 27.

14  Baboo Hursarun Dass, ibid., no. 23. As late as the evening of 11 May, straggling parties of mutineers were still making their way towards Delhi; only some of them were armed, and sowars, *sepoys* and camp-followers alike were riding stolen horses and ponies; see Ram Lall, ibid., no. 24.

15  Ibid., nos. 23–4 and 58.

16  Jat Mall, *Trial*, 32.

17  Metcalfe, ibid., 44. See also Chuni, ibid., 51.

18  Everett, ibid., 111; and Ahsan Ullah Khan, ibid., 20–1 and 24–5.

19  Mrs Fleming, ibid., 85.

20  For the fall of Delhi, see also Mainodin, *Two Native Narratives*; and Mohun Lal, 389–422, Kaye Papers, H/725, APAC. In Dalrymple's *The Last Mughal*, the events of 11 May are explained largely through the prevailing tension within the Mughal capital, whereas I stress the arrival of the Meerut mutineers and the vacillation of the Delhi *sepoys* as decisive factors. It could be said that Dalrymple provides a structural account of the fall of Delhi, while I emphasise the dynamics of the event; it should nevertheless be apparent that our respective interpretations are not incompatible.

21  Vibart, 253.

22  Ibid., 256.

23  Julia Haldane, *The Story of Our Escape from Delhi in 1857* (Agra: s.n., 1888), 2.

24  Hewitt to Chester, 11 May 1857, *Selections*, I, 250; and *Official Narrative of Events in the District of Meerut*, 31.

25  See Mainodin and Jewan Lal, *Two Native Narratives*, 42 and 78; and Tytler, 114. The fact that the letter is expressly stated to have been delivered on the night

of 10 May means that it must have been dispatched quite early in the evening. Even if the message was delivered by two sets of fresh horses, it must have taken more than two hours to cover the 38 miles between Meerut and Delhi. The *dak* coach took five hours to cover the distance; see *Trial*, 139.

26  Mainodin, *Two Native Narratives*, 42.
27  Vibart, 254.
28  Ibid., 11.
29  Tytler, *Trial*, 81.
30  Tytler, 115.
31  Jewan Lal, *Two Native Narratives*, 78 and 238.
32  Vibart, 257.
33  Jewan Lal, *Two Native Narratives*, 235.
34  Ahsan Ulla Khan, *Trial*, 60.
35  Ibid.
36  Ibid., 26.
37  Jewan Lal, *Two Native Narratives*, 235.
38  Makhan, *Trial*, 38.
39  Ahsan Ulla Khan, ibid., 60.
40  Ghulam Abbas, ibid., 10.
41  Ahsan Ullah Khan, ibid., 181.
42  Jewan Lal, *Two Native Narratives*, 237.
43  See also Makhan, *Trial*, 38.
44  Mainodin, *Two Native Narratives*, 42.
45  Chuni Lal, *Trial*, 86.
46  Vibart 41.
47  Forrest, *Trial*, 34.
48  Chuni, ibid., 49–50.
49  Jewan Lal, *Two Native Narratives*, 78 and 238.
50  Metcalfe was eventually protected by Mainodin, who hid him until the Commissioner could escape the city days later; see Mainodin, *Two Native Narratives*, 45–6 and 55–7.
51  Makhan, *Trial*, 39.
52  Bukhtawar Singh, ibid., 47.
53  Ahsan Ullah Khan, ibid., 61.
54  Ibid.
55  See Dalrymple, 120–4.
56  Jewan Lal, *Two Native Narratives*, 80.
57  Jat Mall, *Trial*, 27.
58  Bukhtawar, ibid., 47.
59  Makhan, ibid., 39.
60  Mainodin, *Two Native Narratives*, 47.

61   Mrs Aldwell, *Trial*, 67.
62   Account of James Morley, in Chick, 88–9.
63   Morley in Chick, 89.
64   Mainodin, *Two Native Narratives*, 48.
65   Ram Nath, *Depositions taken at Meerut*, no. 59.
66   Zahir Dehlavi, cited in Dalrymple, 156.
67   Forrest, *Trial*, 34–7.
68   Ibid. See also Vibart, 40–4.

# Chapter 13

1    Tytler, 116.
2    Ibid.
3    Tytler, *Trial*, 81.
4    Ibid.
5    Tytler, in Chick, 48.
6    Ibid.
7    Tytler, 116. The French maid might have been in Paris in 1848.
8    Cited in Vibart, 262. This was supposed to have been sent at 3 p.m.; see Kaye, II, 138.
9    Cited in Vibart, 262.
10   Vibart, 22.
11   Peile, in Chick, 71.
12   Vibart, 18.
13   Paterson, *Trial*, 73.
14   Vibart, 27.
15   Ibid., 21.
16   Ibid., 19.
17   Ibid., 25–6.
18   Ibid.
19   Ibid., 33–4.
20   Ibid., 48–50.
21   Ibid., 57.
22   Chick, 70.
23   Tytler, in Chick, 52.
24   Chick, 61.
25   Peile, in Chick, 71.

26   Ibid., 73.
27   Vibart, 273.
28   Peile, in Chick, 71.
29   Ghulam Abbas, *Trial*, 12.
30   Ahsan Ullah Khan, ibid., 182.
31   Jewan Lal, *Two Native Narratives*, 83.
32   Ghulam Abbas, *Trial*, 12.
33   Ibid., 13. See also Mainodin and Jewan Lal, *Two Native Narratives*, 53 and 83.
34   Ahsan Ullah Khan, *Trial*, 184–7.
35   Ibid., 186–7.
36   *Selections*, I, 230 and Appendix E, cxl and cxlv.
37   Carmichael-Smyth, *Papers regarding the Indian Mutiny*, 15.
38   This is, however, conjectural as no further information is available regarding the role of Gulab Shah/Golaub Khan.
39   Ahsan Ullah, *Trial*, 187. See also ibid., 183.
40   Defence of Prince Mirza Bakhtawar Shah, Kaye Papers, H/725, APAC.
41   See Michael Mann, 'Turbulent Delhi: Religious Strife, Social Tension and Political Conflicts, 1803–1857', *Journal of South Asian Studies*, 28, 1 (2005), 5–34.

# Chapter 14

1   In popular Indian histories, it is often claimed that Mangal Pandey's actions provided the inspiration for the Uprising; see Epilogue below. The only evidence we have that events at Barrackpore affected *sepoys* more generally is Captain Tytler's description of the discontent his men displayed when informed of the execution of Isuree Pandey at Delhi on 11 May; see above. There is no word of Mangal Pandey.
2   For the symbolic significance of the Mughal Emperor, see Thornhill, 7.
3   *FSUP*, I, 342; and *The Delhi Gazette*, 21 Apr. 1857.
4   Kaye and Malleson, I, 431.
5   See *FSUP*, I, 339.
6   Malleson (1857), 30; and Lawrence to Canning, 2 May 1857, *FSUP*, I, 336.
7   See *Selections*, II, 1–11.
8   Similarly at Faizabad, the virulently anti-British Maulavi Ahmad Ollah Shah (and Malleson's chief conspirator) had been arrested by the authorities in February 1857, suspected of stirring up sedition amongst the local population. This alleged

conspirator, however, only joined the Uprising after he was released by mutineers after the outbreak at Faizabad in June; see *FSUP*, I, 381–4 and II, 35.

9    Bayly (1996), 324.

10   Williams, *Memorandum on Meerut*, 10. See also *Selections*, I, 269.

11   Much has been made of the revival in 1857 of the so-called Wahabi networks between Patna and the North-West Frontier, the actual impact of which, however, was vastly exaggerated; see Bayly (1996), 320–1.

12   *FSUP*, I, 353–4.

13   See also ibid., 357–60 and II, 46; and Bayly (1996), 318–23.

14   These alleged conspirators were summarily executed; see *FSUP*, II, 13–14.

15   See ibid., 5–8.

16   *FSUP*, III, 26–7.

17   Ibid., 27.

18   Mainodin, *Two Native Narratives*, 60.

19   Statement of regimental maulavi, Kaye Papers, H/727(a), 758, APAC.

20   See Mukherjee, *Awadh*, 64–6, and Map 1.

21   *Memorandum on Meerut*, 11.

22   *Official Narrative of Events Attending the Outbreak of Disturbances and the Restoration of Authority in the District of Banda* (Allahabad, 1858), II, 3.

23   Berman, in Berman and Lonsdale, *Unhappy Valley*, II, 401.

24   This is at the very heart of Stokes's argument, but does not provide a valid assessment for all the areas affected by the Uprising. See also Sabyasachi Dasgupta, 'The Rebel Army in 1857: At the Vanguard of the War of Independence or a Tyranny of Arms', in *1857: Essays from the Economic and Political Weekly* (New Delhi: Orient Longman, 2008).

25   See also Bayly (1996), 317; and Sugata Bose and Ayesha Jalal, *Modern South Asia: History, Culture, Political Economy* (London: Routledge, 1998), 92.

26   For a different argument, see Ray, *The Felt Community*.

27   See Mahmoud Farooqui, 'The Police in Delhi in 1857', paper presented at the 'New Perspectives on 1857' Mutiny at the Margins Project, University of Edinburgh, 23–6 July 2007.

28   Ahsan Ulla Khan, *Trial*, 60.

29   Jewan Lal, *Two Native Narratives*, 237.

30   Muir, I, 545 and II, 130–1.

31   House of Commons, 27 July 1857, Hansard, vol. 147, 475.

32   Allamah Fadl I Haq, *Journal of the Pakistan Historical Society*, 5, 1 (1956), 23–57: 29–30.

33   *The Delhi Gazette*, 23 Apr. 1857.

34   Ibid., 7 May 1857.

35   See J. C. Heesterman, *The Inner Conflict of Tradition* (Chicago: University of Chicago Press, 1985).

36  Ibid.
37  *Official Narrative of Events Attending the Outbreak of Disturbances and the Restoration of Authority in the Districts of Saugor and Nerbudda* (Allahabad, 1858), 2.
38  Ibid.
39  Gobind Singh, Sheikh Elahee Buksh, and Ghouse Mohomed, *Depositions taken at Cawnpore*, no. 14. See also Kaye Papers, H/725(1), 569, APAC.
40  J. Reid, *Memorandum of Events Immediately Preceding the Outbreak at Faizabad on the Night of the 8th of June, 1857*, cited in *FSUP*, II, 34.
41  *Official Narrative of Events in the District of Banda*, II, 9.
42  Duff, 12–13.
43  'The May Proclamation', cited in Kaye, I, 654; and The King of Delhi's Circular Letter to the Princes and People of India', cited in Salim al-Din Quarashi, *Cry for Freedom* (Lahore: Sang-e-Meel Publications, 1997), 62. The Delhi proclamation is obviously a translation and the original wording is not known.
44  Guha, 101. This interpretation of 1857 is in part inspired by Marshall Sahlins' concept of 'the structure of the conjuncture', first presented in *Islands of History* (1985), and elaborated in his subsequent works.

# Chapter 15

1   Kaye, I, 328.
2   *Official Narrative of Events in the District of Banda*, I, 4.
3   Mainodin, *Two Native Narratives*, 38.
4   Duff, 54–5.
5   See for instance *Illustrated London News*, 4 July 1857.
6   See Peter Hopkirk, *The Great Game: On Secret Service in High Asia* (Oxford: Oxford University Press, 1991).
7   *Official Narrative of Events in the District of Moradabad*, 2.
8   *Official Narrative of Events in the District of Meerut*, 64.
9   Abbott to Waterfield, 13 May 1857, *Selections*, I, 266–7.
10  See also Alex Padamsee, *Representations of Indian Muslims in British Colonial Discourse* (Basingstoke: Palgrave Macmillan, 2005).
11  See Edward Thompson, *The Other Side of the Medal* (London: Hogarth Press, 1925).
12  Dalrymple, 432.
13  Stubbs, 4.

14   *Selections*, I, 251.

15   Lawrence to Penny, 1 Dec. 1857, *Government Records Punjab*, VII, part II, 375.

16   *Selections*, I, 230 and Appendix E, cxlii.

17   Paske to Saunders, 13 Feb. 1858, *Government Records Punjab*, VII, part II, 369.

18   Harriott was subsequently censored by Governor-General Canning for this 'leak' to the media; see Edmonstone to Lawrence, 11 Feb. 1858, ibid., 378.

19   Paske to Saunders, 28 Jan. 1858, ibid., 375.

20   *Trial*, 3–4.

21   Address of Deputy Judge Advocate Major Harriott, 9 Mar. 1858, *Trial*, 139.

22   Ibid., 139–40.

23   Ibid., 143. The Deputy Judge Advocate had himself been witness to events at Meerut.

24   Ibid., 141. This is an oft-repeated claim that is demonstratively incorrect; see for instance Bates, *Subalterns and the Raj: South Asia Since 1600* (London: Routledge, 2007), 65. In order for the *sepoys* to use greased cartridges, they would have had to be in possession of Enfield rifles and only HM 60th Rifles at Meerut had been issued with those by May 1857. Although stores of pre-greased Enfield cartridges may have fallen into the hands of the mutineers at Delhi, they would have been useless for their Brown Bess muskets, which were .75 calibres as opposed to the Enfield's .577.

25   *Trial*, 142.

26   Ibid., 160.

27   Ibid., 160–1. This quote is practically identical to the paragraph from Pearce, *Love Besieged*, reproduced in the Prologue.

28   Ibid., 161.

29   Ibid., 162.

30   Ibid., 166.

31   Ibid., 168.

32   Ibid., 166.

33   Ibid., 172.

34   Ibid., 160.

35   See diary of Colonel Ommaney, 27 Mar. 1858, A, 6301/143, NAM; and Russell, II, 48–51.

36   *Trial*, 161.

37   Minute by Sir John Lawrence on the proceedings against Bahadur Shah, 19 Apr. 1857, *Government Records Punjab*, VII, pt. II, 382.

38   Ibid., 385 and 387. For a similar assessment of the Uprising by a later historian, see Majumdar, 363.

39   Thomas Metcalf, *The Aftermath of Revolt: India 1857–1870* (Princeton: Princeton University Press, 1964), 290.

40   See Ahsan Ullah Khan, Jat Mall, Bukhtawar, Makhan, and Mrs Aldwell in *Trial.*

41   Tytler, 119.

42   Cited in Leckey, 132. For further variations of the story, see Leckey, 126 and 131. As Leckey rightly pointed out, these stories had no factual basis whatsoever.

43   Ibid., 123.

44   See also ibid., 115–18, 128 and 163.

45   See Gautam Chakravarty, *The Indian Mutiny and the British Imagination* (Cambridge: Cambridge University Press, 2005).

46   J. E. Muddock, *The Great White Hand* (London: Hutchinson and Co., 1896). This literary trend continued far into the twentieth century; see for instance John Masters, *Nightrunners of Bengal* (London: Michael Joseph, 1951); and Vivian Stuart, *Mutiny in Meerut* (London: Hale, 1973).

47   *The Great White Hand*, 6–7.

48   Ibid., 9.

49   Ibid., 10–11.

50   Ibid., 13.

51   Ibid.

52   Ibid., 14. *Pagri* is the cloth used for a turban.

53   Ibid., 15.

54   Ibid., 17.

55   Ibid., 18–19.

56   Preface, ibid.

57   Ibid., 31. Flora is abducted by her native admirer but eventually rescued by the heroic Walther, who rises to the occasion.

58   See Nigel Collett, *The Butcher of Amritsar: General Reginald Dyer* (London: Hambledon, 2005).

# Epilogue

1   In 2007 a group of English tourists tried to set up a plaque commemorating the fallen soldiers of HM 60th Rifles at the church in Meerut, but were refused permission by the local authorities, who felt it to be an insult to Indians. The group had to be escorted away by the police when surrounded by an angry crowd; see *Hindustan Times*, 21 Sept. 2007.

2   Badri Narayan, 'Reactivating the Past: Dalits and Memories of 1857', in *1857: Essays from Economic and Political Weekly*, 181.

3  Savarkar, 101.

4  Ibid., 103–6.

5  Amaresh Misra, *Mangal Pandey: The True Story of an Indian Revolutionary* (New Delhi: Rupa, 2005) and *War of Civilizations: India AD 1857* (New Delhi: Rupa, 2008).

6  Misra (2005), 88.

7  Ibid., 101.

8  Misra (2008), I, 165.

9  Ibid., 168

10  Ibid., 172.

11  Ibid., 170.

12  Ibid., 71.

13  *Tehelka Magazine*, 4, 50 (29 Dec. 2007).

14  Ketan Mehta (dir.), *The Rising: Ballad of Mangal Pandey* (2005).

15  It should be noted that anachronistic and politicised histories are as prevalent amongst post-colonisers as they are amongst post-colonised, and many contemporary British writings, popular as well as academic, still trade in nineteenth-century tropes, including Niall Ferguson's controversial *Empire: How Britain Made the Modern World* (London: Penguin, 2003). The same applies to the popular accounts of Saul David (2003) and Julian Spilsbury (2007), both entitled *The Indian Mutiny*, who share more than just the choice of terminology with pre-Independence writers.

16  See also Misra (2008), I, xxxvi.

17  K. C. Yadav, 'Interpreting 1857: A Case Study', in Sabyasachi Bhattacharya (ed.), *Rethinking 1857* (New Delhi: Orient Longman, 2007), 17.

# Select Bibliography

## Manuscripts

### ASIA, PACIFIC AND AFRICA COLLECTIONS, THE BRITISH LIBRARY

Bengal Criminal and Judicial Proceedings, P/131/12.
John Eckford, Mss. Eur. F240/45.
Kaye Mutiny Papers, H/725–7.
MacNabb, Mss. Eur. F206/145.
Martineau, Mss. Eur. C571.
Reade, Mss. Eur. E124, 223.
Vernon-Smith, Mss. Eur. F231.
Waterfield, Mss. Eur. D680.

### NATIONAL ARMY MUSEUM

Ommaney Diaries, 6301/143.
Wilson Letters, 6807/483.

### CENTRE FOR SOUTH ASIAN STUDIES, CAMBRIDGE

Cra'ster Papers.

### NATIONAL LIBRARY OF SCOTLAND

John Charles Brown, MS 15393.
Minto Papers, MS 12756.
Tweeddale, MS 14558 (1–16).

# Primary printed sources

Chick, N. A. (ed.), *Annals of the Indian Rebellion* (Calcutta: Sanders, Cones and Co., 1859).

Forrest, George W. (ed.), *Selections from the Letters, Despatches and Other State Papers Preserved in The Military Department of the Government of India, 1857–58* (Calcutta: Military Dept Press, 1893).

*Gazetteer of the Bombay Presidency* (Bombay: s.n., 1896).

*Hansard, House of Commons Debates*

*House of Commons Parliamentary Papers*

Morley, John, *Indian Speeches (1907–1909)* (London: Macmillan and Co., 1909).

Nayar, Pramod K. (ed.), *The Trial of Bahadur Shah* (Hyderabad: Orient Longman, 2007).

*Punjab Government Records*, VII–I (Lahore: s.n., 1911).

*Report of the Collector of Azimgurh on the Settlement of the Ceded Portion of the District commonly called Chuklah Azimgurh* (Agra, 1837).

*Reports on Cholera in the Meerut, Rohilcund and Ajmere Divisions in the year 1856* (Agra: Secundra Orphan Press, 1857).

'Review of Legislation, 1907: British India', in *Journal of the Society of Comparative Legislation*, 9, 2 (1908).

Rizvi, S. A. A. and Bhargava, M. L. (eds.), *Freedom Struggle in Uttar Pradesh*, I–V (Lucknow: Publications Bureau, 1957–61).

# Official records collected by Lieutenant-Colonel G. W. Williams

*Depositions taken at Cawnpore under the directions of Lieut-Colonel G. W. Williams* (Allahabad, 1858).

*Depositions taken at Meerut by Major G. W. Williams* (Allahabad, 1858).

*Memorandum on the mutiny and outbreak at Meerut in May 1857 by Major Williams* (Allahabad, 1858).

*Official narrative of events attending the outbreak of disturbances and the restoration of authority in the district of Banda; Jhansie; Meerut; Moradabad; Saugor and Nerbudda* (Allahabad, 1858).

# Journals and newspapers

*Bentley's Miscellany*
*The Delhi Gazette*
*Fraser's Magazine for Town etc.*
*The New Monthly Magazine*
*The New York Times*
*The Times*
*Westminster Review*

# Internet sources

Savarkar Newsletter, 5 June 1908, www.satyashodh.com/Savarkar%20Newsletters1A.
htm#d14 (accessed 1 March 2008).

# Printed works

Alavi, Seema, *The Sepoys and the Company: Tradition and Transition in Northern India 1770–1830* (Delhi: Oxford University Press, 1995).
Amin, Shahid, 'A Hanging Twice Over', *Outlook India*, 26 March 2007.
Anderson, Clare, *The Indian Uprising of 1857–8: Prisons, Prisoners and Rebellion* (London: Anthem, 2007).
Arnold, David, 'Looting, Grain Riots and Government Policy in South India 1918', *Past and Present*, 84 (Aug. 1979), 111–45.
——*Colonizing the Body: State Medicine and Epidemic Disease in Nineteenth-Century India* (Berkeley: University of California Press, 1993).
Ball, Charles, *The History of the Indian Mutiny* (London: Printing and Publishing Co., n.d.).
Bandyopadhay, P., *Tulsi Leaves and the Ganges Water: The Slogan of the First Sepoy Mutiny at Barrackpore 1824* (Kolkata: K. P. Bagchi and Co., 2003).
Barrier, N. Gerald, 'The Punjab Disturbances of 1907: The Response of the British Government in India to Agrarian Unrest', *Modern Asian Studies*, 1, 4 (1967), 353–83.

Barthorp, Michael, *Men-At-Arms Series 268: The British Troops in the Indian Mutiny 1857–59* (London: Osprey, 1994).

Bayly, C. A., *Rulers, Townsmen and Bazaars: North Indian Society in the Age of British Expansion* (Cambridge: Cambridge University Press, 1983).

—— 'The Pre-History of "Communalism"? Religious Conflict in India, 1700–1860', *MAS*, 19, 2 (1985), 177–203.

—— *The New Cambridge History of India, II.1: Indian Society and the Making of the British Empire* (Cambridge: Cambridge University Press, 1988).

—— *Empire and Information: Intelligence Gathering and Social Communication in India, 1780–1870* (Cambridge: Cambridge University Press, 1996).

Beik, William, *Urban Protests in Seventeenth-Century France: The Culture of Retribution* (Cambridge: Cambridge University Press, 1997).

Berman, Bruce and Lonsdale, John (eds.), *Unhappy Valley: Conflict in Kenya and Africa* (London: Currey, 1992).

Brass, Paul, *Theft of an Idol: Text and Context in the Representation of Collective Violence* (Princeton: Princeton University Press, 1997).

Buchan, John, *Lord Minto, A Memoir* (London: Nelson, 1924).

Butler, Lewis, *The Annals of the King's Royal Rifle Corps, vol. III* (London: John Murray, 1923).

Butler, William, *The Land of the Veda* (New York: Phillips and Hunt, 1871).

Cadell, Patrick, 'The Outbreak of the Indian Mutiny', *Journal of the Society for Army Historical Research*, 33 (1955), 118–22.

—— 'The Autobiography of an Indian Soldier', *Journal of the Society for Army Historical Research*, 37 (1959), 3–11 and 49–56.

Carey, W. H., *The Mahomedan Rebellion* (Roorkee: Directory Press, 1857).

Carmichael-Smyth, G., *Memorandum, or, A few words on the Mutiny* (Meerut: s.n., 1859).

—— *Papers regarding the Indian Mutiny* (s.n., 1871).

Cave-Browne, John, *The Punjab and Delhi in 1857: Being a Narrative of the Measures by which the Punjab was Saved and Delhi Recovered during the Indian Mutiny* (London: W. Blackwood and Sons, 1861).

Chakravarty, Gautam, *The Indian Mutiny and the British Imagination* (Cambridge: Cambridge University Press, 2005).

Chaudhuri, S. B., *Civil Disturbances during the British Rule in India, 1765–1857* (Calcutta: World Press, 1955).

Chick, N. A., *Annals of the Indian Rebellion* (Calcutta: Sanders, Cones and Co., 1859).

Chirol, Valentine, *Indian Unrest* (London: Macmillan, 1910).

Choudhury, Deep Kanta Lahiri, 'Sinews of Panic and the Nerves of Empire: The Imagined State's Entanglement with Information Panic, India c. 1880–1912', *Modern Asian Studies*, 38, 4 (2004), 965–1002.

Cohn, Norman, *Warrant for Genocide: The Myth of the Jewish Conspiracy and the Protocols of the Elders of Zion* (London: Eyre and Spottiswoode, 1967).

Cole, J. R. I., *Roots of North Indian Shi'ism in Iran and Iraq* (Berkeley: University of California Press, 1988).

Collett, Nigel, *The Butcher of Amritsar: General Reginald Dyer* (London: Hambledon, 2005).

Copland, Ian, 'Christianity as an Arm of Empire: The Ambiguous Case of India under the Company, c. 1813–1858', *The Historical Journal* (2006), 1025–54.

Crooke, W., *An Introduction to the Popular Religion and Folklore of Northern India* (Allahabad: Government Press, 1894).

Cubitt, G., *The Jesuit Myth: Conspiracy Theory and Politics in Nineteenth-Century France* (Oxford: Clarendon Press, 1993).

Das, Veena, *Life and Words: Violence and the Descent into the Ordinary* (Berkeley: University of California Press, 2007).

Dasgupta, Sabyasachi, 'The Rebel Army in 1857: At the Vanguard of the War of Independence or a Tyranny of Arms', in *1857: Essays from the Economic and Political Weekly* (New Delhi: Orient Longman, 2008).

David, Saul, *The Indian Mutiny* (London: Viking, 2002).

Davis, Natalie Zemon, 'Rites of Violence: Religious Violence in Sixteenth-Century France', *Past and Present*, 59 (May 1973), 51–91.

Dodd, George, *The History of the Indian Revolt and of the Expeditions to Persia, China, and Japan, 1856–58* (London: W. and R. Chambers, 1859).

Dowd, G. E., 'The Panic of 1751: The Significance of Rumours on the South Carolina–Cherokee Frontier', *The William and Mary Quarterly*, 3, 53, 3 (July 1996), 527–60.

Downs, Troy, 'Host of Midian: The Chapati Circulation and the Indian Revolt of 1857–58', *Studies in History*, 16 (2000), 75–107.

Duff, Alexander, *The Indian Rebellion: Its Causes and Results. In a Series of Letters* (London: s.n., 1858).

Dunlop, R. H. W., *Service and Adventure with the Khakee Ressalah, or Meerut Volunteer Horse, during the Mutinies of 1857–58* (London: s.n., 1858).

Forbes-Mitchell, W., *Reminiscences of the Great Mutiny* (London: Macmillan and Co., 1893).

Frost, Thomas, *Complete Narrative of the Mutiny in India, from its Commencement to the Present Time* (London: n.s., 1858).

Gilbert, Martin (ed.), *Servant of India: A Study of Imperial Rule from 1905 to 1910 as Told Through the Correspondence and Diaries of Sir James Dunlop Smith* (London: Longmans, 1966).

*The Golden Commemoration of the Indian Mutiny at the Royal Albert Hall, Decr 23rd 1907* (London: W. H. Smith and Sons, 1907).

Gough, Hugh, *Old Memories* (Edinburgh: Blackwood and Sons, 1897).

Greathed, H. H. (Elisa Greathed ed.), *Letters Written during the Siege of Delhi* (London: Longmans, 1858).

Guha, Ranajit, *Elementary Aspects of Peasant Insurgency in Colonial India* (Delhi: Oxford University Press, 1983).

Gupta, P. C., *Nana Sahib and the Rising at Cawnpore* (London: Clarendon, 1963).

Hahn, Steven, '"Extravagant Expectations" of Freedom: Rumour, Political Struggle, and the Christmas Insurrection Scare of 1865 in the American South', *Past and Present*, 157 (Nov. 1997), 122–58.

Haldane, Julia, *The Story of Our Escape from Delhi in 1857* (Agra: s.n., 1888).

Harding, D. F., *Smallarms of the East India Company 1600–1856* (London: Foresight, 1999).

Harfield, Alan, *Meerut The First Sixty Years (1815–1875)* (London: BACSA, 1992).

Heehs, Peter, 'Foreign Influences on Bengali Revolutionary Terrorism 1902–1908', *MAS*, 28, 3 (1994), 533–56.

Heesterman, J. C., *The Inner Conflict of Tradition* (Chicago: University of Chicago Press, 1985).

Hofstadter, Richard, 'The Paranoid Style in American Politics', *Harper's Magazine* (Nov. 1964), 77–86.

Hopkirk, Peter, *The Great Game: On Secret Service in High Asia* (Oxford: Oxford University Press, 1991).

James, Lawrence, *Raj: The Making and Unmaking of British India* (London: Abacus, 1997).

Kaye, John, and Malleson, G. B., *History of the Indian Mutiny* (London: Allen, 1888–9).

Ker, James Cambell, *Political Troubles in India 1907–1917* (Calcutta: Superintendent Government Printing, 1917).

Khan, Syed Ahmed, *The Causes of the Indian Revolt* (1858, trans. Benares: Medical Hall Press, 1873).

Kolff, Dirk H. A., *Naukar, Rajput and Sepoy: The Ethno-history of the Military Labour Market in Hindustan, 1450–1850* (Cambridge: Cambridge University Press, 1990).

Leckey, Edward, *Fictions Connected with the Indian Outbreak of 1857 Exposed* (Bombay: Chesson and Woodhall, 1859).

Lefebvre, George, *The Great Fear of 1789* (orig. 1932; trans. London: New Left Books, 1973).

Lunt, James (ed.), *From Sepoy to Subedar, being the Life and Adventures of Subedar Sita Ram, a Native Officer of the Bengal Army written and related by Himself* (Lahore, 1873; reprint London: Papermac, 1988).

Maclagan, Michael, *'Clemency' Canning Charles John, 1st Earl Canning Governor-General and Viceroy of India 1856–1862* (London: Macmillan, 1962).

MacMunn, George, *The Underworld of India* (London: Jarrolds, 1933).

Macpherson, J., 'Report on Insanity among Europeans in Bengal', *The Indian Annals of Medical Science* (Apr. 1854), 704–5.

Majumdar, R. C., *The Sepoy Mutiny and the Revolt of 1857* (Calcutta: Mukhopadhyay, 1957).

Malcolm, John, *A Memoir of Central India including Malwa and Adjoining Provinces* (London: s.n., 1823).

Malleson, G. B., *The Indian Mutiny of 1857* (London: s.n., 1891).

Mann, Michael, 'Turbulent Delhi: Religious Strife, Social Tension and Political Conflicts, 1803–1857', *Journal of South Asian Studies*, 28, 1 (2005), 5–34.

Martin, Robert Montgomery, *The Indian Empire: With a Full Account of the Mutiny of the Bengal Army* (London: London Printing and Publishing Co., 1861).

Metcalfe, Charles T. (trans.), *Two Native Narratives of the Mutiny in Delhi* (Westminster: A. Constable and Co., 1898).

Minto, Countess of, *India: Minto and Morley 1905–1910* (London: Macmillan, 1934).

Misra, Amaresh, *Mangal Pandey: The True Story of an Indian Revolutionary* (New Delhi: Rupa, 2005).

—— *War of Civilizations: India AD 1857* (New Delhi: Rupa, 2008).

Moore, Kate, 'At Meerut during the Mutiny: A Lady's Narrative of Her Experiences during the Outbreak', *The Nineteenth Century*, XIX–XX, LIV (July–Dec. 1903), 826–38.

Muddock, J. E., *The Great White Hand* (London: Hutchinson and Co., 1896).

Muir, W., *Records of the Intelligence Department of the Government of the North-West Provinces of India during the Mutiny of 1857* (Edinburgh: T. and T. Clark, 1902).

Mukherjee, Rudrangshu, *Awadh in Revolt 1857–1858* (New Delhi: Permanent Black, 2001).

—— *Mangal Pandey: Brave Martyr or Accidental Hero?* (New Delhi: Penguin Books India, 2005).

Muter, Mrs D. D., *My Recollections of the Sepoy Revolt (1857–1858)* (London: Long John, 1911).

Narayan, Badri, 'Reactivating the Past: Dalits and Memories of 1857', in *1857: Essays from Economic and Political Weekly* (New Delhi: Orient Longman, 2008).

O'Callaghan, D., *Scattered Chapters of the Indian Mutiny: The Fatal Falter at Meerut* (Calcutta: s.n., 1861).

Oman, J. C., *Cults, Customs and Superstitions of India* (London: T. Fisher Unwin, 1908).

Padamsee, Alex, *Representations of Indian Muslims in British Colonial Discourse* (Basingstoke: Palgrave Macmillan, 2005).

Pandey, Gyanendra, 'The Bigoted Julaha' in *The Construction of Communalism in Colonial North India* (Delhi: Oxford University Press, 1990), 67–108.

Parker, N. T., *A Memoir of Meerut* (Meerut: s.n., 1904).

Pearce, Charles, *Love Besieged* (1909; reprint Delhi: Oxford University Press, 2007).

Pincince, John, *On the Verge of Hindutva: V. D. Savarkar and the Historical Construction of Hindu National Identity, 1905–24* (unpublished PhD thesis, University of Hawai'i, 2007).

Pionke, Albert D., *Plots of Opportunity: Representing Conspiracy in Victorian England* (Columbus: The Ohio State University Press, 2004).

Popplewell, Richard, *Intelligence and Imperial Defence: British Intelligence and the Defence of the British Empire 1904–1924* (London: Frank Cass, 1995).

Prichard, I. T., *The Mutinies in Rajpootana: Being a Personal Narrative of the Mutiny at Nusseerabad* (s.n., 1860).

Prior, Katherine, 'Making History: The State's Intervention in Urban Religious Disputes in the North-Western Provinces in the Early Nineteenth Century', *MAS*, 27, 1 (1993), 179–203.

Quarashi, Salim al-Din, *Cry for Freedom* (Lahore: Sang-e-Meel Publications, 1997).

Rag, Pankaj, '1857: Need for Alternative Sources', *Social Scientist*, 26, 1/4 (Jan.–Apr. 1998), 113–47.

Ray, Rajat K., *The Felt Community: Commonality and Mentality before the Emergence of Indian Nationalism* (Delhi: Oxford University Press, 2003).

Riley, Glenda, 'The Specter of the Savage: Rumours and Alarmism on the Overland Trail', *The Western Historical Quarterly*, 15, 4 (Oct. 1984), 427–44.

Roberts, Lord, *Forty-one Years in India: From Subaltern to Commander-in-Chief* (London: Bentley, 1897).

Rotton, J. E. W., *The Chaplain's Narrative of the Siege of Delhi from the Outbreak at Meerut to the Capture of Delhi* (London: Smith Elder and Co., 1858).

Roy, Tapti, *The Politics of a Popular Uprising: Bundelkhand in 1857* (Delhi: Oxford University Press, 1994).

—— *Raj of the Rani* (New Delhi: Penguin India, 2006).

Ryder, Stuart, 'Everard Lisle Phillipps VC: First Memorandum Qualifier', Royal United Services Institute, 143, 3 (June 1998), 70–5.

Sahlins, Marshall, *Apologies to Thucydides: Understanding History as Culture and Vice Versa* (Chicago: University of Chicago Press, 2004).

Sattin, Anthony (ed.), *An Englishwoman in India: The Memoirs of Harriet Tytler 1828–1858* (Oxford: Oxford University Press, 1986).

Savarkar, V. D., *The Indian War of Independence, 1857* (London: s.n., 1909; eighth edn., New Delhi: Rajdhani Granthagar, 1970).

Scholberg, Henry, *The Indian Literature of the Great Rebellion* (New Delhi: Promilla and Co., 1993).

Sen, S. N., *Eighteen Fifty-Seven* (Delhi: s.n., 1957).

Sharpe, Jenny, *Allegories of Empire: The Figure of Woman in the Colonial Text* (Minneapolis: University of Minneapolis Press, 1993).

Silvestri, Michael, '"The Sinn Féin of India": Irish Nationalism and the Policing of Revolutionary Terrorism in Bengal', *Journal of British Studies*, 39 (Oct. 2000), 454–86.

Sleeman, W. H., *Ramaseeana, or A vocabulary of the peculiar language used by the Thugs, with an introduction and appendix, descriptive of the system pursued by that fraternity and of the measures which have been adopted by the Supreme Government of India for its suppression* (Calcutta: Military Orphan Press, 1836).

—— *Rambles and Recollections of an Indian Official* (London, 1844; reprint: Westminster: Archibald Constable and Co., 1893).

Spry, H. H., 'Some Accounts of the Gang Murderers of Central India, Commonly Called Thugs; Accompanying the Skulls of Seven of Them', *The Phrenological Journal and Miscellany*, 8 (Mar. 1834), 511–24.

Stokes, Eric (C. A. Bayly ed.), *The Peasant Armed: The Indian Rebellion of 1857* (Oxford: Clarendon Press, 1986).

Stoler, Ann Laura, '"In Cold Blood": Hierarchies of Credibility and the Politics of Colonial Narratives', *Representations*, 37 (Winter 1992), 151–89.

Stubbs, F. W., *Extracts from the Diary of Lieutenant F. W. Stubbs, Bengal Artillery, in 1857–1858* (Woolwich, Royal Artillery Institution, 1894).

Tambiah, S., *Levelling Crowds: Ethnonationalist Conflict and Collective Violence in South Asia* (Berkeley: University of California Press, 1996).

Taylor, P. J. O. (ed.), *A Companion to the 'Indian Mutiny' of 1857* (Delhi: Oxford University Press, 1996).

Taylor, Philip Meadows, *Confessions of a Thug* (London: Richard Bentley, 1839).

Teltscher, Kate, *India Inscribed: European and British Writing on India, 1600–1800* (Delhi: Oxford University Press, 1995).

Thackeray, C. B. (ed.), *A Subaltern in the Indian Mutiny* (London: s.n., 1930–1).

Thompson, Edward, *The Other Side of the Medal* (London: Hogarth Press, 1925).

Thompson, Mowbray, *The Story of Cawnpore* (London: R. Bentley, 1859).

Thornhill, M., *The Personal Adventures and Experiences of a Magistrate during the Rise, Progress, and Suppression of the Indian Mutiny* (London: John Murray, 1884).

Townsend, S. C., *Report on the Cholera Epidemic of 1868* (s.n., 1869).

Trevelyan, G. O., *Competition Wallah* (London: Macmillan and Co., 1866).

—— *Cawnpore* (1865; reprint: London: Macmillan and Co., 1886).

Ward, Andrew, *Our Bones are Scattered* (London: John Murray, 1996).

Wilkinson-Latham, Christopher, *Men-At-Arms Series 67: The Indian Mutiny* (London: Osprey, 1977).

Wood, Evelyn, *The Revolt in Hindustan, 1857–59* (London: Methuen and Co., 1908).

Wood, Gordon, 'Conspiracy and the Paranoid Style: Causality and Deceit in the Eighteenth Century', *The William and Mary Quarterly*, 3, 39, 3 (July 1982), 401–41.

Yadav, K. C., *The Revolt of 1857 in Haryana* (Delhi: Manohar, 1977).

—— 'Interpreting 1857: A Case Study', in Sabyasachi Bhattacharya (ed.), *Rethinking 1857* (New Delhi: Orient Longman, 2007).

Yang, Anand A., 'Disciplining "Natives": Prisons and Prisoners in Early Nineteenth Century India', *South Asia*, 10, 2 (1987), 29–46.

—— 'A Conversation of Rumours: The Language of Popular "Mentalitès" in Late Nineteenth-Century Colonial India', *Journal of Social History*, 20, 3 (Spring 1987), 485–505.

# Index